This book is edited by PrestaShop, Inc. (http://www.prestashop.com/).

PrestaShop
55 rue Raspail
92300 Levallois-Perret

It is printed by Lulu, Inc. (http://www.lulu.com/).

First edition.
Published in July 2014.
Based on PrestaShop 1.6.0.8.

ISBN 978-1-291-93127-3

PrestaShop 1.6 User Guide

PrestaShop 1.6 User Guide

PrestaShop presents a comprehensive, intuitive user administration panel, and gives you hundreds of standard functions that can be adapted or personalized in order to respond to all of your needs.

This user guide will help you familiarize yourself with all of PrestaShop's features. You will also be able to efficiently manage your PrestaShop site. While the majority of it is aimed at shop owners, the first chapter serves as an introduction to the front-office interface, which can be helpful to everyone.

You can post all of your questions directly on our forum:
http://www.prestashop.com/forums/

Table of Contents

Table des matières

PrestaShop 1.6 User Guide 3

Table of Contents 7

Training 31

Customizing your shop 33

Connecting to the PrestaShop back-office 35

Discovering the Administration Area 39

    OVERVIEW OF THE MAIN INTERFACE 39

        The top bar 40

        The menus 41

    THE BUTTONS 43

    CONTEXTUAL HELP 44

    THE DASHBOARD 45

The horizontal bar *45*

The left column *47*

The central column *47*

The right column *49*

First steps with PrestaShop 1.6 51

DEACTIVATE YOUR SHOP 52

DELETE THE CONTENT OF THE DEFAULT SHOP 53

CONFIGURE YOUR SHOP'S INFORMATION 54

The shop's basic settings *55*

Shop languages *58*

Employees information *59*

CONFIGURE YOUR PAYMENT METHODS 60

CONFIGURE CARRIERS AND SHIPMENT 61

CHOOSE YOUR THEME 62

CHOOSE YOUR MODULES 62

CREATE YOUR PRODUCTS AND PRODUCT CATEGORIES 63

CREATE YOUR STATIC CONTENT 63

BUILD YOUR TOP MENU 63

ACTIVATE YOUR SHOP 63

Managing the Catalog 65

Managing Products 65

The Product List 66

The Product Creation Page Global Buttons 68

Filling out the Product Information 69

Setting the Price of a Product 75

Optimizing your product's search engine position (SEO) 79

Managing the Product's Associations 81

Evaluating Shipping Cost: Size, Weight, Carrier 83

Adding Product Combinations 84

Managing Product Quantities 90

Configuring the Product's Images 92

Configuring Product Features 94

Managing Customization 96

Managing Attachments 98

Setting the Product's Supplier 99

Managing Warehouses (advanced) 101

Creating a Pack of Products 103

Creating a Virtual Product 104

Managing Categories 106

Navigating and editing categories 110

Importing and exporting categories *111*

Adding products to a category *111*

MONITORING YOUR CATALOG 112

MANAGING PRODUCT ATTRIBUTES 113

Creating a new attributes *114*

Creating a new value *116*

MANAGING PRODUCT FEATURES 118

Adding a feature *119*

Adding a value to a feature *120*

MANAGING MANUFACTURERS 120

Creating a manufacturer *121*

Adding a Manufacturer's Address *123*

MANAGING SUPPLIERS 124

BUILDING IMAGE MAPS 126

MANAGING TAGS 129

First Solution: When Creating a New Product *130*

Second Solution: Managing Tags *130*

MANAGING ATTACHMENTS 131

Managing Orders **133**

ORDERS 133

 Creating an Order 134

 Viewing an Order's Details 135

 Changing the order 136

 Editing the order details 137

 Attaching a message to the order 142

INVOICES 143

 Invoice Options 145

MERCHANDISE RETURNS 146

 Return process: how the customer sees it 147

 Return process: how you see it 148

 Refunding a customer 149

DELIVERY SLIPS 151

 Delivery Slips Options 152

CREDIT SLIPS 153

 Delivery Slips Options 154

 Creating a Credit Slip 154

STATUSES 155

 Creating a new order status 157

 Creating a new return status 158

ORDER MESSAGES 159

Creating a new message *159*

Sending a message to a customer *160*

Managing Customers **163**

YOUR CUSTOMERS 163

Creating a New Customer Account *165*

Viewing a Customer's Information *168*

Searching for a Customer *169*

CUSTOMER ADDRESSES 171

Adding a new address *172*

Customer Groups *174*

SHOPPING CARTS 176

CUSTOMER SERVICE 179

Handling Customer Service Messages *181*

Customer Service Options *182*

YOUR CONTACTS 184

Creating a new contact *184*

How the customer can contact you *185*

SOCIAL TITLES 186

OUTSTANDING 187

Enabling the Outstanding feature *187*

Current outstanding screen 188

Creating Price Rules and Vouchers 189

CART RULES 190

Creating a New Cart Rule 191

CATALOG PRICE RULES 198

Creating a New Catalog Price Rule 199

MARKETING MODULES 202

Managing Modules and Themes 205

YOUR MODULES 205

Module notifications 205

The modules list 206

Performing Actions on Modules 208

Connecting to Addons 209

MODULES AND THEMES CATALOG 210

Installing a module 212

Updating a module 214

Uninstalling a module 215

Installing a theme 215

Exporting a theme 218

PrestaShop's mobile template 218

FRONT-OFFICE POSITIONS 220

Moving a module within a hook 221

Attaching a module to a hook: Transplanting 222

Editing an attached module 223

Removing a module from a hook 225

Moving a module visually: Live Edit 225

Transplanting a module by modifying its code 227

PAYMENT SETTINGS 228

Installing a payment module 228

Payment Module Restrictions on Currencies 229

Payment Module Restrictions on Groups 231

Payment Module Restrictions on Countries 231

Making the Native Modules Work 233

ADMINISTRATION MODULES 234

1-Click Upgrade - AutoUpgrade 234

Database Cleaner 234

Email alerts 235

Google Analytics API 236

Image watermark 236

Incentivibe 237

Merchant Expertise 238

Newsletters 238

NVD3 Charts 240

Zingaya 240

ADVERTISING AND MARKETING MODULES 240

AddShoppers Social Commerce Platform 240

Advertising block 241

Customer follow-up 241

Feedaty 242

Google AdWords 242

Referral program 242

Search & Merchandising Prediggo 244

SendinBlue (formerly MailinBlue) 244

Trustpilot - Review and online reputation 244

Yotpo Social Reviews 244

ANALYTICS AND STATS MODULES 244

Best manufacturers 245

Google Analytics (ganalytics) 245

BILLING & INVOICING MODULES 245

Avalara - AvaTax 245

European VAT Number 246

DROP SHIPPING MODULES 246

Ecopresto Dropshipping 246

FRONT OFFICE FEATURES MODULES 246

Banner block 246

Add Sharethis 247

Cart block 247

Categories block 247

CMS Block 248

Contact block 249

Contact information block 249

Cross-Selling 250

Currency block 250

Custom CMS information block 250

Customer data privacy block 251

Customer reassurance block 251

Facebook block 252

Facebook sharing block 252

Favorite Products 252

Featured Products on the homepage 252

FIA-NET Sceau de Confiance 252

Home Editorial 253

Image slider for your homepage 253

Language block 254

Layered navigation block 255

Link block 258

Manufacturers block 258

My Account block 258

My Account block for your website's footer 259

New products block 259

Newsletter block 259

Payment logos block 260

Permanent links block 260

Product Comments 260

Product Payment logos block 262

Products category 262

Product tooltips 262

RSS feed block 263

RSS products feed (RSS Feed) 263

Send to a Friend module 264

- Social networking block 264
- Store locator block 264
- Suppliers block 265
- Tags block 265
- Top horizontal menu 265
- Theme configurator 265
- Top-sellers block 266
- Top horizontal menu 266
- User info block 267
- Viewed products block 267
- Wishlist block 267

MARKETPLACE MODULES 267

- eBay Marketplace 267
- Neteven Marketplaces 268

MOBILE MODULES 268

- Brow.si 268
- Shopgate M-Commerce 268

PAYMENT SECURITY MODULES 269

- Certissim 269
- PrestaShop Security (prestafraud) 269

Payments and Gateways modules 270

Adyen   270

Bank wire 271

Cash on Delivery (COD) 272

FerBuy   272

Hipay   272

Kwixo   273

Ogone   273

Payment by check 274

PayPal Europe 274

Realex   274

Skrill   275

Sofort   275

Trustly 275

Pricing and Promotions modules 276

Loyalty Program 276

Specials block 277

SEO modules 277

Google Sitemap 277

Search and Filter modules 278

Quick search block 278

SHIPPING AND LOGISTICS MODULES 278

Carrier Compare 278

Date of Delivery 279

Globkurier 280

GoInterpay 280

Kiala Advanced (Kiala contract holders only) 280

Mondial Relay 281

So Colissimo 281

TNT Express France 282

Tracking - Front office 282

SMART SHOPPING MODULES 283

Shopping Feed 283

Twenga Price Comparison 283

TRANSLATION MODULES 284

Textmaster 284

OTHER MODULES 284

Dashboard Activity 284

Dashboard Goals 284

Dashboard Products 284

Dashboard Trends *284*

Managing Shipping 285

MANAGING CARRIERS 286

Creating a New Carrier *287*

SHIPPING PREFERENCES 293

Understanding Local Settings 297

LOCALIZATION 297

Import Localization Pack *297*

Configuration *299*

Localization *300*

Advanced *301*

LANGUAGES 301

Creating a New Language *302*

ZONES 304

COUNTRIES 305

Adding a New Country *306*

STATES 308

Adding a New State *309*

CURRENCIES 310

Updating the Currency Rates *311*

Adding a New Currency *312*

TAXES 314

Tax Options *315*

Adding a New Tax *316*

TAX RULES 317

Adding a New Tax Rule *318*

TRANSLATIONS 320

Modifying a Translation *321*

Add / Update a Language *325*

Import a Language Pack Manually *326*

Export a Language *326*

Copy   327

Understanding the Preferences **329**

GENERAL PREFERENCES 329

ORDERS PREFERENCES 331

General preferences *331*

Gift options *332*

PRODUCTS PREFERENCES 333

General preferences *333*

Pagination preferences *334*

Product page preferences 335

Products stock preferences 337

CUSTOMERS PREFERENCES 338

THEMES PREFERENCES 339

Your current theme 339

Select a theme for your "[name]" shop 344

Adding and exporting a theme 345

Live from PrestaShop Addons! 349

SEO & URLS PREFERENCES 350

Adding a New Friendly URL 353

Set up URLs 354

Set shop URL 356

Schema of URLs 357

Robots file generation 358

CMS - MANAGING STATIC CONTENT 358

Creating a New CMS Category 359

Creating a New CMS Page 361

IMAGES PREFERENCES 362

Add a New Images Size 363

Images preferences 364

Regenerate Images *365*

STORE CONTACTS PREFERENCES 366

Store list *367*

Parameters *371*

Contact details *371*

SEARCH PREFERENCES 372

Aliases list *373*

Indexation *374*

Search options *375*

Weight   375

MAINTENANCE SETTINGS 377

GEOLOCATION PREFERENCES 377

Options 378

Whitelist of IP address *379*

Understanding the Advanced Parameters 381

CONFIGURATION INFORMATION 381

PERFORMANCE PARAMETERS 382

Smarty   383

Debug mode *383*

Optional features *384*

Combine, Compress and Cache (CCC) 385

Media servers 386

Ciphering 387

Caching 388

E-MAIL PARAMETERS 389

E-mail   389

Test your email configuration 391

MULTISTORE PARAMETERS 391

CSV IMPORT PARAMETERS 392

Data format 396

Uploading the file 398

DB BACKUP 401

Backup Options 402

SQL MANAGER 403

Creating a new query 404

Starting a query 405

Settings 406

Some sample queries 406

LOGS PARAMETERS 408

Logs be e-mail 409

WEBSERVICE PARAMETERS 409

    Adding a new key... *410*

    Configuration... *411*

Administering the Back-Office 413

  ADMINISTRATION PREFERENCES 413

    General   413

    Upload quota... *414*

    Help   415

    Notifications... *416*

  QUICK ACCESS CONFIGURATION 416

    Adding a new link.. *417*

  EMPLOYEES ACCOUNTS CONFIGURATION 418

    Adding a new employee... *419*

    Employees options *421*

  EMPLOYEE PROFILES 422

    Adding a new profile *423*

  PROFILE PERMISSIONS 423

    Setting permissions for a new profile *425*

  ADMINISTRATION MENUS CONFIGURATION 426

    Moving menus *426*

Moving pages 427

Creating a new page or menu 427

MERCHANT EXPERTISE 429

Understanding Statistics 431

STATISTICS 431

Main interface 432

Navigating the statistics 435

SEARCH ENGINES 440

Adding a Search Engine 441

REFERRERS 442

Adding a new referrer 443

Settings 445

Advanced Stock Management 447

GENERAL CONCEPTS 447

Product quantity available for sale 448

Product stocks (physically stored) 448

Using the new stock management feature 449

PRESENTING THE STOCK MANAGEMENT INTERFACE 450

Stock management from the product sheet 451

Warehouses management 456

Stock management *459*

Stock Movement *463*

Instant Stock Status *464*

Stock Coverage *465*

Supply orders *466*

Configuration *472*

STOCK MANAGEMENT RULES 474

Managing Multiple Shops 479

HOW TO DECIDE IF YOU NEED THE MULTISTORE FEATURE 479

ENABLING THE MULTISTORE FEATURE 480

THE MULTISTORE INTERFACE 480

Managing your stores *480*

One back-office to rule them all *481*

CREATING A NEW SHOP GROUP 485

CREATING A NEW SHOP 487

SETTING A SHOP'S URL 491

SAMPLE USAGES AND SPECIFICS 494

Managing a catalog in multistore mode *494*

Data exchange between stores *495*

Managing CMS pages in multistore mode *497*

Managing discounts in multistore mode *498*

Web-service and multistore *498*

Training

This PrestaShop guide is intended to be a practical companion to the PrestaShop software. If you would like to learn even more, PrestaShop offers different training sessions. They are available for anyone who wishes to perfect and to master the PrestaShop software.

We offer three different sessions, tailored to your needs and expertise:

- **PrestaShop User Online**. Learn how to manage your shop on a daily basis from the comfort of your home or office.
  Length of training: this training is a 2-day online course.
- **PrestaShop Beginners Developer & Integrator Online Training**. Discover how to build PrestaShop modules and master PrestaShop's advanced features. You'll also learn how to customize a beautiful and dynamic PrestaShop online store.
  Length of training: this training is a 2-day online course.
- **PrestaShop Advanced Developer & Integrator Online Training**. Become an expert at building online stores with PrestaShop. You'll learn how to develop secure, optimized and beautiful online shops.
  Length of training: this training is a 2-day online course.

If you would like to receive further information and the requirements of participation, please visit the following page:
http://www.prestashop.com/en/training.

Customizing your shop

This guide will teach you about all the various options and features of a standard PrestaShop installation. Diving into PrestaShop means exploring many settings and possibilities, and the power of PrestaShop will little by little be presented to you.

You will soon learn that you can go even further than a standard installation. Indeed, by default your shop has one theme and a hundred of modules, but you can install as many themes and modules as you see fit to expand your shop and make it truly yours.

Themes and modules creators upload their creation on the PrestaShop Addons website, at http://addons.prestashop.com/, the only official PrestaShop marketplace, where shop owners can find many ways to extend and improve their shop.

Creating an account in is free, and many quality add-ons are free too. Browse the many categories, search for a specific keyword, then buy and download the add-on you need and install it on your shop – either in the /modules or /themes folder of your PrestaShop installation.

You do not have to be a PrestaShop expert to start shopping for add-ons: have a look at more than a thousand of modules and more than 900 themes right now!

Visit http://addons.prestashop.com!

Connecting to the PrestaShop back-office

The PrestaShop back-office is the name used to describe the administration panel of your PrestaShop site in this user-guide. You will spend most of your time in this panel, as everything that the user sees is handled directly through the back-office: adding/editing/removing products, handling carriers, building packs, creating vouchers, keeping contact with customers, improving your shop, etc.

During the install process, the /admin folder is renamed into something unique to your shop (for instance, /admin7890), for security reasons. Use that new folder name to access your shop (for example: http://myprestashop.com/admin7890).

> The name change is done automatically by PrestaShop. Be careful to memorize that folder name the first time you access it after the installation!

You will see the login page for your shop's control panel.

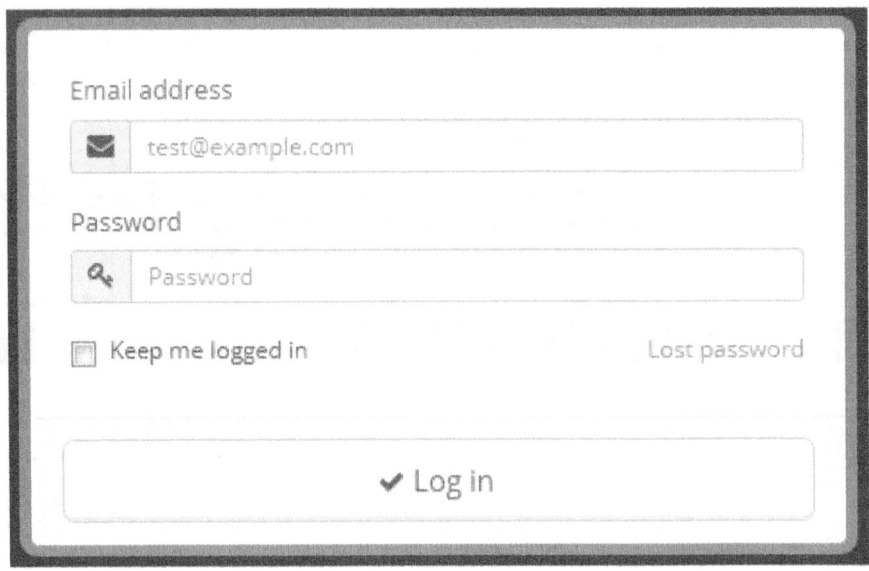

Enter the e-mail address and password that you registered with when you installed PrestaShop. Click the "Log In" button, and you are taken to the back-office's dashboard, a sort of welcome page for this control panel.

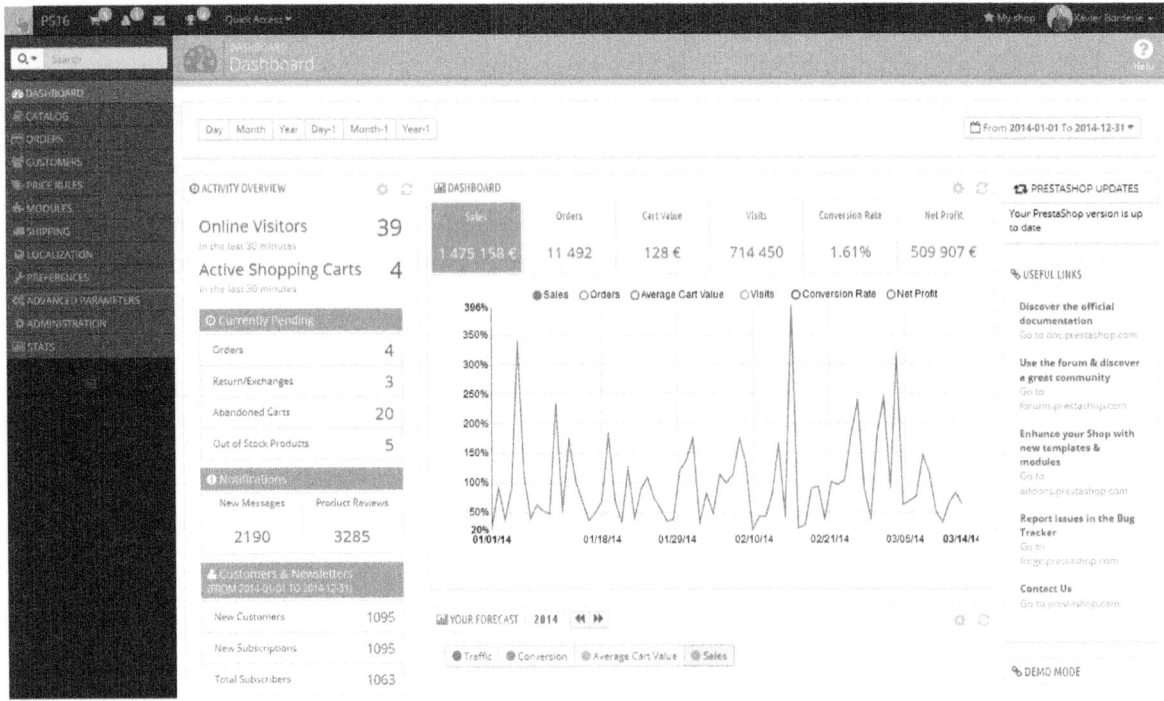

From this step onward, you can begin to configure your shop and sell products to your customers.

Read the next chapter of this user guide, named "First steps with PrestaShop 1.6", to understand all the various sections of the back-office.

Discovering the Administration Area

Now that you have installed PrestaShop 1.6 and that you are properly logged-in to your administration area, you should make sure to easily find your way through its administration interface, understand its notifications and know where to find one specific bit of information.

> The design of the administration area has been completely revamped with version 1.6 of PrestaShop in order to be more intuitive and ergonomic – as well as working better on mobile devices.
>
> While most of the 1.5 pages and options are still where you can expect them to, it might take some time to get used to

We have created this chapter in order to help you make the best of your discovery of PrestaShop's administration interface. It has been designed to be very ergonomic and easy to use, but be aware that you should read the whole guide in order to get a perfect grasp of your new online business tool!

Overview of the main interface

Take the time to survey the Dashboard – that is, the first page you see when logging into your back-office. Not only does it present you with a summary of everything you need to know about your shop at any given time, along with quick links to the main action page, but as a first-timer in PrestaShop, it also gives you tips about what you should have a look at.

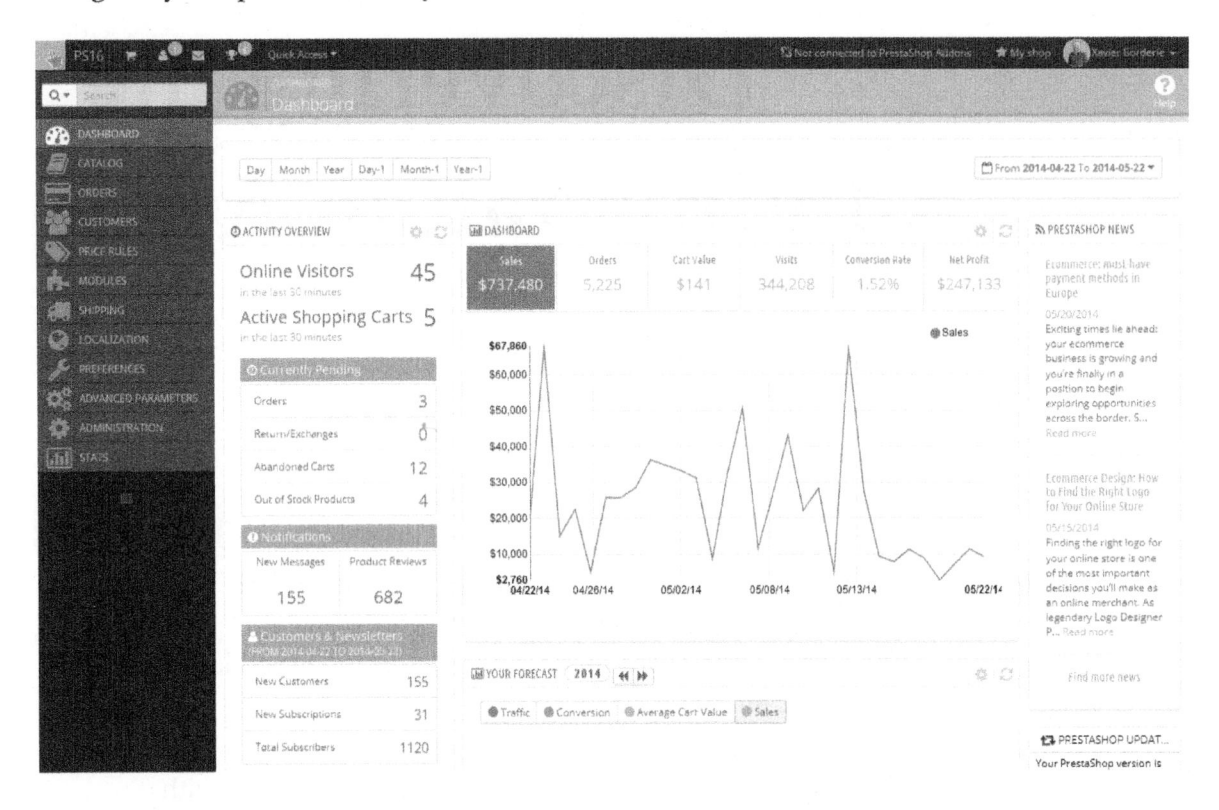

The top bar

At the top of the back-office is a black bar containing a handful of links:

- **(name of your shop)**. From any page, this takes you back to the Dashboard.
- **Cart icon**. A tooltip indicates the number of new orders, if any. Clicking it opens a panel presenting the new orders since you last clicked that icon. From there on, you can either display one of the new orders, or go to the list of orders.
- **Person icon**. A tooltip indicates the number of new customers, if any. Clicking it opens a panel presenting the last registered customers. From

there on, you can either display one of the new customers, or go to the list of customers.
- **Letter icon**. A tooltip indicates the number of new messages, if any. Clicking it opens a panel presenting the last customer service message. From there on, you can either display one of the new messages, or go to the list of messages.
- **Trophy icon.** A tooltip indicates the number of new items, if any. Clicking it opens a panel presenting your progress as a merchant. From there on, you can reach the full page of badges and points, from the "Merchant Expertise" module.
- **Quick Access**. This is the quick links menu, presenting the most useful links, as set in the "Quick Access" page under the "Administration" menu.
- **Not connected to PrestaShop Addons" link**. Opens a modal window enabling you to connect your shop to the Addons marketplace, and thus get updates from the modules and themes you bought.
- **"My Shop" link**. Opens a new browser tab with your shop's front-end.
- **(your name) link**. A simple dropdown panel with a reminder of the administrative account with which you are currently logged-in.
    - **"My preferences" link**. Takes you to your account's preferences page, where you can set some personal options (for instance, the back-office language or your password).
    - **"Log out" link**. Logs you out of the current user account.

The menus

All along your daily activities administrating your shop, you will have to browse through the many pages and options of the back-office.

> By default, the menu system in PrestaShop 1.6 is displayed on the left side of the page. You can switch the menu to the top of the page by using the "Display admin menu" option in your user preference page (which you can access through the link bearing your name in the top bar).
>
> Dashboard Catalog Orders Customers Price Rules Modules Shipping Localization Preferences Advanced Parameters Administration Stats

> In either vertical or horizontal format, the content of each menu is displayed when the mouse hovers the menu label, thus reducing the necessity to load new screens just to access menu options.
>
> In addition to that, the vertical format can be minimized to only its icons by clicking on the "parallel lines" icon at the bottom of it.

Each menu applies to a given set of tasks and contexts:

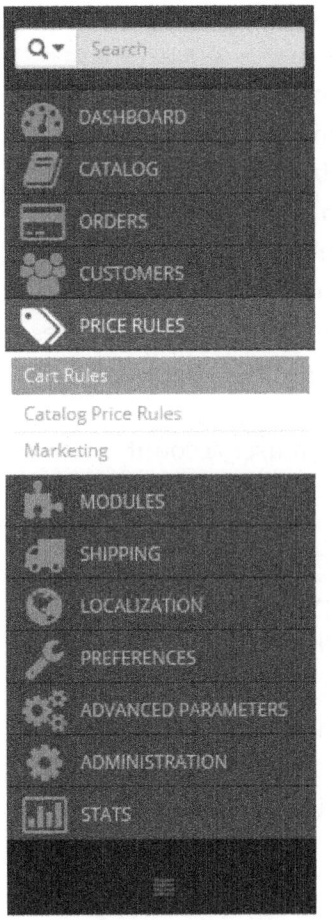

- **Search field with dropdown list**. Enables you to search within the content of your shop.
- **Catalog**. This is the heart of your shop, where you will add products, create categories, set up carriers and suppliers, etc.
- **Orders**. Once clients start adding products in their shopping carts, you will see orders in this menu, with the resulting invoices. This is also where you handle merchandise returns, credit slips and per-order customer service, among other things.
- **Customers**. Here you can access all the information about your clients, and edit their addresses, create groups of customers to which you can apply special discounts, handle customer service, and even manage social titles if need be.
- **Price Rules**. A very specific menu, enabling you to easily create vouchers and price reductions through a set of rules.
- **Modules**. Extend the power and usefulness of your shop by adding and activating modules: more than a hundred are available by default, and many more are available to buy on the Addons marketplace (http://addons.prestashop.com/). This is also where you handle themes, and where you can position the blocks of content from your module on the theme (including the Live Edit feature). One last menu page enables you to apply global settings to payment modules.

- **Shipping**. Everything pertaining to carriers and shipping costs, as well as marketing.
- **Localization**. Helps you customize your shop with local values, such as language and translation, currency, units, taxes and tax rules, and geographical entities (regions, countries, etc.).
- **Preferences**. PrestaShop is a very configurable e-commerce solution, and you can edit just about any of its behaviors using the full-featured preferences.
- **Advanced Parameters**. This menu contains links to tools and informational pages that are too specific to fit in other menus, such as the Web service settings, the database backup tool, or the performance page, among others.
- **Administration**. Here are the settings pertaining to the back-office itself; for instance, the content of the Quick Access menu, the employees list and permissions, or the menu order, among others.
- **Stats**. This menu gives you access to all the numerous statistics and graphics that are gathered and generated by PrestaShop.

These are the default menus. Note that modules can add new options to the existing pages, new pages to the existing menus, and even new menus.

Also, one menu is only available when the proper option is set:

- **Stock**. This menu gives you access to stock management feature, where you can handle warehouses, stock movement and supply orders.
  It can be made available through the "Products" preference page: simply activate the "Enable advanced stock management" option (in the "Products stock" section) and save your change to see the menu appear.

All the default standard menus, including the "Stock" menu, are explained in depth in this user guide.

The buttons

Many of the back-end pages use recurring buttons, either at the top or at the bottom of the screen. For instance, the product edition page can have up to 8 buttons available at the same time.

More than simple shortcuts, they open actual features that you will use very often.

The available buttons vary a lot depending on the context, and therefore two different pages might not feature the same set of buttons. Still, there are a few that you will often see:

- **Add new**. Opens the creation page of the current context.
- **Recommended modules**. Open a pop-in window containing the modules available in the current context.
- **Help**. Opens the online documentation for the current page.

The "Recommended modules" button presents you the modules which apply to the current context. For instance, in the "Shipping > Carriers" page, it will display the modules from the "Shipping & Logistics" category of modules. This is very helpful when you need to quickly find which module to install and configure in order to get a given result.

Many of the back-office forms are validated with buttons at the bottom of the screen:

- **Save**. Saves the content of the current page and returns to the list of existing items.
- **Save and stay**. Saves the content of the current page and keep the page open.
- **Cancel**. Returns to the list of existing items.

Contextual help

Since version 1.6.0.7 of PrestaShop, the software's documentation is directly embedded into administration interface: clicking on the "Help" button from any back-office page reduces the main interface's width in order to add a new column on the right, which contains the documentation for that section of the back-office.

Another click on the "Help" button closes the contextual help. If you do not close the help column, PrestaShop understands that you want it displayed on every page of the back-office, and thus will maintain the column open until you have clicked to close it.

> If the browser's display zone is lower than 1220 pixels width, then PrestaShop will open the contextual documentation in a new browser window rather than reducing the screen space dedicated to the main interface.

At the bottom of the help column, a small form enables you to tell the PrestaShop team whether the help section has been helpful to you or not. Rate the help page by clicking on one of the 5 levels of satisfaction. If you click on one of the two lowest levels, PrestaShop will open a short form allowing to detail your thoughts? You can either fill it and click on the "Submit" button, or close the form by clicking on the cross, in which case only your rating will be sent to our server.

The Dashboard

Let's now explore the content of the Dashboard itself. It can feel crowded to a first-time user, but you will find that it gives an excellent summary of your shop's daily activities at a glance.

The Dashboard is divided in 4 main areas: a horizontal bar, and three columns.

> By default, the Dashboard uses fake data so that you can better visualize what the various stats are for.
>
> When using PrestaShop for a real online store, you must disable this fake data so that your real data is used: click on "No" in the "Demo mode" block at the bottom right of the screen.

The horizontal bar

At the top of the Dashboard is a single bar which helps you choose the period of time for the currently displayed dashboard statistics. Three sets of options are available:

- Current day, month or year.
- Previous day, month or year.
- Precise date selection (the button on the right, which opens a date selector).

Choosing an option updates all the blocks of content that are on the Dashboard so that they display data for the chosen period of time only. Blocks that are not stats-based do not change.

In order to choose a period of time, you can either click the first and last date of that period in the calendar (the clicking order does not matter), or you can type the dates in the YYYY-MM-DD format in the text boxes. Click "Apply" to see the Dashboard change according to your settings.

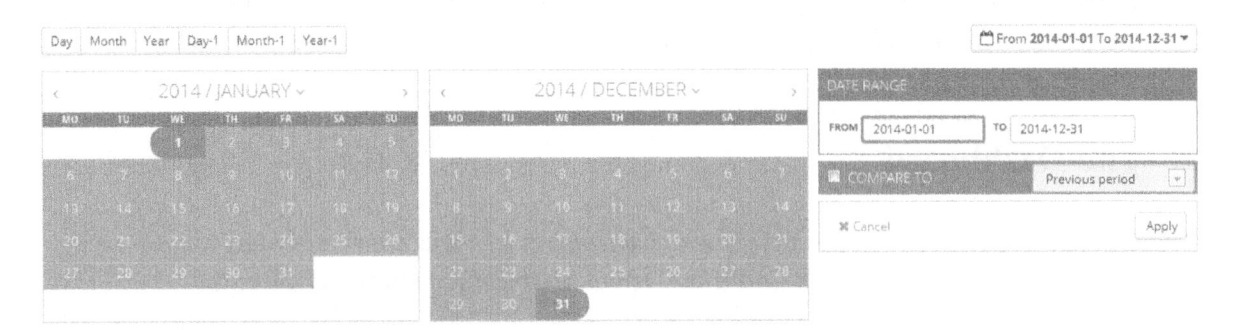

You can also compare two periods of time together by checking the "Compare To" box. Select the second period as would do for the first one (the two can even overlap), then click on the "Apply" button.
When comparing two periods, some of the content blocks will update to indicate the evolution of the data (see for instance the main "Dashboard" block, which presents data from the Dashboard Trends module).

The left column

By default, this column presents you with data from the Dashboard Activity module, which gives the main figures from your database in a quick glance:

- Online visitors in the last 30 minutes.
- Active shopping carts in the last 30 minutes.
- Currently pending orders, return/exchange inquiries, abandoned carts and out of stock products.
- Notifications for new messages, order inquiries and product reviews.
- New customers and new newsletter subscriptions.
- Traffic statistics: visits, unique visitors, traffic sources and direct links.

The central column

The central column is where the term "dashboard" takes its importance: this area of the Dashboard presents the user (you) with the most important numbers pertaining to his shop's daily activities, along with a graph of sales and a list of the latest orders. Every time you log into your shop's administration area, you will be first and foremost looking at the evolution that these numbers take. This is where you see your shop live and breathe.

By default, there are three blocks of content in this column, which are handled by modules:

- **Dashboard** (Dashboard Trends module). This is the main block of information on the dashboard. With its various graphics, it really helps you see if your shop is headed in the right direction or not. Click on one of the graphic type to display it. Additionally, when comparing two time periods, it displays the evolution of each figure in percentages. Hover the graphic with your mouse to see the details.

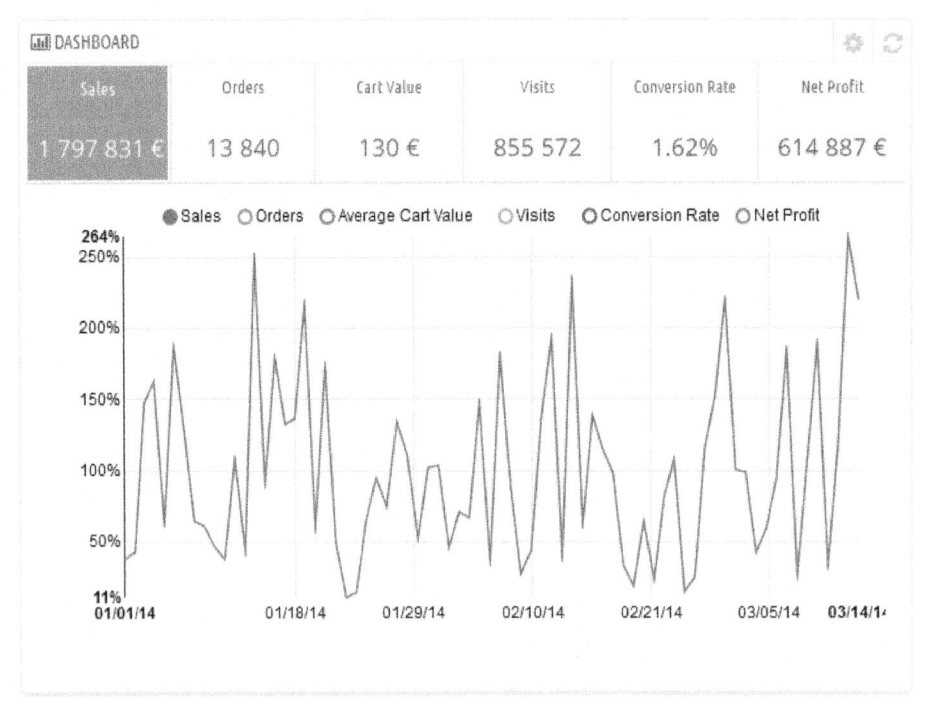

Clicking on its configuration icon (top right) open a new page where you can set various expenses that your shop has (bank wire fee, average shipping fee, hosting expenses, etc.), in order to better indicate your trends.

- **Your Forecast** (Dashboard Goals module). This block presents you with the goals you have for the coming months, and how your shop is doing as compared to them. Hover the graphic with your mouse to see the details.

Depending on your monthly results, you should update your

forthcoming goals. You can set your goals in the block's configuration form (top right of the block), and fill in your expectations month per month in terms of traffic, conversion rate, and average cart value. The "Sales" column will be updated according to the goals set in the other columns (for instance, for a 1000 visitors with a 2% conversion rate and a $10 average cart, you would get 1000*(2/100)*10 = $200). You can change the currency in the "Currencies" page under the "Localization" menu.

- **Products and sales** (Dashboard Products module). This block presents you with a table of your latest orders and a ranking of your products: best sellers, most viewed and top searches (as searched in your shop's search form, not from search engines).

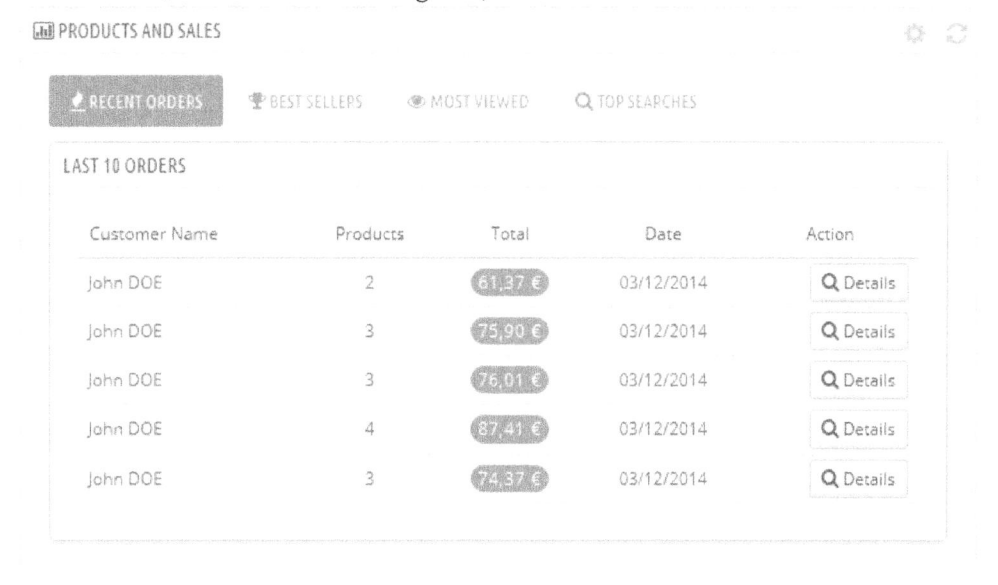

Customer Name	Products	Total	Date	Action
John DOE	2	61,37 €	03/12/2014	Q Details
John DOE	3	75,90 €	03/12/2014	Q Details
John DOE	3	76,01 €	03/12/2014	Q Details
John DOE	4	87,41 €	03/12/2014	Q Details
John DOE	3	74,37 €	03/12/2014	Q Details

You can set the number of items to display in each by opening the block's configuration form

The right column

This last column is an informational one: it gives you the latest news from PrestaShop.com, notifications about new PrestaShop versions, and useful links.

It also features the "Demo mode" block, from which you can disable the fake data used by default on the Dashboard and use your own data (as gathered by PrestaShop's statistics system).

First steps with PrestaShop 1.6

You must spend a good amount of time making sure every part of your future online shop is properly set up, secured, validated and ready for business.

While PrestaShop makes it easy for you to install it and build your business online, it cannot possibly be a 5-seconds work: you are dealing with products, customers, carriers, and most importantly with real actual money that will be flowing from your customers to your bank account. We dare say you want to make sure nothing fails in the process of validating an order, having the products be found in your storage location, then be packaged, and shipped to your customers without a single glitch, or even without anything unpredicted happening without your knowledge.

PrestaShop is a very complete tool, and the number of possibilities can feel overwhelming. This chapter will therefore lead you through some basic actions to perform in order to set up your shop before the big launch. A lot can and must be done before you launch your shop, but these steps are the essential configuration steps of any shop.

Deactivate your shop

We will consider that you are still within the first hour following your installation of PrestaShop, in a single-shop instance.

Deactivating your shop means making sure that no one can access it while you are busy making changes, creating products, settings prices and taxes, installing payment modules and a new theme, setting carriers... This is called "putting your shop in maintenance mode".

Enable Shop	YES NO
Maintenance IP	[ ] + Add my IP

In your back-office, go the "Preferences / Maintenance" page. This page features two simple settings:

- **Enable Shop**. Simply set it to "No", and your front-end will display the maintenance page to your visitors, which simply states that your shop will soon be back online.
- **Maintenance IP**. This is where you must put your own IP address, so that you can still get access to your front page, and browse your shop as if it was available to all. This is a must-do every time you put your shop in maintenance mode, as you will always need to browse your front-end so as to make sure everything is in place as intended.
  Simply click on the "Add my IP" button. You can add more IP addresses by separating them with commas.

> If you have already decided what your theme and products are, you can simply put your shop in Catalog mode. This means that customers can browse your shop, but no price will be displayed, and they won't be able to add anything to their cart until you disable the Catalog mode.
>
> You can activate the Catalog mode by going to the "Preferences / Products" page, where it is the first option.

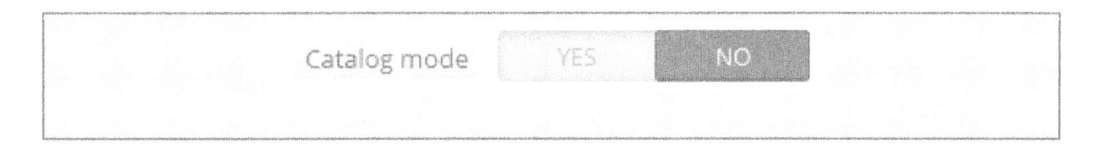

Delete the content of the default shop

The default installation features a handful of products – mainly women's clothing. Their only use is to help you explore the organization of a real store. After you've learned the intricacies of the ties between products, categories, orders and customers, you should delete all these items in order to start your shop with a clean slate.

You must therefore delete all the default data, which means:

- products and their...
    - categories
    - attributes
    - features
    - manufacturers
    - suppliers

- image mappings
  - tags
- orders
  - order messages
- customers
  - customers shopping carts
- carriers
  - price ranges
  - weight ranges
- contact & stores (delete or adapt to your business' needs)
- CMS pages (delete or adapt to your business' needs)

This would mean browsing through the many various screens of the back-office and deleting content one page after the other, but there is much easier way:

1. Go to the "Modules > Modules" page.
2. Find the "Database Cleaner" module and click its "Install" button.
3. You are directly taken to its configuration page (if not, click its "Configuration" button).
4. Read and accept the warning, then click the "Delete Catalog" button: it will delete all your products and their attributes, manufacturers, etc.
5. Read and accept the warning, then click the "Delete Orders & Customers" button: it will delete all your customers and their orders, carts, etc.
6. Click the "Check & fix" button to refine your database integrity constraints.
7. Click the "Clean & optimize" button to reorganizes the physical storage of table data and associated index data, to reduce storage space and improve I/O efficiency when accessing the tables.

THERE IS NO WAY BACK. Be sure to only click these buttons if you do intend to wipe your database from its default content.

Configure your shop's information

Now that you have a clean shop, you can start making it your own, and that implies setting everything up to your likings, starting with your personal information and your preferences.

The shop's basic settings

You should pay attention to the following settings, most of which are important because they are displayed on the front-office, and therefore in plain sight of your customers.

Some of these settings require you to configure a module instead of changing one of PrestaShop's preferences.

Configuring a module is easy:

1. Go to the "Modules" page under the "Modules" menu.
2. Type the name of the module (or part of it) in the module search box. It should display results as you type.
3. When the module is found, click its "Configure" button, and follow the instructions.

For each module presented here, you should read their documentation for more information.

Setting	Description	Where to find it
Shop name	Defines your brand, most notably on search engines (Google, Yahoo!, Bing...).	"Preferences" menu, "Store Contacts" page, then in the "Contact details" section, edit the "Shop name" option.
Shop logo	Defines your brand visually. The default logo says "YourLogo" as an incentive to use yours. Displayed at the top left of every page of your store, as well as in your invoices and other automatic e-mails.	"Preferences" menu, "Themes" page, "Appearance" section, then change the various default images to your logo.
Default shop currency	The currency in which you want to set the default price for your products.	"Localization" menu, "Localization" page, "Configuration" section.

		If the currency is not available, you must import localization pack for its country first: use the "Import a localization pack" tool from the same page.
Customer service info	A block presenting the phone number for your customer service, and a button to send you an e-mail. Displayed in the front-office's right column.	"Contact block" module.

Setting	Description	Where to find it
Company info / Contact info	A block presenting your contact address, the phone number for your customer service, and a link to send you an e-mail. Displayed in the front-office's footer.	"Block contact info" module.
Advertising	A block presenting an image with a link to another site. Displayed in front-office, left column.	"Advertising block" module.
Image slider	The slider presents several images, scrolling one after the other. It is a strong visual signature for your store and products. Usually placed front and center of the homepage	"Image slider for your homepage" module.
CMS pages	The content of static pages, such as "About Us", "Delivery", "Legal Notice", "Terms and Conditions", and "Secure Payment". Some of them have default content,	"Preferences" menu, "CMS" page, then edit and create pages at will.

	which you should adapt to your business; some others are empty, and you should paste your own text. Displayed in the "Information" block in the left column, and in the "Information" section of the footer.	
Social networks	A block presenting three links: your company's Facebook page, your company's Twitter account, and the RSS feed for your company's blog (or "current events" site). By default, all these links lead to the PrestaShop company's own sites. It is important that you change it to your own. Displayed in the "Follow us" section of the footer.	"Social networking block" module.
Top menu	The top of the default theme uses a top menu to indicate categories that the visitor can go to, as well as links to other locations – for instance, the default installation has a "Blog" link which sends the use to the official PrestaShop blog.	"Top horizontal menu" module.
Homepage content	The default theme contains a lot of demo content: texts, images, links, etc. If you intend on using that theme for your own store instead of buying your theme, you	"Theme configurator" module: this module handles a lot of things on your theme. Mainly, it enables you to switch some feature off and on (social sharing buttons, top banner, payment logos, etc.), and perhaps more

| | should make sure to remove all the default content first. | importantly, it lets you easily add/change images on your home-page.
"Custom CMS information block" module: this module helps you manager the two last blocks at the bottom of the home-page, right before the footer: the "Free shipping etc." one and the "Custom block" one. |

These are the most visible default settings on your front-end – at least with the default theme.

The "Where to find it" column enables you to see where you can find the interface to change these aspects of your store. This user guide will provide you with more details for each interface.

Shop languages

PrestaShop is able to work with many languages, both on the front-office and the back-office. As soon as more than one language is enabled in your back-office, each back-office text-field is accompanied with a language code selector, which indicates the current language, and which you can click in order to choose another language in which to write that field's content.

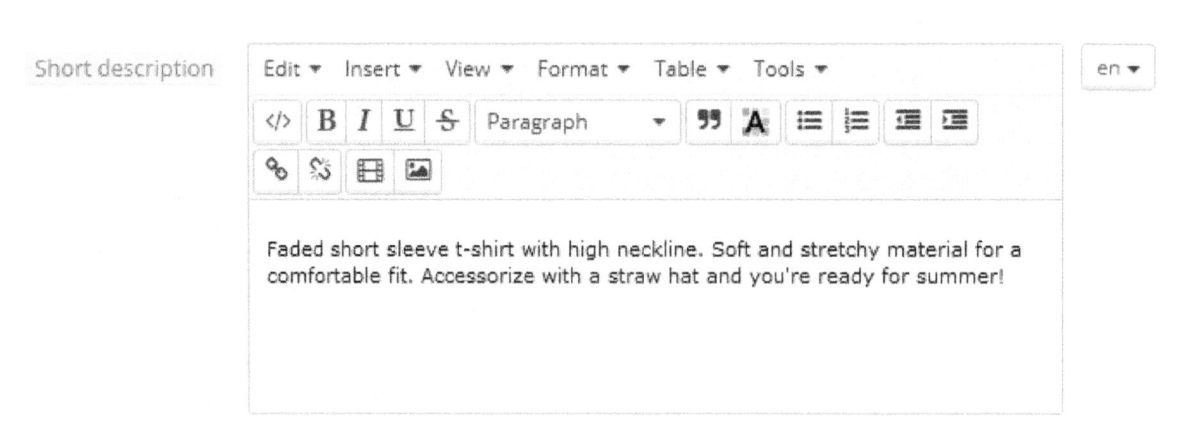

By default, PrestaShop is installed with two languages: the one used when installing the software, and French. To manage the currently installed languages, go to the "Localization / Languages" page. It presents you with a table of the available languages.

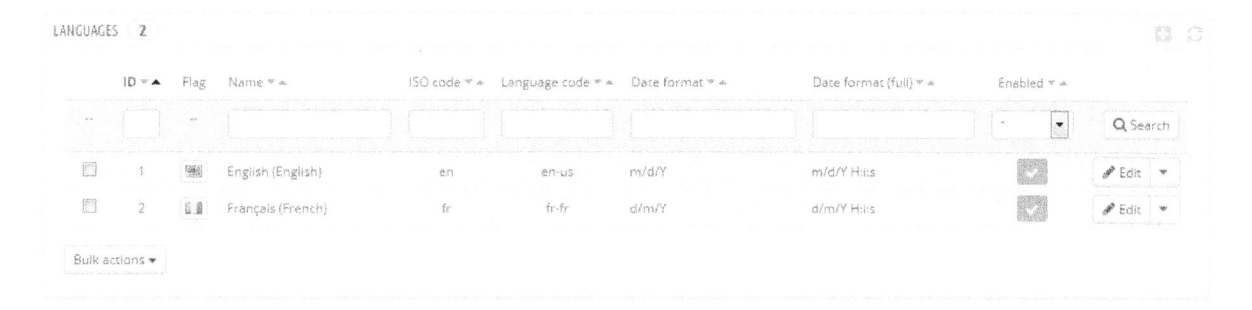

ID	Flag	Name	ISO code	Language code	Date format	Date format (full)	Enabled
1		English (English)	en	en-us	m/d/Y	m/d/Y H:i:s	Yes
2		Français (French)	fr	fr-fr	d/m/Y	d/m/Y H:i:s	Yes

The currently enabled language(s) have a green "Yes", while the others have a red "No". Click on a "Yes" to disable the selected language; click on a "No" to enable it back.

> You can install and enable many languages if you think your shop needs them, but be aware that you will have to translate your content for all of the enabled languages: product names, descriptions, tags, category names and descriptions, static content (CMS pages), module settings, etc.

You can easily import many more languages in the "Localization / Localization" page, and then enable them in the "Localization / Languages" page.

Employees information

Should you have people helping you with your shop (whether they are your family, your friends, or paid employees), you should make sure to create an employee account for each of them – if only to know who has performed which recent action. The other advantage is that you can give them specific profiles and specific access rights to the administration pages: for instance, you might not want everyone to have access to your statistics, your invoices or your payment settings.
You can create as many profiles as needed.

To create a new employee account, go to the "Administration" menu, select "Employees", and click the "Add new employee" button. Give it a name, such as "Martin Doe" or "Shipping handler", and save.

An account can be used for as many people as needed – but we do advise you to create one for each helping person.

Now that you have a proper account for this employee, you should give that account specific permissions, tailored to the employee's tasks. By default, a new profile cannot do much. It is up to you to set exactly the parts of your shop to which that profile should have access. It can be a tedious task, but it is an important one.

To assign permissions to an employee account, you must use the "Profile" option in the account creation page: this menu lets you pick the account's profile (SuperAdmin, translator, etc.)

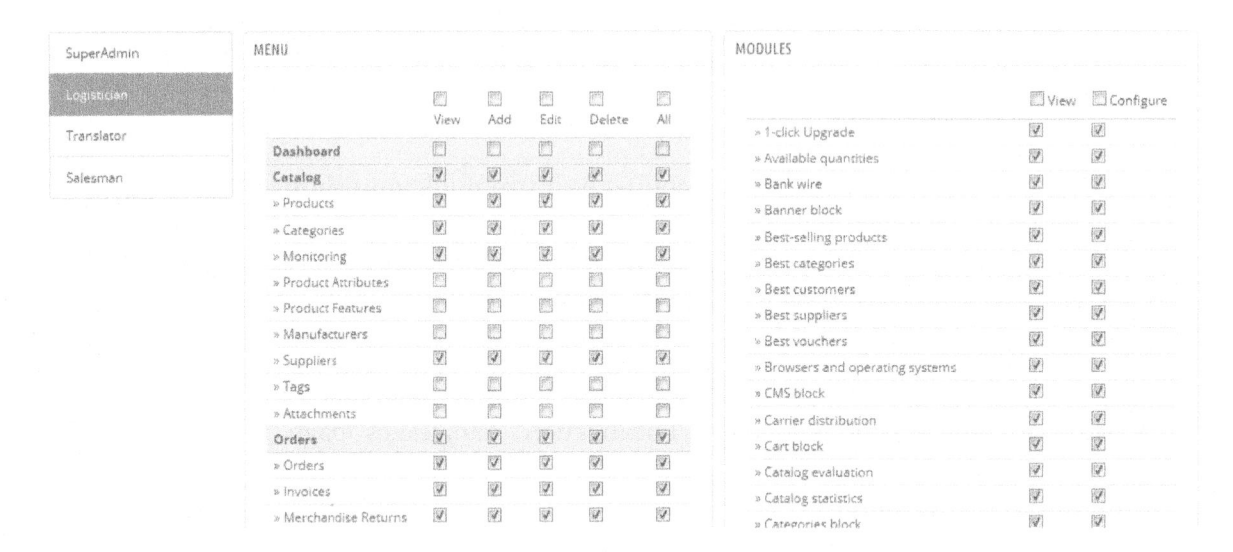

You can edit these permissions this way: go to the "Administration" menu, select "Permissions", and select the profile you want to change. A long list of permissions appears: edit them at will. Your changes are saved automatically.

Configure your payment methods

Your shop is meant to earn money, and this can only become a reality if you use at least one payment module. Several modules are already available in the default install, which you can install and configure (from the "Modules" page under the "Modules" menu, in the "Payments & Gateways" category), and create restrictions for them (in the "Payment" page under the "Modules" menu). Many payment modules require you to first set up an account on the service they were built for.

See the "Payment" section of the "Making the Native Modules Work" chapter of this guide in order to learn about them all.

You can also install other payment modules, downloaded from the Addons marketplace: http://addons.prestashop.com/en/4-payments-gateways-prestashop-modules

> Check and bank wire are the only two payment methods which are enabled by default. If you choose to keep them, you **need** to configure them with your information: check order and address, account owner, bank details (IBAN, BIC, etc.).
>
> These payment methods are configured through the "Bank Wire" and "Payment by check" modules, which you can find in the "Payments & Gateways" category of the modules list.

Configure carriers and shipment

Products sold on your shop must be shipped to your customers – unless you only sell downloadable products, in which case the "Shipping" menu will be of little use to you.

Whether you are sending your products yourself by regular post office mail, or you have set up a contract with a carrier, you should set this information within PrestaShop.

See the "Managing Shipping" chapter of this guide in order to learn about shipping and carriers.

> **Merchandise return is not enabled by default.** If you want to allow your customers to return products and get a refund or a voucher, you can do it in the "Merchandise return (RMA) options" of the "Merchandise return" page, under the "Orders" menu.
> Merchandise return is explained in the "Managing Orders" chapter of this guide.

Choose your theme

Your shop should have its own theme in order to have a distinctive style, and therefore be more recognizable, separating it from the numerous other online shops.

There are many themes to choose from on the PrestaShop Addons marketplace: http://addons.prestashop.com/en/3-templates-prestashop.

You can also choose to create your own theme, or have it created for you by a developer. Refer to the PrestaShop Designer Guide for help.

Once your theme is installed, you should explore it fully in order to know it by heart and be able to help customers out of a situation. Read its documentation carefully.

You can and should customize some of the theme's aspects, most notably its logo in various situations (header, mail, invoice, etc.). This is done using the "Themes" preferences page, which you can find under the "Preferences" menu.

Choose your modules

PrestaShop comes bundled with more than a hundred modules. These are very varied: analytics, front-office features, payment, shipping... You should explore the available modules in full, in order to know which ones you might want to enable, and which you'd rather keep disabled.

See the "Managing Modules" and "Making the Native Modules Work" chapters of this guide in order to learn about them all.

You can also find many other modules on the Addons marketplace: http://addons.prestashop.com/en/2-modules-prestashop

> Every time you activate and configure a module, make sure that it does work well within the confines of your theme, in case its features impact your shop's front-end.

Create your products and product categories

This is described in details in the "Adding Products and Product Categories" chapter.

Create your static content

If you haven't done this already, you should take the time to write the content for the various static pages which are either already available in your PrestaShop installation, or ones that you feel are needed.

Some pages already exist, but their content should really be triple-checked, as they can have a lot of impact on your shop's legal status, among other things.

The default pages are "About Us", "Delivery", "Legal Notice", "Terms and Conditions", and "Secure Payment". Some of them have default content, which you should update; some others are empty, and you should paste your own text.
To edit these pages, go to the "Preferences" menu, click the "CMS" page, then choose the page you want to edit, or create new ones.

You can create as many pages as you feel are necessary.

Build your top menu

Now that you have product categories and CMS pages, you should arrange them in a logical and compelling way in the top menu.

This is done using the "Top horizontal menu" module: go to the "Modules" page, type "menu" in the module search form, and you should find the module. Enable it if it is disabled, then configure it: remove the pages or categories you deem unnecessary, add other pages, and move the content around, until you are satisfied with your menu's hierarchy.

Activate your shop

Now that all is set and done, you can finally open your shop to the public.

Go the "Preferences / Maintenance" page, and change the two options:

- **Enable Shop**: set it back to "Yes".
- **Maintenance IP**: remove your IP from the list. This is optional: your shop will still work if you leave the field as it is.

Your shop should now be fully ready to receive its first visitors... and take its first orders!

Managing the Catalog

The foundation of a PrestaShop site is its catalog, which contains products and product categories. Building and improving your catalog is the main way you will make your website live in the eyes of the customer. This is where your shop becomes a reality, creating content, and thus giving value to your online presence.

As the heart of your shop, your catalog deserves a great deal of your attention. Adding products does not only mean adding an image and some text, and then validating your content. It means knowing your product by heart: price, weight, size, features, specifications, details, manufacturer, supplier and so much more. You should not start adding products to your Catalog without knowing exactly what you want to present to the customer, and thus need to have a set plan about your products and the way they will be displayed. This also means knowing your shop's front-office like the back of your hand in order to properly fill in the required fields.

The "Catalog" section can be accessed by opening the menu with the same name, which lists all the product-related pages. This is where you manage your products and their characteristics throughout your PrestaShop shop.

Managing Products

You can manage the products in your shop using the "Products" page, in the "Catalog" menu.

The Product List

Clicking on the "Products" option of the "Catalog" menu takes you to the list of your current products, displayed with their main details: ID, photo, name, reference, category, etc.

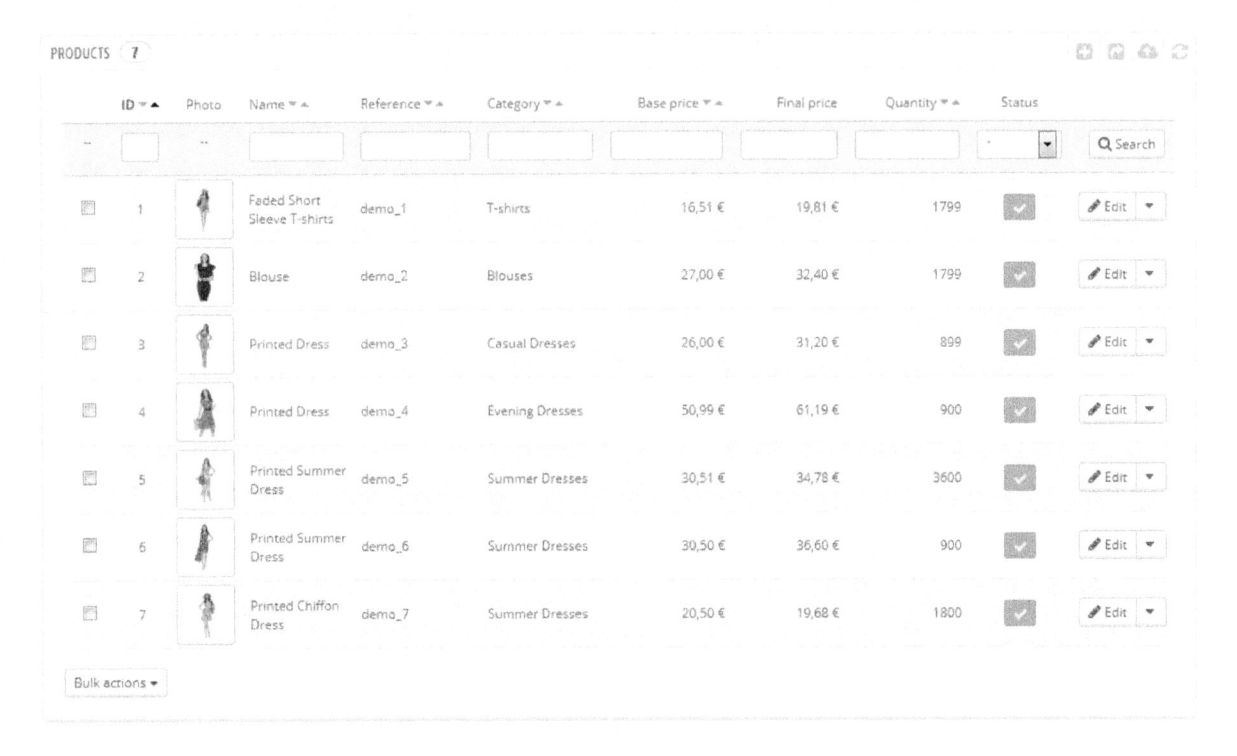

ID	Photo	Name	Reference	Category	Base price	Final price	Quantity	Status	
1		Faded Short Sleeve T-shirts	demo_1	T-shirts	16,51 €	19,81 €	1799	✓	Edit
2		Blouse	demo_2	Blouses	27,00 €	32,40 €	1799	✓	Edit
3		Printed Dress	demo_3	Casual Dresses	26,00 €	31,20 €	899	✓	Edit
4		Printed Dress	demo_4	Evening Dresses	50,99 €	61,19 €	900	✓	Edit
5		Printed Summer Dress	demo_5	Summer Dresses	30,51 €	34,78 €	3600	✓	Edit
6		Printed Summer Dress	demo_6	Summer Dresses	30,50 €	36,60 €	900	✓	Edit
7		Printed Chiffon Dress	demo_7	Summer Dresses	20,50 €	19,68 €	1800	✓	Edit

Beside the product list, this page presents you with four statistics from your store:

- Percentage of in-stock items,
- Percentage of average gross margin,
- Percentage of sales during the last 30 days,
- Number of disabled products.

The "Filter by category" option enables you to only display products pertaining to you current search, as well as reorganizing the position of products within a category.

Product position

You cannot reorganize the whole list of products. The products are displayed as is in your store (by increasing ID number), and the customer can choose the product's order using the available sorting algorithms: lowest price first, highest price first, product name A to Z, product name Z to A, in-stock first, lowest reference first, highest reference first.

You can organize products on a per-category basis by clicking on the "Filter by category" checkbox. This opens a small interface listing all your categories and sub-categories. Selecting one category automatically filters the list of products to only display products from the selected category. It also adds a "Position" column to the table, with which you can order the product on the category page. This is done either by moving the rows up and down, or by clicking the arrows.

Your product order can then be overridden by the user's sorting choice.

Note that when you change the display order in the product list in the back-office (by clicking on column name's arrow in order to sort products according to that column), the "Position" column does not display arrows nor can you use it to move rows around anymore. Instead, it displays the position number of the product. In order to be able to position products again, click on the "Reset" button.

Finally, the top of the product list presents four buttons:

- **Add new product**. Creates a new product.
- **Export**. Downloads a CSV file of all the products in your catalog.
- **Import**. Sends you to the CSV Import option page, from where your can import your CSV files.
- **Refresh List**. Reloads the list of products to display the latest changes.

You can add new products by clicking on "Add new". A form appears, with several tabs in the left column and two buttons at the top: "Back to list" and "Help".

The Product Creation Page Global Buttons

By default, the product creation page has two buttons that you will find on most the administration pages: "Recommended modules" and "Help".

At the bottom of the each page are three buttons:

- **Save**. This saves any change you have made to any of the data for the current product, and takes you back to the product list.
- **Save and stay**. This saves any change you have made to any of the data for the current product, and keeps you on the current tab. This is particularly useful when you want to switch tabs without losing your changes to the current tab, or in order to see your changes get applied immediately.
- **Cancel**. It simply takes you back to the list of product, without saving any change you have made in any of the tab from this page.

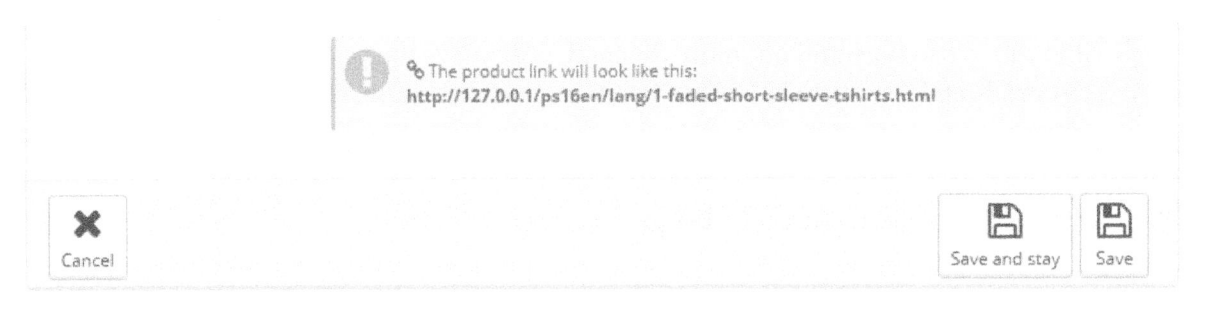

As soon as you give your new product a name and click on the "Save and stay" button at the bottom, more buttons appear at the top of the product page:

- **Preview**. Displays the front-page page of your product. This is very handy, as it works even if the product is disabled ("Information" tab).
- **Duplicate**. Creates an exact copy of the current product. This is very useful when you'd rather use the current product's data as a template for another new product, and not have to create every data of the new product by hand. For instance, two products might be very different, but could share the same associations, carriers or supplier settings.

> **Don't over-duplicate!**
>
> If you need to create different versions of the same product, because of its variety of colors, capacity, size, etc., then you should create product combination for the current product rather than duplicating it X times. See the "Combinations" tab on the left, which is explained in the "Adding Product Combinations" section of this chapter.

- **Product sales**. Redirects you to the "Product detail" page of the statistics dashboard ("Stats" menu), which gives you a graphic of both the visits to this product's page, and also its sales.
- **Delete this product**. Removes all the data for the current product, including its images, combinations, features, etc.

Filling out the Product Information

The first tab contains the basic information about the product.

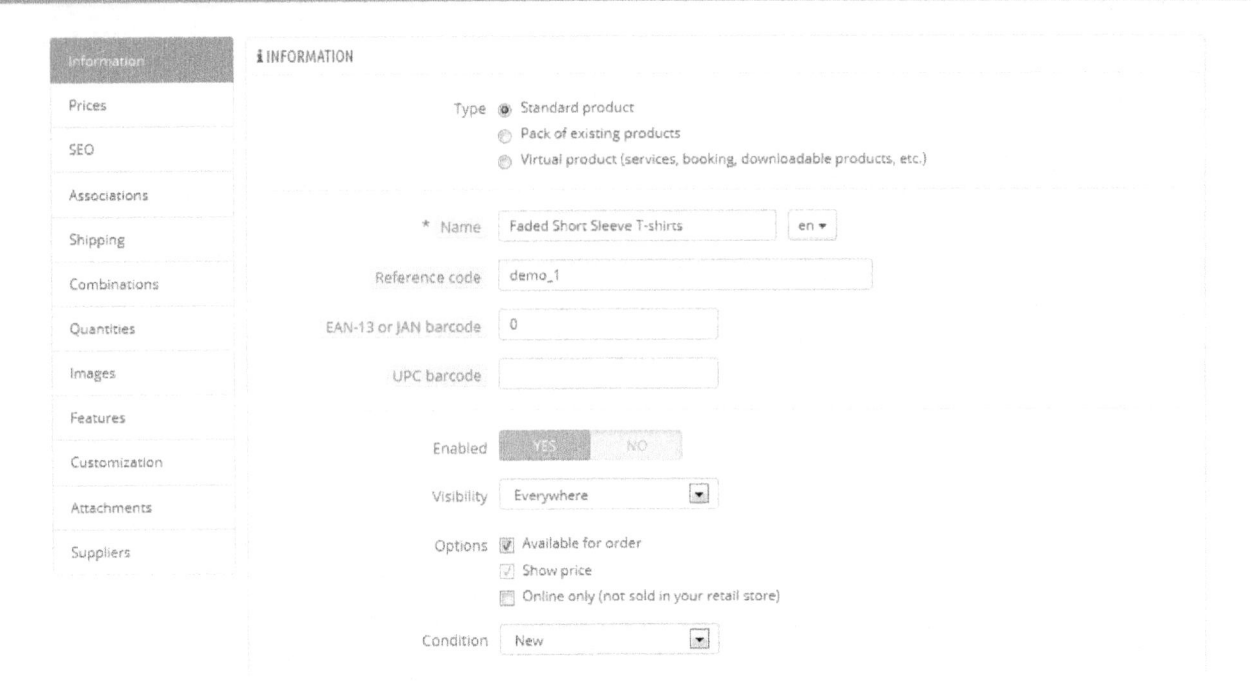

Information
Prices
SEO
Associations
Shipping
Combinations
Quantities
Images
Features
Customization
Attachments
Suppliers

i INFORMATION

Type: ● Standard product
○ Pack of existing products
○ Virtual product (services, booking, downloadable products, etc.)

* Name: Faded Short Sleeve T-shirts [en ▼]

Reference code: demo_1

EAN-13 or JAN barcode: 0

UPC barcode:

Enabled: YES / NO

Visibility: Everywhere

Options: ☑ Available for order
☑ Show price
☐ Online only (not sold in your retail store)

Condition: New

The first line is an essential one: indicate whether the product is a pack (a combination of at least two existing products), a virtual product (downloadable file, service, etc.), or simply a classic, mail-sent product. For now, we will only explore the first option of these three, and deal with packs and virtual products in their own sections of this chapter.

> There are many more product-related options in the "Products" page from the "Preferences" menu:
>
> - Number of days for which the product is considered 'new'.
> - Default product order.
> - Enable advanced-stock management.
> - etc.
>
> You should really check that these global settings are set as you wish.

You begin with four text fields:

- **Name**. The first thing to complete is the product name, which will appear in the search engine results. Next to the field you will find a language code, which enables you to choose the language into which you wish to edit or create the name.

> You **must** give the product a name in at least the default language before you can save it. You won't be able to save until it has a name – and many other tabs require the product to be saved in order to be accessible.
>
> Make sure to translate each field in every language that your shop supports. In order to do that, click on the language code next to the field, and choose the language in which you wish to edit the text.

- **Reference code**. This is your own internal reference. It might be a number, or its reference from the storage location or its supplier, or anything that makes it unique.
- **EAN-13 or JAN barcode**. These are the numbers of the product's barcode, which are used worldwide in order to identify it. You can use either an EAN-13 or a JAN number.
    - An EAN-13 is the product's 13-digit international article number. Read more on Wikipedia: http://en.wikipedia.org/wiki/International_Article_Number_%28EAN%29.
    - A JAN is specific to Japan, but is compatible with the international EAN. Read more on Wikipedia: http://en.wikipedia.org/wiki/Japanese_Article_Number.
- **UPC**. A 12-digit barcode, more widely used in North America, UK, Australia and New-Zealand. Read more on Wikipedia: http://en.wikipedia.org/wiki/Universal_Product_Code.

Then come four options:

- **Enabled**. If you do not want this product to be immediately available or visible to your customers, switch the option to "No".
- **Visibility**. You can further choose to have the product available through different channels:
    - **Everywhere**. Customers can get to the product by browsing the catalog, search for the product's name, or directly using its URL.
    - **Catalog**. Customers can get to the product by browsing the catalog or directly using its URL.

- **Search**. Customers can get to the product by searching for its name or directly using its URL.
- **Nowhere**. Customers can only get to the product using its URL. They won't find it by browsing through the catalog or by searching for its name. This is great for creating private products, that only a few trusted visitors can access, even temporarily (you can change this setting at any time).
  - **Options**. A couple of specific options.
    - **Available for order**. If you uncheck this box, customers will not be able to add this product to their cart. This makes it more like a single-product Catalog mode (in comparison with the "Catalog mode" preference).
    - **Show price**. If the "available for order" option above is unchecked, you can either choose to display the product's price nevertheless (even though visitors won't be able to buy it), or choose to not display it.
    - **Online only (not sold in store)**. If your business does have brick-and-mortar stores, this option will prove invaluable when a product is only sold online, not in store – this prevents customers from checking a product price online, then come to your store hoping to buy it directly, and thus avoid shipping cost.
  - **Condition**. Not all shops sell new product. This option enables you to indicate the condition of the product:
    - **New**. The product is brand new, sealed in its original packaging.
    - **Used**. The product has been sold at least once before, and probably used by someone else (second hand). It should come in its original packaging, which might be closed with tape.
    - **Refurbished**. The product has been returned for various reasons ("scratches, dents or other forms of cosmetic damage which do not affect the performance of the unit"). Read more on Wikipedia: http://en.wikipedia.org/wiki/Refurbishment_%28electronics%29.

Now that these details are set in stone, you can start adding a description for your product.
Describing your product well is essential, both for the customer (the more information, the better) and search engines (it will help your shop appear in more search requests).

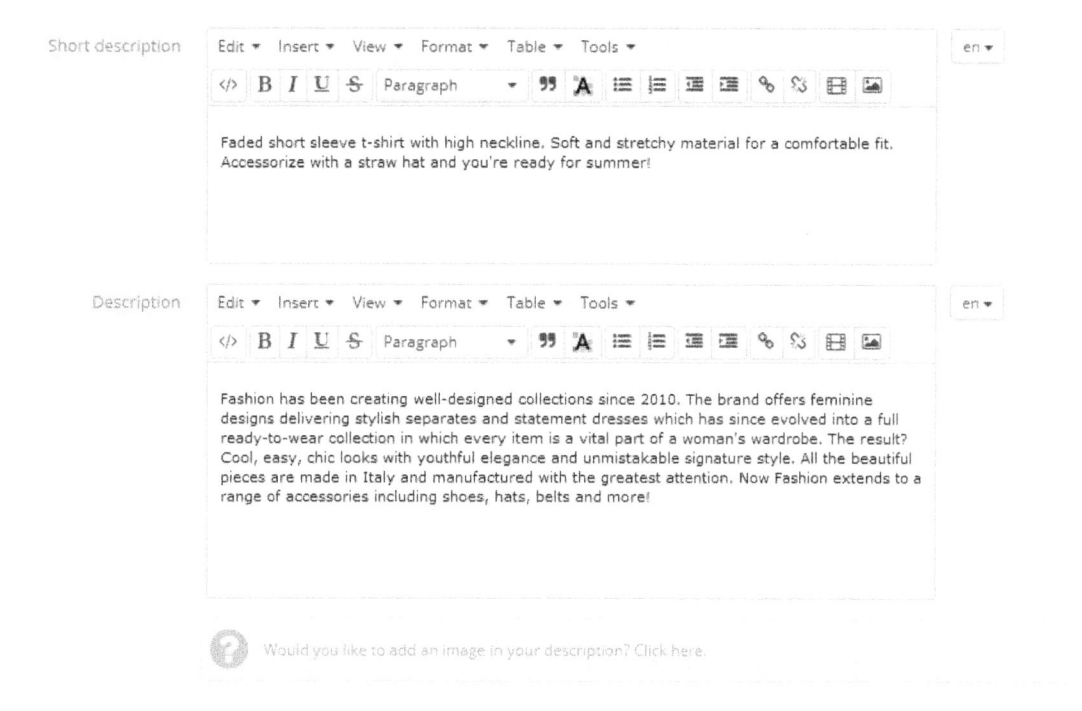

At the bottom of the screen, the two description fields each serve different purposes:

- The **"Short description"** field enables you to write a short description that will appear in search engines and in the category description for your product.
  This field is limited to 400 characters by default: if you exceed that limit, PrestaShop will warn you with a message in red below the field. You can change that limit in the "Products" preference page, where you will find the "Max size of short description" option.
- The **"Description"** field enables you to write a full description of your product, which will appear directly on the product page. The text editor offers a wide range of options for creating visually attractive descriptions (font, size, text color, etc.).
  While the second field has no limits, there is such thing as too much content: strive to provide the essential information in a compelling way, and your product should be good to go.

Below the "Description" field, you can find a small tool to add one of the images you attached to the product (through the "Images" tab) to the "Description", using image tags. Click on "Click here" to open it.

Simply select the image you want, choose its position according to the text and its size, and PrestaShop will generate an image tag which you can then put right into the description (preferably between two paragraphs, or at the very beginning of a paragraph).

In the "**Tags**" field, add some terms and keywords that will help your customers easily find what they are looking for.

They are displayed on the store in the "Tags" block (if available). If you do not want the tag block displayed, simply disable the "Tags block" module (in the "Modules" page).

> ### Differences with PrestaShop 1.4
>
> PrestaShop 1.4 enabled you to indicate the product's manufacturer right in this tab. Since version 1.5, this setting is to be found in the "Associations" tab on the left. Same for the "Default category" field, the associated categories, and the "Accessories" field.

> Version 1.4 also enabled you to indicate the size and weight of the final package. Since version 1.5, these settings are to be found in the "Shipping" tab on the left.
>
> The "Location" field of version 1.4 can be found in the optional "Warehouses" tab on the left, which is only available if you have enabled Advanced Stock Management ("Preferences" menu, "Products" page, "Products stock" section).

Once you have filled out all this information, save your work, after which you will be sent to your list of products. If you save by clicking on "Save and Stay", you will be able to continue working on your product's presentation.

Setting the Price of a Product

This is all done in the "Prices" tab on the left. The pricing section can be quite intimidating, with fields influencing each other and taxes to take into account – but it is in fact quite simple.

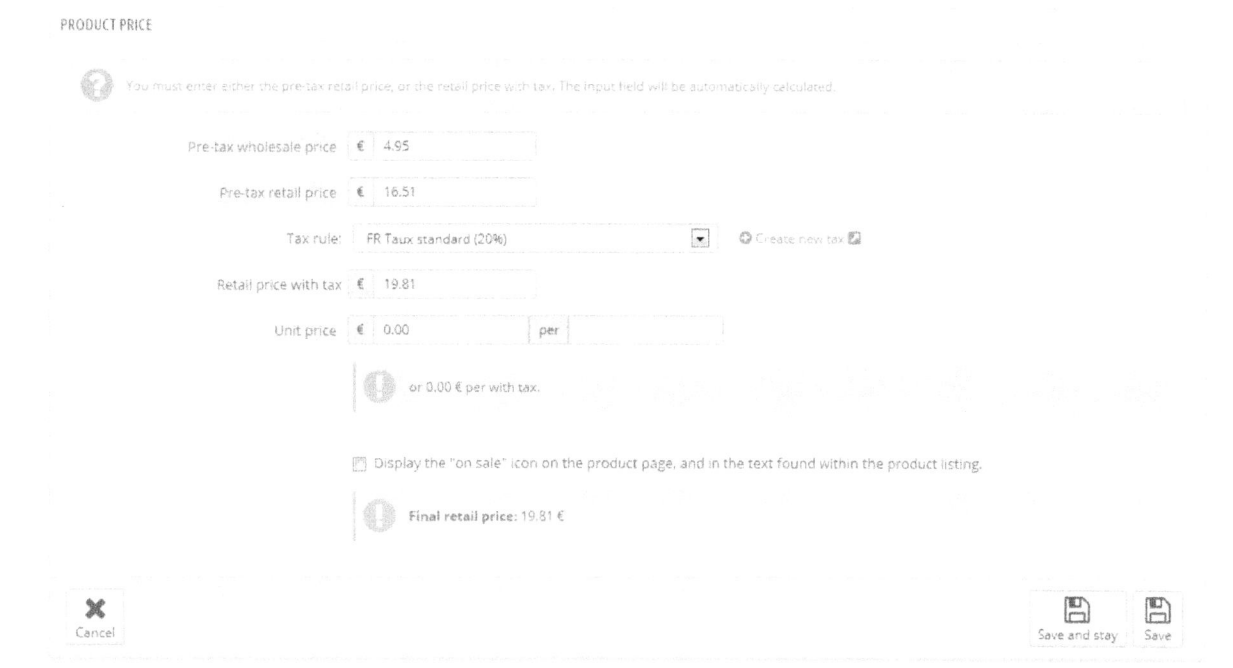

PRODUCT PRICE

You must enter either the pre-tax retail price, or the retail price with tax. The input field will be automatically calculated.

Pre-tax wholesale price	€ 4.95
Pre-tax retail price	€ 16.51
Tax rule:	FR Taux standard (20%) ⊕ Create new tax
Retail price with tax	€ 19.81
Unit price	€ 0.00 per
	or 0.00 € per with tax.
	☐ Display the "on sale" icon on the product page, and in the text found within the product listing.
	Final retail price: 19.81 €

Cancel   Save and stay   Save

Set the price that will appear in your store by following the instructions below:

- **Pre-tax wholesale price**. Enables you to instantly know your wholesale, factory price, and thus compare it to your selling price in order to easily calculate your profit.
- **Pre-tax retail price**. The price of your product before taxes.
- **Tax rule**. The tax applicable to the product. Choose between the different rates that you have registered.
  If you need to create new tax rates, click the "Create New Tax" button. Tax creation is done in the "Localization" menu, "Taxes" page; it is fully explained in the "Understanding Local Settings" chapter of this guide.
- **Eco-tax (tax incl.)**. The value of the ecotax for this product. This value is already included in your retail price. You are supposed to declare that tax to your country's tax agency.
  Note that this field is not displayed by default. If you have to include an ecotax, you must first enable it: go to the "Localization" menu, "Taxes" page, "Tax options" section (bottom of the page), and choose "Yes" for the "Use ecotax" option.
- **Retail price with tax**. Displays the price of the product with taxes included. You can edit the value, and it will automatically update the "Pre-tax retail price" field according to the tax rule that you chose.
- **Unit price**. Enables you to conform to local legislations that require products to be displayed with their unit price.
  For instance, if you are selling a pack of 6 cans of soda, then you should fill this field with the price per can, and indicate "can" in the text field. The description on the same line will update accordingly.
- **Display the "on sale" icon on the product page and in the text found within the product listing**. Check that box to show that your product is on sale, both on the product page and in the text on the product listing. An "On sale" icon will appear under the product. You can modify this logo by changing the following file: themes/default/img/onsale_en.gif
- **Final retail price**. This price, including the discount taken, will update as you type.

You can fill out the "retail price with tax" field and choose the tax rate to apply, and the field will automatically calculate the pre-tax retail price. The opposite operation is also available.

At this point, you are done with the essential information for a basic product page. You can save it and have it immediately available for sale on your shop!

But keep reading, as there are many more details you can add to your product to make it more attractive to customers.

Specific prices: Managing Quantity Discounts

You can changes the total price of the product depending on the quantity of products your customer buys, the user group, the country, etc. This is done with the "Specific prices" section of the "Prices" tab. Click on the "Add a new specific price" button to reveal the creation form.

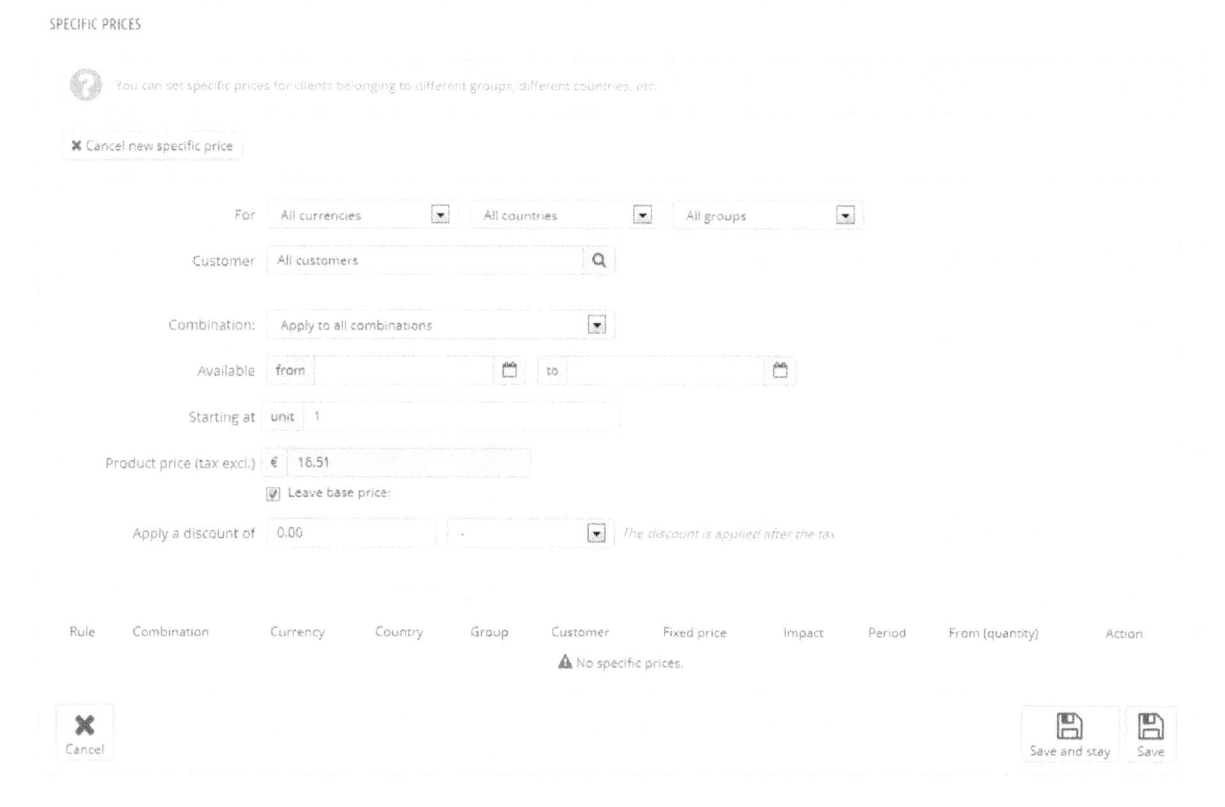

This is a very easy way to create a discount price for this product (and all its combinations).

Click "Add a New specific price", and a form appears.

- **For**. This enables you to be very specific about the various groups to which this price applies, including currencies, countries and even your customer groups (which we'll discuss in a later chapter).

- **Customer**. You can choose to be even more specific and directly set at who the discount you are creating is targeted. Start typing the first letters of the clients' first name or last name, and select the ones you want.
- **Combination**. You can choose to have this specific price apply to all of the product's combinations, or only one. If you wish to apply to more than one combination but not all of them, you will have to create a specific price for each combination.
- **Available from/to**. Here you can define a range of dates between which the discount price is active. Clicking each selector will open a calendar, simplifying the process.
- **Starting at [] unit**. Contains the value from which the discount should be applied. Default is "1", which means any quantity.
- **Product price (tax excl.)**. This is where you can set an arbitrary price, independent of calculations and regular prices. Keep this field at "0" to use the default price.
  Leave base price. Check this box to reset the "Product price" field and prevent yourself from editing it.
- **Apply a discount of**. The discount that will be applied once the client has chosen a quantity of product. Use the selector to set the type of discount (either a specific amount in the default currency, or a percentage of the default price).

Once you have chosen your values click on "Save and stay": the summary of your discount settings appears below. The discount will be immediately visible on the store.
If you wish to delete a value, click on the trashcan icon in the table.

If you want to build more complex discounts, go read about the "Price rules" menu in the "Creating Price Rules and Vouchers" chapter of this guide.

Managing Price Priority

A customer might fit into multiple prices or discount rules, even when you have set detailed prices and quantity discounts, with custom groups and shops (if in a multistore context). PrestaShop therefore uses a set of priorities in order to apply a single price rule to such customers. You might want the user group to be more important than the currency, for instance.

You can change PrestaShop default settings using the "Priority Management" section.

PRIORITY MANAGEMENT

Sometimes one customer can fit into multiple price rules. Priorities allow you to define which rule applies to the customer.

Priorities: Shop > Currency > Country > Group

☐ Apply to all products

[Cancel] [Save and stay] [Save]

The default order of importance is:

1. Shop (when in a multistore context).
2. Currency.
3. Country.
4. Group.

A checkbox at the bottom enables you to update the settings for all products. If the checkbox remains unchecked, then your changes only apply to the current product.

Optimizing your product's search engine position (SEO)

To improve your product listing as well as increase your store's visibility we suggest that you carefully fill out the various SEO fields: meta titles, meta descriptions, and keywords and friendly URLs.

> "SEO" itself stands for "Search Engine Optimization. Read more on Wikipedia:
> http://en.wikipedia.org/wiki/Search_engine_optimization
>
> Get to know the best SEO practices for e-commerce! Download and read PrestaShop's free "Complete Guide to SEO":
> http://www.prestashop.com/en/white-paper-seo

To access the product's SEO information, open the "SEO" tab on the left.

The fields in this page enable you to directly optimize your catalog's visibility on search engines.

- **Meta title**. This is the most important field, as the title that will appear on all search engines. Be very factual: you must convince the search engine user to click your link, not one from another site. Make sure the title is unique to this product within your site.
    - Good example: "Levi's 501® Original Jeans - Tidal Blue - Original Fit".
    - Bad example: "Item #02769869B bestseller".
- **Meta description**. A presentation of the product in just a couple lines (ideally, less than 155 characters), intended to capture a customer's interest. This will appear in results for some search engines, depending on the search request: some search engine might choose to display the searched keywords directly in the context of the page content. Make sure the description is unique to this product within your site.
- **Friendly URL**. This is another extremely important field. It enables you to rewrite the web addresses of your products as you wish. For example, instead of having an address such as http://www.myprestashop.prestashop.com/index.php?id_product=8&controller=product
you can have:
http://www.myprestashop.prestashop.com/8-name-of-the-product.html.
All you need to do is indicate in the "Friendly URL" field the words that you wish to see appear instead of the default name, separated by dashes. The "**Generate**" button makes it easy to produce a proper friendly URL based on the product name. Once generated, you can edit the URL produced if necessary.

> Friendly URLs will only work if URL rewriting is enabled. You can do this in "SEO & URLs" preference page, in its "Set up URLs" section.
>
> You will find more information on the "SEO & URLs" preference page in the "Understanding the Preferences" chapter of this guide.

Managing the Product's Associations

Creating associations for your product means pairing it with other content in your database:

- Product categories.
- Other products (accessories).
- Manufacturer.

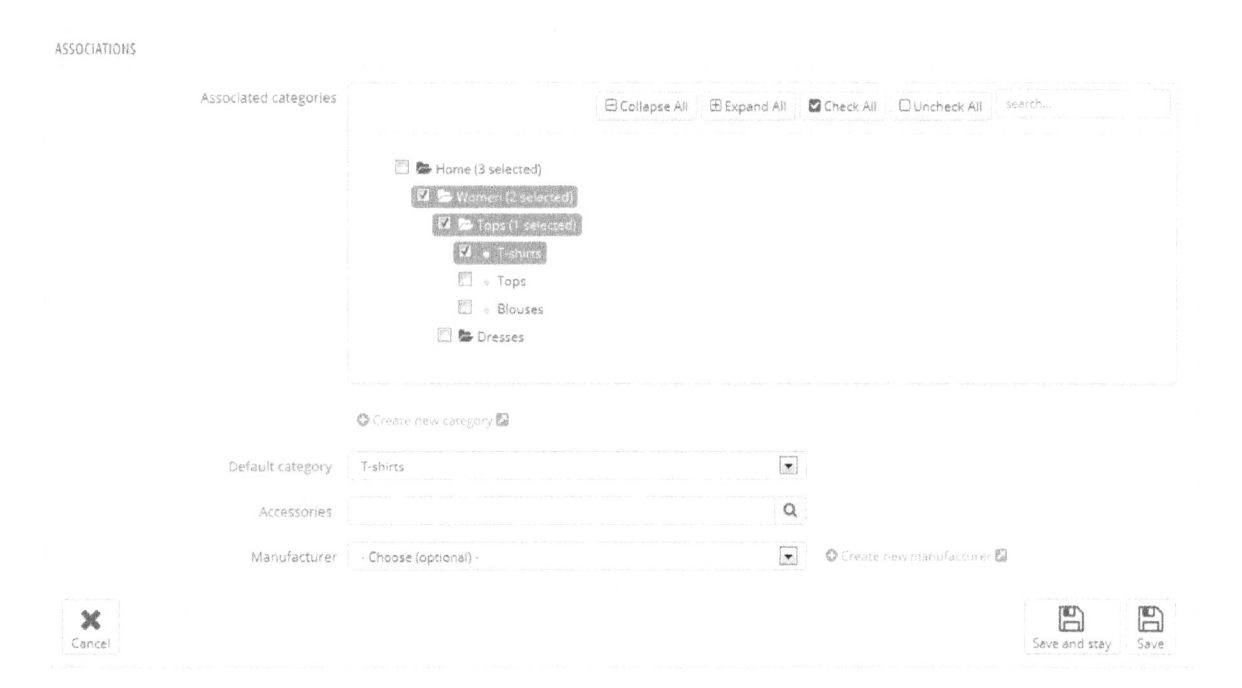

Product categories

The "Associated categories" section enables you to select in which category the product should appear. You can select more than one, but keep in mind that it is better for the customer if the category only contains equivalent and comparable products. Therefore, you should prevent from selecting root categories, and

prefer child categories.
For instance, the "telephone" category can feature sub-categories of "brands" (Apple, Samsung, Nokia, etc.) and as well as "characteristics" (smart-phone, flip-phone, etc.). It is up to you to indicate the category most useful to your customers.
If you feel you need to add a category, save the current state of your product before clicking the "Create new category" button. Category creation is explained in another section of this guide.

The "Default category" selector is useful when an article is filed under several categories. It serves mainly to clarify which category to use in case your customer arrives at your site from a search engine, since the name of the category will appear in the product's URL.

> **Featured List**
>
> Checking the "Home" box enables you to highlight the product on your shop's homepage, provided your theme supports it. To remove a product from the Featured list, simply uncheck the "Home" box.

Accessories

The "Accessories" field gives you the option of choosing relevant products to associate with this product, to suggest them to your customers when the visit the product's page (if the theme supports it). Type in the first letters of product and select it. The product is then added at the bottom of the field.

Accessories
✖ Printed Dress (ref: demo_3)

You can associate a product with as many other products as you deem necessary. Click on the cross to delete the product association.
An association goes one way only: the associated product will not feature an association to the current product in its setting page.

> Accessories addition/removal is not automatically saved! Do not forget to click on the "Save" button.

Manufacturer

A product can only be associated with one manufacturer. Choose one in the dropdown menu, or create a new manufacturer if it is needed (but do save your current product before clicking the "Create a new manufacturer" link).

Evaluating Shipping Cost: Size, Weight, Carrier

Shipping costs are not be neglected: they can easily double the final cost of an order, and you should be very upfront about them – customers hate bad surprises.

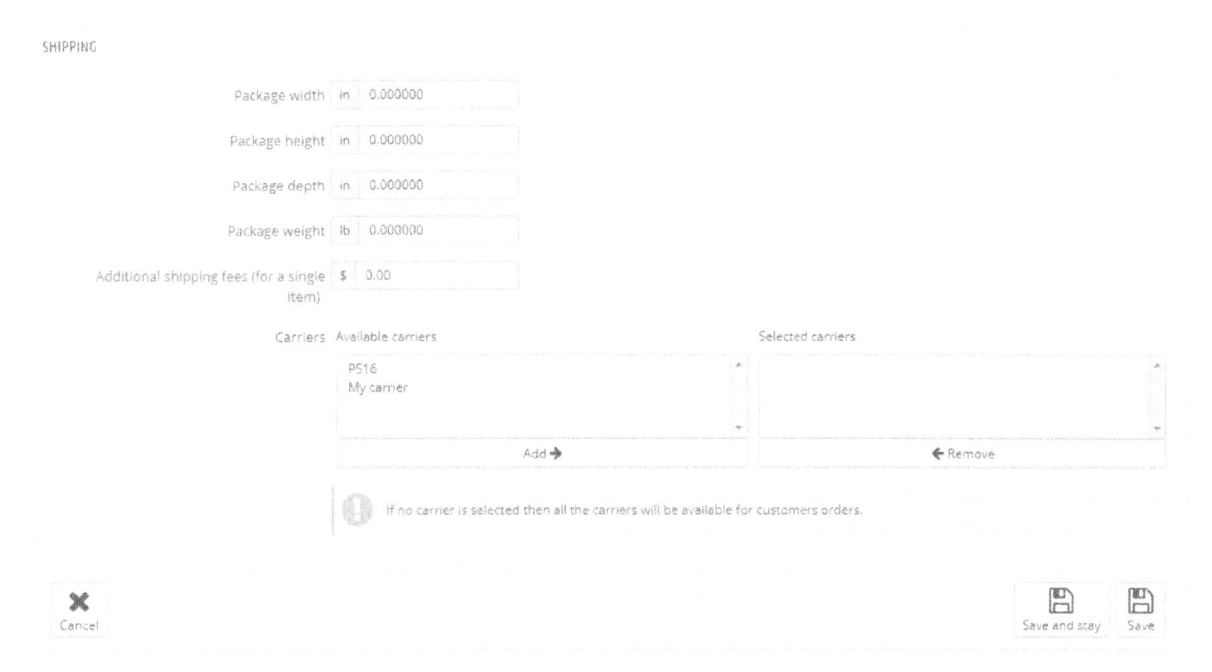

The "Shipping" tab on the left enables you to give some precious details about your product's package:

- **Package width, height, depth & weight.** You should strive to fill each field, because knowing the exact size and weight of a package is not only useful to you, but PrestaShop can also direct specific sizes/weights to specific carriers automatically, based on these settings. The order's final price will appear to the customer once PrestaShop (or the customer) has selected a carrier.

> These values use the default weight, volume, distance and dimension units, as set in the "Localization" page of the "Localization" menu.
>
> These values do not have to be integers. If your products weight less than 1 lbs, you can simply use a period (.) to indicate the fractions:
>
> 123 lbs
> 1.23 lbs
> 0.23 lbs (equals 3.68 oz)
> etc.

- **Additional shipping fees**. This can prove very useful to you for specific products that are particularly tricky to package, or really heavy.
- **Carriers**. You can choose to have the current product only be shipped by a selection of carriers. If no carrier is selected then all the carriers will be available for customer orders.

Adding Product Combinations

You will often sell the same product under different versions: they share the same overall name, but they might differ by their color, their capacity, their screen size, and other attributes. Most of the time, these attributes come together: you could have the red version of the product available with either 1 Gb capacity or 2 Gb, or with 12" screen or a 15" screen. This is why PrestaShop calls these versions "combinations": your stock of products can be made of several variations of a single product, which in effect are simply its attributes combined in specific ways.

> You cannot create combinations if you do not already have product attributes properly set in PrestaShop.

> Also, you should not create combination for features that your customers should not be able to choose from.
>
> Attributes creation is done in the "Product Attributes" page from the "Catalog" menu, and is explained in details in the chapter of the same name of this guide.

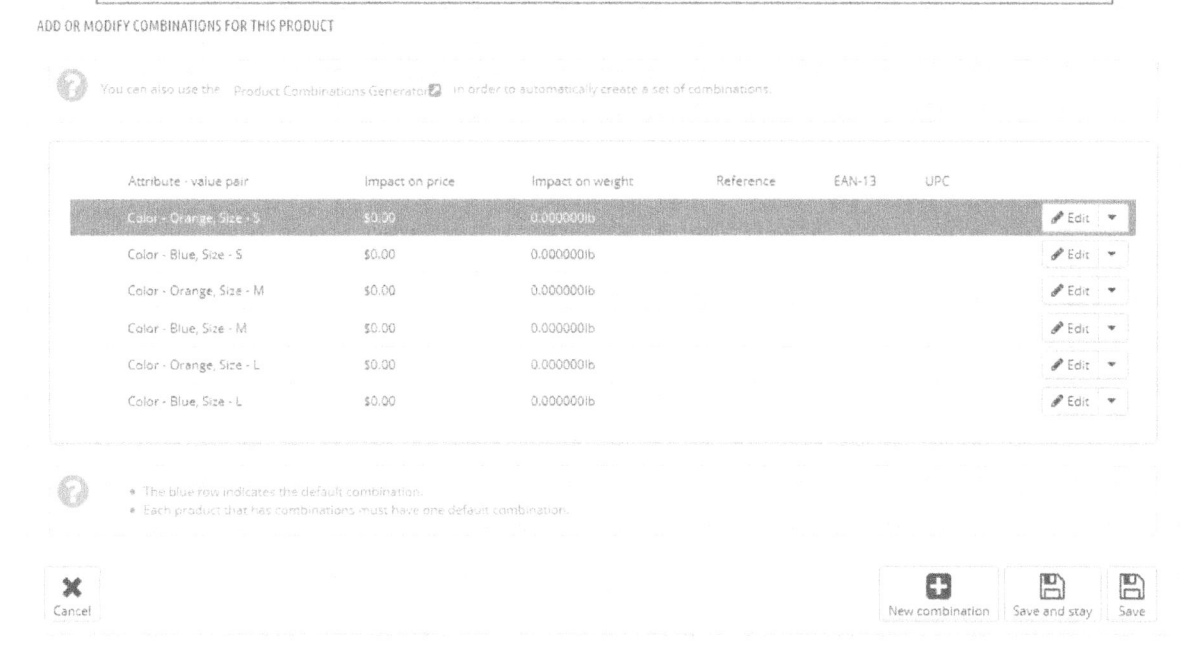

ADD OR MODIFY COMBINATIONS FOR THIS PRODUCT

You can also use the Product Combinations Generator in order to automatically create a set of combinations.

Attribute - value pair	Impact on price	Impact on weight	Reference	EAN-13	UPC	
Color - Orange, Size - S	$0.00	0.000000lb				Edit ▾
Color - Blue, Size - S	$0.00	0.000000lb				Edit ▾
Color - Orange, Size - M	$0.00	0.000000lb				Edit ▾
Color - Blue, Size - M	$0.00	0.000000lb				Edit ▾
Color - Orange, Size - L	$0.00	0.000000lb				Edit ▾
Color - Blue, Size - L	$0.00	0.000000lb				Edit ▾

- The blue row indicates the default combination.
- Each product that has combinations must have one default combination.

[Cancel]   [New combination]   [Save and stay]   [Save]

How your product attributes are combined into combinations is up to you, and PrestaShop gives you two methods to achieve this.

Manual method

This method helps you create combinations one after the other. Therefore, it is to be reserved to either products with few combinations, or products with very specific combinations that can't be created reliably using the automatic method (see next section).

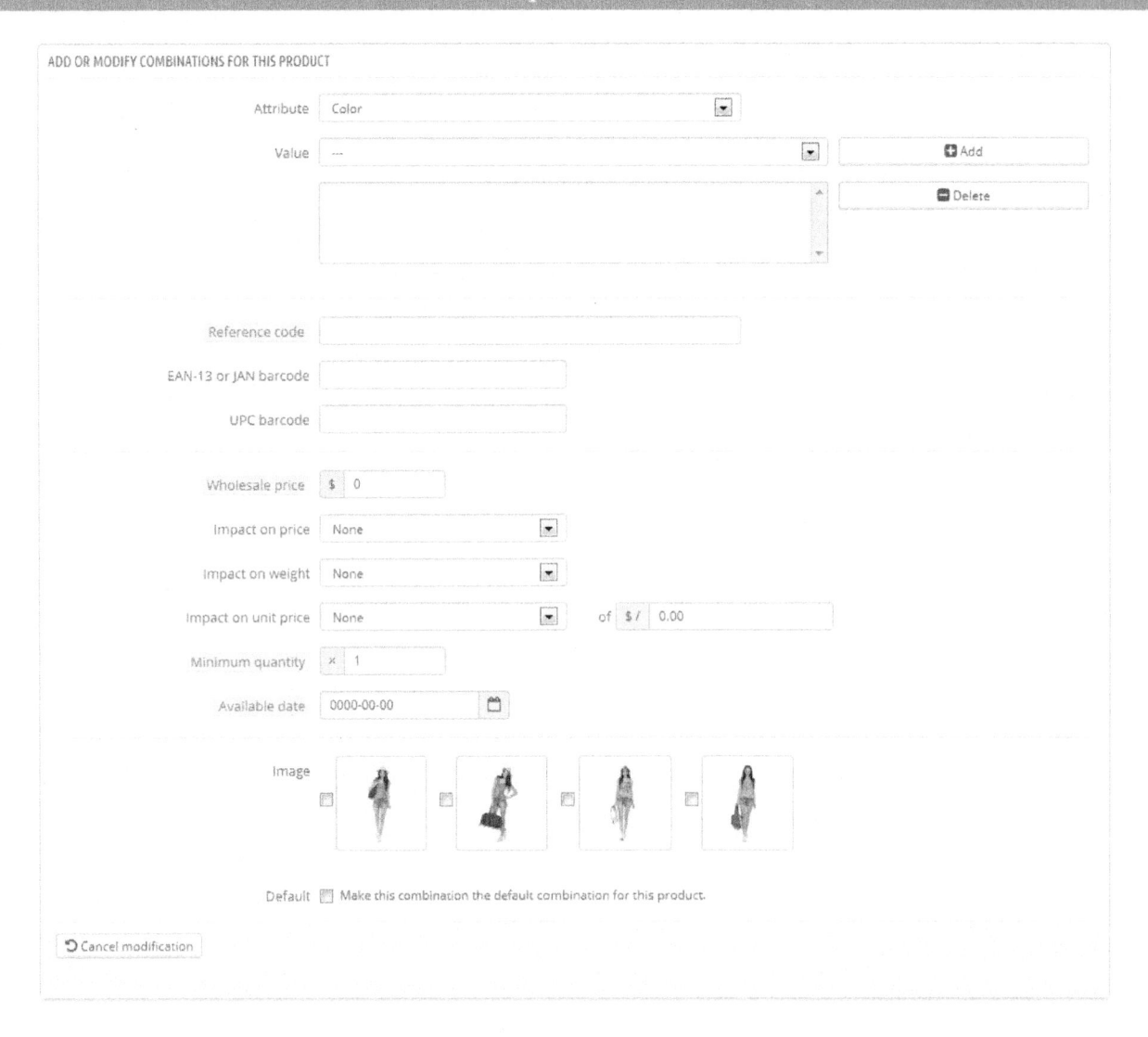

Adding a new variation to your product takes just a few steps. Click on the "New Combination" button at the bottom of the page, next to the "Save" buttons. A form appears:

- **Attribute-value pair**.
    1. From the drop-down menu, choose a group of attributes, such as "Color" for example. The content of the "Value" dropdown list updates accordingly.
    2. Choose the attribute value that you would like to include, for example "Blue".

3. Click on the "Add" button and it will appear in the selector.
   You can add as many attribute-value pairs as necessary to one combination.
   You can only add one pair per attribute to one combination: it is impossible to have both "Color: Blue" and "Color: Red" in your pairs; if this is necessary, you will have to create new attributes, for instance "Primary color" and "Secondary color".
   You can delete an attribute-value pair by selecting it and clicking on the "Delete" button.
- **Reference, EAN-13 & UPC**. If necessary, indicate the combination's reference, EAN-13 and/or UPC numbers into each field, as if you were creating a brand new product in PrestaShop. These numbers may be used by your warehouse or your carrier, so make sure to fill these fields, they are often essential to your business.
- **Wholesale price**. This field is useful if the original price of the product changes simply because this is a combination.
- **Impact on price/weight/unit price**. If the combination is supposed to have an impact on the product's original price/weight/unit price, choose the appropriate dropdown menu, select "Increase" or "Reduction" depending on the context, and fill the field that appears with the value of that impact.
- **Ecotax**. The specific ecotax for this combination (if the ecotax option is enabled).
- **Minimum quantity**. You might prefer this combination to only be sold in bulk. Use this field to set the number of items to be sold in bulk.
- **Available date**. If this is a temporary or promotional product combination, you can indicate the date at which this product should not be available for sale anymore.
- **Image**. The images that are linked to the original product (as uploaded using the form in the "Images" tab on the left) are displayed. Check the box for the images that best represent this combination.
- **Default**. Check this box if you want the combination you are creating to actually be the main one for this product.

When you have set all of the combination's details, save your product changes using the "Save and stay" button. Your combination will appear in the attributes list at the bottom of the screen.

> **Differences with PrestaShop 1.4**
>
> In PrestaShop 1.4, there used to be a "Color picker" form at the bottom of the list of combinations, where you could choose to display a color picker or not on the product page.
>
> Since PrestaShop 1.5, this option has been moved and improved. When creating a new attribute (in the "Catalog" menu, "Attributes & Values" page), you can use the "Attribute type" drop-down list to choose whether the front-page should display it as a drop-down list, a radio button list, or a color picker.

Automatic method

If you have too many different products versions or varieties, you can use the "Product Combinations Generator." This tool allows you to automatically generate all of the combinations and possibilities.

Clicking the "Product combinations generator" takes you to the complete form.

ATTRIBUTES GENERATOR

[Screenshot of the Combinations Generator interface showing attribute selection lists (Color, Shoes Size, Size) on the left, and on the right the selected Color values (Orange, Blue) and Size values (S, M, L) with Tax Excluded/Tax Included price impact fields and product weight impact fields, plus Default Quantity and Default Reference inputs, and a "Generate these Combinations" button.]

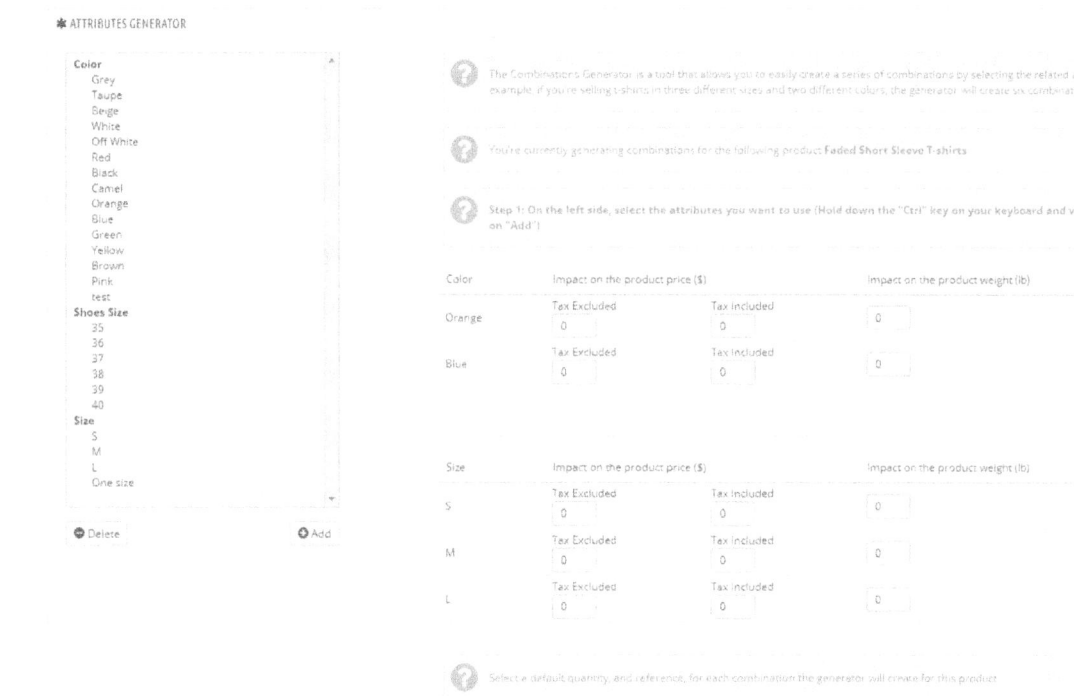

> A warning window might appear, saying "You will lose all unsaved modifications. Are you sure that you'd like to proceed?" This means your product already had some combinations created. If you agree to this, this will delete the combinations that have not yet been saved. Be careful, and always save your work before using the generator!

On the left side of this page are your attributes and their values. Select the combinations by clicking on the value names (if want to select more than one value, hold the Ctrl key while clicking), then click on "Add".
For example, you might select the "Blue", "S, M, L" values.
To remove an existing attribute selection, simply select their values and click on "Delete".

Once the varieties have been selected, you can edit the impact on product price and on product weight for each selection. You do not have to: they might simply be the same price and weight.

Insert the quantity of each product in the "Default quantity" field at the bottom. **Be careful, it needs to be the same for every combination.** For instance, 200 products in each combination = 2 colors * 1 size * 200 = 400 items in all.

You may add a default reference for this combination if it serves your administrative needs.

Click the "Generate these Combinations" button, and PrestaShop sends you back to the "Combinations" tab, with all the generated combinations. If you need to, you can now edit them one by one.

As you can see, the combination generator helps you save a lot of time when you have numerous attributes to assemble, such as sizes and materials. It automatically creates **all of the possible combinations**, which will then appear under the product's public page, in the "Combinations" tab (if the theme supports it).

If you do not want to keep all generated combinations or if they are in fact not all exactly the same (different references, prices, available dates...), you can delete them (trashcan icon) or modify them (file icon) from the product's combination list. The star icon turns the selected combination into the default one – in which case it is highlighted in blue.

Managing Product Quantities

Product quantities are managed in a single tab. The way it works is quite easy: the page presents you with a table of all the combinations for the current product (if there are no combinations, the table simply has a single row). It is up to you to set the initial stock for all the combinations. PrestaShop will use this to determine when a product is soon out-of-stock or unavailable anymore.

Stock Management Options

The quantities tab supports the advanced stock management feature, if activated. This means that if the current product's combinations are distributed among several storage locations, PrestaShop is able to handle the exact location of each combination, even within a given warehouse.

[ ] I want to use the advanced stock management system for this product.
⚠ This requires you to enable advanced stock management.

Available quantities ○ The available quantities for the current product and its combinations are based on the stock in your warehouse (using the advanced stock management system). - This requires you to enable advanced stock management globally or for this product.
● I want to specify available quantities manually.

Quantity	Designation
299	Faded Short Sleeve T-shirts - Size - S, Color - Orange
300	Faded Short Sleeve T-shirts - Size - S, Color - Blue
300	Faded Short Sleeve T-shirts - Size - M, Color - Orange
300	Faded Short Sleeve T-shirts - Size - M, Color - Blue
300	Faded Short Sleeve T-shirts - Size - L, Color - Orange
300	Faded Short Sleeve T-shirts - Size - L, Color - Blue

When out of stock ○ Deny orders
○ Allow orders
● Default: Deny orders as set in the Products Preferences page

✖ Cancel   💾 Save and stay   💾 Save

By default, you have to manage the current product's quantities by hand, for each combination, from this page. With the advanced stock management feature activated, you can rely on PrestaShop's stock management feature to handle this.

To use advanced stock management for the current product, checking the box for "I want to use the advanced stock management system for this product". Once this is done, an option becomes available: "Available quantities for current product and its combinations are based on warehouse stock". Click it, and you cannot edit the current product's quantities from the "Quantities" page anymore: it has new become dependent of your stock management.

When out of stock

The "When out of stock" option enables you to set PrestaShop behavior when the product is out of stock: deny orders (the product is not available for sale anymore) or allow order (in essence, you are doing pre-sales). The third and default option simple uses the global default setting ("Preferences" menu, "Products" page, "Product Stock" section, "Allow ordering of out-of-stock products" option).

Availability Settings

At the bottom of the page, you can set the exact behavior of PrestaShop depending on the availability of the current product.

The options are:

- **Displayed text when in-stock**. Enables you to display a message to your visitors when your product is in stock, for example "Item available". It reassures them that your shop can immediately send them the product.
- **Displayed text when allowed to be back-ordered**. Enables you to display a message to your visitors when your product is out of stock but they can still order it (as set using the "**When out of stock**" selector), for example "Pre-order now!". It reassures them that your shop will send them the product immediately once it is in stock.

You can also configure the general settings applied to all of your products: the default option is to deny orders, but this can be modified under the "Products" preference ("Allow ordering of out-of-stock products" option), which is fully explained in the "Understanding the Preferences" chapter of this guide.

Configuring the Product's Images

The "Images" tab on the left is for including photos on your product page. You should upload all the images for this product, including all of its combinations (color, size, shape, etc.).

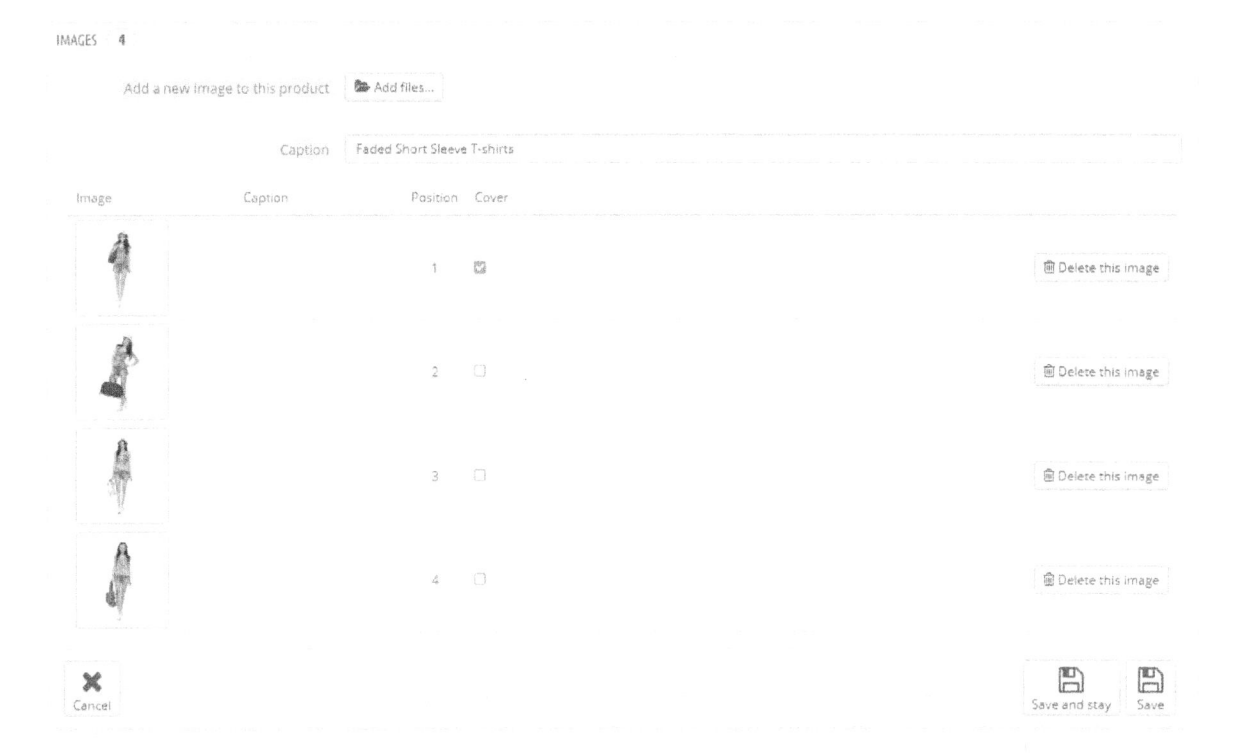

To add one or more images to your product:

1. Click the "Add files" button and then select at least one image file from your computer to upload. You can select as many images as necessary by keeping the Ctrl-key pressed while selecting files, or you can make your selection one by one. PrestaShop will display the chosen images in a list, with their size and a button to remove some.
   The default maximal size for an image file is set by PrestaShop according to your server's PHP settings. This size can be lowered in the "Images" preference page, "Product images" section.
2. Give the image a caption. It will be displayed if the image cannot be displayed – which can be very good for your search engine optimization.
3. Click on the upload button to put your file online.
4. The uploaded images appear in a table below the button. If you have more than one image, you can choose which image is to be used as the default/cover image by clicking on the red "no entry" button and turn it into a checkmark. That cover image will also appear automatically on the product page of your shop.
   You can click on a thumbnail to display the image in full size.

Once you have uploaded all your product images, you can modify the image order by drag-and-dropping each table row when the mouse cursor changes to a "movable" cursor.

Configuring Product Features

The "Features" tab is where you specify your products' features (i.e. weight, material, country of origin, etc.).

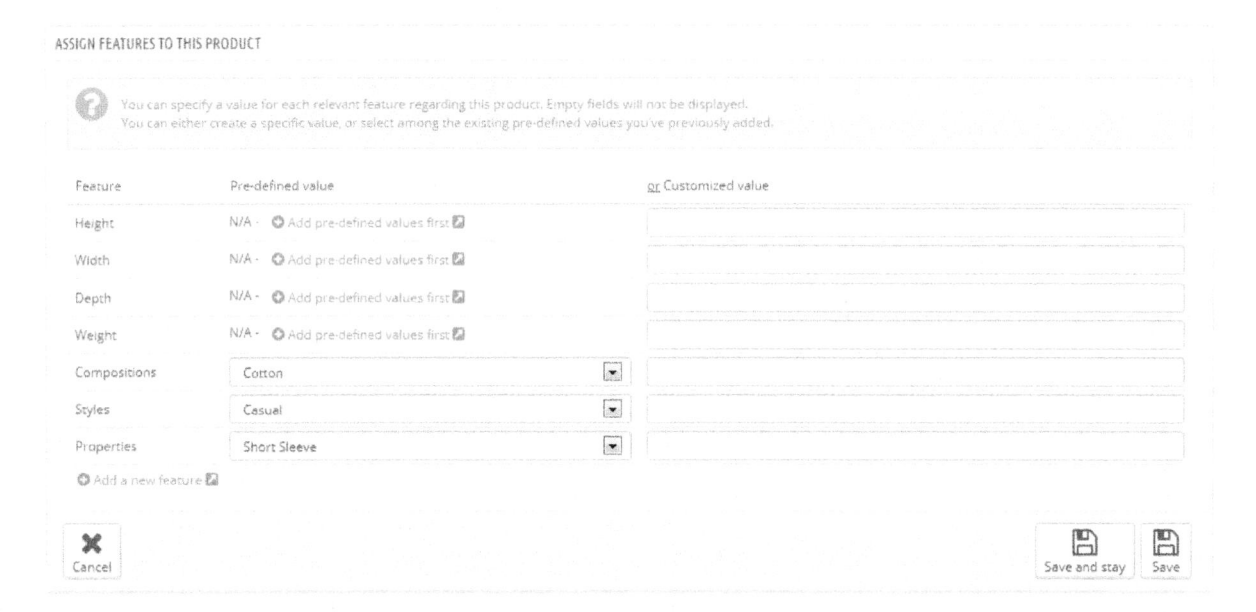

When you create features and values (i.e. wool knit and micro-fiber materials), you assign them to the products when it is appropriate. This means that you do not have to fill out the features fields for each of your products but instead simply fill in the necessary values and apply them later.

> PrestaShop's comparison engine relies entirely on product features: this is what gets compared.
>
> Also, since product comparison works on a per-category basis, you should make sure that all the products in a given category do share the same features, with various values to be compared between each other.

Be aware that **contrary to the combinations, these values do not change, and**

are valid for the general product (meaning: all your combinations will share these same features).

Creating a feature

Before adding a feature to a product, you must create it for general use in your shop. You either go to the "Features" page of the "Catalog" menu, or directly click on the "Add a new feature" button. A warning will appear, "You will lose all unsaved modifications. Are you sure that you'd like to proceed?" – make sure all your changes are saved before validating.

Feature and feature value creation are explained in details in the dedicated section of the guide.

Assigning a value and feature to a product

We will assume here that you have already set all your features and feature values.

In the current product's "Features" tab on the left, a table is displayed, listing all of your shop's features. Not all of them pertain to this product: PrestaShop will only take as relevant the features where you actually set a value.

You can either set a value manually, in the field on the far right a feature's row, or you can use one of the pre-defined values (as set when creating the feature) if there are any available.
If no value is available for a feature, the mention "N/A" appears (short for "not available" or "not applicable"), followed by a "Add pre-defined values first" button.

If you choose to use a custom value, do not forget to set it for every language that your shop supports. Use the language code selector to change language.

If there are pre-defined values available, they will appear in a dropdown list. Simply click it and choose the correct value.

Once you have set all the relevant features, save your changes to see them immediately applied in the front-page.

Remember: If a feature does not have any value assigned to it, it will not be taken into account for this product, and will not be visible on your shop.

Managing Customization

PrestaShop makes it possible for your customers to customize the product that they will buy.

Example: You are a jewelry retailer and your customers have the possibility to engrave their jewelry with a text or an image. Your customers can submit the text and/or the image when they place their order.

The advantage of this function is that it offers your customers a personal service, which they will without a doubt appreciate!

Let's look at how to configure this function. In the "Customization" tab on the left, you can indicate what type of context (file and/or text) can be personalized.

- **File fields**. Puts the indicated number of file upload buttons on the order page. Each button accepts only one file, so put as many field as you allow your customers to upload.
- **Text fields**. Puts the indicated number of text fields on the order page. You can add as many text fields as necessary.
  Example: If you allow your customer to use a 5-line text with each line limited to 14 characters, you can add 5 fields and indicate the number of allowed characters in the field's label. You cannot limit the number of characters in the string.

Once you have added the needed number for each field, click "Save and stay". The page will reload and display as many text fields as necessary. Fill every one of them with the appropriate public label: this will be an indicator for the customer, so be very specific about what you expect.

For instance, if you allow images for a book cover, you could use the following:

- "Front cover (20.95 x 27.31 cm, color)".
- "Back cover (20.95 x 27.31 cm, black and white)".
- "Spine (20.95 x 1.716 cm, color)".

Same for text: if customers can engrave words to a product, you could use the following:

- "First line (24 chars)".
- "Second line (24 chars)".
- "Last line, signature (16 chars)".

Removing fields. If in the end you added too many fields, simply change the number of needed fields for each of the two types and click "Save and stay". The page will reload with the right number of fields, with the first ones preserved.

Once all the label fields have been filled, do not forget to save your changes.

On the customer's side

Once a product has customizable properties set, its front-end product page has a new tab, next to the "More info" tab: "Product customization".

The customer must choose the file(s) and/or add some text and save them before they add the product in the cart.

The custom image(s) and text(s) will appear in the final cart.

The rest of the purchase process is the same as usual.

On the merchant's side

Once the order has been validated by the customer, the merchant gets a notification of the order in the back-office.

He can then check on the order, which will indicate the image(s) and the text(s) in the list of products, for each product. The merchant then simply has to download the image(s) (simply by clicking on the image in the order) or copy/paste the text and use that in its customization tool.

The rest of the order and delivery process is the same as usual.

Managing Attachments

PrestaShop enables you to make some files available to your customers before their purchase. This is done in the "Attachments" tab on the left.

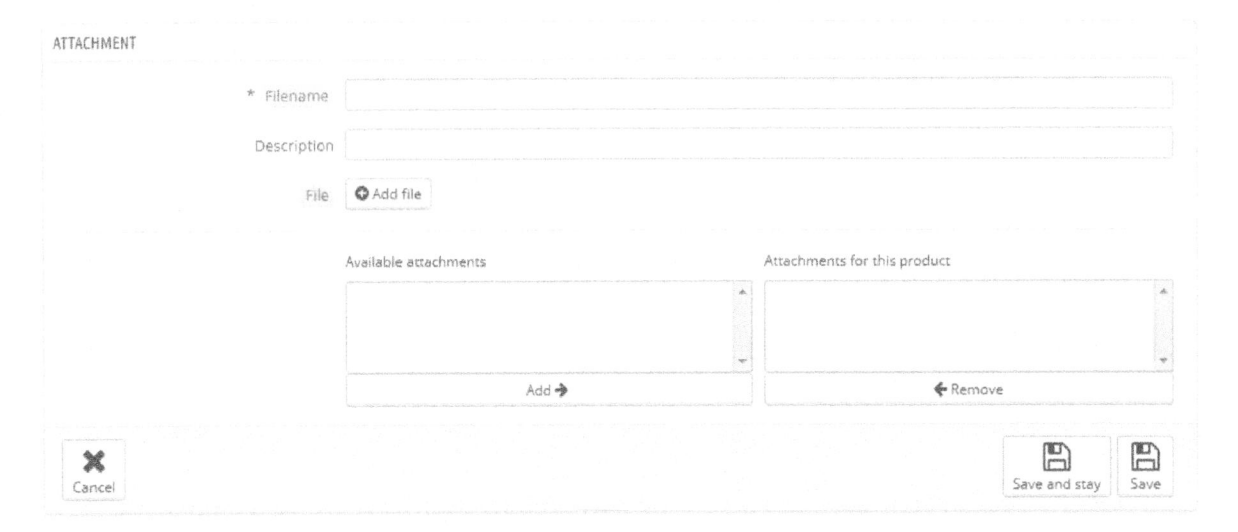

For example, let's say you sell electronics, and you would like to urge your customers to read a document on how a product works. You can upload a document for that purpose.
You could also simply have the product's PDF manual directly available for download right on the product page.

Adding an attachment is really quick:

1. Fill out the file name of your attachment (it doesn't have to be the same as the original file name).
2. Give it a description. This will help you distinguish between your uploaded files with certainty.

3. Click on "Add file" to select a file on your computer to upload. As soon as you choose the file, PrestaShop uploads it, then displays it in the list
4. The attachment appears in the "Available attachments" list: you have to select it then click on the "Add" to move it to the "Attachments for this product" list.
5. Save your product with either the "Save" button or the "Save and stay" one.

Now the "Download" tab will appear on the product's page (if the theme supports it), and your customers can download the file(s) that you just uploaded.

If you need to remove an attachment, select it in the "Attachments for this product" selector and click on the "<- Remove" button. The file will be moved to the "Available attachments" selector if you need to set it back online later on.

You can view all of your store's attached files, add some more and remove some, by going to the "Attachments" page under the "Catalog" menu. This also makes it possible to use the attachments that you already uploaded for other files: if you need to apply the associated one file with many products, you will thus only have to upload it once.

Setting the Product's Supplier

Indicating the product's supplier is not really important to your customers (very much less so than its manufacturer in any case), but it may turn out to be an essential part of your own internal management, not the least when managing your stock: you simply need to know who you bought the product from. The supplier of the current product is to be set from the "Suppliers" tab on the left.

SUPPLIERS OF THE CURRENT PRODUCT

This interface allows you to specify the suppliers of the current product and eventually its combinations. It is also possible to specify supplier references according to previously associated suppliers.

When using the advanced stock management tool (see Preferences/Products), the values you define (prices, references) will be used in supply orders.

Please choose the suppliers associated with this product. Please select a default supplier, as well.

Selected	Supplier Name	Default
☑	Fashion Supplier	⊙

+ Create a new supplier

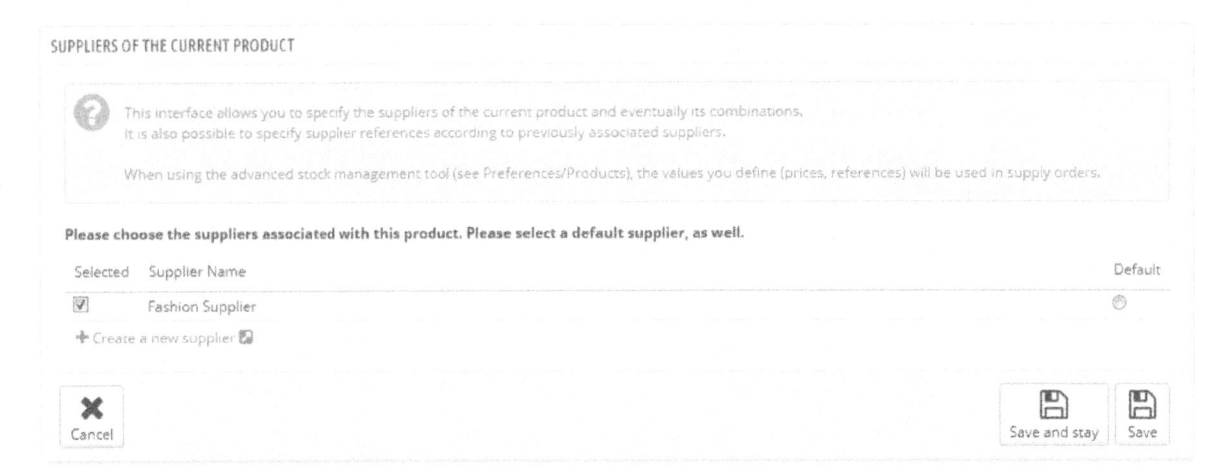

[Cancel] [Save and stay] [Save]

> You cannot use this feature if you do not already have at least one supplier registered in your shop. Suppliers are created from the "Suppliers" page, under the "Catalog" menu.
>
> The complete supplier registration process in explained in details in the current chapter of this guide.
> You can access the creation page directly by clicking on the "Create a new supplier" button.

Associating the current product with one or more suppliers is really easy: simply click the box corresponding to the supplier, and save your changes.

If the product is associated with more than one supplier, you can choose which one should be the default one using the radio button on the right.
Note: the "Default" radio buttons are unavailable by default. In order to select them, you must first click the "Save and stay" button" in order to select another supplier as default.

Product reference(s)

The product's supplier page also features a table that enables you to set the precise reference and unit price/currency for each product combination. If the product has more than one supplier, the table only opens the combination tied to the first supplier, the others being closed by default. Click on a supplier's name in order to open its references table, and close the others.

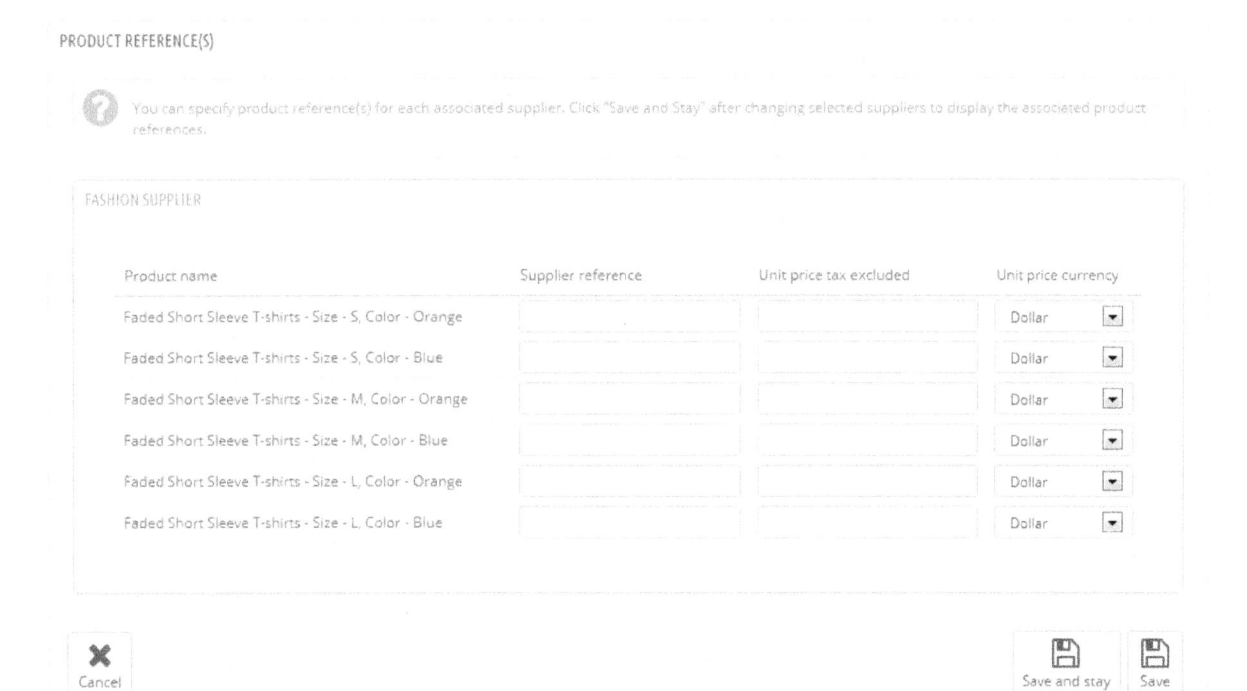

Managing Warehouses (advanced)

Once you have enabled the advanced stock management option (in the "Products" preference page), this new tab gets available for all products, and enables you to indicate in which warehouse the current product is stored.

PRODUCT LOCATION IN WAREHOUSES

This interface allows you to specify the warehouse in which the product is stocked.
You can also specify product/product combinations as it relates to warehouse location.

Please choose the warehouses associated with this product. You must also select a default warehouse.

Create a new warehouse

001 - MAIN WAREHOUSE

Stored	Product	Location (optional)
☐	Faded Short Sleeve T-shirts - Size - S, Color - Orange	
☐	Faded Short Sleeve T-shirts - Size - S, Color - Blue	
☐	Faded Short Sleeve T-shirts - Size - M, Color - Orange	
☐	Faded Short Sleeve T-shirts - Size - M, Color - Blue	
☐	Faded Short Sleeve T-shirts - Size - L, Color - Orange	
☐	Faded Short Sleeve T-shirts - Size - L, Color - Blue	

☑ Mark / Unmark all product combinations as stored in this warehouse.

002 - SECONDARY WAREHOUSE

Stored	Product	Location (optional)
☐	Faded Short Sleeve T-shirts - Size - S, Color - Orange	

> You cannot use this feature if you do not already have at least one warehouse registered in your shop. Warehouses are created from the "Warehouses" page, under the "Stock" menu.
>
> The complete warehouse registration process in explained in details in another chapter of this guide, "Managing Stock".
> You can access the creation form by clicking on the "Create a new warehouse" button.

The "Warehouses" tab presents you with a table that enables you to set the precise location for each product combination (if any) in each warehouse. If you have registered more than one warehouse, the table only shows the first one by default, the others being closed by default. Click on a warehouse's name in order to open its sub-table, and close the others.

For each warehouse, you can set which combination of the current product is stored, and a text field enables you to indicate precisely where it is stored in that warehouse. You can write anything in that field: "Aisle 5", "Next to the Radiohead albums", "A07 E08 H14", or anything that helps you or your packaging team to find the product as quickly as possible.

Creating a Pack of Products

You may wish to sell a pack of products made of several items. I.e.: a computer start-up pack composed of the computer itself, a monitor, and a printer. PrestaShop makes it easy for you to create a "pack" product and add other products from your catalog to this pack.

Packs enable you to simplify preparing orders. They also allow customers to take advantage of special prices and offers.

> You cannot currently add combinations or virtual products to a pack.
> If you need to have packs with combinations, you will have to create single products for each combination. This is a known limitation that will be fixed in a coming version of PrestaShop.

> You cannot add an existing pack within a new pack, or import the content of an existing pack into a new pack.

The process to create a pack is similar to the one for creating a regular product:

1. Go to the "Products" page, under the "Catalog" menu.
2. Click the "Add New" button.
3. From the "Information" tab on the left, change the product type to "Pack of existing products ".

A new tab appears on the left, titled "Pack". This tab only features two text fields and a button:

- The first field is used to search for products that are already registered in your shop.
- The second field is used to indicate the quantity of chosen product should be added to the pack.
- The button adds the product to the pack.

PACK

> You cannot add combinations to a pack.

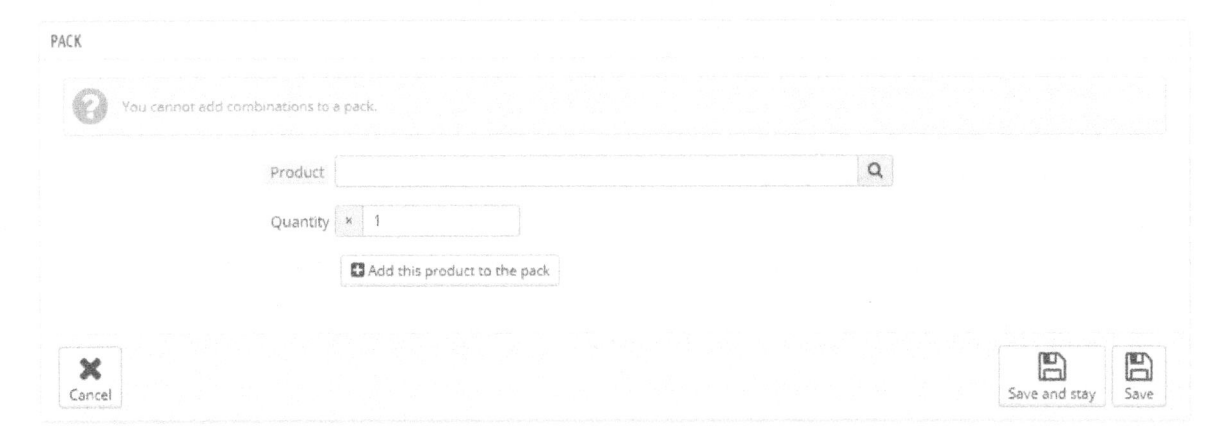

Product: [   ] 🔍
Quantity: × 1
[+ Add this product to the pack]

[✗ Cancel] [💾 Save and stay] [💾 Save]

You can add as many products as you would like to the pack.

You can remove a product from the pack simply by clicking the trashcan icon next to it.

Once you are done with the "Pack" tab, you can edit the content of all the other available tabs as if you would for a regular product.

Creating a Virtual Product

Your shop may feature (partly or exclusively) virtual products – that is, products that are not shipped, but rather downloaded: entertainment tickets, e-books/PDF files, real-life services...
PrestaShop makes it easy for you to create a virtual product

The process to do this is similar to the one for creating a simple product:

- Go to the "Products" page, under the "Catalog" menu.
- Click the "Add New" button.
- From the "Information" tab on the left, change the product type to "Virtual Product".

The tabs on the left change:

- The "Virtual Product" tab appears, to which you will be redirected as soon as you change the product type.
- The "Shipping product" tab disappears.

The new tab only features one option at first: it asks if the virtual product you are creating has a file attached (i.e., if your customer will pay to download something).

- If not, leave it at that: you are selling a service, and nothing needs to be downloaded.
- If yes, click the "Yes" option.

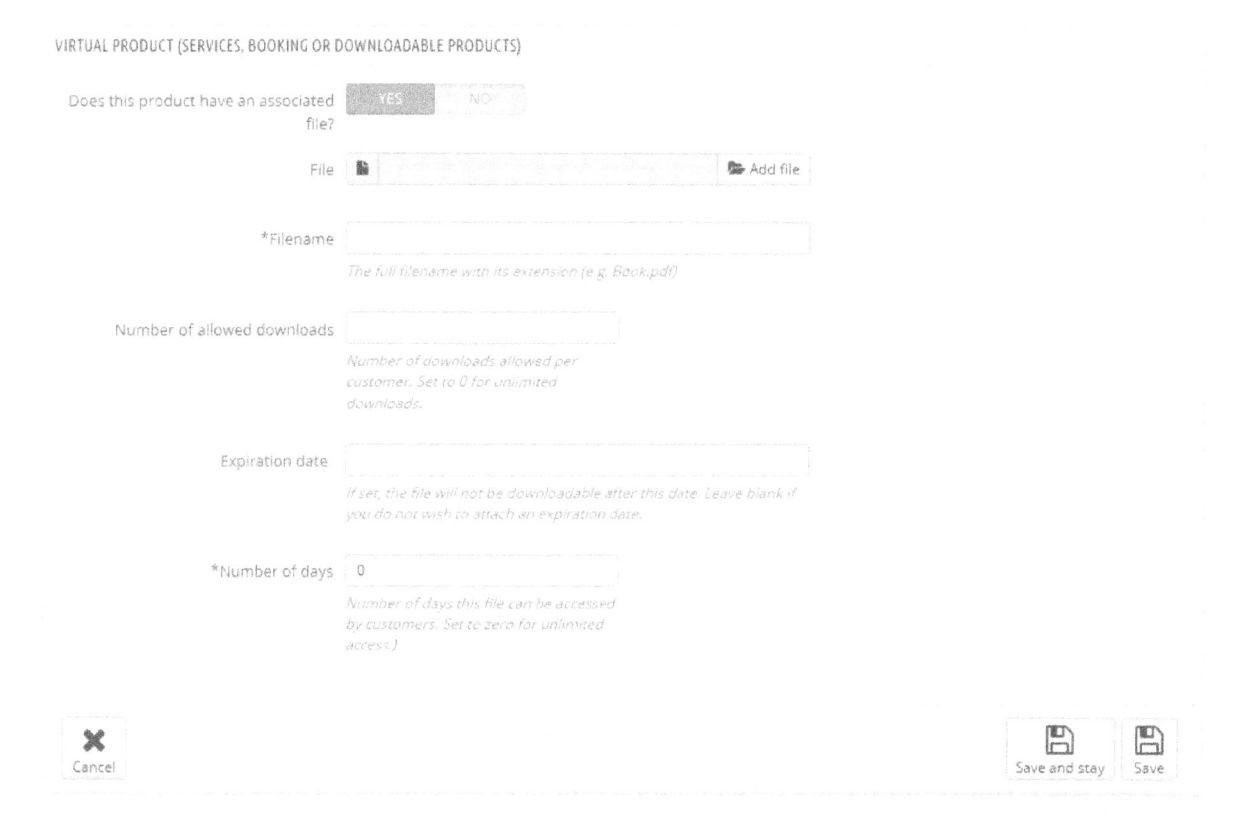

VIRTUAL PRODUCT (SERVICES, BOOKING OR DOWNLOADABLE PRODUCTS)

Does this product have an associated file?	YES NO
File	Add file
*Filename	
	The full filename with its extension (e.g. Book.pdf)
Number of allowed downloads	
	Number of downloads allowed per customer. Set to 0 for unlimited downloads.
Expiration date	
	If set, the file will not be downloadable after this date. Leave blank if you do not wish to attach an expiration date.
*Number of days	0
	Number of days this file can be accessed by customers. Set to zero for unlimited access.)

Cancel | Save and stay | Save

When you click "Yes", PrestaShop opens a new form within the tab, from which you can upload the file you intend to sell:

- **Filename**. The name of the file. This field is automatically filled after the file has been uploaded. It is not recommended to change it to another value.
- **File**. Click the "Browse" button to find the file on your hard drive. As soon as you have selected a file, the upload begins.

> The maximum file-upload size setting depends on your server's settings, and cannot be increased from PrestaShop.
>
> If you have access to your server's php.ini file, these are the values you should change:
>
> - upload_max_filesize = 20M
> - post_max_size = 20M
>
> If you do not have access to the php.ini file, contact your web host about this.

> You should compress your file in zip format, in order to avoid the browser misinterpreting .exe or .jpg file formats. Browsers automatically download zip files for the customer, no question asked.
>
> If you are selling a high resolution image, uploading it using this form does not prevent you from uploading its thumbnail in the "Images" tab on the left.

- **Number of allowed downloads**. You can set the number of time the file can be downloaded once the customer has bought it. You might prefer to limit this to 1, or 5. If you want to keep it unlimited, set the text field to 0.
- **Expiration date**. Virtual files can be of promotional nature, or lose their selling value after a certain date. If so, you can set the expiry date after which the product will not be available on your shop anymore. Leave it blank if there is no expiry date.
- **Number of days**. You can set the number of days after which the download link becomes non-functioning. If there is no limit, set the text field to 0.

Once you are done with the "Virtual Product" tab, you can edit all the other available tabs as if you would for a regular product.

Managing Categories

Categories are essential, as they enable you to group equivalent products. This helps customers find their way through the variety of your catalog, and narrow down their search when looking for a specific type of product. Categories also make it easy for the customers to find and compare them (thanks to PrestaShop's product-comparison feature).

You should create a new category from the moment you have at least two products with equivalent attributes. Products in a category should be comparable, if not interchangeable. Keep this idea in mind when adding new products and creating new categories.

> You may choose to not create any category, and have all products grouped into a single global category, "Home". But then customers won't be able to compare products.
>
> You may also decide that you are not interested in the comparison feature, and would rather build your categories freely. In that case, you should disable the comparison feature: go the product preference page, and put 0 for the "Product comparison" option.

> When creating a product category, you should focus on one thing: **the products in this category must be comparable** through their attributes (not their features). This is not only useful for your customers, but it is also a necessity for PrestaShop's product-comparison feature.

Categories are managed in the "Categories" page of the "Catalog" menu. This page displays a table with the currently existing categories, with the main information displayed.
In order to display sub-categories, click on the parent category or select "View" in the action menu.

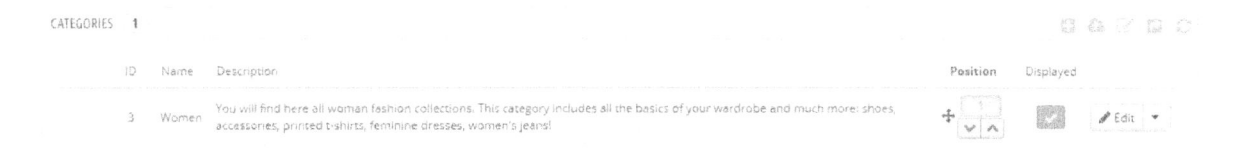

ID	Name	Description	Position	Displayed
3	Women	You will find here all woman fashion collections. This category includes all the basics of your wardrobe and much more: shoes, accessories, printed t-shirts, feminine dresses, women's jeans!		Edit

Using the icon in the "Displayed" column of the table, you can indicate the ones you want hidden from the customer by clicking on the green check-mark icon, thus turning it into a red "x" mark.

All the categories are actually sub-categories of the "Home" category.
To edit the "Home" category (or any currently selected category), click on the "Edit" button in the button bar when the table displays the root categories.

To create a new category (or a sub-category of an existing category), click on the "Add New" button from any level of categories.

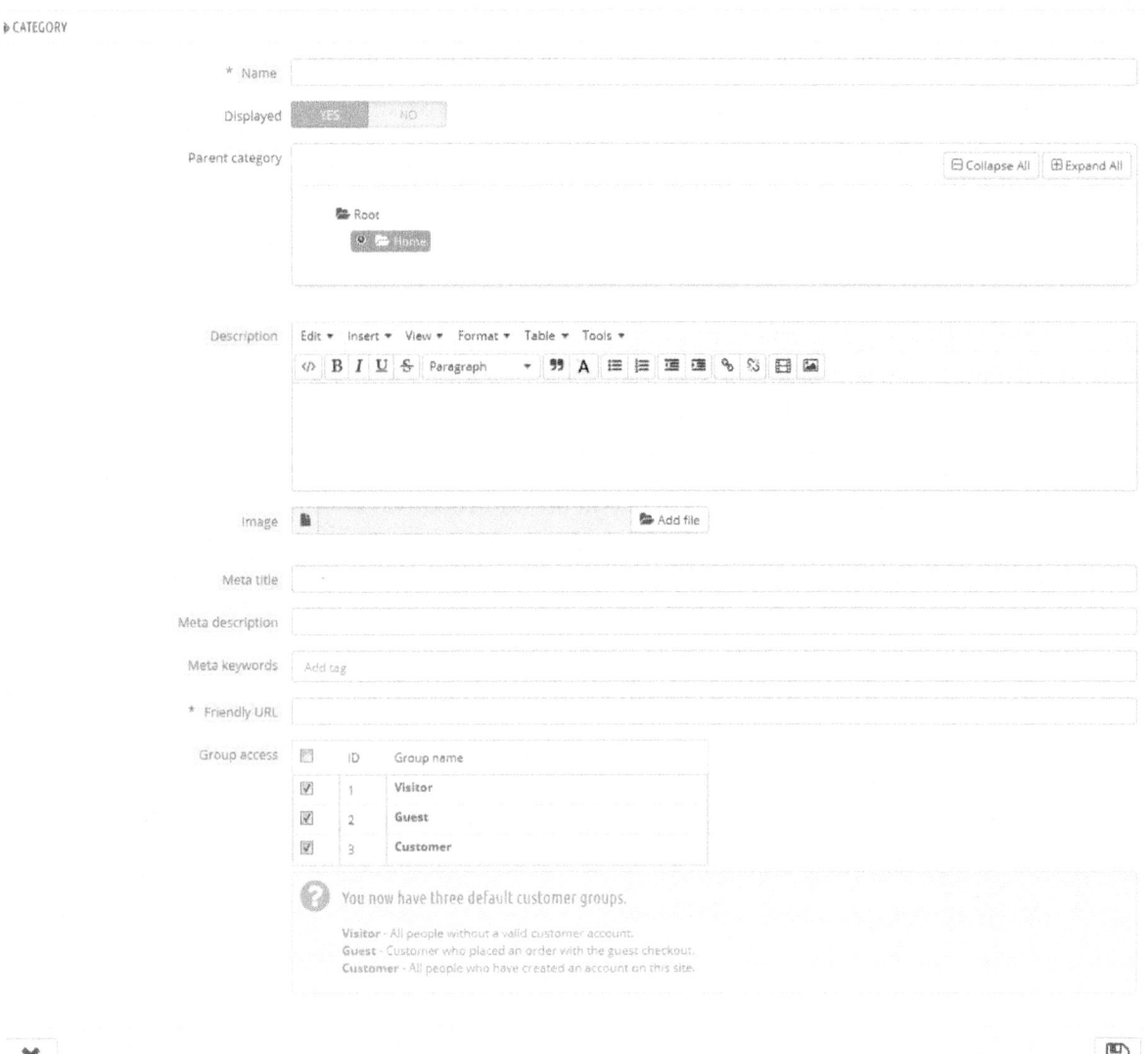

> **Translate your categories!**
>
> Make sure to translate each field in every language that your shop supports. In order to do that, click on the language button next to the field, and choose the language in which you wish to edit the text.

First of all, you must enter a set of general information:

- **Name**. Give your category a name. Make it very short and descriptive, and choose your words wisely: your customers will rely on it when browsing your shop.
- **Displayed**. Indicate if it is "displayed" (i.e., whether or not it will be available to your customers). For example, you may want to postpone displaying a new category to your customers because you have not quite completed it.
- **Parent Category**. *Does not appear when creating a root category.* If you wish to create a subcategory belonging to a category other than the home page, choose the category under which it will appear.
  The form is the same when creating a root category or a sub-category. The only difference is that when clicking "Add New" from a sub-level of categories, PrestaShop understands that you want to create a sub-category, and therefore sets the "Parent category" option accordingly.
- **Description**. You should fill this field, because not only will it be useful to you or your employees, but some themes might also make use of it, displaying it to your customers.
- **Image**. Click on "Add file" to upload an image from your computer which will represent this category.
- **Meta title**. The title that will appear on the search engines when a request is made by a customer
- **Meta description**. A presentation of your category in just a few lines, intended to capture a customer's interest. This will appear in search results
- **Meta Keywords**. Keywords that you must define in order to have your site referenced by search engines. You can enter several of them, separated by commas, as well as expressions, which must be indicated in quotation marks.
- **Friendly URL**. Enables you to rewrite the addresses of your categories as you wish.

For example, instead of having an address such as http://www.example.com/category.php?id_category=3, you can have http://www.example.com/123-name-of-the-category.
In this case, all you would need to do is indicate in the field marked "Friendly URL" the words that you wish to see appear instead of "name-of-the-category" separated by dashes.

- **Group access**. Restricts access to the category and its products to certain shoppers. To see these categories, your shoppers must belong to a user group. Check out the "Groups" page in the "Customers" menu for more information.
- **Root Category**. *Only appears when creating a root category*. You might want to use this new category as the new root category, instead of "Home". If so, check this option that applies.

> The root category is very useful in multi-shop mode. Imagine you have 3 stores with different or partly different products and categories: you might want to use a different root category for each store.
>
> The root category thus reflects the "home" category of each store so if you do not want to have the same products in the homepage category of each store, you need different root categories.
> This way it is easier to assign categories to each store and you can have different products in the home category.

Once you have finished configuring your category, save it, and you are ready to fill it with products.

Navigating and editing categories

The "Edit" button in the button bar enables you to edit the parent category of the currently-displayed sub-categories. This means that when you are viewing the main sub-categories, clicking the "Edit" button will enable you to edit the "Home" category.

You can click on any category in the table: this will open that category, and display all of its sub-categories. In effect, this will change the context of the interface: clicking the "Edit" button will edit the current parent category, and clicking the "Add new" button will open the category creation form with the "Parents category" option set to the current parent category.

Importing and exporting categories

Besides the "Add new" and the "Edit" buttons, the list's button bar also features three buttons:

- **Export.** Enables you to download the list of all categories, in CSV format.
- **Import.** Opens the "Advanced Parameters > CSV Import" page, with the expect data type set to "Categories". Go to the "Understanding the Advanced Parameters" chapter to learn more about importing CSV files. You will need your CSV file to follow this format:

    ID;Name;Description;Position;Displayed;
    3;iPods;Now that you can buy movies from the iTunes Store and sync them to your iPod, the whole world is your theater.;1;1;
    4;Accessories;Wonderful accessories for your iPod;2;1;
    5;Laptops;The latest Intel processor, a bigger hard drive, plenty of memory, and even more new features all fit inside just one liberating inch. The new Mac laptops have the performance, power, and connectivity of a desktop computer. Without the desk part.;3;1;

    The category identifier is the ID, not the category's name.

- **Refresh list**. Reloads the list of categories with all the changes that you made.

More import options are available in the "CSV Import" page of the "Advanced parameters" menu.

Adding products to a category

In order to add a product in a category, you must open the product configuration page and go to its "Association" tab on the left. This is where you can set the categories to which the product belongs.

> The "Home" category is a special category, where you can highlight/promote products from any other category by making them appear in the "Featured products" bloc. By default, you can only display 8 products in the homepage.

The "Featured products" block depends on the "Featured products on the homepage" module. If you want more (or less) products on the homepage, configure this module (from the "Modules" page in the "Modules" menu).

Note: you do not have to remove a product from its original category in order to put it on the homepage. A product can have as many categories as needed.

Monitoring Your Catalog

The "Monitoring" page lists the sections of your shop to which you must pay the most attention in order to best manage your catalog, and make sure nothing goes out of control.

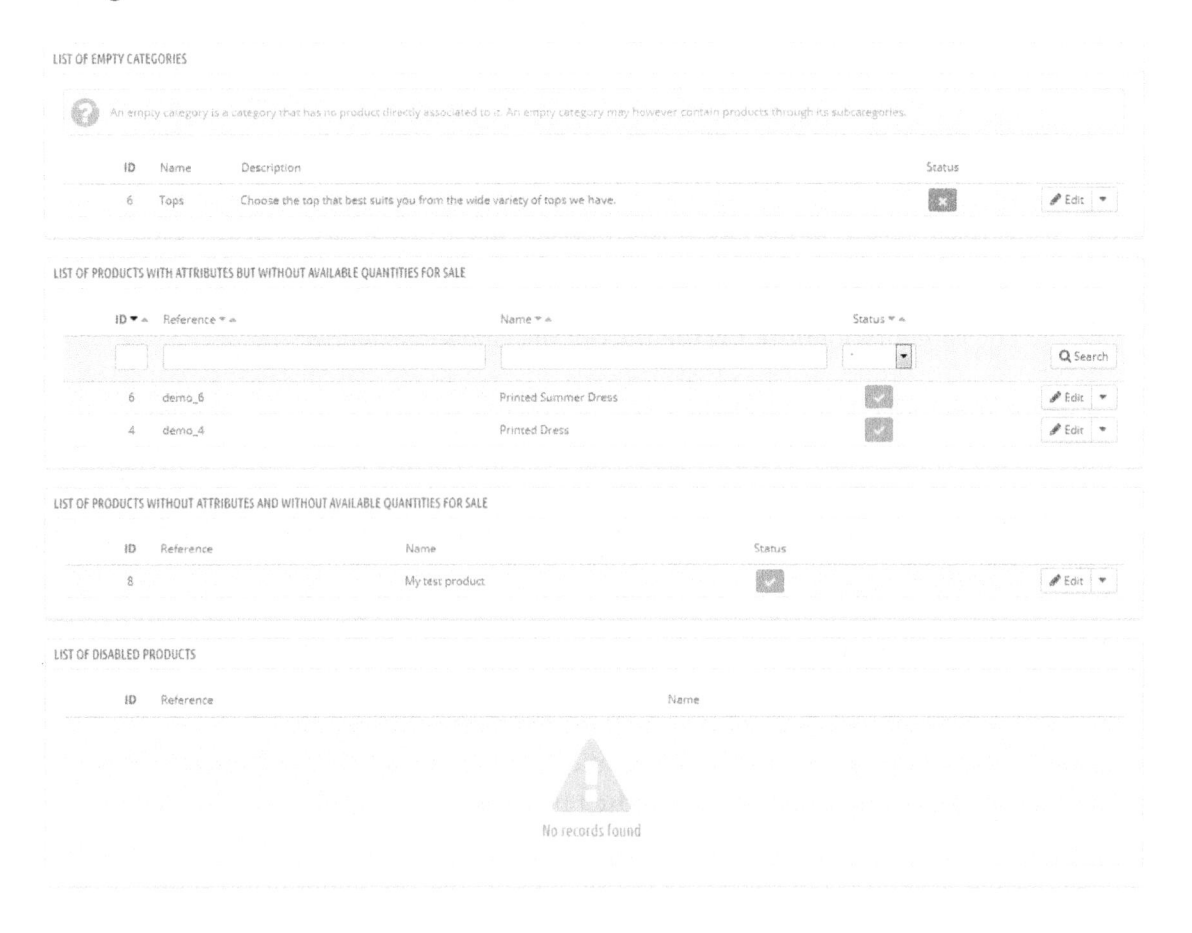

Four sections are shown:

- **List of empty categories**. Gives you the categories that do not have any products. You should either delete these empty categories, or fill them with at least one product. This prevents customers from finding themselves in an empty category in your shop.
- **List of products with attributes and without available quantities for sale**. Gives you which products are no longer for sale. If you do not see any good reason for them not being for sale, then put them back online
- **List of products without attributes and without available quantities for sale**. Likewise, gives you which products are no longer for sale. Find the reason why, or put them back up.
- **List of disabled products**. Gives you the products that have been disabled in the store and that aren't visible to your customers. Consider either enabling them (maybe after restocking them) or deleting them from your catalog.

The "Monitoring" page should be checked regularly in order to improve your catalog management.

Managing Product Attributes

Attributes are the basis of product variations (or "combinations" in PrestaShop's interface): you can only create variations of a product if at least one of its attributes changes.
You should think of attributes as properties of a product that may change between variations, while still keeping the same product name: color, capacity, size, weight, etc. You can use anything that varies between versions of the same product, except the price.

> The difference between an attribute and a feature depends on the product itself. Some products might share the same property, one being an attribute built for building product variations, another one being simply an invariable feature.
>
> For instance, a customer can buy an iPod variation based on attributes (color, disk space) but not on features (weight, size).
>
> Likewise, another shop might sell t-shirts variations based on attributes (color, size, gender) but not on features (weight).

Attributes are configured on a per-product basis, from the "Products" page under the "Catalog" menu, but they must first be registered on your shop using the tool on the "Product Attributes" page under the "Catalog" menu.

This page presents a list of all your currently registered attributes. You can edit or delete each using the actions on the right of the table, or display their values by clicking on the "View" action, which opens a new table.

	ID	Name	Values count	Position	
	1	Size	4	0	Edit
	2	Shoes Size	6	1	Edit
	3	Color	14	2	Edit

You can also set the attributes front-office presentation order by clicking on the arrow icons, or by drag-and-dropping each row when the mouse hovers the "Position" column.

Creating a new attributes

To add an attribute, or in other words, to add a group of variation possibilities (colors, capacity, material, etc.), click on "Add new attribute". A new page appears.

ATTRIBUTES

Fill out the form:

- **Name**. The exact description of the attribute. This needs to be short but precise, so as to not confuse it with another attribute.
- **Public name**. The attribute name, as displayed to the customers on the product page. Since some attributes might have the same name for varying content, this field enables you to still present it correctly within the product's context, while being able to easily tell an attribute from another with a similar name but different meaning.
- **Attribute type**. Enables you to choose whether the product's page should display this attribute's values as a drop-down list, a radio button list, or a color picker.

> Three more options are available when you enable the Layered Navigation Block module. They are not strictly tied to the layered navigation: they provide a direct URL to each of a product's variations. This way, not only is the customer able to send a correct link to a friend, but this also helps enhance your search engine placement.
>
> - **URL**. The word to use in the URL. By default, PrestaShop uses the attribute's public name.
> - **Meta title**. The word to use in the page's title. By default, PrestaShop uses the attribute's public name.
> - **Indexable**. Whether search engines should index this attribute or not.

> The customer can get the URL simply by clicking on an attribute from the product sheet: the URL will change to add a final detail, for instance #/color-metal or #/disk_space-16gb/color-green.
>
> The layered navigation generator does make use of these too, hence the description text "Specific URL format in block layered generation" and "Use this attribute in URL generated by the layered navigation module".

Save your new attribute to return to the attributes list. You must now add values to your attribute.

Creating a new value

Click on "Add new value". A new page appears.

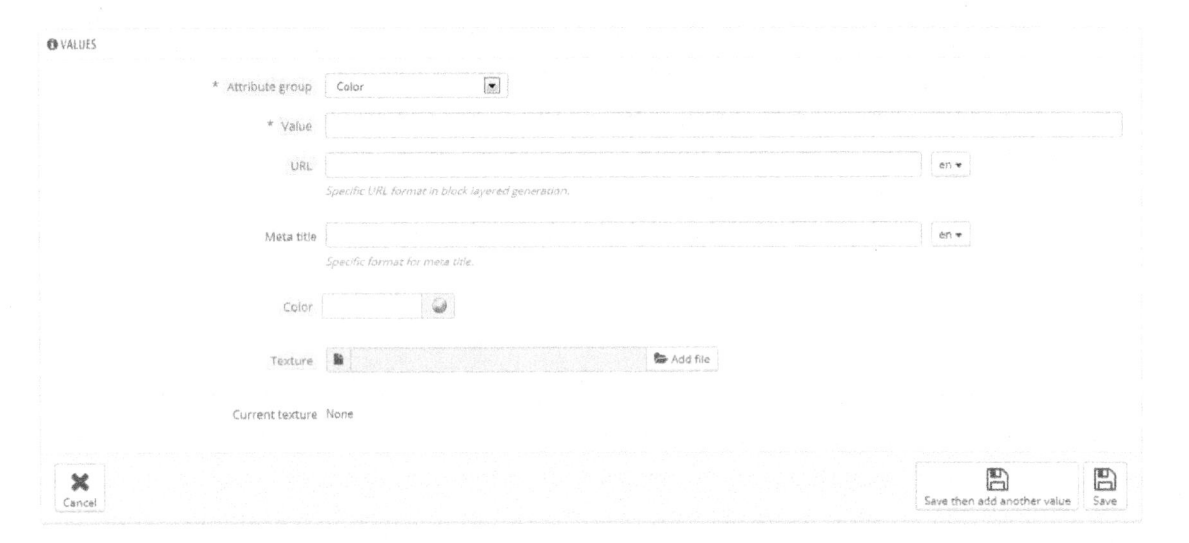

Fill out the form:

- **Attribute type**. From the dropdown list, select one of the available attributes.
- **Value**. Give a value to the attribute: "Red", "16 Gb", "1.21 gigowatts"...

The next fields are only shown if the attribute is a color type.

- **Color**. If the attribute is a color, you can enter its value in HTML color code (i.e. "#79ff52" or "lightblue"), or use the color picker to precisely show the correct hue.
- **Texture**. If your product does not use a solid color but rather a textured one (i.e. tiger stripes), you can upload a small image file that will be displayed on the product's page. Note that this will replace the HTML color from the field above. Click on the "Save" button is order to start the upload.
  You can also use this option to let the customer choose color variety from a picture of your product rather than a color. How it is displayed on the front-end depends on the theme you are using...
- **Current texture**. Once you have uploaded a texture file, it is displayed in this section as a reminder.

You can add more values for the same attribute type by saving your changes with the "Save then add another value" button.

Two more options are available when you enable the Layered Navigation Block module. They are not strictly tied to the layered navigation: they provide a direct URL to each of a product's variations. This way, not only is the customer able to send a correct link to a friend, but this also helps enhance your search engine placement.

- **URL**. The word to use in the URL. By default, PrestaShop uses the value's name.
- **Meta title**. The word to use in the URL. By default, PrestaShop uses the value's name.

The customer can get the URL simply by clicking on an attribute from the product sheet, and the URL will change to add a final detail, for instance #/color-metal or #/disk_space-16gb/color-green.

The layered navigation generator does make use of these too, hence the "Specific URL format in block layered generation" description text.

Once your attributes are in place and their values are set, you can create product variations (or "combinations") in each product's "Combinations" tab, from the "Products" page under the "Catalog" menu.

Managing Product Features

Features are a product's intrinsic characteristic: they remain the same throughout the product's variations (or "combinations").
You should think of features the same way you think of product attributes (see above), with the notable difference that you cannot create product variations based on features.

> The difference between an attribute and a feature depends on the product itself. Some products might share the same property, one being an attribute built for building product variations, another one being simply an invariable feature.
>
> For instance, a customer can buy an iPod variation based on attributes (color, disk space) but not on features (weight, size).
>
> Likewise, another shop might sell t-shirts variations based on attributes (color, size, gender) but not on features (weight).

Features are configured on a per-product basis, from the "Product" page under the "Catalog" menu, but they must first be registered on your shop using the tool on the "Features" page under the "Catalog" menu.

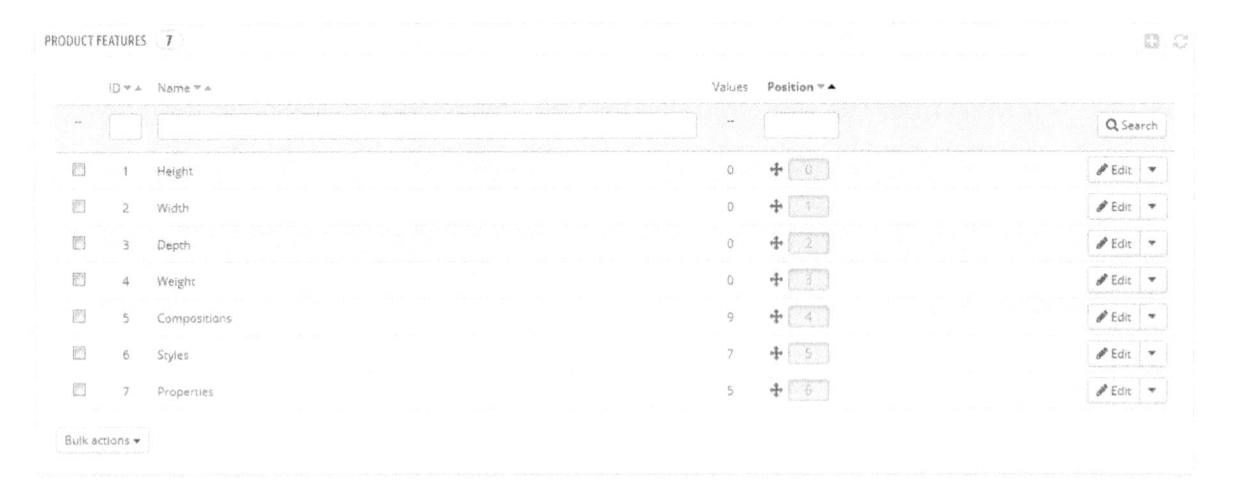

	ID	Name	Values	Position	
	1	Height	0	0	Edit
	2	Width	0	1	Edit
	3	Depth	0	2	Edit
	4	Weight	0	3	Edit
	5	Compositions	9	4	Edit
	6	Styles	7	5	Edit
	7	Properties	5	6	Edit

You can set the features' order using the arrows in the "Position" column.
The "Actions" column gives an Edit action, a Delete action and a View action

which you can click to display the available values for this feature. From there, you can sort, edit and delete values if you need to.

Adding a feature

Click on "Add new feature". A very simple form appears. This is where you name the feature itself: for example, the types of headphones provided with a music player.

Give a name to this new feature, and save your new feature to return to the attributes list.

> Three more options are available when you enable the Layered Navigation Block module. They are not strictly tied to the layered navigation: they provide a direct URL to each of a product's variations. This way, not only is the customer able to send a correct link to a friend, but this also helps enhance your search engine placement.
>
> - **URL**. The word to use in the URL. By default, PrestaShop uses the attribute's public name.
> - **Meta title**. The word to use in the page's title. By default, PrestaShop uses the attribute's public name.
> - **Indexable**. Whether search engines should index this attribute or not.

The customer can get the URL simply by clicking on an attribute from the product sheet: the URL will change to add a final detail, for instance #/color-metal or #/disk_space-16gb/color-green.

The layered navigation generator does make use of these too, hence the description text "Specific URL format in block layered generation" and "Use this attribute in URL generated by the layered navigation module".

Adding a value to a feature

Click on "Add new feature value". Another form appears.

Fill out the form:

- **Feature**. From the dropdown list, select one of the available features.
- **Value**. Give a value to the attribute: "5 lbs", "27 cm", etc.

...and save your feature value. You can add more values for the same feature type by saving your changes with the "Save and add another value" button.

Managing Manufacturers

Unless you make your products yourself, you should always register your products' manufacturers in PrestaShop.

In PrestaShop, a manufacturer is the brand behind a product. If you sell your own products, you must at least create your company as a manufacturer: this

> helps your customer find what they are looking for, and this can bring some valuable search engine points.

> On the front-end of your store, manufacturers are sorted alphabetically. You cannot change that order.
>
> New manufacturers are automatically disabled. You must enable them in order to have them appear online – even if they do not contain any product yet.

By entering information about the manufacturers, your site's visitors can have rapid access to all of a given manufacturer's products. This makes navigating around your site easier for them. In terms of visibility, filling out these fields will improve your position in search engines.

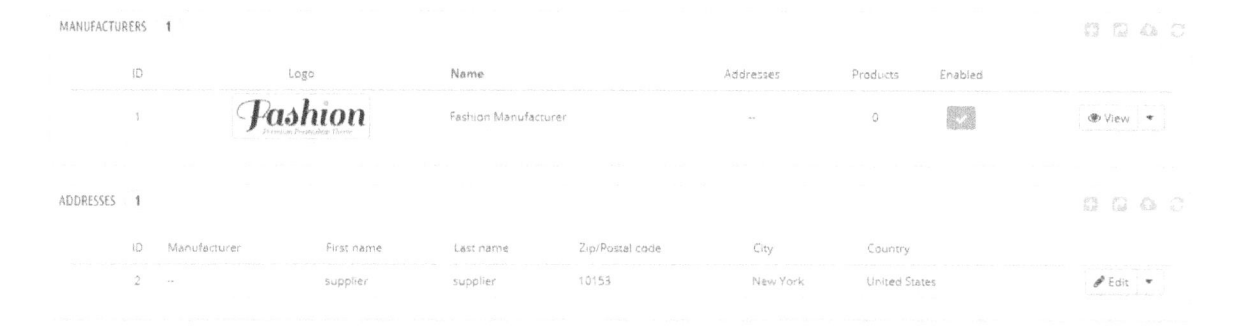

ID	Logo	Name	Addresses	Products	Enabled	
1	Fashion	Fashion Manufacturer	--	0	✓	View ▼

ADDRESSES 1

ID	Manufacturer	First name	Last name	Zip/Postal code	City	Country	
2	--	supplier	supplier	10153	New York	United States	Edit ▼

Creating a manufacturer

Click on the "Add new manufacturer" button, and a creation form appears.

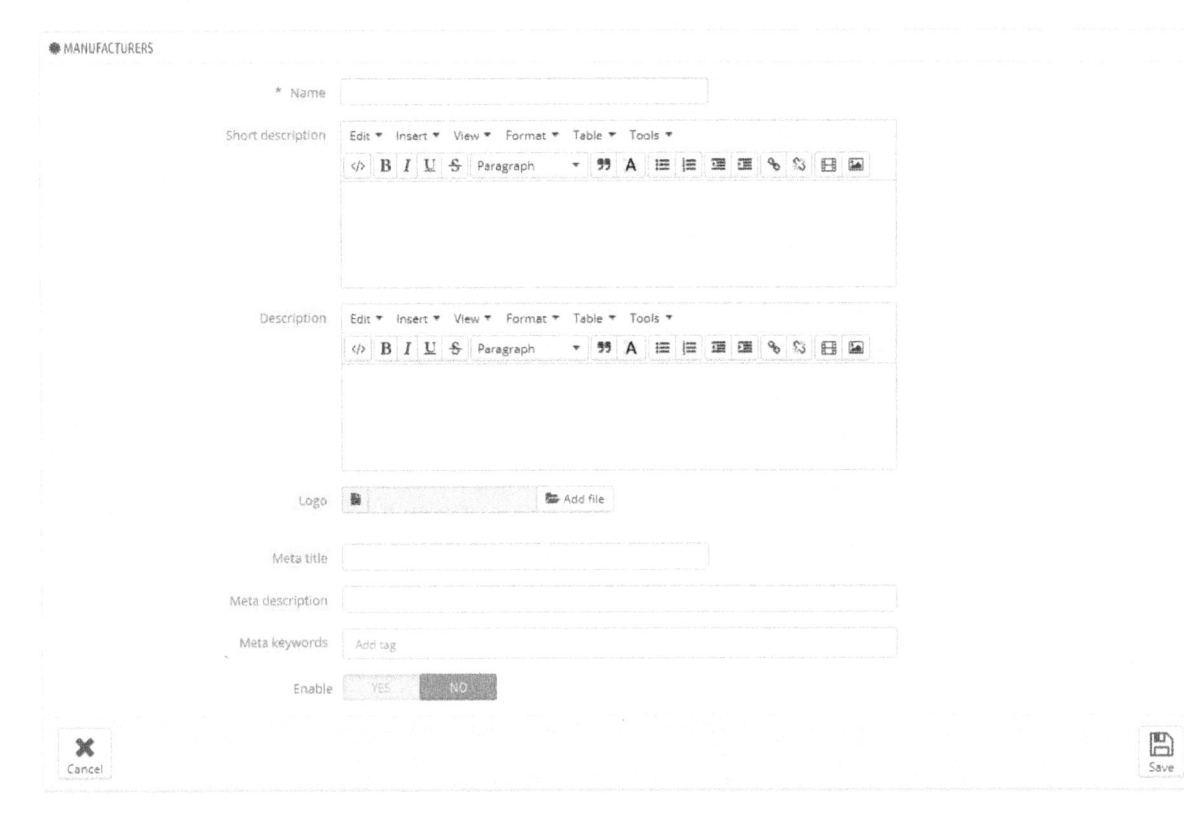

Fill out all of the fields:

- **Name**. Indicate the name of the manufacturer in order to simplify your visitor's searches.
- **Short description**. The description that will appear on the search engines when a user make a request. Limited to a 100 characters.
- **Description**. Add a more complex description of your manufacturer and their activity and products.
  You can detail their specialties and promote the quality of their products. The manufacturer's description will be shown in your store among the others.
- **Logo**. Having a manufacturer logo is essential: it leads the customers' eyes to trust your shop almost as much as they trust that manufacturer/brand.
- The SEO fields (Title, Meta description, and Meta Keywords) provide the same functionality as they do in the categories.
    - **Meta title**. The title that will appear on the search engines when a request is made by a customer

- o **Meta description**. A presentation of your site in just a few lines, intended to capture a customer's interest. This will appear in search results
    - o **Meta Keywords**. Keywords that you must define in order to have your site referenced by search engines. You can enter several of them, separated by commas, as well as expressions, which must be indicated in quotation marks.
- **Enable**. You can disable a manufacturer, even temporarily. This will only remove it from the manufacturers list on your shop's front-end.

Save your changes in order to be taken back to the manufacturers list. From there, you can:

- Click on a manufacturer's name or logo, and get a list of all the products associated with it. If there are none, then you associate products to that manufacturer, working on a per-product basis, from the "Products" page under the "Catalog" menu, using each product's "Associations" tab on the left.
  The same result is achieved by clicking the "View" icon on the right of the current page.
- Disable the manufacturer, by clicking on the green "Yes". Once disabled, a red "No" appears in its place: click to re-enable the manufacturer.
- Edit/delete the manufacturer by clicking on the respective buttons on the right of the row.

Adding a Manufacturer's Address

At the bottom of the "Manufacturers" page is an "Addresses" section. Each manufacturer can have its own address registered with PrestaShop. This serves mainly as a reminder for yourself: this way, you'll always have the contact address for a manufacturer available directly within PrestaShop.

Click on the "Add new manufacturer address" button to open the creation form.

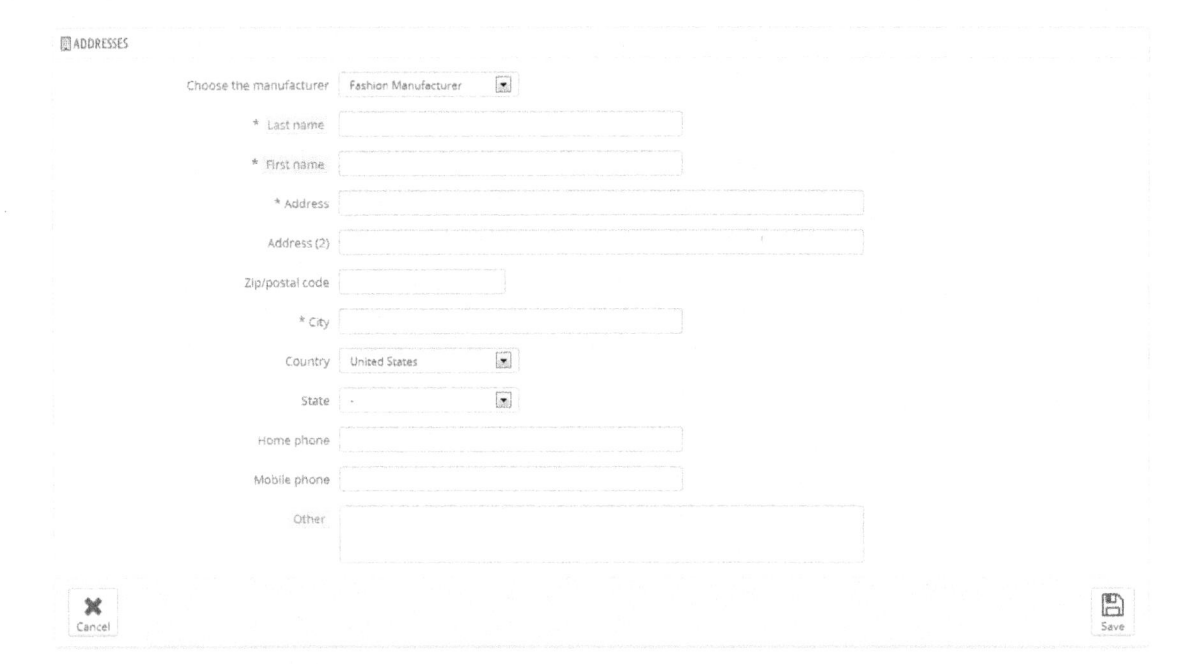

Make sure to choose the correct manufacturer, and to fill as many fields as possible.

Managing Suppliers

Having suppliers registered is optional if you already have manufacturer who directly supply you with their products. It all depends on your needs, but if your product supplier is not the same as the product manufacturer, then you should make sure to have both registered in your system, and associated with each product.

> In PrestaShop, a supplier is the company which provides you with a product.
>
> Even if you sell your own products, you must at least create your company as a supplier.

Just as for manufacturers, your site's visitors can have rapid access to all of supplier's products. This makes navigating around your site easier for them. In terms of visibility, filling out these fields will improve your position in search engines.

SUPPLIERS	1					
ID	Logo	Name	Number of products	Enabled		
1	Fashion	Fashion Supplier	7	✓		View ▼

Click on "Add new supplier", and a creation form appears.

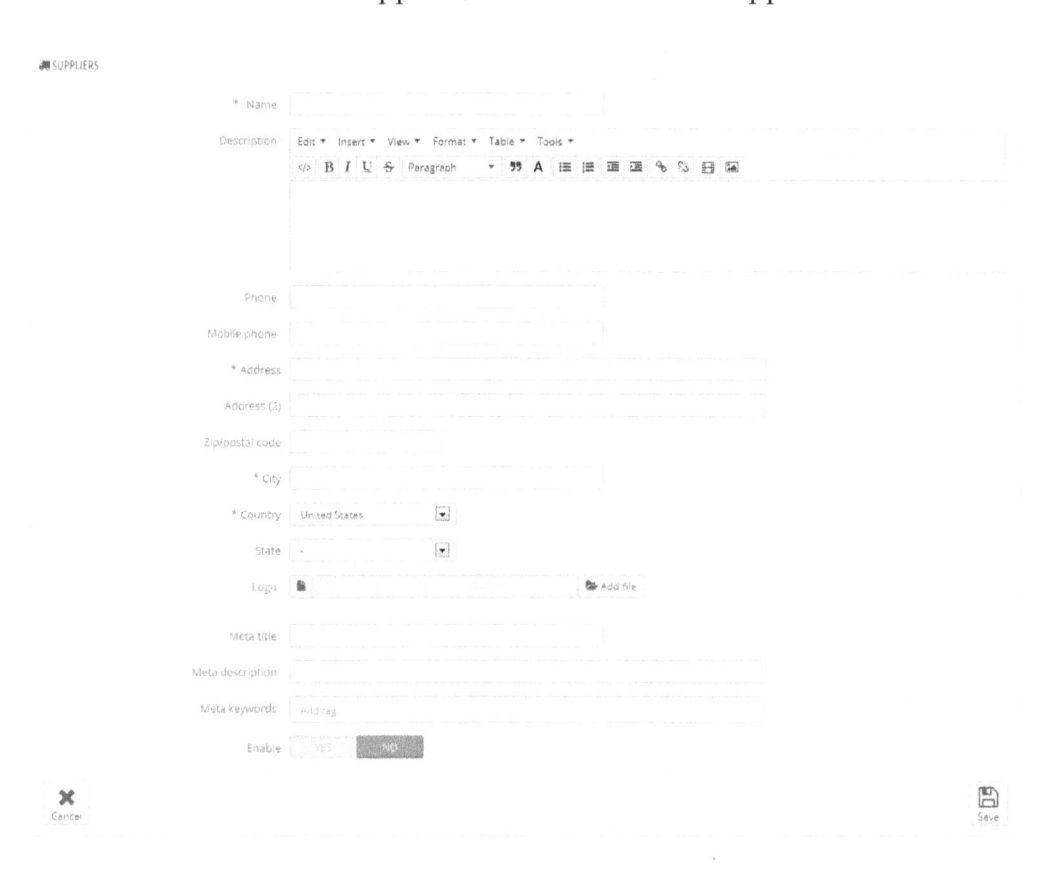

[Supplier creation form with fields: Name, Description, Phone, Mobile phone, Address, Address (2), Zip/postal code, City, Country, State, Logo, Meta title, Meta description, Meta keywords, Enable]

Fill out all of the fields:

- **Name**. Indicate the name of the supplier in order to simplify your visitor's searches.
- **Description**. Add a more complex description of your supplier and their activity and products.
  You can detail their specialties and promote the quality of their products. The supplier's description will be shown within your shop.

- The address fields (Phone, Address, Postcode, City, State, and Country). The "State" field only appears for relevant countries.
- **Logo**. Having a supplier logo is essential: it leads the customers' eyes to trust your shop almost as much as they trust that supplier/brand.
- The SEO fields (Title, Meta description, and Meta Keywords). Provides the same functionality as they do in the categories.
    - **Meta title**. The title that will appear on the search engines when a request is made by a customer
    - **Meta description**. A presentation of your site in just a few lines, intended to capture a customer's interest. This will appear in search results
    - **Meta Keywords**. Keywords that you must define in order to have your site referenced by search engines. You can enter several of them, separated by commas, as well as expressions, which must be indicated in quotation marks.
- **Enable**. You can disable a supplier, even temporarily. This will only remove it from the suppliers list on your shop's front-end.

Save your changes in order to be taken back to the suppliers list. From there, you can:

- Click on a supplier's name or logo, and get all the products associated with it. If there are none, then you should work on a per-product basis, from the "Products" page under the "Catalog" menu, using each product's "Associations" tab on the left.
  The same result is achieved by clicking the view icon on the right.
- Disable the supplier, by clicking on the green check-mark. Once disabled, a red "X mark appears in its place: click to re-enable the supplier.
- Edit/delete the supplier by clicking on the respective buttons on the right of the row.

Building Image Maps

Image maps was a feature that was introduced with version 1.1 of PrestaShop, and available up to version 1.5 included.

> **New installations of PrestaShop 1.6 do not have this feature available, but stores upgraded to version 1.6 can still use it.**
>
> If you have made a fresh installation of PrestaShop 1.6 and you still want to use image maps, here's how:
>
> 1. Open the Administration > Menus page.
> 2. Click on "Add a menu"
> 3. In the form, give the page a name (a priori, "Image Maps"), and type "AdminScenes" in the "Class" field. Leave the "Module" field empty, and choose "Catalog" for the parent page.
> 4. Save the form. The image maps page now appears in the chosen page.
>
> **Note that this feature is deprecated, and not supported anymore.**

Image mapping consists of assigning multiple clickable zones to an image so that different product pages can be opened by clicking on one single image. This feature makes your site very attractive by easing your customers' navigation.

Before creating an image map, you must have an image which features variations of a product, or different products altogether.

Clicking on the "Image Mapping" menu option takes you to a new page, which lists the currently-registered image maps, if any.

To create a new map, click on the "Add new image map" button. You are taken to the creation screen.

- **Image map name**. Enter a name for the image map.
- **Status**. Whether the image map is available or not. You can choose to delay its availability until you are done settings all the links.
- **Image to be mapped**. Select the image that you want to represent the image map, then click "Save and stay". The page will then reload, with the photo that you uploaded and many more options.

Now we are going to learn how to set up an image map. Click anywhere on your image and drag your mouse over one of the products presented, in order to highlight/cut out the part of the image you want to be clickable to the user.

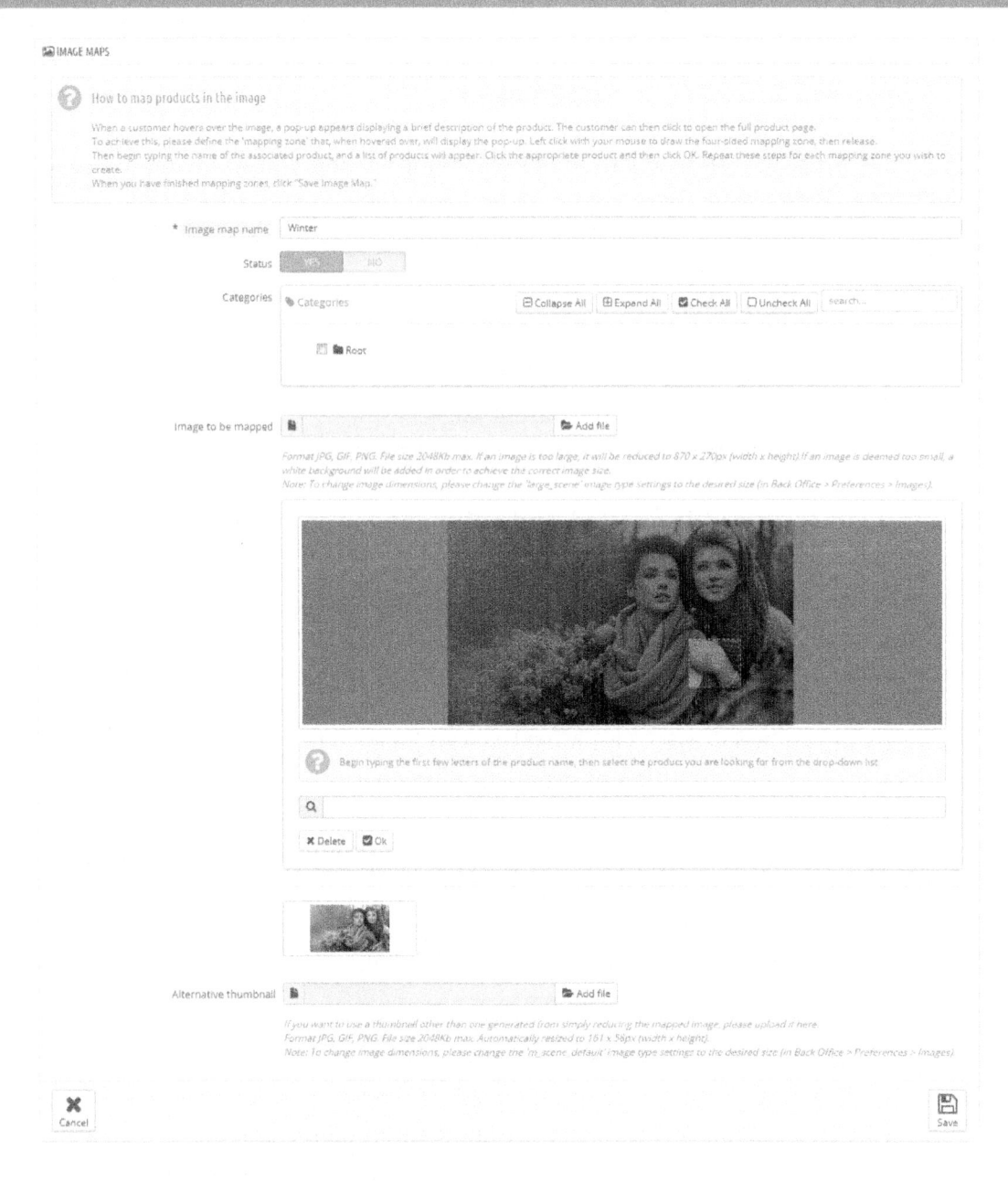

Your selection will be clear and illuminated while the rest of the image will darken. Pay attention to carefully align the frame of your selection with the zone onto which your customer will be able to click.

Once this is done:

1. In the field just underneath the image, type the first few letters of the product associated with your selected zone.
   In our example, we would type "dress" and several choices would appear. We would then choose "Printed dress".
2. Confirm your choice by clicking "OK". Your image map is now created.

Repeat this process for all of the products on this image that you wish to make accessible with a click.

The clickable zones are visible thanks to the "+" icon. Hovering over the image with your mouse cursor, you can see a little window that presents the image's name, default image, short description, and price.

If you have made a mistake on your clickable area, you can resize by grabbing its sides or corners.

If you wish to delete a clickable area, just select the area, and click the "Delete" button within the image.

Finally, you must assign your Image Map to a category. This is done by checking the boxes on the "Categories" table.

Once all of the modifications have been done, save all of your settings.

Your image map is now available on your store, in the chosen categories.

Managing Tags

The tagging feature enables you to associate your products with keywords. Your customers can use the keywords to easily and quickly find the products they are looking for.

For instance, let's say customer wants to find a MP3 player in your shop. In order to find the product corresponding to his or her search, there needs to be a tag to associate "MP3 player" with "iPod Nano".

> Products tags are not the same as page keywords: they have no direct impact on search engine placement.
>
> To work on your search engine placement, open the "SEO" tab of each product's create sheet.

You have two ways to set up this feature.

First Solution: When Creating a New Product

You can associate several tags to your product from the moment you create it in PrestaShop, directly in the "Tags" field in the product's "Information". See the previous chapter of this guide, "Adding Products and Product Categories".

Second Solution: Managing Tags

The "Tags" page under the "Catalog" menu enables you to create new tags and manage existing tags. Once you have given tags to your products, you will get a very important list of tags. The "Tags" page will help you manage them all.

To create a new one, click on "Add New", and a creation page appears.

This interface enables you to add tags to one or many of your products.

- **Name**. Give your tag a name. It should be short and to the point, so as to actually help you customers find the associated products instead of hindering them.

- **Language**. Indicate in what language the tag should appear on your shop. PrestaShop is clever enough not to display keywords in Spanish to customers who chose to see the French version of the site, for instance.
- **Products**. Select the products from the right column to which you would like to apply the tag. Hold on the Ctrl key on your keyboard in order to select several products at once.

Once you save the page, the named tag will be applied to all the products listed in the list on the right.

To add the same tag for another language, just repeat the operation, only this time, change the language.

After saving the tag, you are redirected to the list of tags, where you can edit or delete them, or even bulk delete them using the button at the bottom of the list. Next to the edit and trash icons, a number indicates how many products use the tag.

From now on, when your customers make a search query on your site, the results they will receive will also depend on the tags that you have associated with the products.

Managing Attachments

PrestaShop enables you to make some files available to your customers before their purchase.

For example, let's say you sell electronics, and you would like to urge your customers to read a document on how a product works. You can upload a document for that purpose.
You could also simply have the product's PDF manual directly available for download right on the product page.

Each product can have attachments, which can be individually set in their own "Attachments" tab on the left, as explained in the previous chapter of this guide, "Adding Products and Product Categories". That page gives you access to all the attached files of the shop: if you need to apply the associated one file with many products, you will thus only have to upload it once.

You can also upload attachments on their own, before associating them to products. This is done from the "Attachment" page, under the "Catalog" menu.

The process to register a new attachment to your shop is straightforward:

1. Click on the "Add new". A form appears.
2. **Filename**. Give your attachment a name, in all the needed languages.
3. **Description**. Give it a quick description, also in as many languages as needed.
4. Click on "Add file" to select a file on your computer to upload.
5. Click on "Save".

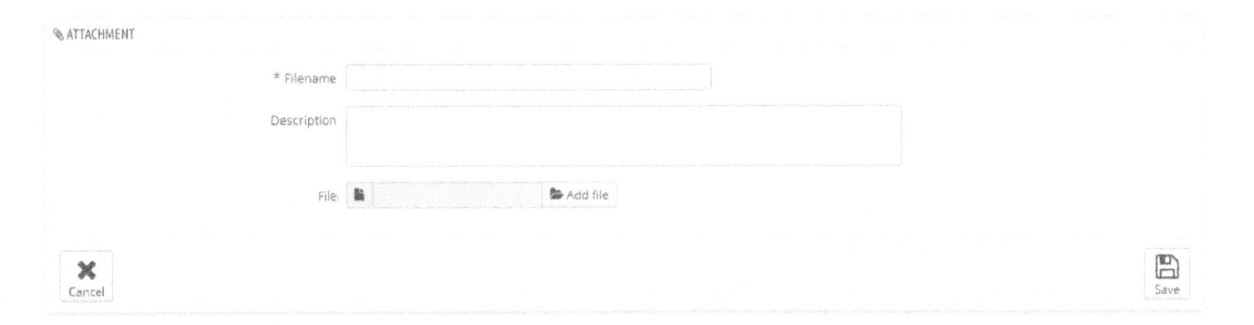

You are then redirected the attachment list, where your file now appears. It is now available to all products, through their "Attachments" tab.

Now the "Download" tab will appear in your online shop and your customers can download that file if needed.

Managing Orders

As a shop manager, you will have to deal with heaps of orders and their accompanying invoices and customer support requests – at least, that's what we wish for you. The daily task of handling numerous orders can be daunting. Fortunately PrestaShop does its best to help you wade through them all and successfully handle your customers' purchases, along with credit slips and the unavoidable merchandise returns.

Orders

The "Orders" page under the "Orders" menu enables you to see all of the information about all the purchases from your shop. All of your shop's transactions are available there, organized by date (by default, it is set to sort from newest to oldest).

You can filter the results and easily find the orders you're looking for by using the fields above. For instance, to identify Mr. Doe's orders, type "Doe" into the "Customer" field and then click "Filter".

> YOU CANNOT DELETE AN ORDER. It is illegal to be able to remove payment or ordering information and/or invoice information from a business in Europe. Therefore, implementing a "Delete" button for orders would render PrestaShop illegal in Europe.

> To safely delete the default order, install the "PrestaShop cleaner" module (which is available in the default installation since v1.5.4), open its configuration screen and check the "Orders and customers" box before you click on the "Check & fix" button.

You can export a list of your orders by clicking on the "Export" button at the top. You cannot import orders.

Creating an Order

One of the great features of PrestaShop is the ability to create an order directly from the back-office. For instance, this is tremendously useful when a customer wants to buy a product but does not succeed, and you need to take the hand and make the order while on the phone or during an e-mail conversation with the customer.

Clicking "Add new order" opens a new page with a single text field, labeled "Search customers". When creating a new order through the back-office, your first task is to associate that order with a customer. Type the first letters of the customer first name, last name or e-mail address, and PrestaShop will display the matching accounts.

> If the customer you are creating this order for does not even have a user account already, you can create one on the fly: click the "Add a new customer" button to open a window with the main account details ready to fill. Once the account is saved, it becomes the chosen account for the order.
>
> Note that you will also have to register the customer's address – an "Add new address" button is available at the bottom of the page, in the "Addresses" section.

Click the "Choose" button for the correct customer, and the whole order form appears. Its main section, "Cart", is where you will make all the necessary product decisions for this order. You can also choose to use a previous order from the customer, or a previously abandoned cart.

The "Search a product" field enables you to dynamically find products to add: type the first letters of its name and PrestaShop will fill a drop-down list with

matching products. Choose a product, select a quantity, and click "Add to cart" button. You can of course choose among the many combinations of a product, if any, in the "Combination" drop-down list that appears in that case.
Note that PrestaShop gives you an indication of the remaining stock for a given product, which enables you to tell the customer that you are out of stock for said product right from the order form.

The page also enables you to see the previous carts and orders from that customer, if any. If it turns out you are dealing with a cart that a customer somehow cannot validate, you can use that cart for this order by clicking on the "Use" action button.

If needed, you can also grant that order a voucher/cart rule, and even create one on the fly by clicking on the "Add new voucher" button.

Finally, you need to specify to which address the order should be delivery (and possibly billed). Here, again, you can create new addresses on the fly using the "Add new addresses" button.

Viewing an Order's Details

In order to process the orders you receive, you have to view the information they contain.
Click on the line containing the order, or click on the button to the right of the order.

The order detail sheet fills a full page.

At the top of the page is a quick summary of the order: date it has been validated, number customer service discussions about it, number of products in the order, and total amount of money.

The detail sheet of the order gives you access to:

- On the left, order information:
    - The status and status history of the order.
    - The shipping information: total weight of order and carrier chosen by the customer.
- On the right, customer information:

- Name of buying history.
- Shipping and invoice addresses (with a rough location map using Google Maps).
* The method of payment that was used, the cost of the products, and the shipping costs.
* Various details on the ordered products.

In the "Shipping address" section of the page, you can see a "G" icon: the enables you to use Google Maps to locate the address on a map.

Changing the order

Orders are definitive. There are many reasons why you would need to change an order before its products are gathered, packed and sent to their new owner: one of the product is out of stock, the customer changed his or her mind, etc.

Adding a product

At the bottom of the "Products" list, you can find the "Add a product" button, which adds a field to the order.

When adding a product, the products table gets a new row added with a handful of fields. The first text field is actually a small search engine: type the first letters of a product to see a list of corresponding products. Select the one you want to add, and the grayed-out field of the row becomes available.
If the product has combinations, you can select it in a drop-down list that appears below the name: the unit price update accordingly.
Set the quantity of products, and then click the "Add product" button: the product is added

You cannot add more product quantity than there is of available product.

Removing products

To cancel a product, go to the product list, and either delete the product by clicking on the "Delete" action, or by clicking on the "Edit" action if all you need is to remove some quantity of a product.

You can edit the quantity of many products at the same time.
If a product's quantity reaches 0, it is removed from the order altogether.
You cannot remove more than the quantity of product.
Click the "Cancel" button to cancel your edit.

Editing the order details

Many sections of the order sheet can be edited, enabling you to update or correct some of the data provided by the customer.

Order Status

The first drop-down list in the order page enables you to change its status. It is a very important part of the whole order monitoring process, as with each status change, new functionalities and documentation will be made available for the order.

You can choose between the following statuses:

- Awaiting bank wire payment.
- Awaiting cheque payment.
- Awaiting PayPal payment.
- Canceled.
- Delivered.
- On backorder.
- Payment accepted.
- Payment error.
- Payment remotely accepted.
- Preparation in progress.
- Refund.
- Shipped.

In order to get a better view of the order's activity, every status change is recorded, and the log appears right below the status change drop-down list. Therefore, you should only change a status if it has been clearly confirmed: do not mark an order as "Delivered" when you have sent the package, use "Shipped"; do not use "Preparation in progress" when in fact you have only taken a quick glance at the order, etc.

Actions Buttons

The action buttons change depending on the order's status. For instance, once the order is in the "Delivered" state, the "Add a product" and "Remove products" turn into two new buttons: "Return products" and "Partial refund".

> Product return is not activated by default. To activate it, go to the "Product returns" page under the "Orders" menu, and activate the option in the option at the bottom of the page. This will apply to all products and all orders.

- **Standard refund**. Available once the order reaches the "Payment accepted" status. Not available once the products have been sent.
  To be used when you need to refund the totality of the order, and can be done as long as the products are still in your warehouse.
  Click the "Standard refund" button and a new column will appear in the product list, titled "Refund". Set the amount and quantity for each of the affected products, choose one of the option at the bottom of the list (see below), and click the "Partial refund" button at the bottom of the table.
- **Partial refund**. Available once the order reaches the "Payment accepted" status.
  To be used when you need to refund only part of the order and not the whole order, either because the customer returned the ordered product, or simply as a sign of goodwill for a damaged product that the customer chose to keep anyway.
  Click the "Partial refund" button and a new column will appear in the product list, titled "Partial refund". Set the amount and quantity for each of the affected products, choose one of the option at the bottom of the list (see below), and click the "Partial refund" button at the bottom of the table.
- **Return products**. Available once the order reaches the "Shipped" status. PrestaShop must be set to accept merchandise returns, which is not in the Orders > Merchandise Returns page, with the "Enable returns" option.
  To be used only when the customer has effectively returned products: once the returned product has been received, you can mark it as returned directly in the order form.
  Click the "Return products" button and a new column will appear in the

product list, titled "Return". Check the box of the affected products, indicate the quantity of items that were returned, and click the "Return products" at the bottom of the table.

When you set a product as returned or to be refunded, four options are available below the list of products:

- **Re-stock products**. When checked, PrestaShop will consider that the returned product as available for sale again, and will therefore increase the stock for this product. You should not click this when a product is returned due to it being broken...
- **Generate a credit slip**. When checked, a credit slip will be created for the selected items. A credit slip is an acknowledgment from your shop that merchandise has been returned and that a refund has been issued. The customer can then use it as a credit slip for his or her next purchase.
- **Generate a voucher**. When checked, a voucher will be created for the amount of the selected items. A voucher takes the form of a discount code that the customer can enter during the checkout process.
  You can edit the customer's existing vouchers by viewing the customer's page: from the current order's page, click on the link under the customer's name in the "Customer information" section; once in the customer's page, reach the "Vouchers" section. You can edit each voucher by clicking on the "Edit" icon.

> In PrestaShop, vouchers are part of a special kind of discount feature: "cart rules". They can be created and edited from the "Cart Rules" page, under the 'Price rules" menu. The cart rules creation process in the next chapter, "Creating Price rules And Vouchers".

- **Repay shipping cost**. You can also choose to refund the shipping cost of the returned product, which is always an appreciated gesture.

If the customer paid the order using a credit card, the payment system should refund the cart automatically. If the order was paid using a check or a bank transfer, you have to issue the refund yourself, then mark the order as having been refunded manually in the back-office (in the order's page).

> **Difference between a credit slip, a voucher and a cart rule**
>
> A credit slip is first and foremost a written proof that a product has been returned. Most of the time, the customer can use it as a voucher.
>
> A voucher is a discount code which does not have to be tied to a merchandise return or a refund, and which can take more forms than a simple credit slip:
>
> - A discount on an order (percentage).
> - A discount on an order (amount).
> - Free shipping.
>
> You can apply a voucher to all customers, or a group of customers, or a single customer; you can set its expiration date;
>
> A cart rule is basically an advanced version of a voucher: in addition to what a voucher could do in PrestaShop 1.4, the cart rules system introduced in PrestaShop 1.5 enables you to:
>
> - Name the discount.
> - Allow the customer to use only a portion of the discount.
> - Assign priorities between cart rules.
> - Set the compatibility between cart rules.
> - Have the discount only work with some carriers.
> - Have the discount only work with a selection of products and/or categories and/or manufacturers and/or suppliers and/or attributes... or all of these at the same time if necessary!
> - Have the discount be applicable for free shipping and/or a discount on an order and/or a free gift... or all of these at the same time if necessary!

Documents

You can get many PDF documents out of the order page. When available, they are listed in the "Documents" section of the page.

By default, you can download the order itself as a PDF, by clicking on the "Print order" button on right.

You can get an invoice for the order by clicking on the "Generate invoice" button from the "Documents" section. The invoice is also generated once you put the order in the "Payment accepted" status.
Once it is generated, the "View invoice" button below gets activated the top-bar.

> You can customize the invoice layout easily: the PDF template files are located in the /pdf folder. These .tpl files are actually HTML files with Smarty tags for dynamic data. You can change the invoice's layout by editing the file named invoice.tpl.

When you put the order in the "Preparation in progress" state, a delivery slip PDF is generated, which you can then download from the "Documents" section.

Shipping

The shipping details of the current order can be partly edited. More specifically, you can change the tracking number: in the "Shipping" section, click on the "Edit" icon in the "Tracking number" column, and enter the new number.

Shipping Address

The "Shipping address" section enables you to edit the destination address of the package your team is about to send. You can either use the drop-down list to choose another of the addresses that the customers has already registered on your shop, or you can use the "Edit" icon to edit the currently chosen address.

If you need to send the package to an address that is not already registered in PrestaShop, you must first create it. To do this, go to the "Customers" menu, open the "Addresses" page, and click in the "Add new" button. Do not forget to put the correct e-mail of the customer, as this is the way PrestaShop will know to associate that new address with your existing customer! Once done, go back to the order's page, and change the address using the drop-down list.

Note that a small "G" icon enables you to visualize the destination of the package on Google Maps.

Invoice Address

The "Invoice address" section enables you to edit the payment address of the order. Just as for the shipping address, you can either choose the drop-down menu to choose another of the addresses that the customers has already registered on your shop, or you can use the "Edit" icon to edit the currently chosen address.

If you need the payment to be tied to an address that is not already registered in PrestaShop, you must first create it. To do this, go to the "Customers" menu, open the "Addresses" page, and click in the "Add new" button. Do not forget to put the correct e-mail of the customer, as this is the way PrestaShop will know to associate that new address with your existing customer! Once done, go back to the order's page, and change the address using the drop-down menu.

Discount

In the "Products" section, at the bottom of the products listing, you the "Add new discount" button. This creates a simple discount, not as advanced as the vouchers/cart rules system but still useful.

Clicking it will open a new form, with the following items:

- **Name**. Give the discount a short name. This will be public to the customer.
- **Type**. Choose the discount type: "percent", "amount" or "free shipping".
- **Value**. For the "percent" or "amount" types, set the value of the discount.
- **Invoice**. Select to which invoice from this order this discount should be applied. When there is more than one invoice, you can check the box to apply the discount to all the invoices.

The discount will be applied to the total before the shipping costs.

Attaching a message to the order

In the "New Message" section, on the right of the page, you can attach a comment on the order for your team.

You can also have this comment be sent to the customer, in order to give him or her information concerning the order, a delay, a surprise, or keep him or her informed on offers and specials. This is a key point of customer relationship.

There are two links available:

- **Click here to add a comment or send a message to the customer**.
    - You can add a message simply by writing in the message box and clicking "Send". The message will be stored in the client's profile in your Customer Service database, which you can access either by going to the client's page, or to the Customer Service page. The message can also be sent to the client's e-mail address should you choose to.
    - Pre-written messages can be saved and used multiple times, saving you the hassle of writing them over and over again. If you would like to send one of these messages, select it from the dropdown list. You can then add further details to the pre-written message if needed.
    You can create more pre-written messages using the tool in the "Order messages" page, under the "Orders" page.
- **Click here to see all messages**. This link will take you to the "Customer service" page of the "Customers" menu. This is fully explained in the "Managing Customers" chapter of this guide.

Invoices

Each time an order from your shop is validated, an invoice is sent out to the customer. You can download the invoices for a single order from the order's page. The "Invoices" page under the "Orders" menu enables you to download a selection of invoices from past orders in PDF format, all at the same time (in the same PDF file).

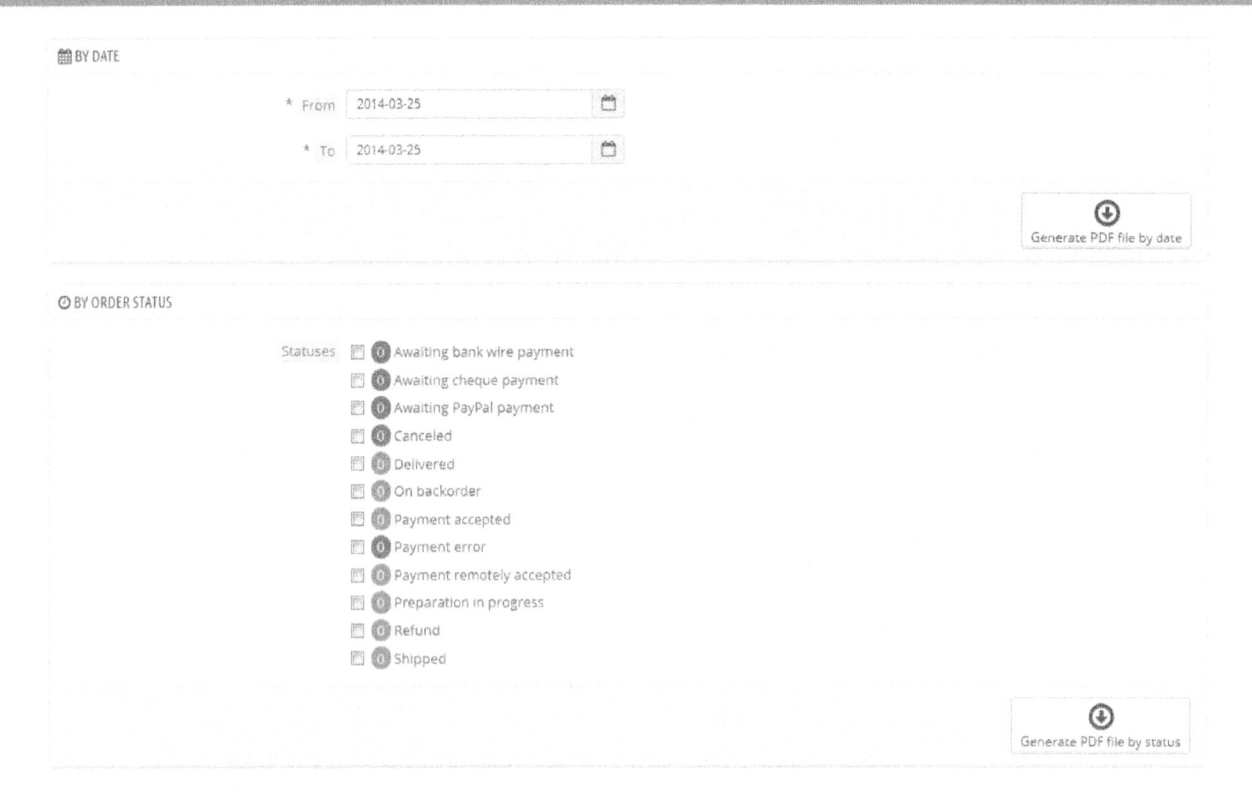

You can get a PDF file containing several invoices depending on two main criteria:

- **By date**. Very useful when you need to print all invoices for a given month or a given quarter. Select the start and end date, and click on the "Generate PDF file by date" button in the top bar.
- **By order status**. A must-have when you need to print precisely which orders are canceled, refunded or on backorder. PrestaShop helpfully indicates the number of invoices tied to each status in parentheses.

In both cases, the invoices are generated into a single PDF file, each with their own pages. You cannot get a single PDF file for each invoice of the given period or statuses using this page.

> If you want to customize the look of your store's invoices, you must change its template files.
>
> PDF template files are located in the /pdf folder. Open the invoice.tpl file and edit it to your likings: it is an HTML file with Smarty tags.

Invoice Options

You can choose whether or not invoices should available to your customers as soon as the order is made, as well as the Invoice Prefix and the invoice number you want listed on the printed version of the invoice. This feature can help you simplify the management of your account.

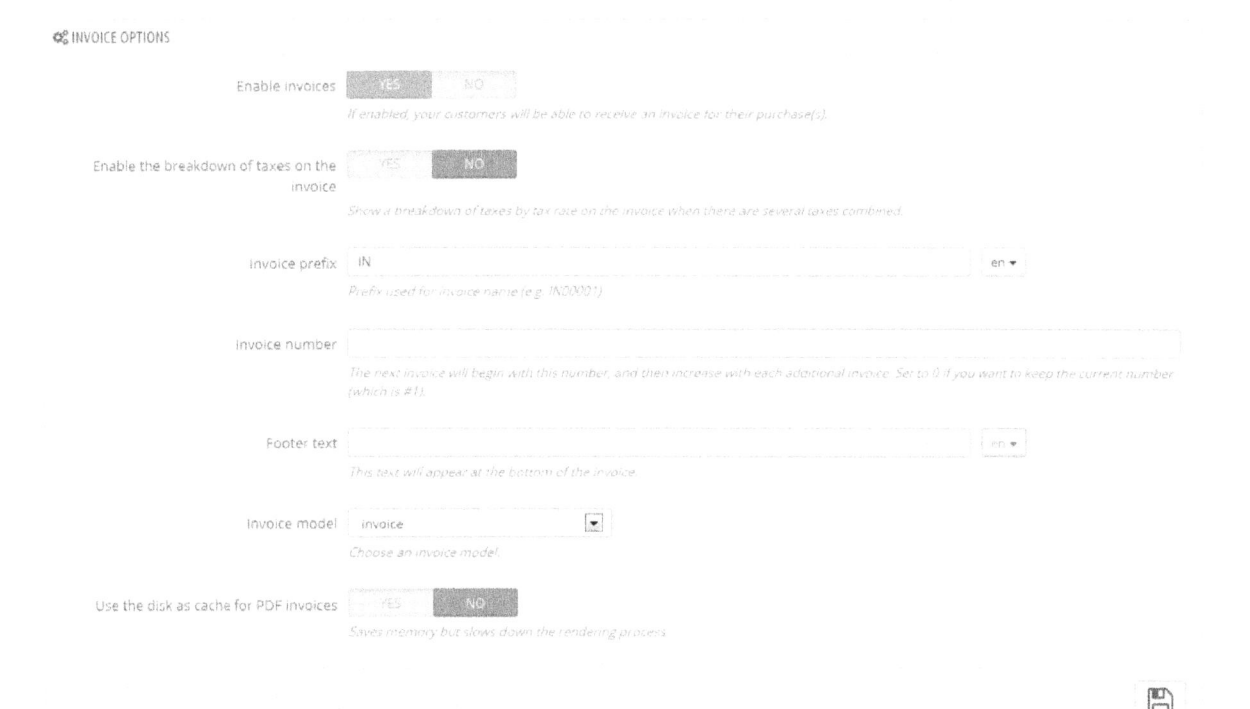

- **Enable invoices**. When disabled, your customer will not receive an invoice after their purchase. You will be responsible for handling the invoices, if your customers ask for one.
- **Enable the breakdown of taxes in the invoice**. *New in 1.6*. When enabled, the invoice lists all the various taxes that were applied to the order, instead of just one percentage.
- **Invoice prefix**. By default, PrestaShop has language-adapted invoice prefixes: "IN" in English, "FA" in French (for "*facture*"), "CU" in Spanish (for "*cuenta*"), etc. You could choose to have language codes instead: "EN", "FR", "SP", etc. Of course, you can also choose to have a single prefix for every language, or to not have a prefix at all.

PrestaShop will then generate the invoices number according to you settings: "#IN000001", "#FA000002", etc.
- **Invoice number**. If your business has already had orders and invoices before you started using PrestaShop, you can use this option to start your invoice number from a higher number.
- **Footer text**. You can use to have a custom text at the bottom of all your invoices. The text will appear below the name of your shop in the invoice.
- **Invoice model**. Depending on your themes, you might be able to use more than one style of invoice. Test them with a fake order, in order to choose the one you prefer. If you know how to code in HTML, you can add your own invoice models or edit the existing ones: they are located in the /pdf/ folder of your PrestaShop installation.
- **Use the disk as cache for PDF invoices**. You can choose to store generated invoices on PrestaShop's server disk rather than in its server cache. While it saves on memory usage, it slows down the PDF generation itself, so use it knowingly.

Do not forget to save your changes.

When your customers ask for their invoices, you can redirect them to the "Order History" section of their user accounts, which keeps all of their invoices available for them.

Merchandise Returns

The "Merchandise Returns" page gives you a list of all the RMA process (Return merchandise authorization).

At the bottom of the page, you have the possibility of enabling customers to send products back to you ("Enable returns" option). Simply make a choice, indicate the number of days during which a return request can be made, and save your settings: customers now have the ability to ask for a return authorization.

MERCHANDISE RETURN (RMA) OPTIONS

Enable returns: YES / **NO**
Would you like to allow merchandise returns in your shop?

Time limit of validity: 7
How many days after the delivery date does the customer have to return a product?

Save

Return process: how the customer sees it

Once you have activated the RMA option in your back-office, the customer can choose to return an item (provided the order is still in the time of validity). In order to do this, s/he must do the following:

1. Access the "Orders History" section of his or her account.
2. Select the order from which he wants to return an item.
3. Select the product(s) that s/he wishes to return by checking the box next to its name(s).
4. (optional) Add an explanation, in order for the shop team to better understand why the customer wants to return this product.

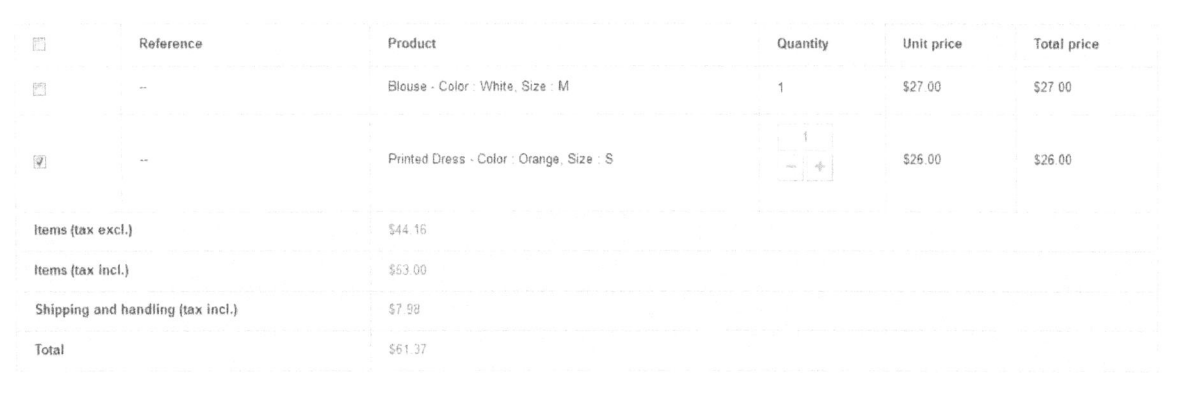

	Reference	Product	Quantity	Unit price	Total price
☐	--	Blouse - Color : White, Size : M	1	$27.00	$27.00
☑	--	Printed Dress - Color : Orange, Size : S	1	$26.00	$26.00

Items (tax excl.)	$44.16
Items (tax incl.)	$53.00
Shipping and handling (tax incl.)	$7.98
Total	$61.37

MERCHANDISE RETURN

If you wish to return one or more products, please mark the corresponding boxes and provide an explanation for the return. When complete, click the button below

Already bought one from you

Make an RMA slip >

Once the form is complete, the customer clicks on "Make an RMA slip", and the request is sent to the store manager (you). The request appears as "Waiting for confirmation" in the customer's "Return Merchandise Authorization" page, accessible from the account page.

Return process: how you see it

The return request appears in your back-office. At first, the RMA has the "Waiting for confirmation" status.

The refund process can take several steps, which are indicated by the RMA status. There is just a handful of statuses, which can follow the whole RMA process:

- Waiting for confirmation.
- Waiting for package.
- Package received.
- Return denied.
- Return completed.

RETURN MERCHANDISE AUTHORIZATION (RMA)

Customer	John DOE
	View details on the customer page
Order	Order #1 from 03/25/2014
	View details on the order page
Customer explanation	Already bought one from you.
Status	Waiting for confirmation ▼
	Merchandise return (RMA) status

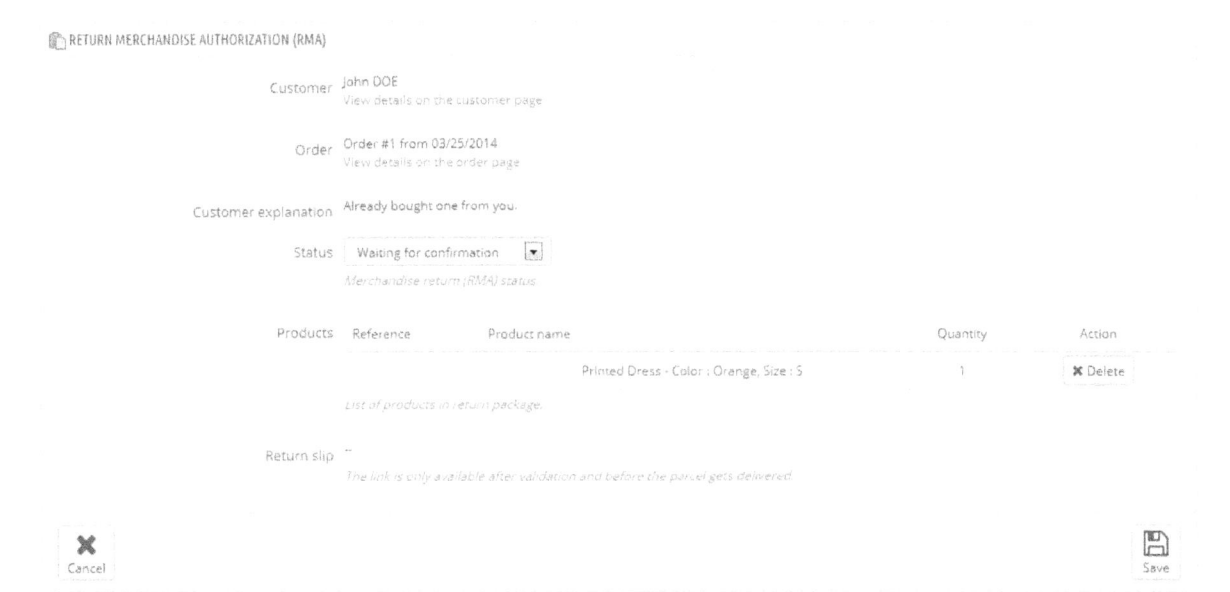

Products	Reference	Product name	Quantity	Action
		Printed Dress - Color : Orange, Size : S	1	✘ Delete

List of products in return package.

Return slip —
The link is only available after validation and before the parcel gets delivered.

[Cancel] [Save]

It is now up to you to accept it or deny it:

1. Click on the name of the return request to see more details.
2. Change the status to continue with the return process or stop it.
    - If you want to stop the return process (and deny the customer a refund), simply choose the "Return denied" status.
    - If you agree with the product being returned and the customer being refunded, follow each step precisely:
        1. Choose the next step in the process: "Waiting for package". This will send an e-mail to the customer indicating that the product can be sent back to you.
        2. Once you have received the package, change the RMA's status to "Package received".
        3. Finally, once the whole process is over (either the customer has been refunded or you have issued a credit slip), change the RMA's status to "Return completed".
3. Validate.

Refunding a customer

An order can be refunded, either partially or totally. This is done using two actions buttons located in the top bar of the order's page itself rather than in the RMA page.

The action buttons change depending on the order's status. For instance, once the order is in the "Delivered" state, the "Add a product" and "Remove products" turn into two new buttons: "Return products" and "Partial refund".

> Product return is not activated by default. To activate it, go to the "Product returns" page under the "Orders" menu, and activate the option in the option section at the bottom of the page. This will apply to all products and all orders.

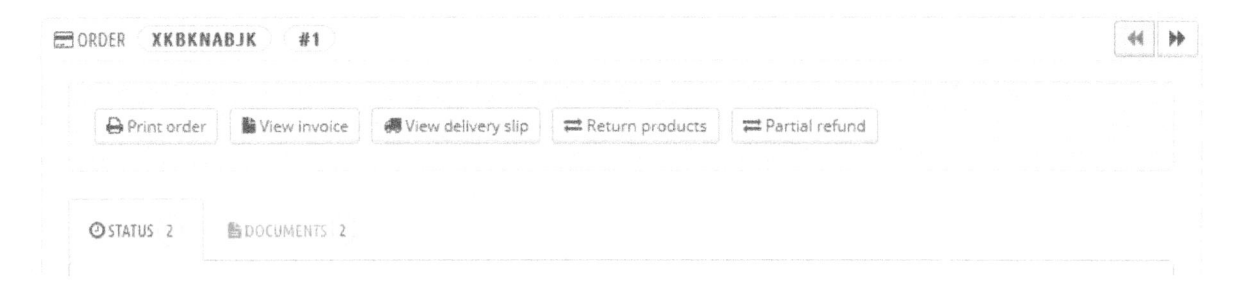

- **Return products**. To be used only when the customer has effectively returned products: once the returned product has been received, you can mark it as returned directly in the order form. Click the "Return products" button and a new column will appear in the product list, titled "Return". Check the box of the affected products, indicate the quantity of items that were returned, and click the "Return products" button at the bottom of the table.
- **Partial refund**. To be used when you need to refund only part of the order and not the whole order, either because the customer returned the ordered product, or simply as a sign of goodwill for a damaged product that the customer chose to keep anyway. Click the "Partial refund" button and a new column will appear in the product list, titled "Partial refund". Set the amount and quantity for each of the affected products, choose one of the option at the bottom of the list (see below), and click the "Partial refund" button at the bottom of the table.

When you set a product as returned or to be refunded, four options are available below the list of products:

- **Re-stock products**. When checked, PrestaShop will consider that the returned product as available for sale again, and will therefore increase

the stock for this product. You should not click this when a product is return due to it being broken...
- **Generate a credit slip**. When checked, a credit slip will be created for the selected items. A credit slip is an acknowledgment from your shop that merchandise has been returned and that a refund has been issued. The customer can then use it as a credit slip for his or her next purchase.
- **Generate a voucher**. When checked, a voucher will be created for the amount of the selected items. A voucher takes the form of a discount code that the customer can enter during the checkout process.
  You can edit the customer's existing vouchers by viewing the customer's page: from the current order's page, click on the link under the customer's name in the "Customer information" section; once in the customer's page, reach the "Vouchers" section. You can edit each voucher by clicking on the "Edit" icon.
- **Repay shipping cost**. You can also choose to refund the shipping cost of the returned product, which is always an appreciated gesture.

If the customer paid the order using a credit card, the payment system may refund the cart automatically, or you may have to do it yourself. If the order was paid using a check or a bank transfer, you have to issue the refund yourself, then mark the order as having been refunded manually in the back-office (in the order's page).

Delivery Slips

A delivery slip is a notification of delivery. It can also be called "delivery note" or "advice note".
It is supposed to be put in the shipped package, along with the ordered products. It will have your shop's logo, and indicate the content. On receiving the package, the customer will be able to use the delivery slip in order to double-check the content of the package, see that nothing is missing from the order.

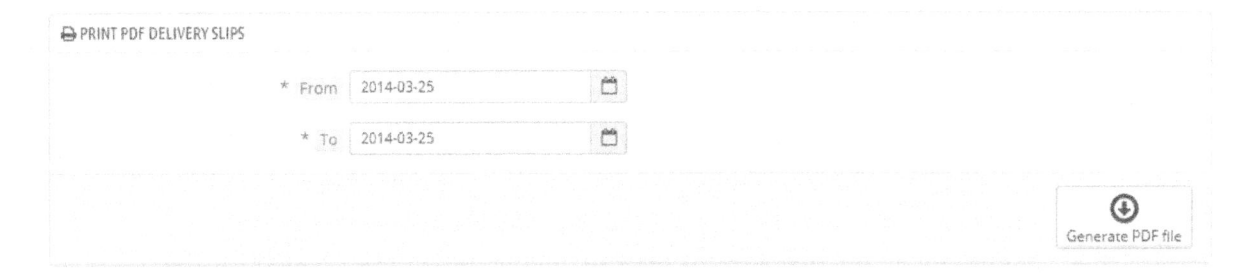

Getting a delivery slip is exactly like getting an invoice. Select the dates, as well as the options you would like, and then confirm them to create your documents.

You can get a PDF file of several delivery slips depending only by date, which is very useful when you need to print all delivery slips for a given day or a given quarter. Select the start and end date, and click on the "Generate PDF file" button.

Delivery Slips Options

The two options are the same as for the invoice options:

- **Delivery prefix**. You might like to have language-tagged delivery slips: "DE" in English, "LI" in French (for "livraison"), "EN" in Spanish (for "entrenga"), etc. Or you could directly choose to have language codes: "EN", "FR", "SP", etc. Of course, you can also choose to not have a prefix at all.
- **Delivery number**. If your business has already had orders and delivery slips before you started using PrestaShop, you can use this option to start your delivery slip number from a higher number.

PrestaShop will then generate the delivery slips number according to you settings: "#DE000001", "#LI000002", etc.

Do not forget to save your changes.

Credit Slips

Following your agreement on a product return, you should receive a package from the customer. Once you have received that package, you **must** create a credit slip from the order's page. It can also be called "credit note" or "credit memo".
Credit slips are not created in the "Credit Slips" page, but only listed there. This page is also used to generate a PDF of your credit slips.

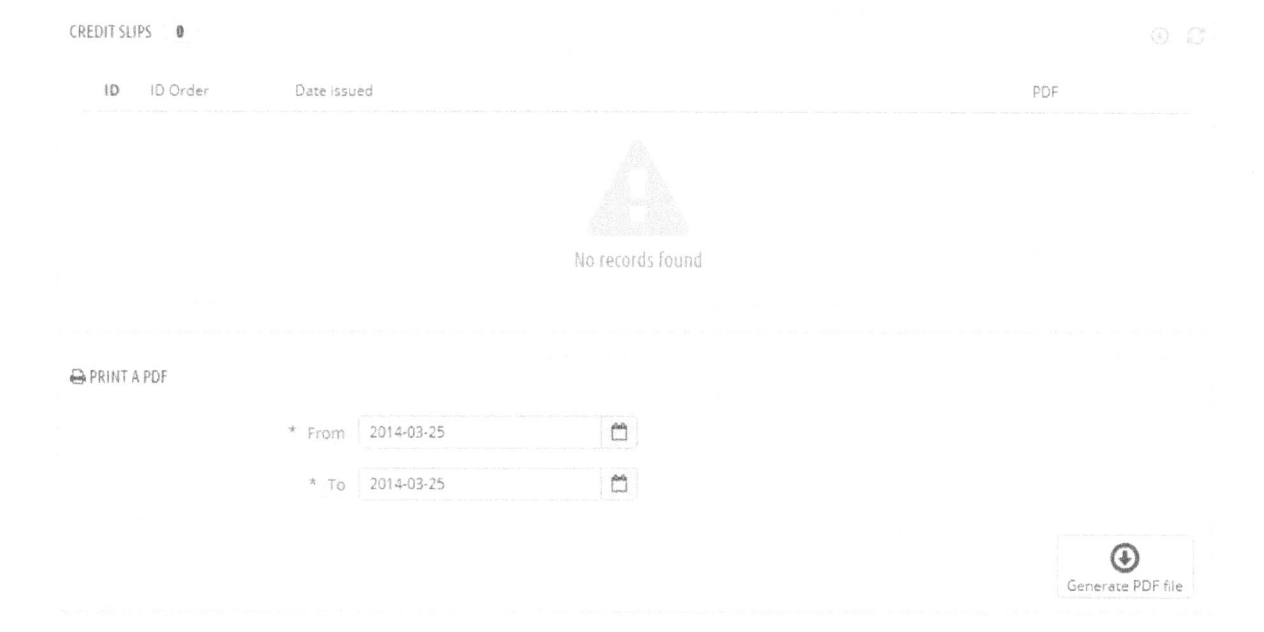

Delivery Slips Options

There is only one option on the page:

- **Credit slip prefix**. You might like to have language-tagged delivery slips. Of course, you can also choose to not have a prefix at all.

PrestaShop will then generate the credit slips number according to you settings.

Do not forget to save your changes.

Creating a Credit Slip

In your list of orders ("Orders" page), click on the order for which the customer is returning some items for more details – this will only work if have already indicated that the customer can send products back.

Below the "Products" table, do the following:

1. Check the returned item(s).
2. Check the box "Re-stock Products" if you wish to put the product back in your stock.
3. Check the box "Generate a Credit Slip."
4. To make a customer happy after committing an error in their order, consider giving him a voucher by checking the box next to "Generate a Voucher."
5. You can also reimburse his shipping costs by clicking next to "Include Shipping."

Once you have selected all the options you want, confirm by clicking on "Return products."

The credit slip is now created and will be available in the Order Details well as in the "Credit Slips" page.
From there, you can click the link to download the PDF file.
The customer will see the slip in his or her "My Account" section.

If you have created a voucher, customers will see it in the "My vouchers" section of their account. If they click on it, it should look something like this:

The amount of the returned item(s) is added to the voucher. The customer can use the discount code (listed in the far left of the column) next time he or she places an order.

Statuses

Having different order or return statuses enables you to easily manage your orders and returns, and keep you customers informed of the evolution of their purchase.

The various available statuses are visible and editable in the "Statuses" page, under the "Orders" menu.

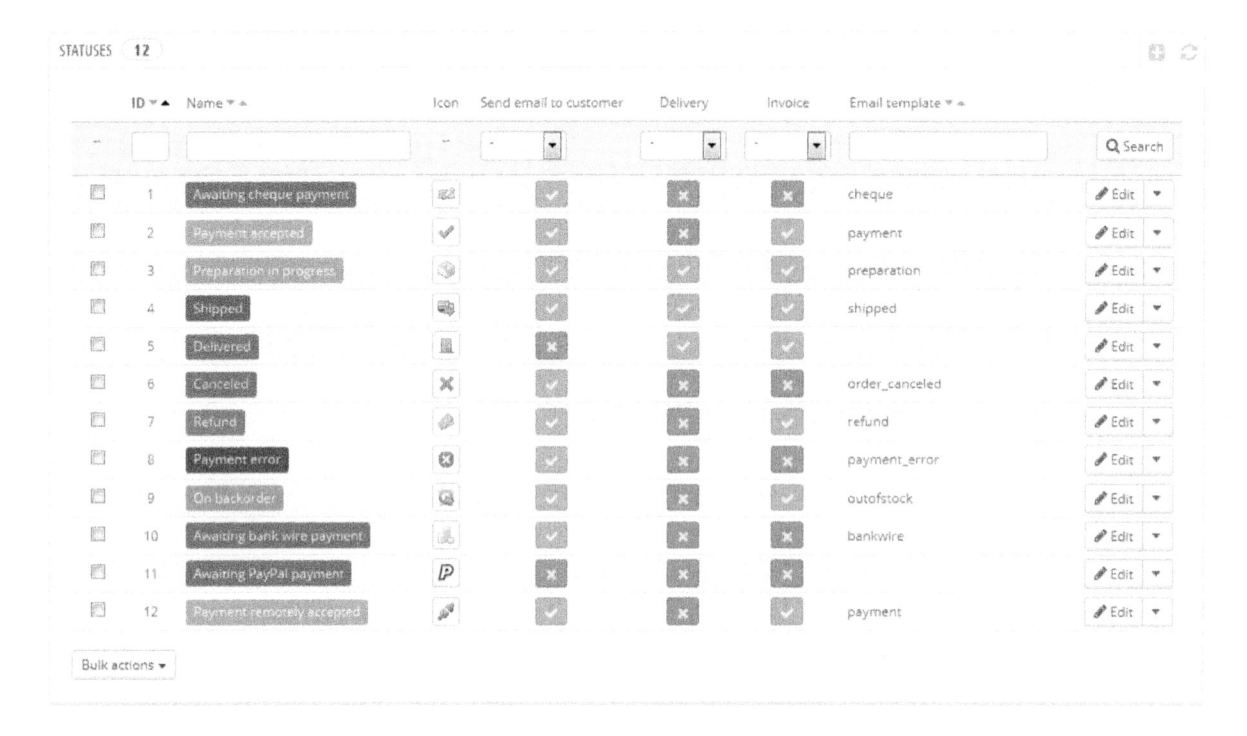

STATUSES	12								
	ID	Name	Icon	Send email to customer	Delivery	Invoice	Email template		
	1	Awaiting cheque payment	📧	✓	✗	✗	cheque	Edit	
	2	Payment accepted	✓	✓	✗	✓	payment	Edit	
	3	Preparation in progress	📦	✓	✓	✓	preparation	Edit	
	4	Shipped	🚚	✓	✓	✓	shipped	Edit	
	5	Delivered	🏠	✗	✓	✓		Edit	
	6	Canceled	✗	✓	✗	✗	order_canceled	Edit	
	7	Refund	🔄	✓	✗	✓	refund	Edit	
	8	Payment error	⊗	✓	✗	✗	payment_error	Edit	
	9	On backorder	🔍	✓	✗	✓	outofstock	Edit	
	10	Awaiting bank wire payment	🏦	✓	✗	✗	bankwire	Edit	
	11	Awaiting PayPal payment	P	✗	✗	✗		Edit	
	12	Payment remotely accepted	✏️	✓	✗	✓	payment	Edit	

Bulk actions

The page displays a list of the currently registered order statuses, along with:

- Their distinctive colors: existing status have colors that help quickly decide if there's an issue with the order or if it all goes well.
- Their icons.
- Their ties to three PrestaShop behaviors (more are available):
    - Should the customer receive e-mail when the order gets this status?
    - Is this a delivery status?
    - Does this status allow the customer to download and view a PDF version of the order's invoice?
- The name of their e-mail template: you can edit these templates, language by language, in the "Translations" page under the "Localization" menu. In the "Modify translations" section of that page, choose "E-mail template translations" in the drop-down menu, and then click on the language code of the language in which you wish to edit these templates.

- Their action icons: "edit" and "delete".

The return status list features less information, because those statuses are merely labels with no impact on the order.

RETURN STATUS	5		
1	Waiting for confirmation		Edit
2	Waiting for package		Edit
3	Package received		Edit
4	Return denied		Edit
5	Return completed		Edit

Creating a new order status

You can create a new status with the "Add New" button at the top. The creation form opens.

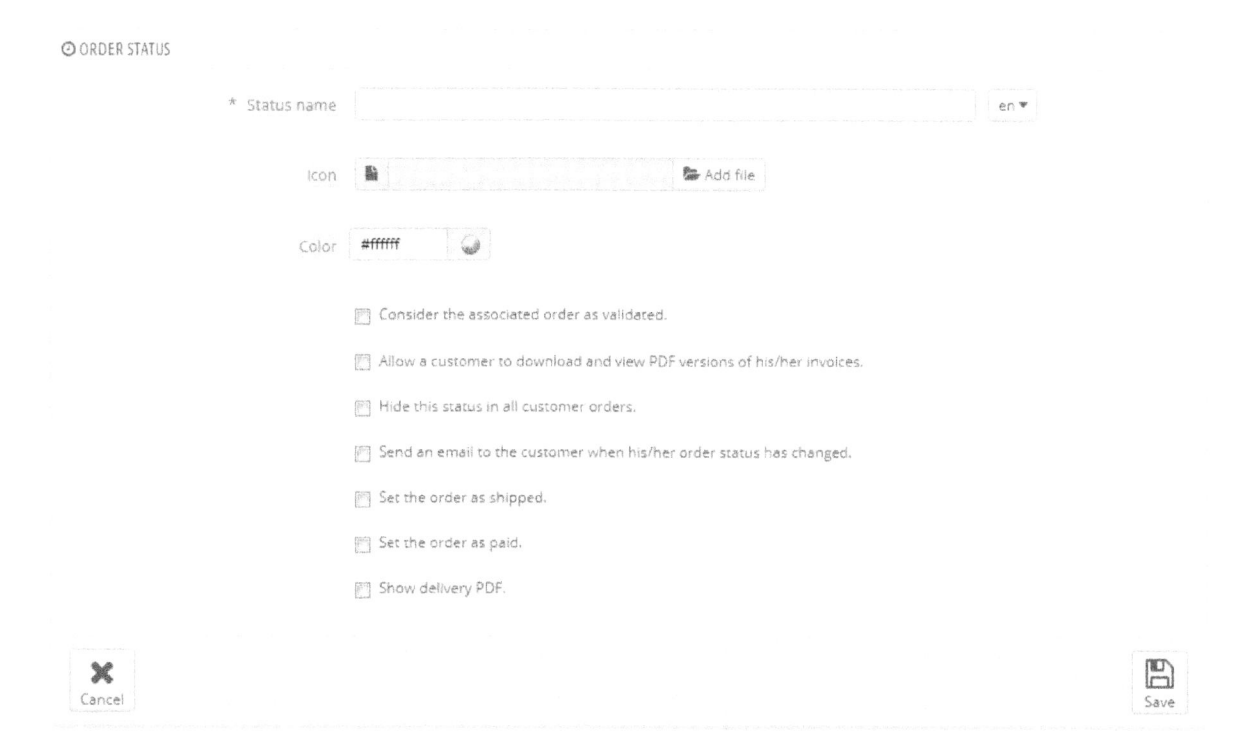

ORDER STATUS

* Status name: [_____] en ▼

Icon: [Add file]

Color: #ffffff

- ☐ Consider the associated order as validated.
- ☐ Allow a customer to download and view PDF versions of his/her invoices.
- ☐ Hide this status in all customer orders.
- ☐ Send an email to the customer when his/her order status has changed.
- ☐ Set the order as shipped.
- ☐ Set the order as paid.
- ☐ Show delivery PDF.

[Cancel] [Save]

Fill out the form:

- **Status name**. Keep it very short and distinctive.
- **Icon**. You can use any 16*16 icon; for instance, the excellent and free FamFamFam Silk icon set: http://www.famfamfam.com/lab/icons/silk/.
- **Color**. You should strive to have the status' color match the existing colors (if relevant). The default color usages are:
    - Red/Orange: canceled or refunded orders,
    - Crimson red: payment error,
    - Blue: orders which are still awaiting payment,
    - Light green: paid orders,
    - Dark green: delivered orders,
    - Purple: shipped orders,
    - Pink: backordered orders.
- Options:
    - **Consider the associated order as validated**. If enabled, this status marks all associated orders as "paid", and puts them in this same status.
    - **Allow a customer to download and view PDF versions of their invoice**. If disabled, you will have to send customers their invoice yourself.
    - **Hide this state in all customer orders**. This enables you to create internal statuses, for you and your team. Customers will never see this in their order status page.
    - **Send an e-mail to customer when his/her order status has changed**. When enabled, a drop-down menu appears to let you choose which mail template to use.
    - **Set the order as shipped**. Be careful: once an order is set as "shipped", it cannot be set back to the previous status.
    - **Set the order as paid**. Same here: once an order is set as "paid", it cannot be set back to the previous status.
    - **Show delivery PDF**. Displays the delivery PDF.

Creating a new return status

You can create a return status with the "Add New" button at the bottom. The creation form opens.

⊙ RETURN STATUS

* Status name
Color #ffffff

[Cancel] [Save]

It only features two fields:

- **Status name**. Set your desired status name.
- **Color**. Set its color

Finally, save your creation.

Order Messages

When you have to send a message to your customers using the PrestaShop interface (from the order page), you can choose to save this message in order to send it out again to other customers with similar questions, comments, or concerns.

To do this, go to the "Order Messages" page under the "Orders" menu. One default message is already saved: "Delay".

ID	Name	Message	
1	Delay	Hi, Unfortunately, an item on your order is currently out of stock. This may cause a slight delay in delivery. Please accept our apologies and rest assured that we are working hard to rectify this. Best regards,	Edit ▼

Creating a new message

To add other message, click on the "Add New" button. You can also edit the default message.

ORDER MESSAGES

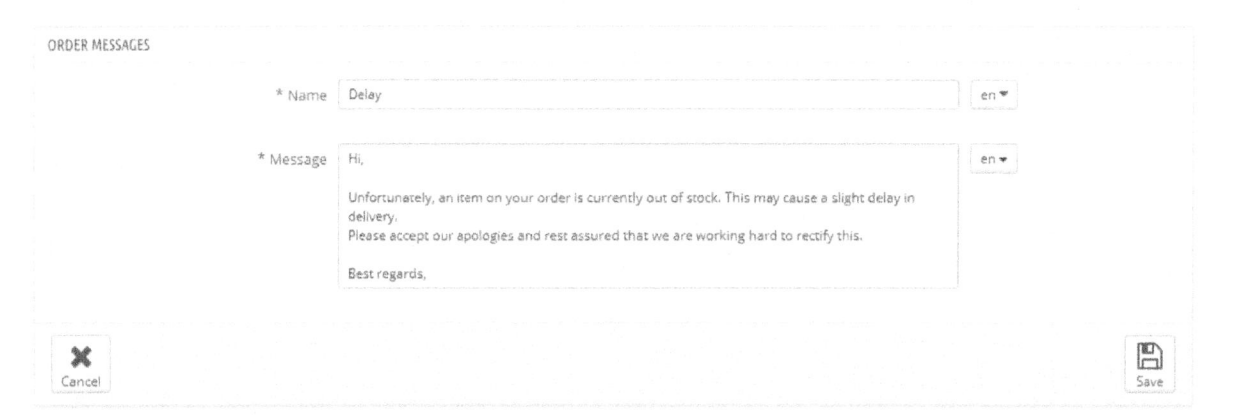

* Name	Delay
* Message	Hi, Unfortunately, an item on your order is currently out of stock. This may cause a slight delay in delivery. Please accept our apologies and rest assured that we are working hard to rectify this. Best regards,

[Cancel] [Save]

The form goes to the essentials:

- **Name**. Give your message a descriptive name so that you can easily find it again later.
- **Message**. Write out the content that you wish to send to your customers.

Once done, click on "Save".

You can create as many messages as needed.

Sending a message to a customer

Once you pre-written messages are all set, you can send them by going directly into a customer's order:

1. Select the pre-written message.
2. Edit it if needed, in order to tailor it to the order or the customer.
3. Enable the "Display to customer?" option.
4. Click "Send message".

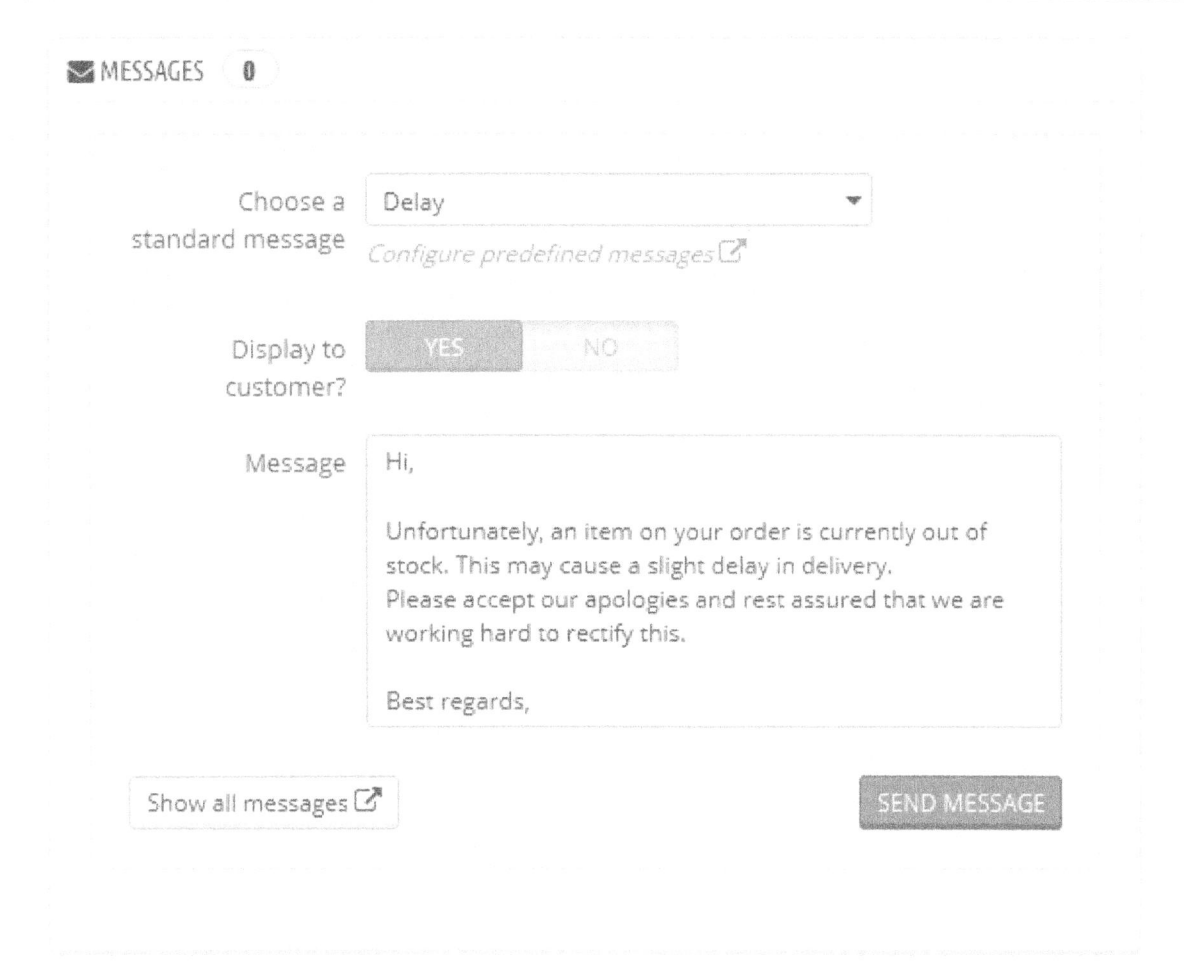

✉ MESSAGES 0	
Choose a standard message	Delay ▼
	Configure predefined messages ⤴
Display to customer?	YES NO
Message	Hi, Unfortunately, an item on your order is currently out of stock. This may cause a slight delay in delivery. Please accept our apologies and rest assured that we are working hard to rectify this. Best regards,
Show all messages ⤴	SEND MESSAGE

Your customer will receive the message on the email address associated with this account. To follow-up on the conversion, go to "Customer Support" page, in the "Customers" menu.

Managing Customers

You have to take good care of your customers. That means making sure their profile contains all the information you need to have a package shipped to them, following up on their support requests, creating special discount groups, knowing which orders have been completed and which have been abandoned, and much more.

The "Customers" menu enables you to check on your customers' details, create groups to which you can apply discounts, view the current shop carts, handle customer service, etc.

Your customers

The first page under the "Customers" menu gives you a list of all the registered users on your shop.

This gives you a bird's eye view of your customers, with some details thrown in which you can use to sort and search accounts:

- **Title**. Customers can declare their social title, which are matched with a genre and can help you better customize your customers' experience. There are three default social titles (Mr., Ms., and Miss), but you can create more in the "Titles" page under the "Customers" menu.
- **Age**. Knowing the age of you customers can also help you better target your demographics, and choose to sell products that appeal more to them.
- **Enabled**. Indicates whether the customer is active or not. You can disable an account by clicking on the green "Yes".
- **News.**. Indicates whether the customer is subscribed to your shop's newsletter or not. You can unsubscribe from it by clicking on the green "Yes".
- **Opt.**. Indicates whether the account has accepted to receive e-mails from your partners or not. You can unsubscribe it clicking on the green "Yes". **Do not subscribe a user to these e-mails without their consent, as this is considered spam**.
- Registration date and last visit can always be useful when sorting user accounts.
- **Actions**. You can edit the user's account, simply view it in full (with its messages, orders, addresses, vouchers, etc.), or trash it forever.

When installed for the first time with sample data, PrestaShop has a default user, named John DOE.

You can use this fake user to test some of your shop's features, and generally browse your shop and see it the way a regular user would.

To log in to your shop using this public account, use these credentials:

- E-mail address: pub@prestashop.com
- Password: 123456789

Before you open your shop to the public, make sure to delete this default user, or at least change its credentials! If not, malicious visitors could use it to make fake purchases and more.

Below the customers table is the "Set required fields for this section" button. It opens a form where you can indicate if a database field is necessary or not by checking the appropriate boxes: this way, you can make it so fields such as "newsletter" or "optin" are mandatory when a visitor is creating a customer account on your shop.

You can export a list of your clients by clicking on the "Export" button at the top. You can also import customers using the "Import" button. You will need your CSV file to follow this format:

ID;Title;Last name;First Name;Email address;Age;Enabled;News.;Opt.;Registration;Last visit;

2;1;Gorred;Francis;francis@example.com;-;1;0;0;2013-07-04 15:20:02;2013-07-04 15:18:50;

1;1;DOE;John;pub@prestashop.com;43;1;1;1;2013-07-02 17:36:07;2013-07-03 16:04:15;

More import options are available in the "CSV Import" page of the "Advanced parameters" menu.

Creating a New Customer Account

To create a customer account manually, select "Add New". A form appears.

Fill out the customer's information:

- **Title**. Choose between the ones available, or create another one in the "Titles" page under the "Customers" menu.
- **First name**, **Last name**, **E-mail address**. Those are essential: the names are used in the confirmation e-mails that PrestaShop sends, and the e-mail address is used for log-in.
- **Password**. Choose a password, at least 5 characters long.
- **Birthday**. This information can be used for birthday e-mails and temporary discounts.
- **Status**. You may wish to create an account, but not have it yet active.
- **Newsletter**. Can be used by the "Newsletter" module, for sending regular information to those customers who requested it.
- **Opt-in**. Can be used by modules for sending regular partner promotions to those customers who requested it. **Do not subscribe a user to these e-mails without their consent, as this is considered spam**.
- **Group access**. Having customer groups enables you to create group discounts. Many other PrestaShop feature can also be group-restricted.

You will learn more about group in the "Groups" section of this chapter of the PrestaShop user guide.
- **Default customer group**. No matter how many groups that customer belongs to, s/he should always have one main group.
-

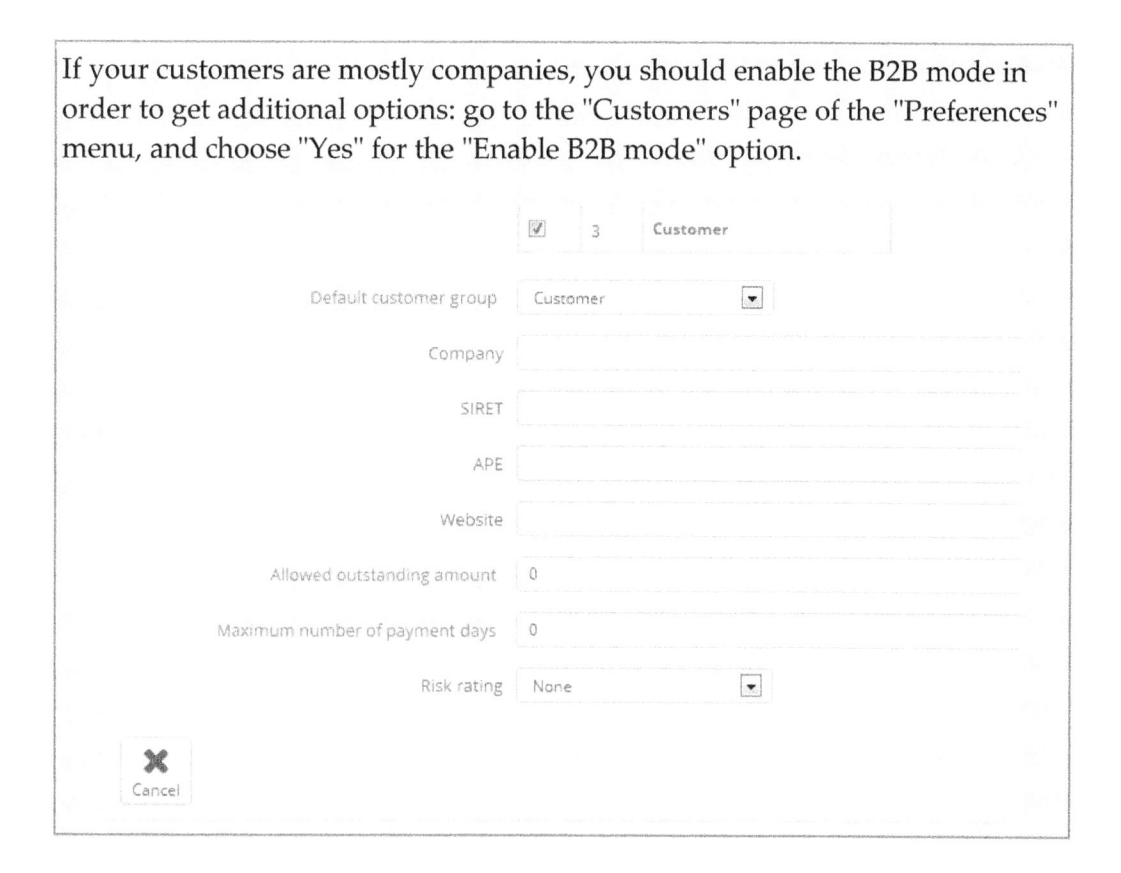

If your customers are mostly companies, you should enable the B2B mode in order to get additional options: go to the "Customers" page of the "Preferences" menu, and choose "Yes" for the "Enable B2B mode" option.

The B2B mode adds a few company-specific fields:

- **Company**. The name of the company.
- **SIRET**. Its SIRET number (France only).
- **APE**. Its principal activity code (*Activité principale exercée* - France only).
- **Website**. Its website.
- **Allowed outstanding amount**. The amount of outstanding money that the company is allowed.
- **Maximum number of payment days**. The number of days that the company is allowed.

- **Risk rating**. Your risk rating of this company: Low, Medium or High.

Viewing a Customer's Information

In the case where you would like to have more information on a given customer, you can click on the "view" button, located at the end of the row in the customer's list. A new page appears.

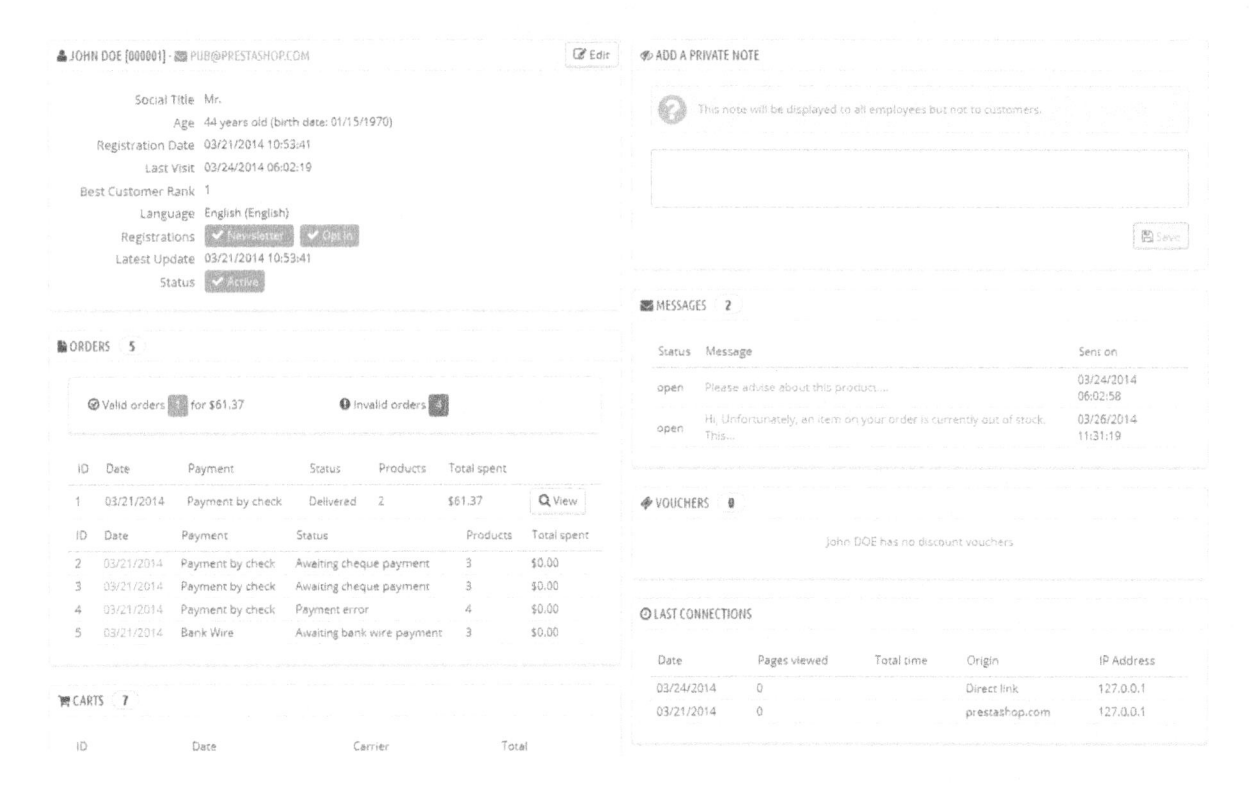

The various sections provide you with some key data on the user:

- Customer information, first and last name, e-mail address, ID, sign-up date, date of last visit, rank.
- Information regarding the subscription to the store's newsletter and subscription to ads from partnering companies, the age, date of last update, and whether or not the account is active.
- Private notes from the store's employees (i.e. you or your team).
- Messages sent by the customer to the shop's team (through customer service).
- The groups to which the customer belongs.

- Summary of the customer's past purchases. Amount spent, type of payment, order status. For more information about each order, click on the icon in the "Actions" column.
- Summary of the products that were ordered by a customer. Among other things, this enables you to know when a customer is very fond of a product, and maybe create a special discount for the 10th purchase. Clicking on a product directs to the order to which that product is tied.
- Registered addresses.
- Available vouchers / cart rules.
- Carts that the customers has created (but not necessarily validated) since sign-up. When your customer is currently on your shop, you can see what is being added to the cart in real time.
- Previous connection to the shop.

Searching for a Customer

Searching for a customer on your PrestaShop shop can be done two different ways.

The first method consists of entering the information you have into the PrestaShop search bar, which is found in the top center of your back-office. By selecting "everywhere", "by name" or "by ip address", you can perform a search based on:

- ID. The numbers that is assigned to the customer in the database.
- First or last name. Note that you cannot search for both: choose either "john" or "doe", as "john doe" won't work.
- E-mail address.
- IP address. You can search using the IP of the latest connection to your shop.

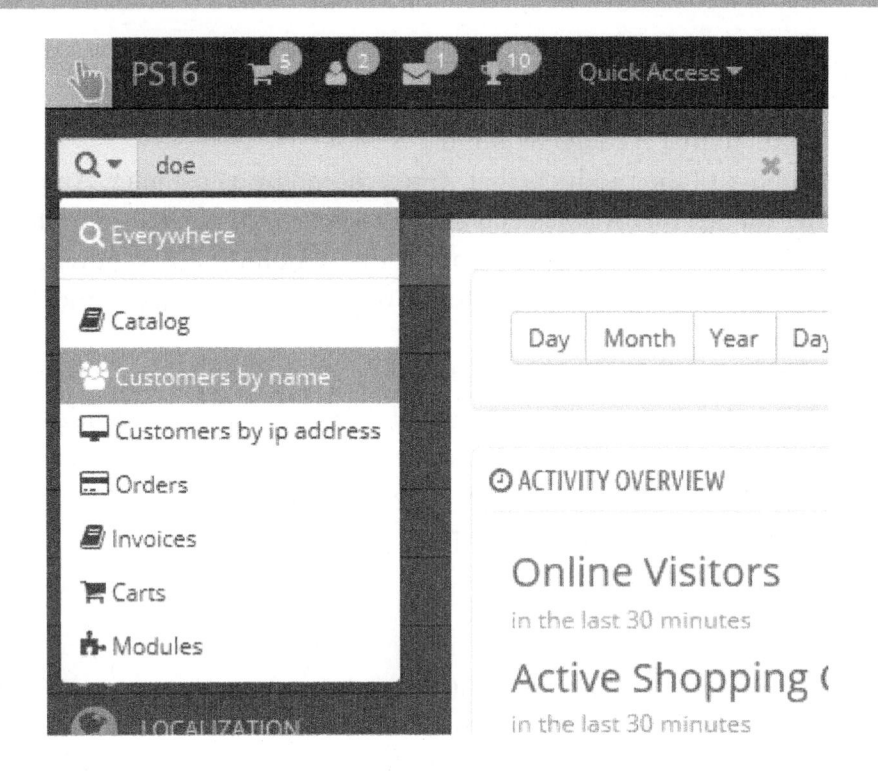

The results, if any, are then presented: the list presents you with the users' ID, social title, e-mail, birthday, registration date, amount of orders and whether or not the user's account is active. From there on, you can view the whole user's page, or edit its details.

The second method consists of going to the "Customers" page, and listing all of your customers.

On this page, you can complete the fields at the top of the list, in order to filter it according to the following criteria: ID, social title, first name, last name, e-mail address, age, account status (enabled or disabled), subscription to the newsletter, subscription to partnering ads, registration date, and last connection date. Enter your criteria and click the "Filter" button in the top right-hand corner of the table. You can then sort the list for some of the columns.

Click the "Reset" button to go back to the complete list.

Customer addresses

By clicking on the "Addresses" page, you will have access to the list of your customer's addresses (home, work, etc.). You can edit them using the "Edit" button, or delete them altogether.

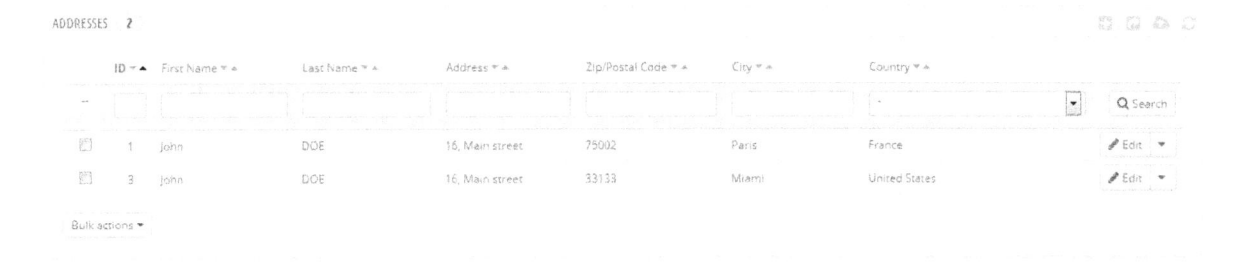

Below the addresses table is the "Set required fields for this section" button. It opens a form where you can indicate if a database field is necessary or not by checking the appropriate boxes: this way, you can make it so fields such as "company" or "phone number" are mandatory when a customer is registering a new address on your shop.

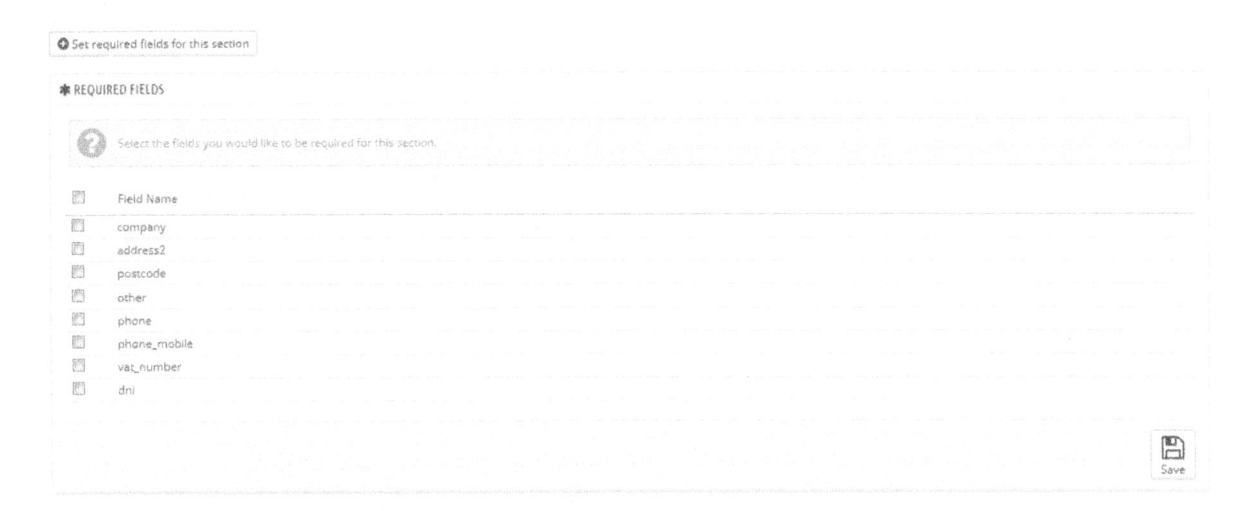

	Field Name
☐	company
☐	address2
☐	postcode
☐	other
☐	phone
☐	phone_mobile
☐	vat_number
☐	dni

Adding a new address

You have the possibility to create new addresses for a client yourself with the "Add new address" button. It opens a form with the kind of field you might expect.

[Screenshot of address form with fields: Customer email, Identification Number, Address alias, First Name, Last Name, Company, Address, Address (2), City, Zip/Postal Code, Country, State, Home phone, Mobile phone, Other; with Cancel and Save buttons]

Some fields, however, require special care:

- **Customer email**. This field is essential: if you are adding an address for an existing customer, you MUST identify this customer using her/his email address. Otherwise, PrestaShop will not know who to assign this address to.
- **Identification number**. The national ID cart number of this person, or a unique tax identification number. This field is of course optional.
Note: the field's title gives a singular hint: "DNI / NIF / NIE". Those are Spanish acronyms: DNI stands for "Documento Nacional de Identidad", NIF stands for "Número de Identificación Fiscal" and NIE stands for "Número de Identidad/Identificación de Extranjero".
- **Address alias**. A short description, in order to help the customer choose the correct address: "Home", "Office", "Aunt Beth's", etc.
- **Other**. Some additional information that might be useful to the shipment.

Customer Groups

PrestaShop enables you to give your customers certain privileges, by assigning them to Groups. You can create as many customer groups as needed, and assign a user to as many groups as you like.

This is all done from the "Groups" page, under the "Customers" menu.

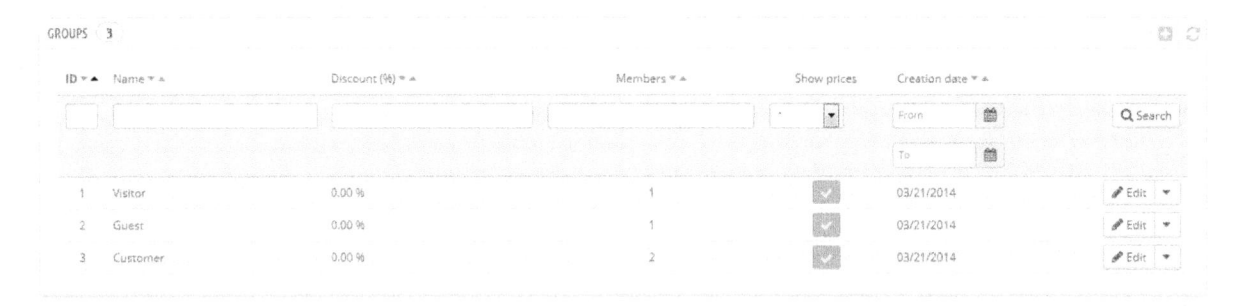

By default, three special groups are available:

- **Visitor**. All persons without a customer account or unauthenticated.
- **Guest**. Customer who placed an order with the Guest Checkout – that option needs to be enabled.
- **Customer**. All persons who created an account on your shop, and are authenticated.

> These three groups cannot be deleted.

To create more groups, click the "Add New" button: you will get a creation form.

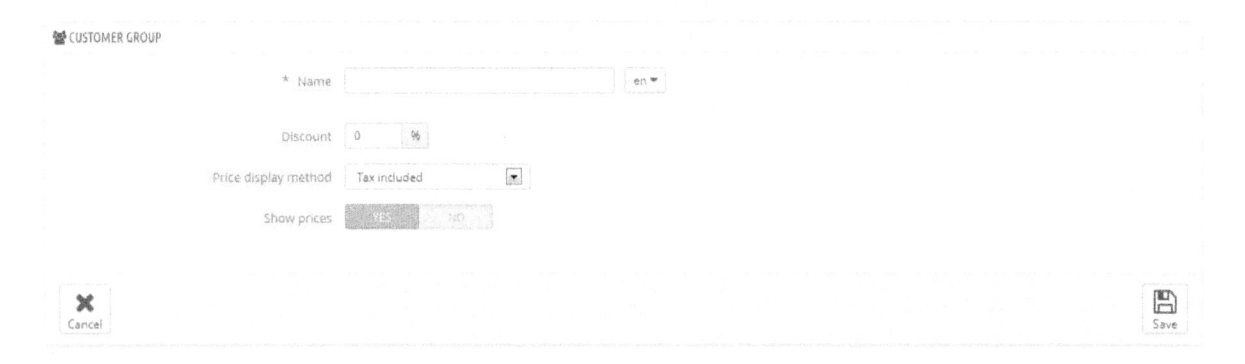

- **Name**. Use a short and descriptive name.
- **Discount (%)**. The discount that you set for members of this group applies to all products on your shop.
  You may prefer to not set any discount value, and create cart rules. You can learn more about cart rules in the next chapter of this guide, "Creating Price Rules and Vouchers".
- **Price display method**. PrestaShop is frequently used in the Business to Business (B2B) sector. You can create a group of customers who can buy products without paying the tax. The drop-down list gives you a choice between "tax included" and "tax excluded".
- **Show prices**. By default, all users of your shop can view the prices. You may prefer some to not have access to your product prices. For instance, you could make it so users can only view prices if they have an account: from the groups list, click on the green "Yes" in the "Show prices" column for the "Visitors" group to turn it into a red "No".

Once these settings are in place, you can save the group as-is, or add per-category and/or per-module settings. In that second case, after the group has been saved, open it again: the form will load with two more options:

- **Category discount**. Click on the "Add a category discount" to bring up a new window, which contains a list of all your categories. You can pick one, and apply a specific discount which will apply for that group of customers only, and to that category only.
  Note that:
    - Only products which have this category as their default category will be affected by the discount. Products which have this category as a secondary category will not be affected.
    - This category discount will replace any other discount that members of this group would otherwise enjoy on this category.
    - You can add as many category discounts for this customer group as you need – thereby enabling to entirely give this group a whole set of different discounts if you feel the need.
- **Authorized modules**. This section enables you to block members of this group to access and use some of your shop's modules. For instance, you might prefer some customers to not be able to see your top-sellers or to your specials.

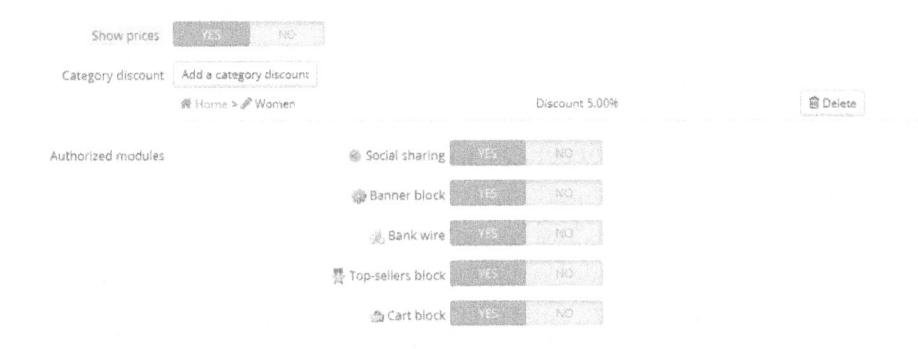

You can add a customer to a group of your choice by editing the customer's details: from the list of customers (in the "Customers" page under the "Customers" menu), click on the Edit button on the customer's row. Then, in the "Group access" table, select the group(s) to which you want your customer to belong. If you assign the customer to more than one group, remember to set their main group with the "Default customer group" option.

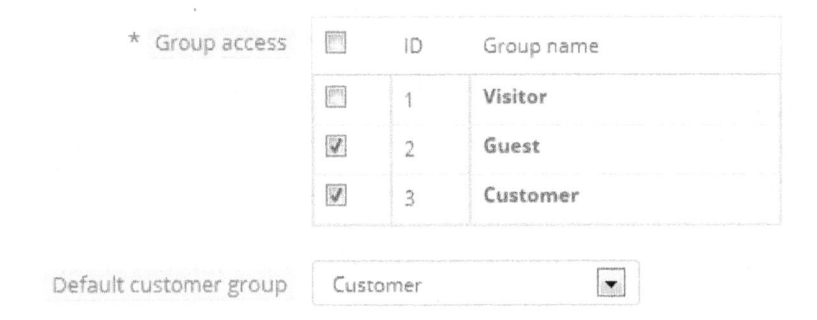

Shopping Carts

PrestaShop contains some very powerful marketing features that enable you to see the products that customers are adding to their carts in real time. There are two ways to achieve this:

1. Go to the "Clients" page in the "Clients" menu, find the customer you are looking for, and view his or her customer profile. In that profile, scroll down to the "Shopping carts" section, where you can see all the carts created by this customer.
2. Go to the "Shopping carts" page in the "Clients" menu. The carts are sorted by ID. Find the customer you are looking for.

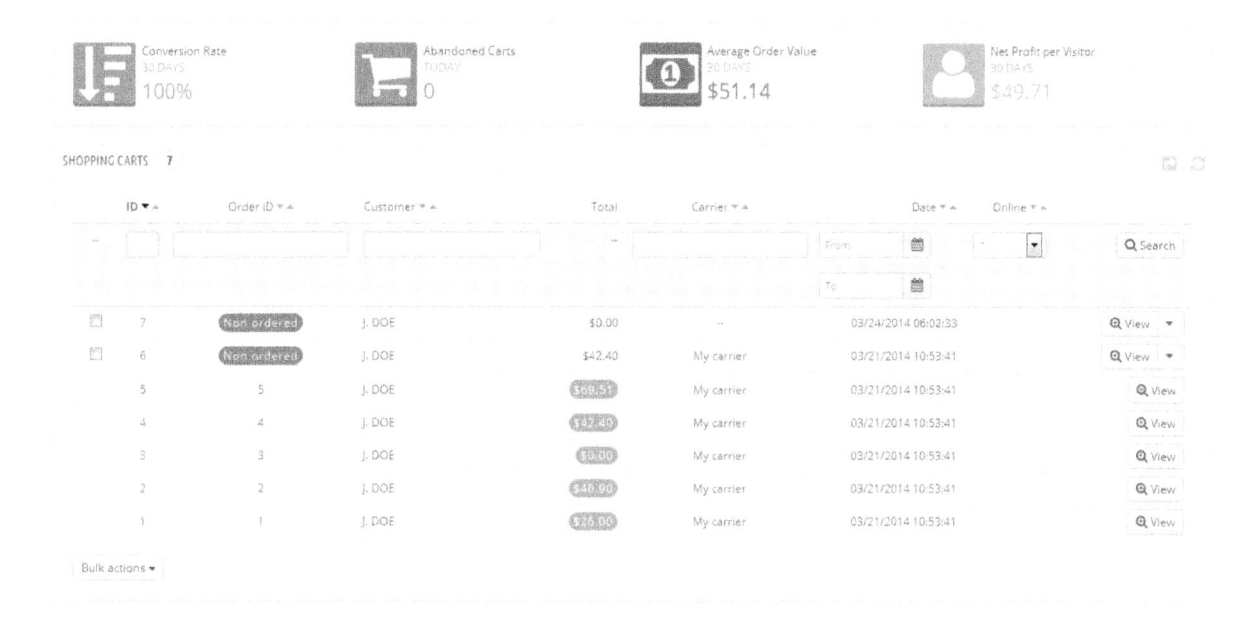

In both cases, you can click the "View" icon to see the content of your client's cart, and use this information to improve your commercial performance.

Cart #000005				
JOHN DOE ON 03/21/2014				
$71.51				

CUSTOMER INFORMATION

John DOE   pub@prestashop.com

Account registration date: 03/21/2014

Valid orders placed: 1

Total spent since registration: $61.37

ORDER INFORMATION

Order #5

Made on 03/21/2014

CART SUMMARY

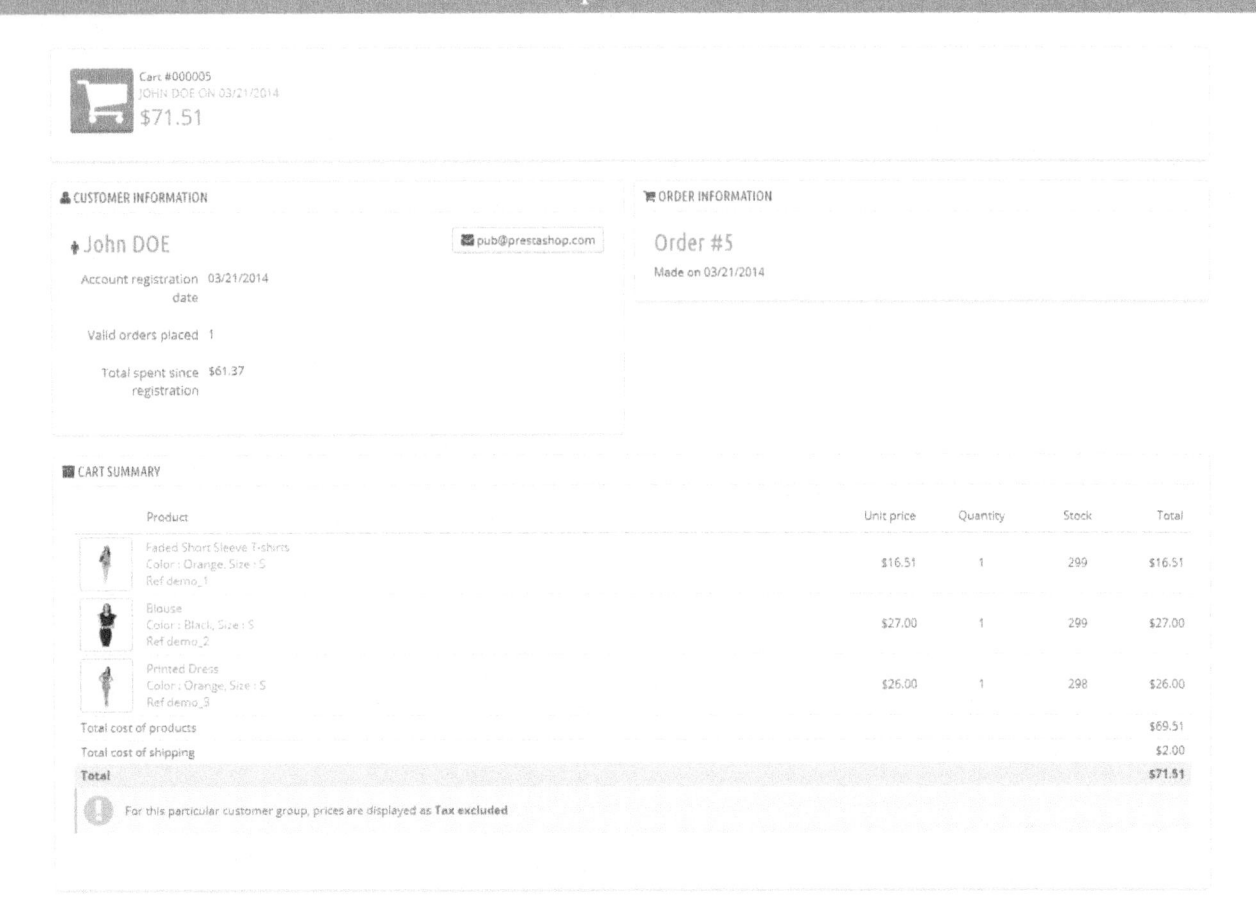

Product	Unit price	Quantity	Stock	Total
Faded Short Sleeve T-shirts Color : Orange, Size : S Ref demo_1	$16.51	1	299	$16.51
Blouse Color : Black, Size : S Ref demo_2	$27.00	1	299	$27.00
Printed Dress Color : Orange, Size : S Ref demo_3	$26.00	1	298	$26.00
Total cost of products				$69.51
Total cost of shipping				$2.00
Total				**$71.51**

For this particular customer group, prices are displayed as **Tax excluded**.

In the cart's page, the most important information is in the "Cart Summary" section, where you can see what products the customer chose to purchase, the price of each item, the quantity they put in their cart, and the total value of their cart.

> ## Managing abandoned carts
>
> Cart abandonment often means that a sale has been lost. The "Shopping cart" page indicates the carts that have not been turned into proper orders, and it is up to you to remind the customer that they can still come back to finish their purchase.
>
> Abandoned carts (or "ghost carts") will have a delete link at the end of each row, while carts without delete links are processed carts, i.e. the purchase has been confirmed and you are supposed to send the products.

> By default, it is up to you to contact the customer about his abandoned cart. You can install the Customer Follow-up module, which is available in the default installation and enables you to send vouchers to those who have abandoned their shopping carts, or to those who you want to thank for their order, to the best clients to thank them for their purchases and for being faithful... Note that this can lead to abuse: some customers might abandon carts on purpose in order to receive a voucher...
>
> You can also buy PrestaShop's Abandoned Cart Reminder module for a complete tool: http://addons.prestashop.com/en/checkout-modules/16535-abandoned-cart-pro.html.

Customer Service

PrestaShop enables you to centralize all the customers' request within its confines. This helps you keep track of which discussion threads needs answering, rather than having to check with all the recipients of the mail to see if someone did answer it.

In practice, the contact form of your shop, available under the "Contact us" link at the bottom of your front-office, presents the customer with two contacts by default: "Webmaster" and "Customer Service". The customer only has to choose who to contact, and then fill the rest of the fields. The message is then recorded in PrestaShop's customer service tool.

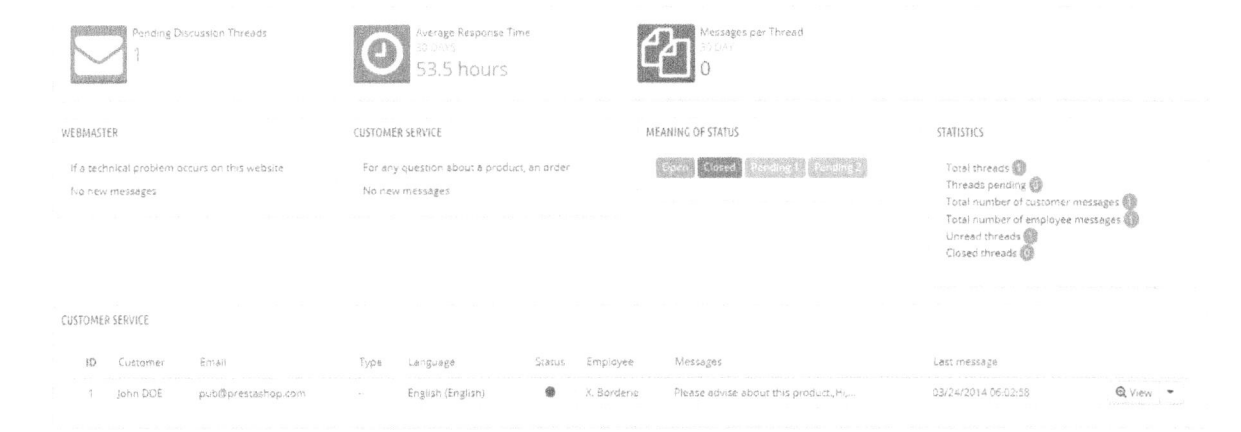

> Discussion threads are only included in the customer service tool if the contact has the "Save Message?" option enabled. You can change this setting, or add more contacts, by going to the "Contact" page, under the "Customers" menu. This page is explained in detail in the next section of this chapter of the PrestaShop User Guide.
>
> If the option is disabled for the contact that the customer chooses, the message is simply sent to the contact's e-mail address, and is not stored in PrestaShop.
>
> You also need to properly configure your IMAP settings, so that PrestaShop can retrieve the customer's answers to e-mail that were sent from the customer service tool. This is done in the "Customer service options" section, at the bottom of the screen.

On this page, each contact has its own box, where you can quickly see if a there are new messages (meaning, those that have not yet been read). By default there are two, and adding more contacts will move the "Meaning of status" and "Statistics" boxes further to the left and down.

These two last boxes are handy when you need to handle new messages daily:

- **Meaning of status**. A simple reminder of the color codes that your team can apply to a discussion thread.
- **Customer service: statistics**. An overview of the global activity of your customer service since the beginning.

Further below is the list of received messages, both old and new.

You can edit a couple options at the bottom of the page, which apply to all contacts:

- **Allow file uploading**. Whether the customer can attach a file to the message. This can be useful in case of visual issues on the front-page, as the customer can send you screen captures.
- **Pre-defined message**. The default template for your employees' answer. Keep it simple, so that it can adapt to many situations, even if it needs a little editing for each case.

Finally, the bottom of the page features the "Customer service options" section, where you can set many options pertaining to your mail (IMAP) server.

Handling Customer Service Messages

Each conversation with a customer can be entirely handled through PrestaShop's complete interface, without having to use an e-mail client such as Outlook or Thunderbird.

In the conversation list, click on a row to view the conversation's details:

- You can apply a handful of actions to a discussion, in order to quickly sort them and thus handle them quicker. There are 4 available actions:
    - **Mark as "handled"** or **"Re-open"**. Changes the discussion's status to "Closed" or "Open".
    - **Mark as "pending 1"** and **Mark as "pending 2"**. These two statuses are internal: their meaning is up to your team. You may even choose to not use them, and only rely on "Closed" and "Open".
    - **Forward this discussion to another employee**. From the moment an employee has started replying to a customer message, he becomes in charge of the customer's request. If during the discussion it turns out another employee should handle it instead of you, you can use that button to attribute it through a drop-down list. That other employee will receive a notification about it. If the person you want to forward this discussion to is not available in the list, choose "Someone else" in the dropdown list

and two options will appear, enabling you to indicate the email address of the recipient and a comment about your message.
- **Reply to the next unanswered message in this thread**.

Essential details are available:

- Customer name and email, which you can click on to access the customer's information
- Number of orders, total amount spent and date of registration for the customer.
- Time and date of the message.
- Finally, the message itself.

To reply to this thread, simply use the form with your default message (as set in "Contact options" section of the "Customer service" page), and click "Send".

At the bottom of the page, the "Orders and messages timeline" gives you a clear chronological view of the events pertaining to this discussion thread.

Customer Service Options

This section basically enables you to precisely configure PrestaShop's access to your e-mail server through its IMAP interface. You should make sure all fields are filled in order for the customer service tool to work properly. Most of this information should be provided by your webhost.

CUSTOMER SERVICE OPTIONS

IMAP URL	
IMAP port	143
IMAP user	
IMAP password	
Delete messages	YES / NO
Create new threads	YES / NO
IMAP options (/norsh)	YES / NO
IMAP options (/ssl)	YES / NO
IMAP options (/validate-cert)	YES / NO
IMAP options (/novalidate-cert)	YES / NO
IMAP options (/tls)	YES / NO
IMAP options (/notls)	YES / NO

- **IMAP URL, IMAP port, IMAP user** and **IMAP password**. Essential details to access the e-mail server using the IMAP protocol.
- **Delete message**. If enabled, messages on the server will be deleted as soon as PrestaShop has retrieved them. Use with caution: this would make your messages unavailable to other e-mail clients.
- **/norsh**. If enabled, the connection to your e-mail server will not pre-authenticated. Not recommended.
- **/ssl**. If enabled, the connection to your e-mail server will not be encrypted. Not recommended.
- **/validate-cert**. If enabled, PrestaShop will force the validation of the server's TLS/SSL certificate.
- **/novalidate-cert**. If enabled, PrestaShop will never try to validate the server's TLS/SSL certificate. Essential for servers with self-signed certificates.

- **/tls**. If enabled, PrestaShop will force use of StartTLS to encrypt the connection. Servers that do not support StartTLS will be rejected.
- **/notls**. If enabled, PrestaShop will not use StartTLS to encrypt the session, even with servers that support it.

Your Contacts

To facilitate communication with your clients, you can create multiple contact accounts. For example: customer service, technical support, sales department, etc. This feature allows your customers to directly contact the right person according to their needs.

Creating a new contact

In order for the message to be redirected to the intended recipient, you must configure the contacts in your shop.

By clicking on the "Contacts" page under the "Customers" menu, you can access the existing list of contacts.

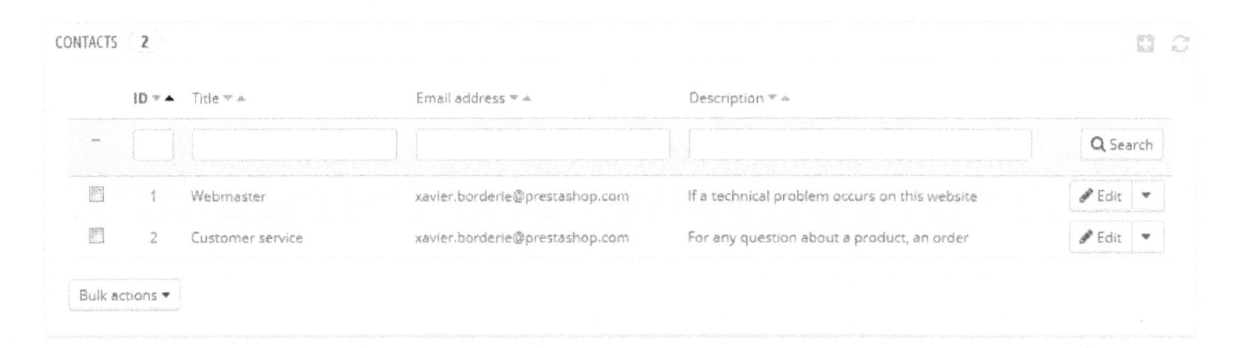

ID	Title	Email address	Description	
1	Webmaster	xavier.borderie@prestashop.com	If a technical problem occurs on this website	Edit
2	Customer service	xavier.borderie@prestashop.com	For any question about a product, an order	Edit

Click the "Add new" button to access the contact creation form:

- **Title**. The name of the contact: either a person's name, or the name of the service itself. You could also choose to use a phrase, such as "I have a problem with my order", "I want to return a product" or "I want to become a partner".
- **E-mail address**. The address can be the same as another contact. In fact, all contacts can share the same address if you don't really have a team –

customers will never know, but having many contacts helps them trust your shop, as it means there are many people working for your shop.
- **Save messages?**. Indicate if the e-mail is to be saved in the "Customer Service" tool, or simply sent to the e-mail address. If disabled, PrestaShop will not help you handle customer service for this contact. This might be useful for "Partner e-mail", as you might not want your customer service employees to have access to these.
- **Description**. Make it short, no more than a single line, as it is displayed to the customer in the contact form.

How the customer can contact you

To contact the appropriate team of employees from your shop's front-office, the customer clicks either on the "Contact" link at the top of the page, or on the "Contact Us" link at the bottom of the page. The contact form appears.

The customer is then asked to choose the service to contact, enter the e-mail address and then complete the message. A drop-down menu makes it possible to choose which order is being discussed, and even which product from that order.

Social Titles

The social title tool helps you better define your customers: in the customers list, you can choose to only display customers having a given social title. Modules may also rely on social titles for certain features.

Clicking on the "Add new" button brings you to a form:

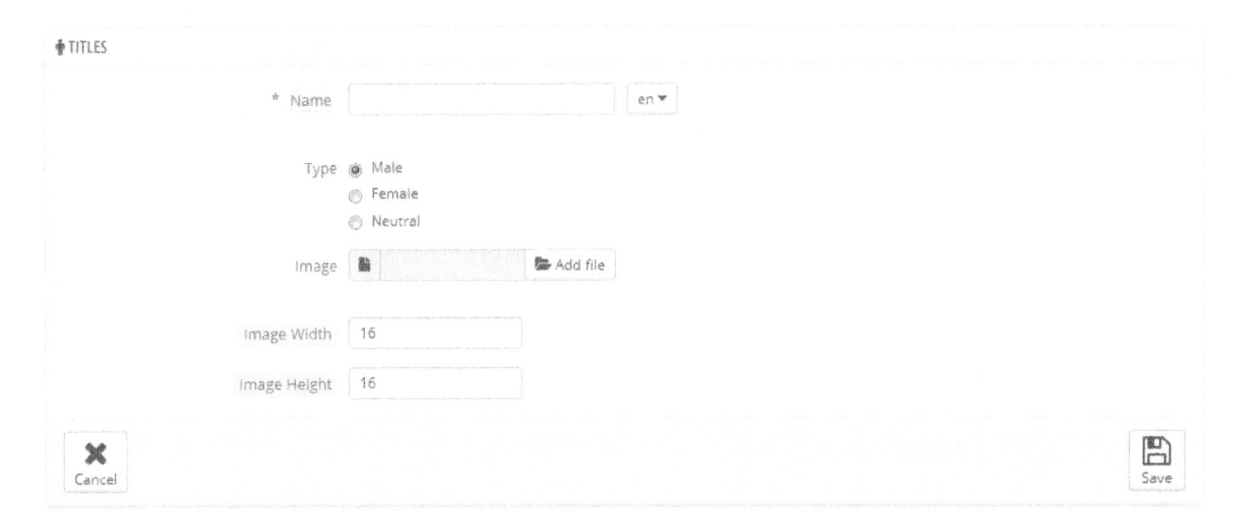

- **Name**. You can choose anything, from the very common ("Sir", "Lady", "Gentleman", etc.) to the very unusual ("Jedi", "Magnificent One", "Money carrier"...). The important thing when departing from the commonly accepted titles is to reflect your shop's true identity.
- **Type**. Some names may apply to both male and female customers, or to neither. Be sure then to set that option to "Neutral".

- **Image**. A 16*16 image file representing the title. Classic gender symbols are the Mars and Venus ones (♂ and ♀), but there are many other possibilities. PrestaShop enables you to characterize your creation with a unique image.
- **Image width** and **Image height**. PrestaShop works best with 16*16 image, and will resize your image if it bigger than that. Nevertheless, you might feel necessary to use bigger images, and these two options enable you to set the exact size required by your image. If you enter "0", PrestaShop will simply use the image's original size.

Outstanding

> This page is only available when you enable PrestaShop's B2B features. To do that, go to the Customer Preferences page, and choose "Yes" for the "Enable B2B mode" option.

This page displays the outstanding report for some of your customers, meaning the amount of money you are allowing them to buy your products before they have to actually pay you.

Enabling the Outstanding feature

When the B2B mode is enabled (Preferences > Customers page), three fields are added to the customer creation form:

- **Allowed outstanding amount**. The maximum amount of money this customer can use as an outstanding.
- **Maximum number of payment days**. The maximum number of days the customer can go before having to pay his outstanding.
- **Risk rating**. The risk factor for this customer: None, Low, Medium or High. It is up to you to decide if a customer is a risky benefactor of your outstanding feature, or if he will assuredly pay on time.

You should fill these fields for all professional customers.

Current outstanding screen

Once a customer with outstanding allowance buys from your shop, it appears in the Customers > Outstanding page. This enables you to get an overview of your current outstanding invoices.

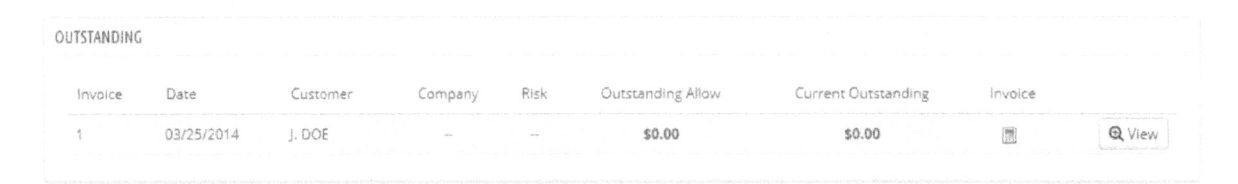

Invoice	Date	Customer	Company	Risk	Outstanding Allow	Current Outstanding	Invoice	
1	03/25/2014	J. DOE	--	--	$0.00	$0.00		View

Creating Price Rules and Vouchers

Vouchers play an important role in your daily relationships with your customers. Typically, customers like two things when shopping:

- Feeling special, unique.
- Getting good prices.

Both can be achieved with personalized discounts, and this is precisely where vouchers come into play – or more precisely, price rules.

"Price rules" can take two forms:

- **Cart rules**. These are actually the successors to vouchers, as they were known in previous versions of PrestaShop.
  Basically, it enables you to create per-customer voucher codes, but also much more.
- **Catalog price rules**. Enables you to assign price reductions by category, manufacturer, supplier, attribute or feature.
  For instance, you can set a rule that would say that for Spanish customers belonging to the "Good clients" group would get 10% off on your Electronics category and all Sony products for the first week of July.

Cart Rules

The "Cart rules" page gives you access to an advanced tool that succeeds and builds upon the voucher system from PrestaShop 1.4. Seasoned users of PrestaShop will not be surprised with the features that were added, but will have to adapt to the new name: when this guide mentions vouchers, we are actually talking about cart rules – which, in themselves, are quite different to credit slips.

> ### Differences between a credit slip, a voucher and a cart rule
>
> A credit slip is first and foremost a written proof that a product has been returned. Most of the time, the user can use it as a voucher.
>
> A voucher is a discount code which does not have to be tied to a merchandise return or a refund, and which can take many more forms than a simple credit slip:
>
> - A discount on an order (percentage).
> - A discount on an order (amount).
> - Free shipping.
>
> You can apply a voucher to all customers, or a group of customers, or a single customer; you can set its expiration date.
>
> A cart rule is basically an advanced version of a voucher: in addition to what a voucher could do in PrestaShop 1.4, the cart rules system introduced in PrestaShop 1.5 enables you to:
>
> - Name the discount.
> - Allow the customer to use only a portion of the discount.
> - Assign priorities between cart rules.
> - Set the compatibility between cart rules.
> - Have the discount only work with some carriers.
> - Have the discount only work with a selection of products and/or categories and/or manufacturers and/or suppliers and/or attributes... or all of these at the same time if necessary.

> - Have the discount be applicable for free shipping and/or a discount on an order and/or a free gift... or all of these at the same time if necessary!
>
> In this user guide, "cart rule" and "voucher" are synonymous and interchangeable.

The "Cart rules" page lists the currently existing cart rules, which you can enable or disable by clicking on the icons in the "Status" column.

ID	Name	Priority	Code	Quantity	Until	Status	
1	Cart rule 1	1	QGMRA2S8	7	05/01/2014 09:00:00	✓	Edit ▼

Creating a New Cart Rule

A voucher can be created automatically after a product return, but you can create a new voucher at any time manually, and be very specific about its properties.

The creation form has three tabs, enabling you to precisely build new rules and vouchers.

Information Tab

The first tab, "Information", contains the rule's identifiers and main settings.

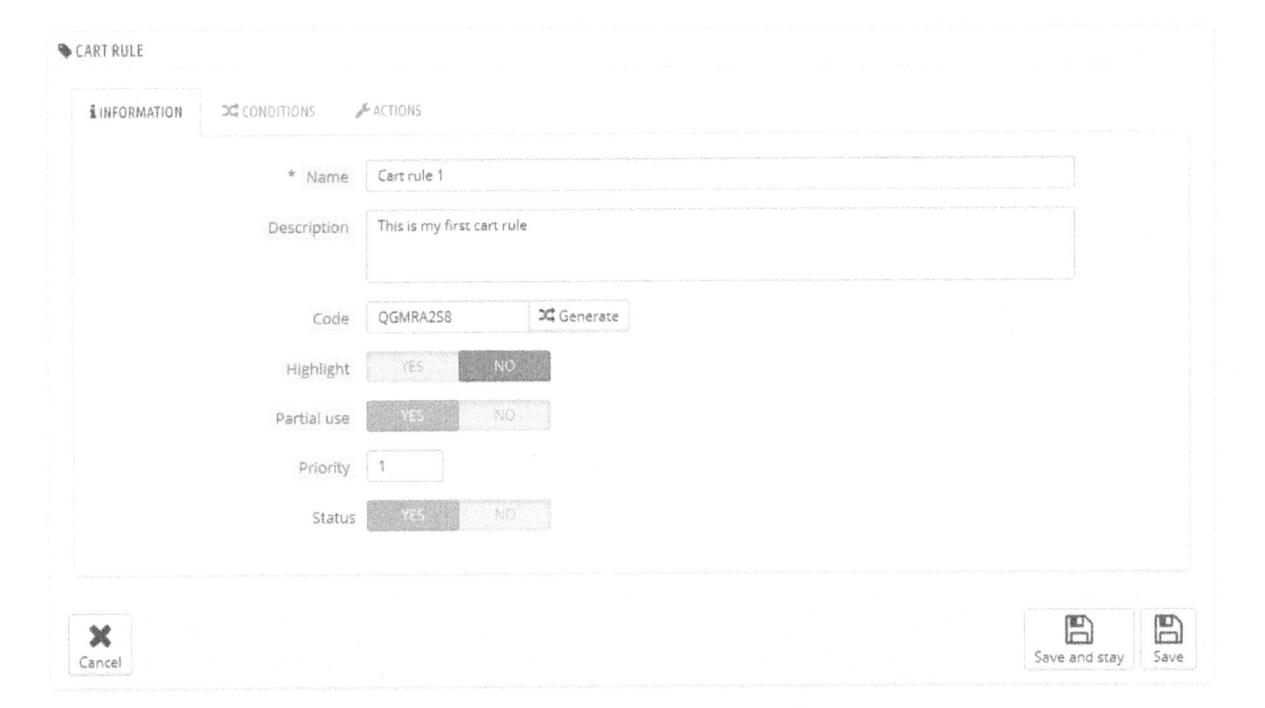

- **Name**. The name is public, so you should keep it casual.
- **Description**. The description is not public. It helps your shop employees understand why the rule was created.
- **Code**. Give your rule a unique code. You can either create one manually (and therefore use readable words, like 1VOUCH4JOE), or have PrestaShop generate one unique string by clicking the "Generate" button. Of course, you can also use any other string generator (such as http://www.random.org/strings/).
  Note that if no code is set, the rule will apply to any customer fitting the other conditions:
    o If there is a code, then customer have to enter it during the ordering process.
    o If there is no code, then the rule is automatically applied to benefiting customers.
- **Highlight**. If enabled, PrestaShop will let the user know that a voucher corresponding to the items in the cart is available and can be added.
- **Partial use**. If disabled, the rule/voucher can only be used once, even if it is not completely used. If enabled, a new voucher is created when the current one is not completely used.

- **Priority**. If a customer (or group of customers) is eligible for more than one voucher, or if more than one voucher can be applied to an order, then PrestaShop applies said voucher one by one in the alphanumerical order. You can change that order by placing a lower priority to you voucher. By default, they all have a priority of 1. If you set it to a higher number, the voucher will be applied after vouchers with a lower number.
- **Status**. You can disable and enable a rule whenever you feel is necessary.

Conditions Tab

The second tab, "Conditions", contains a large set of possibilities, enabling you to precisely target who should be able to benefit from this rule.

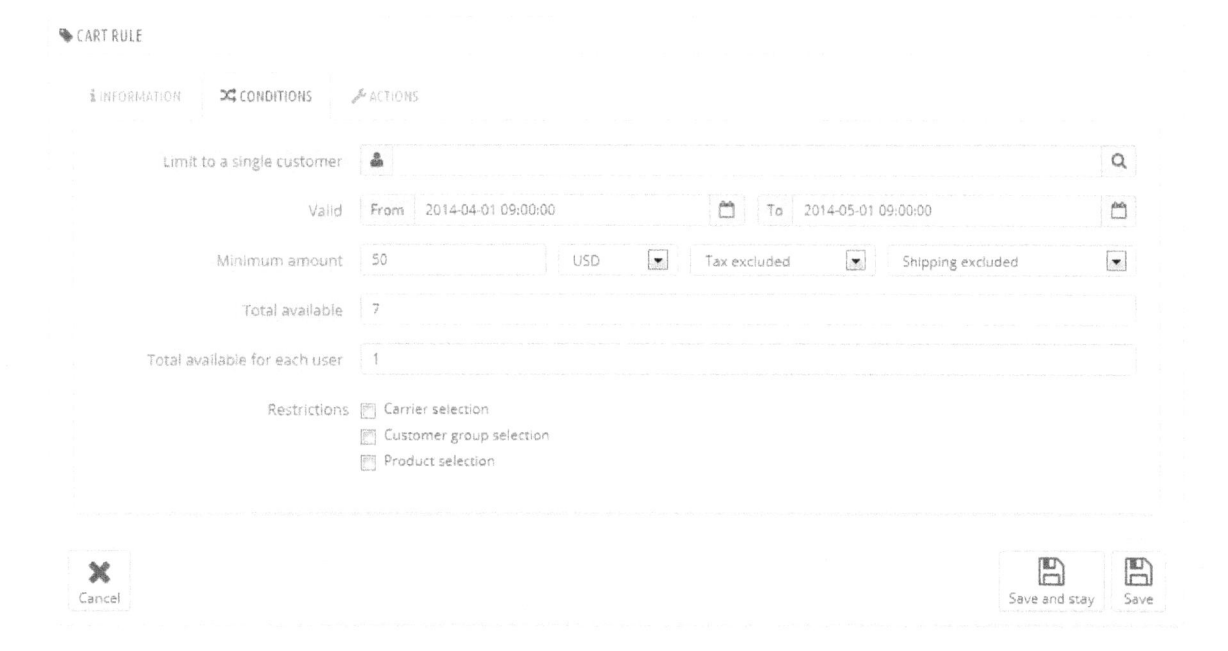

- **Limit to a single customer**. This is where you indicate that the voucher you are creating is for one customer only. For instance, if you had a delivery delay and you want to make a gesture of goodwill, you can create a voucher for this customer that only he or she can access. To quickly find the customer, type in the first few letters of their first name, last name or e-mail in the text field.
  If empty, PrestaShop will understand than any customer can use it...

unless you have added a customer group as a further condition (see "Customer group selection" check-box below).
- **Validity**. The default validity is one month, but you can reduce that to one week or even one day.
- **Minimum amount**. The minimum order amount from which the voucher is applicable. Your voucher will only be applicable if the customer's order is above the given amount. You can choose if that amount should include taxes and/or shipping costs.
- **Total available**. Set a quantity of available vouchers: either "1" if it is intended for a single customer, or any number if the voucher is for whoever uses one first.
- **Total available for each user**. You can set the number of times a voucher can be used for each user. That number must be at least equal to the quantity of available vouchers above ("Total available" field).
    - If that number is inferior to the total quantity of available vouchers, then one single customer will not be able to use all of them.
    - Keeping it to "1" makes sure that each of your customers can only use the voucher once. In that case, make sure the voucher applies to a group rather than a customer...

The check-boxes at the bottom of the section are very important, as they help you further filter to what or to whom the rule is to be applied.

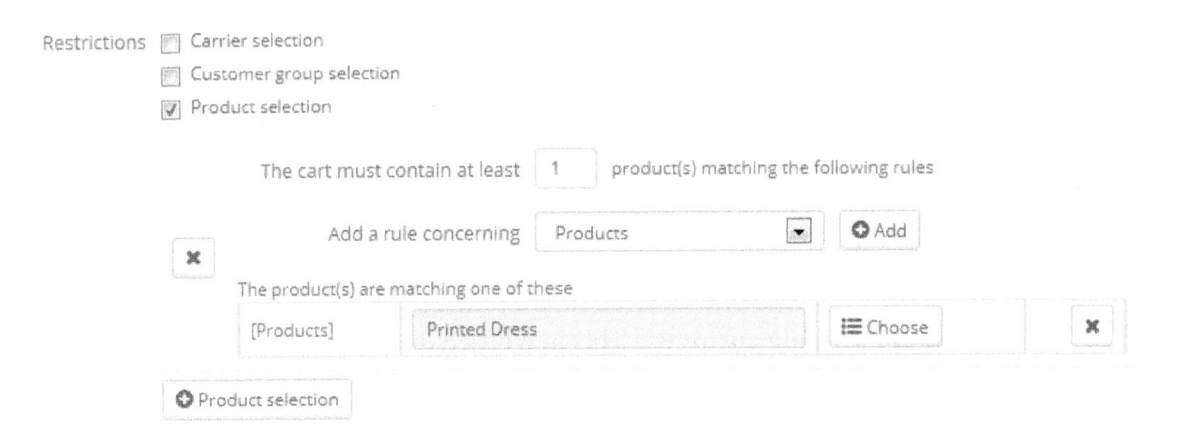

Restrictions
- [ ] Carrier selection
- [ ] Customer group selection
- [x] Product selection

The cart must contain at least [1] product(s) matching the following rules

Add a rule concerning [Products ▼] [+ Add]

[×] The product(s) are matching one of these
[Products] [Printed Dress] [≡ Choose] [×]

[+ Product selection]

- **Carrier selection**. You can make it so that the customer will have a discount if he or she chooses a specific carrier for the package delivery.

- **Customer group selection**. This is very useful. Thanks to PrestaShop's group creation tool, you can create discount that apply to a range of users, and build other conditions on top of that discount thanks to the cart rule creation tool.
- **Compatibility with other cart rules**. By default, an order can benefit from any number of cart rules. With this option, you can tell PrestaShop that this rule cannot be combined with a selection of other rules. This option only appears if you have more than one cart rule.
- **Product selection**. Another very useful tool, which enables to create automatic vouchers for cart which contain specific products. The tool is explained in more detail below.
- **Shop selection**. By default, a cart rule applies to all your stores. With this option, you can make it so that rule only applies to a selection of your stores.

The "Product selection" option brings a whole new form, and enables you to create not only per-product vouchers, by also per-categories, per-manufacturers, per-suppliers and even per-attribute. As a bonus, you can combine all these in order to specify your customer target as much as possible.

For instance, you can create automatic vouchers for your customer in the form "Buy at least 3 Apple product, get free shipping!"
This is really a tool within the cart rule too, and its configuration is quite specific. You can add as many product selections as needed, following this path:

1. Click the "Product selection" link to add a new section.
2. Indicate the number of products needed for the discount to activate.
3. Add at least one rule, of the type you want: products, attributes, categories, manufacturers, suppliers. You can add as many rules per product selection as you want, even one for each type if necessary.
4. Clicking the "OK" adds a new line in the selection. For each type, you must give details on the content the rule applies to. Click the "Choose" link and a window opens, listing the content available for this type (products, categories...). Move the content from the left panel to the right one by clicking on the "Add" button, and close the window by clicking on the "X" at the top right. If only one content is selected, the content field will give its name; otherwise, it will indicate the number of selected content.

You can add as many rules within a selection as necessary. These rules are cumulative: either they all apply, or the discount is not granted.

Product selections are independent: you can add as many as needed, and they will not influence each other. This enables you to create a whole range of products to which the cart rule will apply.

Actions Tab

The third and last tab, "Actions", is where you choose what the discount actually consists of.

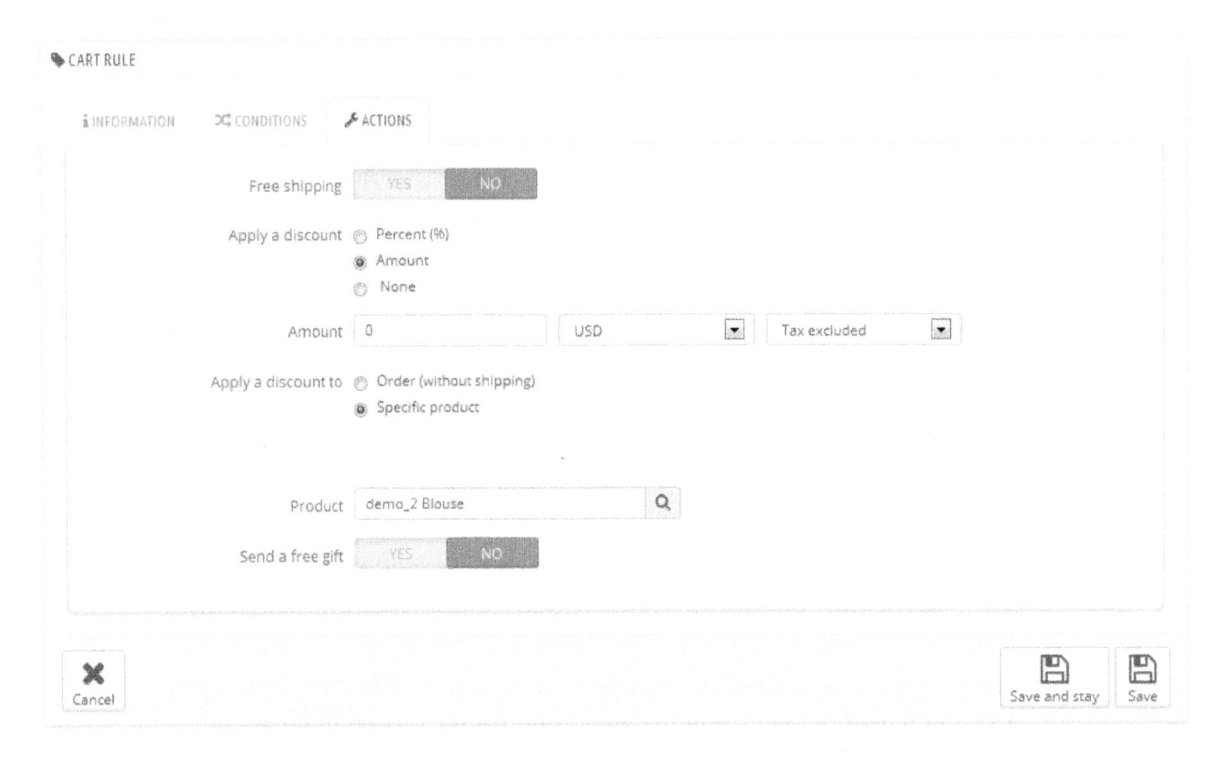

- **Free shipping**. The rule treats benefiting customers to free shipping.
- **Apply a discount**.
    - **Percent (%)**. The rule applies to a percentage of the order total. For instance, let's say the order is valued at $200 before taxes. The rule has a value of 15%. Customer who benefit from this rule will only have to pay $170 (before taxes and shipping costs).
    - **Amount**. The rule applies a monetary discount on the order total. For instance, let's say the order is valued at $200 before taxes. The

discount offers $20 off the purchase. Customer who benefit from this rule will only pay $80 before (before shipping costs). You can choose whether taxes are applied to the discount or not.
    - **None**. The rule does not offer any discount on the order. Choosing this option makes the next section, "Apply discount to", disappear.
- **Apply discount to**.
    - **Order (without shipping)**. The discount applies to the whole order.
    - **Specific product**. You can choose to which product the discount should apply: type the first letters of the product, and choose in the list of matching names.
    - **Cheapest product**. Only available for the "Percent (%)" option.
    - **Selected product(s)**. The customer can choose on which products the discount should be applied. Only available for the "Percent (%)" option.
- **Send a free gift**. You can choose to offer a gift for some conditions (and skip the discount altogether). A field appears: type the first letters of the product, and choose in the list of matching names.

Once everything has been saved, you can send your voucher code to your customers, or let the system handle the cart rules automatically, depending on your settings.

Your voucher will appear in the "Cart Rules" page, under the "Price rules" menu. You can delete or edit it at any time. If the voucher was set to a specific group or customer, then it will appear in the Front-Office, in the customer's "Vouchers" section of his account as well as in the cart (if you chose to), where they can choose which one to apply to their order.

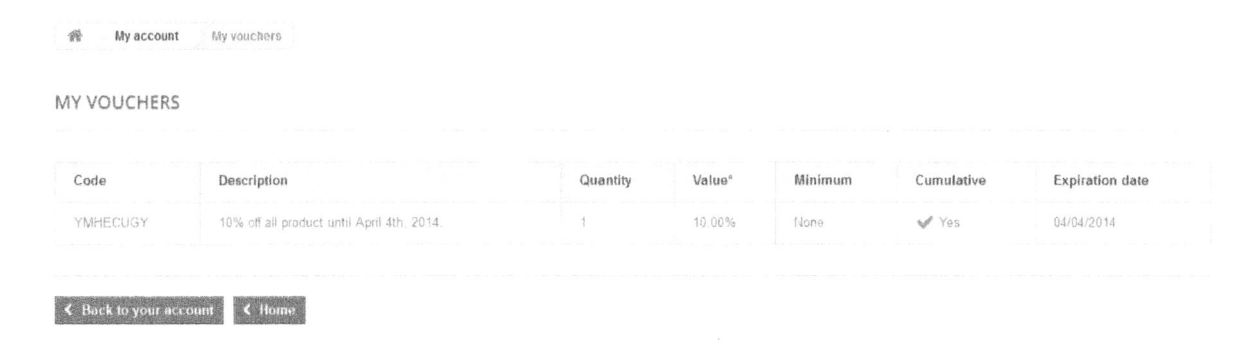

MY VOUCHERS

Code	Description	Quantity	Value*	Minimum	Cumulative	Expiration date
YMHECUGY	10% off all product until April 4th, 2014.	1	10.00%	None	✔ Yes	04/04/2014

Cart rules that are set to apply to all customers do not appear in the customer's "My vouchers" page: he or she has to know about them in order to use them. It is up to you to let them know about these public discounts.

In order to apply the cart rule, the customer needs to visit his cart and enter the voucher in the "Vouchers" field and click "Add". The customer will not be able to apply the voucher if the check-out is already validated.

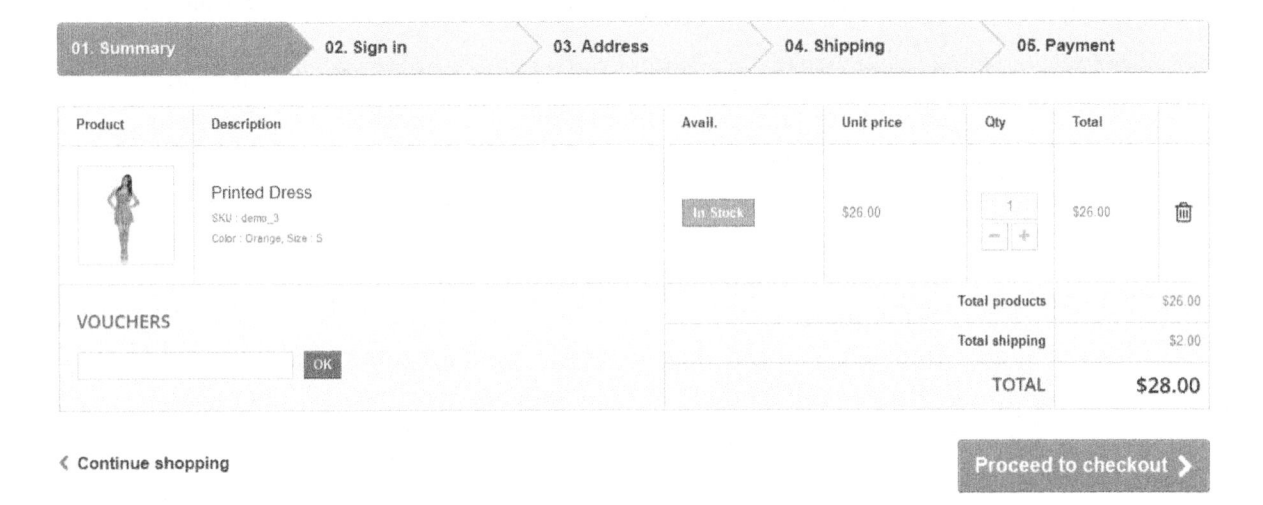

Once applied, the cart summary displays the voucher's impact on the order's amount.

Catalog price rules

Catalog price rules enable you to assign price reductions by category, manufacturer, supplier, attribute or feature. As its name implies, this type of rules applies to a range of products; it cannot be used for a single product. If you need a discount applied to a single product, you must create a cart rule instead or create a specific price (in the "Price" page of the product's edition page).

For instance, you can set a rule that would say that for Spanish customers belonging to the "Good clients" group would get 10% off on your Electronics category and all Sony products for the first week of July.

The "Catalog price rules" page lists the currently existing rules, which you can edit or delete by clicking on the icons in the "Status" column. If you need to disable a rule, simply change its end date to the day before.

Creating a New Catalog Price Rule

The creation form page has two sections, enabling you to precisely build new rules.

Specific price rules

The first form is easy to understand.

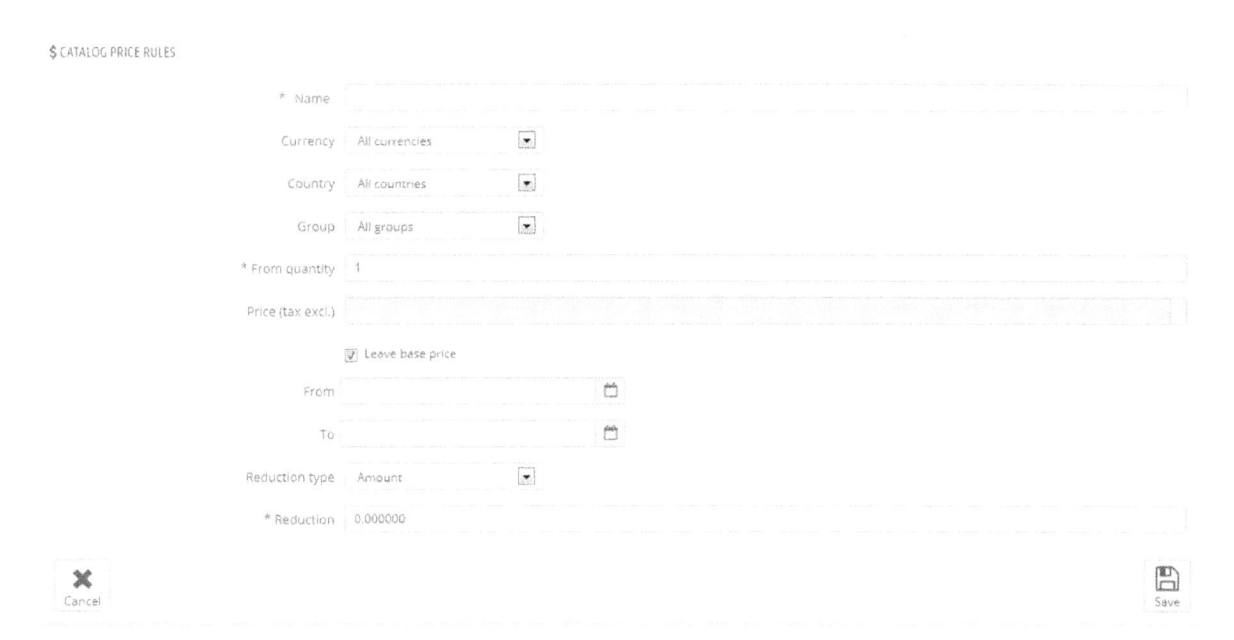

$ CATALOG PRICE RULES

* Name	
Currency	All currencies
Country	All countries
Group	All groups
* From quantity	1
Price (tax excl.)	
	☑ Leave base price
From	
To	
Reduction type	Amount
* Reduction	0.000000

Cancel   Save

This is where you set who should benefit from the rule, what the discount should be, and other details.

- **Name**. The name is public, so you should keep it casual.
- **Shop**. *Multistore mode only.* The rule applies to customers who buy through a specific shop. Only available if you have at least two shops.
- **Currency**. The rule applies to customers who set to pay with a specific currency.
- **Country**. The rule applies to customers from a specific country.
- **Group**. The rule applies to customers who belong to a specific customer group.
- **From quantity**. The rule applies the order has at least a specific number of matching products.
- **Price (tax excl.)**. The new price for the product. Here you can set the public price of the product that matches the rules that you are putting in place. By default, the rule applies to the base price.
- **From** and **To**. The rule applies in this time frame.
- **Reduction type**. The discount can either be an amount of money, or a percentage of the order total.
- **Reduction**. The value of the reduction. Depending on the "Reduction type" above, putting "10.0" in the field can either mean "$10 off" (depending on the default currency) or "10% off".

You can of course combine all of these rules.

Conditions

The "Conditions" section is where you set the products to which the category price rule applies. You only appears if you click on the "Add a new condition group" button.

CONDITION GROUP 1

Type	Value	
Attribute	Color: Grey	✖ Delete

AND

| Manufacturer | Fashion Manufacturer | ✖ Delete |

OR

CONDITION GROUP 2

Type	Value	
Attribute	Shoes Size: 35	✖ Delete

AND

| Feature | Height: 2.75 in | ✖ Delete |

AND

| Manufacturer | Fashion Manufacturer | ✖ Delete |

➕ Add a new condition group

CONDITIONS

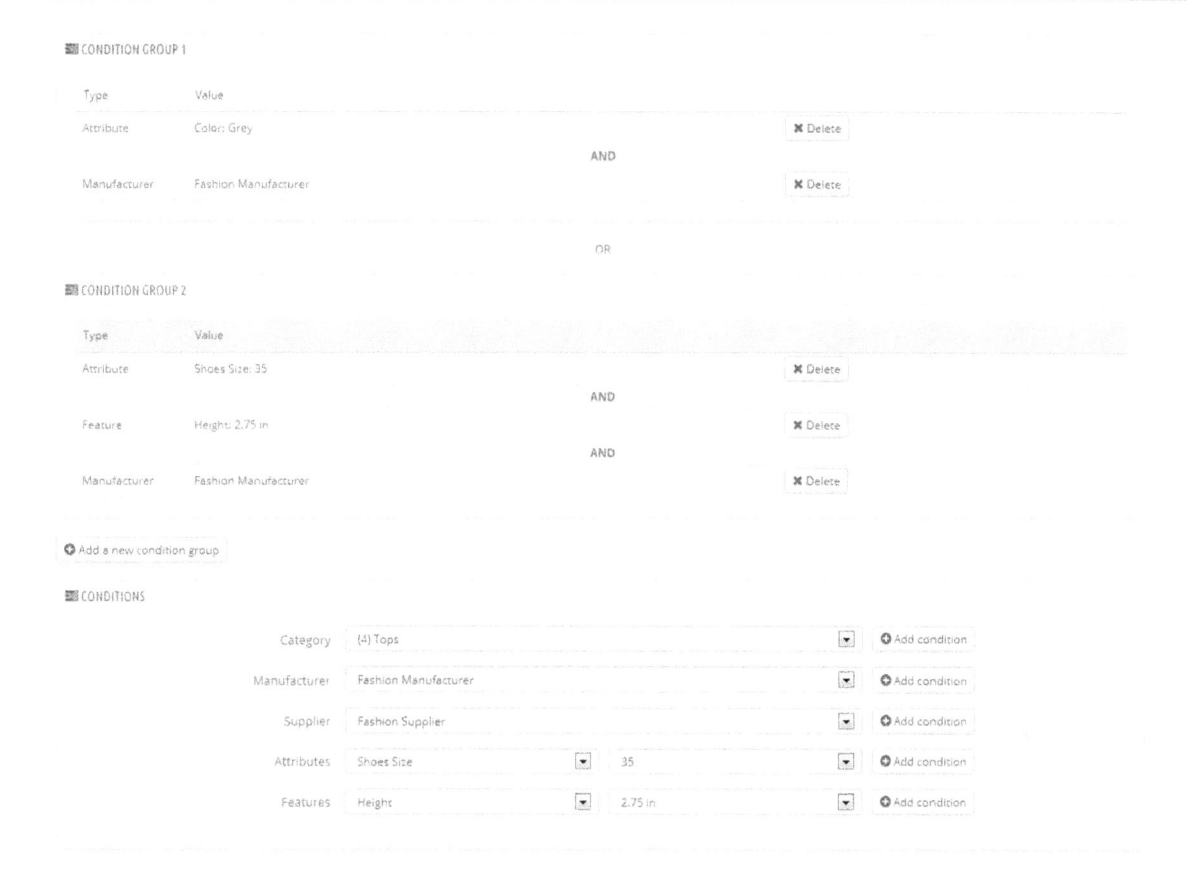

Category	(4) Tops			➕ Add condition
Manufacturer	Fashion Manufacturer			➕ Add condition
Supplier	Fashion Supplier			➕ Add condition
Attributes	Shoes Size		35	➕ Add condition
Features	Height		2.75 in	➕ Add condition

Conditions are built around condition groups, meaning that your data from the "Specific price rule" section above can be applied to many different ranges of products.

Conditions are grouped in an inclusive manner: all conditions of the group have to apply for the catalog price to apply. Hence the "AND".

Meanwhile, condition groups are exclusive: only one group has to apply for the catalog price to apply. Hence the "OR".

The default condition group is empty. You can add conditions to it using the drop-down menus in the lower part of the section:

- Choose a category or any other type of selection, and then click on the "Add condition" button.
- The condition will appear in the condition group. You can put many conditions in a condition group.

- Once a group is completed and you want to create a new condition group, click on the "Add new condition group". A new group will then appear, which you can fill in the same way.

By default, new conditions are added to the condition group that was created last. If you need to add conditions to a previous group, click on that group to highlight it, and then add your conditions.

You cannot currently delete a condition group.

Marketing modules

This page gathers in one place some of the most marketing-wise important modules available in your installation of PrestaShop. It serves as a shortcut to certain categories of modules from the "Modules" page.

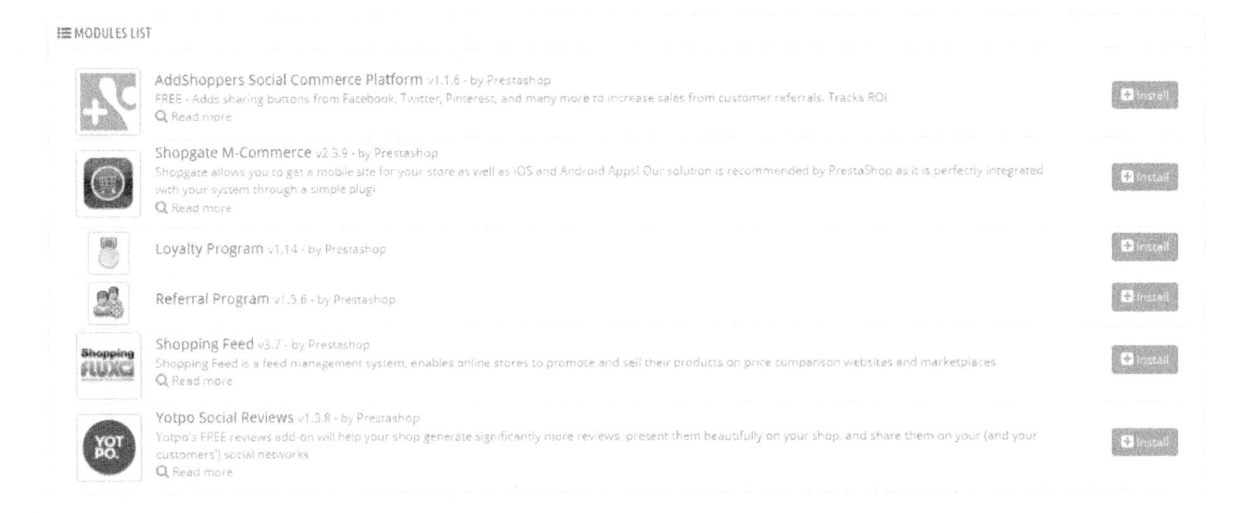

MODULES LIST

- **AddShoppers Social Commerce Platform** v1.1.6 - by Prestashop
  FREE - Adds sharing buttons from Facebook, Twitter, Pinterest, and many more to increase sales from customer referrals. Tracks ROI
  Read more

- **Shopgate M-Commerce** v2.3.9 - by Prestashop
  Shopgate allows you to get a mobile site for your store as well as iOS and Android Apps! Our solution is recommended by PrestaShop as it is perfectly integrated with your system through a simple plugi
  Read more

- **Loyalty Program** v1.14 - by Prestashop

- **Referral Program** v1.5.6 - by Prestashop

- **Shopping Feed** v3.7 - by Prestashop
  Shopping Feed is a feed management system, enables online stores to promote and sell their products on price comparison websites and marketplaces
  Read more

- **Yotpo Social Reviews** v1.3.8 - by Prestashop
  Yotpo's FREE reviews add-on will help your shop generate significantly more reviews, present them beautifully on your shop, and share them on your (and your customers') social networks
  Read more

The modules in this page come from the "Advertising and Marketing" and "Smart Shopping" sections in the "Modules" page.

You can install modules directly from this page. When you click the "install" button, the module is installed and you are taken to the "Modules" page, where you can open the module's configuration page by clicking on its "Configure" link. You can also return to the "Marketing" page in order to open the configuration page, or delete, disable, reset or uninstall the module, depending on its status.

Managing Modules and Themes

PrestaShop 1.6 comes bundled with over 120 modules that can be installed/uninstalled and configured as desired, in order to customize and complete your shop.

The range of actions is virtually unlimited: the extensibility of PrestaShop makes it possible to turn your shop into exactly what you intend it to do, instead of you having to comply with constraints that you did not choose – provided you can find the module that does exactly what you need.

Your Modules

The "Modules" page under the "Modules" menu gives you access to the list of modules. On this page you can install, uninstall, and configure each module. All the native modules are explained in depth in their own chapter, "Making the Native Modules Work". This chapter simply explains how the Modules page works.

Module notifications

Below the page title, you will at times get notifications from installed modules. Most of the time, the notification help you complete the configuration of modules that are installed but not yet ready to be used: updating their setting should make the notification disappear... and your module work properly.

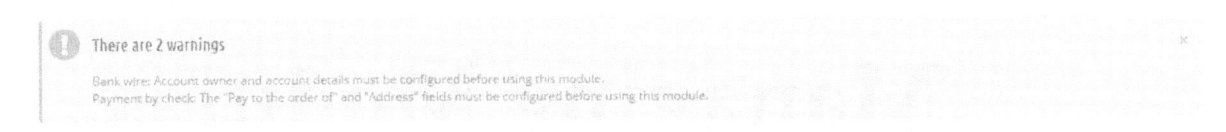

When one of your module has an update available on the Addons site, PrestaShop will let you know about it, and a "Update all" button will appear at the top of the page. Click on this button to update them all.

Above the table of modules are two buttons, titled "Normal view" and "Favorites view". They radically change the way modules are listed.

The modules list

This list enables you to quickly find the module you want to install or edit the settings of.

The first section is where you can search for a specific module, or filter down modules until you find the one you are looking for.

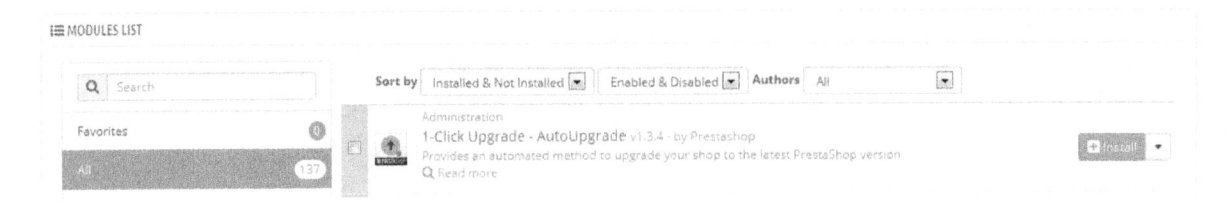

- **Search field**. Modules are displayed while you type their name, which makes it even more intuitive and fast.
- **Sort selectors**. The list automatically reloads when you make a selection, and displays modules according to all the current settings.

- o **Installed & Not Installed**. Most of the time, you will want to perform an action on an installed module, or install a new one. This filter is the most commonly used.
- o **Enabled & Disabled**. Installed module are the only ones that can be configured, hence the importance of this selector.
- o **Authors**. You can filter the modules by author. By default, only "PrestaShop" is available, but as add more modules, this selector will prove very useful.

On the left is a list of all the module categories, with the number of modules for each in brackets. Click on a category in order to display the modules for this category.
One of the categories is named "Favorites" and is empty by default. This enables you to gather the modules you most often use, and to access them quickly. You can set your favorite modules using the "Mark as Favorite" action.

Modules can have one of 4 statuses:

- Non-installed.
- Installed but disabled
- Installed and enabled.
- Installed and enabled, but with warnings.

Some module have a "Popular" badge. This modules are actually from the Addons website. They are not free: the "Install" button is replaced by a shopping cart button, with the price of the module. Clicking that button open the module's page on the Addons website, where you can buy the module.

Difference between disabling and uninstalling

When you do not have a use for a module anymore, you can either disable or uninstall it. The results of both actions are seemingly the same: the module is not available anymore, its options do not appear in your back-office and any element it added to your front-end have disappeared.

The difference is that disabling a module keeps its configuration safe for later re-enabling, while uninstalling it removes all of its configuration and database data.

Therefore, you should only uninstall a module if you do not care about its data or if you are certain that you would not need it. If you are really sure you do not want that module on your shop, you can even click on its "Delete" link.

Performing Actions on Modules

Here are the available actions, depending on the module's status:

- Uninstalled modules:
    - **Install**. This will trigger the installation of the module on your installation of PrestaShop. The module will be automatically enabled. It might add new options to your back-office.
    - **Mark as favorite**. This will add the module to your Favorites list.
- Installed modules:
    - **Configure**. Some modules have a configuration page. In that case, they offer a "Configure" link to access a new interface where the user will be able to adjust all its settings.
    - **Disable**. When installed, a module is enabled by default. You can disable it, which will remove its options from your back-office, but will keep its settings for a later re-enabling.
        - **Disable/display on mobile**. This will disable the front-office view of the module only for mobile devices (smartphones, etc.).
        - **Disable/display on tablets**. This will disable the front-office view of the module only for tables.
        - **Disable/display on computers**. This will disable the front-office view of the module only for desktop computers.
    - **Reset**. This will restore the module's settings to their defaults.
    - **Uninstall**. This will disable the module and delete its data.
    - **Mark as favorite**. This will add the module to your Favorites list.
    - **Delete**. This will remove the module from the modules list, and delete its files and folders from your server.

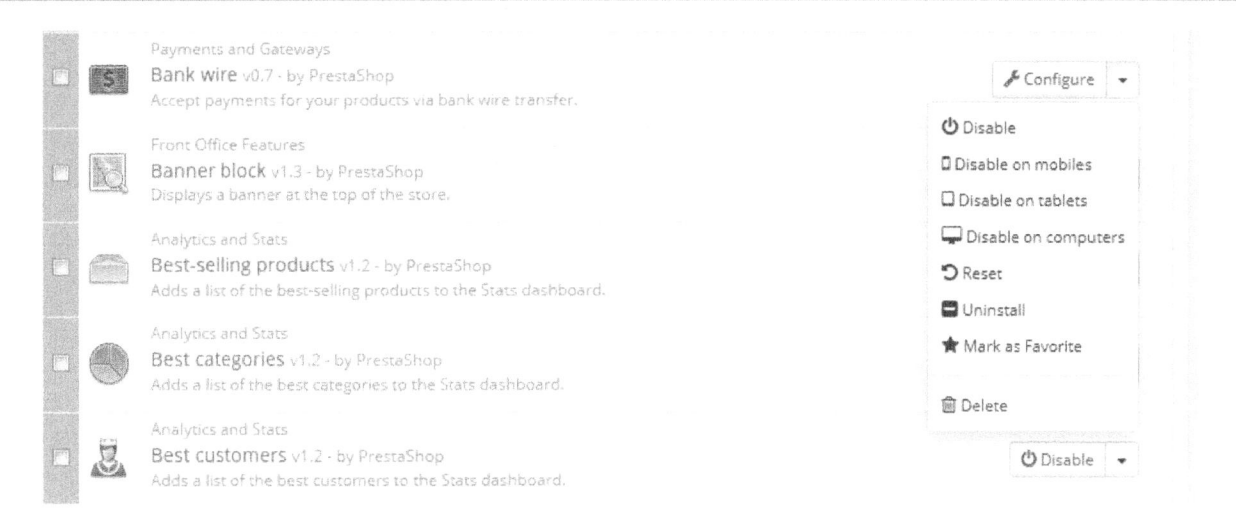

		Payments and Gateways	
☐		**Bank wire** v0.7 - by PrestaShop Accept payments for your products via bank wire transfer.	🔧 Configure ▾
			⏻ Disable
		Front Office Features	☐ Disable on mobiles
☐		**Banner block** v1.3 - by PrestaShop Displays a banner at the top of the store.	☐ Disable on tablets
			🖥 Disable on computers
		Analytics and Stats	↻ Reset
☐		**Best-selling products** v1.2 - by PrestaShop Adds a list of the best-selling products to the Stats dashboard.	⊟ Uninstall
		Analytics and Stats	★ Mark as Favorite
☐		**Best categories** v1.2 - by PrestaShop Adds a list of the best categories to the Stats dashboard.	🗑 Delete
		Analytics and Stats	
☐		**Best customers** v1.2 - by PrestaShop Adds a list of the best customers to the Stats dashboard.	⏻ Disable ▾

> Top ranking modules from Addons can be promoted to your module list, depending on your country settings. They appear among regular modules, but their action buttons are not labeled "Install" but instead "30 €", for instance. Clicking on the button takes you to the module's Addons page, from which you can log in, buy and download the module. From there on, you can install it on your shop.

Connecting to Addons

In the basic configuration, the modules' page will only let you update the default modules, the ones that were included in PrestaShop. If you have bought modules on Addons, the PrestaShop marketplace, and you want those to update automatically too, you have to connect your PrestaShop to Addons.

Click on the "Addons" link at the top of the screen: this will open a model window with a log in form. Simply fill in the form with your Addons connection details, and PrestaShop will now know (and update) the modules you have bought. Click on the "Addons" again, and it will display your account login.

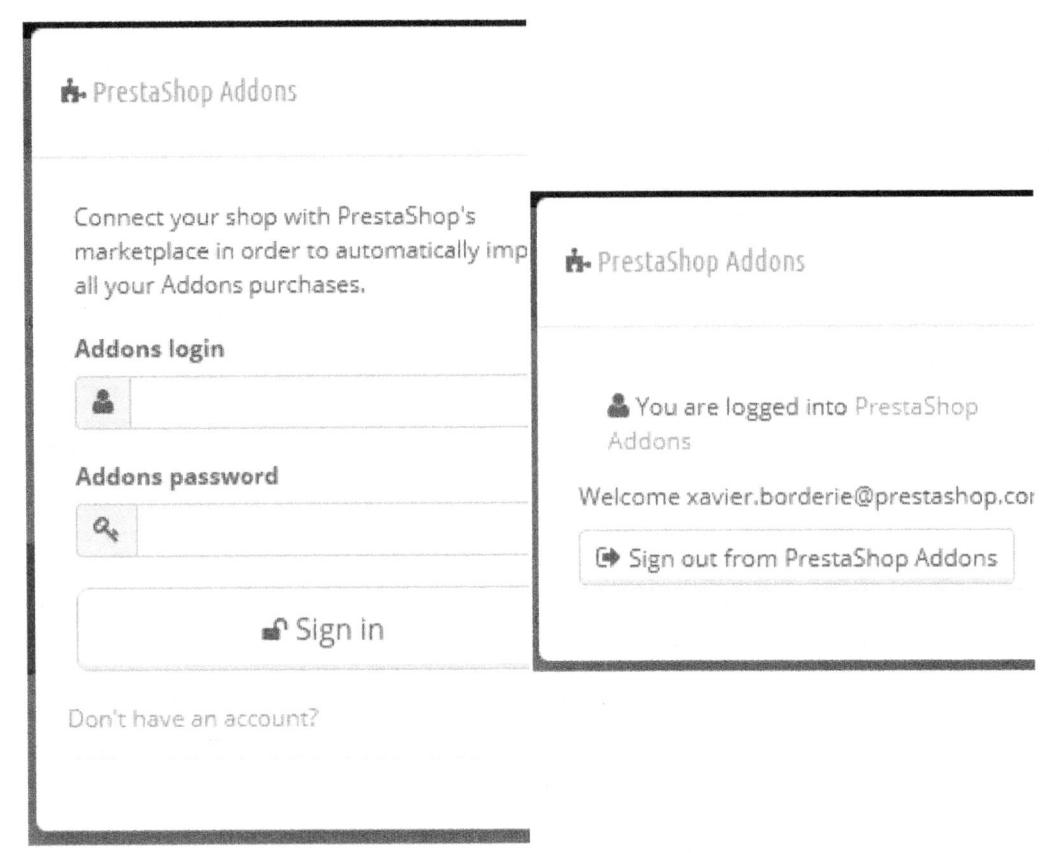

If the modules you have bought on Addons are not updating, do check that you are connected through this form!

Modules and Themes Catalog

PrestaShop comes bundled with more than 100 modules, but even that number might seem limiting, or you could want to explore other directions.

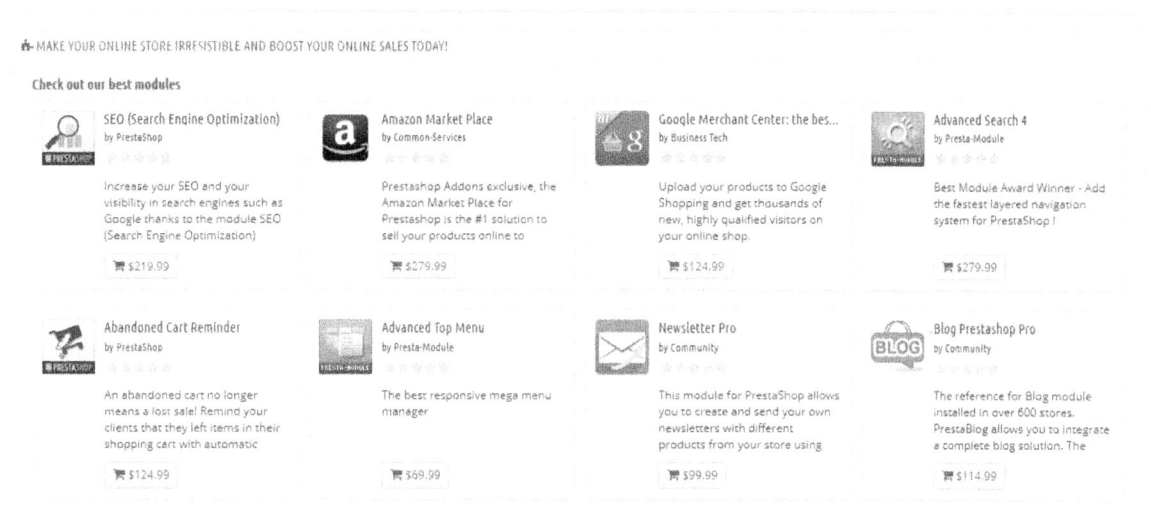

There are many more modules available on the PrestaShop Addons website (http://addons.prestashop.com/). Some are free, others are for-pay, and you are sure to find something that suits your needs! Once you are a seasoned module developer/theme designer, you can even submit your own creations, and sell them on Addons!

The "Modules & Themes Catalog" page gives you a quick and easy access to the online Addons database of modules and themes. Its interface is pretty straightforward:

- A search field, with which you can search the whole content of the Addons website.
- A list of 8 modules that you can buy directly.
- A list of 12 themes that you can buy directly.

A search query will send you to the Addons website, where more options are available.

Clicking on an item will open its Addons page in a new browser tab.

Addons is the official marketplace for PrestaShop Modules and Themes. This is where shop owners can get all the necessary items to customize their shop, and where authors can share their creations with the community.

Modules and themes can either be free or for-sale: the price is set by the author. Take the time to browse the available modules and themes, because expensive does not always mean better.

You must be logged-in before you can download or rate anything. Creating an account is free.

Installing a module

Once you have downloaded a module from the Addons online shop to your computer, it is up to you have it installed on your PrestaShop site.

There are two ways to install a module: either using the dedicated form, or using your FTP client.

Installing using the dedicated form

To install a new PrestaShop module automatically, click on the "Add new module" link at the top of the list of modules, in the "Modules" page. A new section will slide open.

ADD A NEW MODULE		
The module must either be a zip file or a tarball.		
Module file		Choose a file
	Upload this module	

The form in this section enables you to upload the archive file of the module, as downloaded from Addons. You can either upload a zip file, or a tar.gz one (tarball). The form is straightforward: simply browse to the module's file that you downloaded, and click the "Upload this module" button. Do not point to the module's uncompressed folder or any of its unpacked files: only the archive file!

Once you have clicked the button, PrestaShop will upload the module from your computer to its server, unpack it, place the files in the correct location, and update the page, all this in a handful of seconds. PrestaShop will then display "Module downloaded successfully".

Modules are not installed by default: you still have to click the module's "Install" button, and then possibly configure its settings.

Once configuration is complete, be sure to test the module immediately to confirm that it works as planned.

Installing using a FTP client

To install a new PrestaShop module manually:

1. Unzip (decompress) the module archive file (.zip or tar.gz). This should result in a new folder.
2. Using your FTP client, connect to PrestaShop web server, and place the unpacked module folder in PrestaShop's /modules folder.
   Pay attention NOT to upload that folder in another module's folder (which can happen when drag-and-dropping items). Upload both the folder and the files it contains, not just the files.
3. Go to your back-office, in the "Modules" menu.
4. Locate the new module in the modules list. You might have to scroll down; you can also use the list's search engine, which should give you a dynamically updated list of matching module names.
5. In the row for the new module, click the "Install" button.
6. Your module is now installed and should be activated too. If necessary, click on the module's "Configure" link. Also, pay attention to any warning message that might be displayed by PrestaShop.

Once configuration is complete, be sure to test the module immediately to confirm that it works as planned.

Modules can come from many sources, and not all of them are reliable. This is why PrestaShop 1.6.0.7 introduced a warning window for "Untrusted" modules

– that is modules that have not been verified by PrestaShop through its Addons marketplace. This screen window lets you choose whether to proceed with the installation with no further notification, or to stop the installation process.

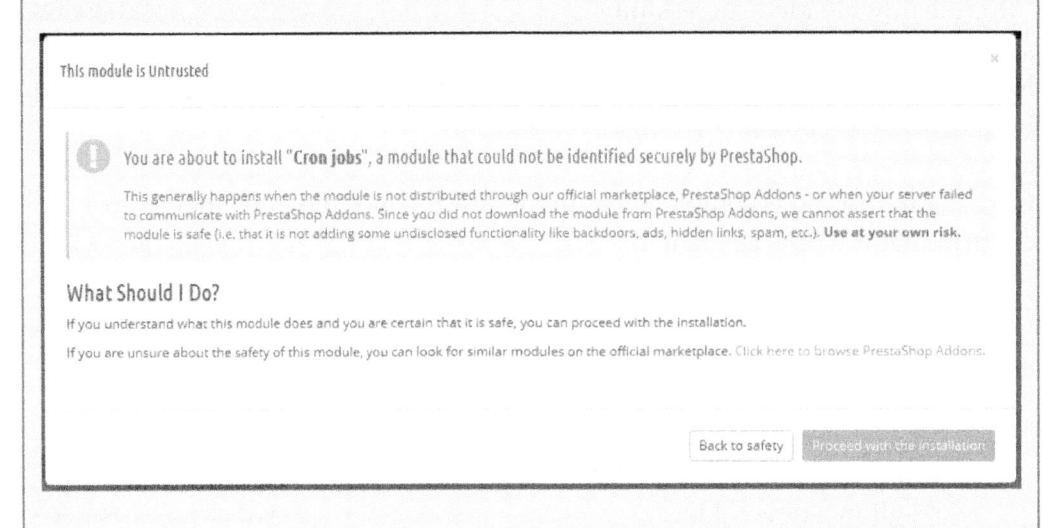

This module is Untrusted

You are about to install "**Cron jobs**", a module that could not be identified securely by PrestaShop.

This generally happens when the module is not distributed through our official marketplace, PrestaShop Addons - or when your server failed to communicate with PrestaShop Addons. Since you did not download the module from PrestaShop Addons, we cannot assert that the module is safe (i.e. that it is not adding some undisclosed functionality like backdoors, ads, hidden links, spam, etc.). **Use at your own risk.**

What Should I Do?

If you understand what this module does and you are certain that it is safe, you can proceed with the installation.

If you are unsure about the safety of this module, you can look for similar modules on the official marketplace. Click here to browse PrestaShop Addons.

Back to safety Proceed with the installation

Installing a native module or a module obtained through Addons will not trigger the display of this window.

Updating a module

Your PrestaShop installation regularly checks with the Addons server if there is any update for your modules. If so, PrestaShop displays a "Update it!" link for the affected modules. Simply click it, and PrestaShop will take care of downloading and updating the module.

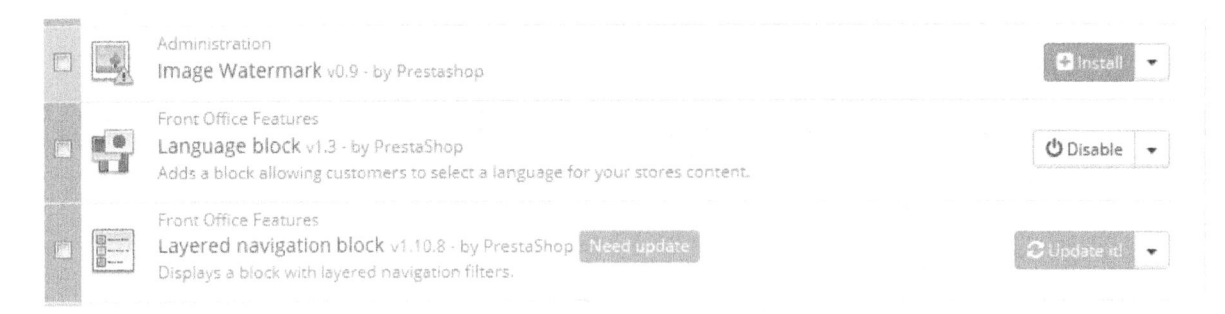

Uninstalling a module

> **Do not ever delete a module by directly trashing its folder using your FTP client!** You must let PrestaShop take charge of it.

When you need to temporarily stop using a module, but still wish to keep its configuration, you can simply disable it: just click on the "Disable" link. The actions will turn into "Enable" and "Delete", but the "Uninstall" button can still be seen.

If you do not care about the module's configuration, click on the "Uninstall" button: your module's folder will still be in the /modules folder, but the module will not have any impact on your shop anymore.
If you wish to entirely remove the module from your server, click the "Delete" link: PrestaShop will get rid of its folder and all its files.

> Make sure that the disabling or removal of the module does not break the theme.

Installing a theme

Once you have downloaded a theme from the Addons online store, it's up to you have it installed on your PrestaShop site.

Installing using PrestaShop's theme installer

This is the recommended method, as it preserves all the blocks' positions on their respective hooks.

PrestaShop has a native theme importer, which you can reach from the "Themes" page, under the "Preferences" menu. Click the "Add new theme" button at the top of the screen (not the "Add new" button above the list of themes, which is used to create a new theme). This screen presents you with 3 methods to install (or "import") a new module: from your computer, from a public website, or from your own FTP server. It also gives you a method to create a new theme from scratch.

Importing a theme

Whatever the method, the process remains the same: indicate the location of the theme's Zip archive, then click "Next".

> **Import from your computer**: using the file explorer to find the archive.
> **Import from the web**: indicate the direct public URL to the archive.
> **Import from FTP**: using your FTP client, upload the archive in the following folder: /modules/themeinstallator/import/ .

A quick summary is displayed in the next page, indicating what that importer is about to do.

Click "Next" again to validate your choice. The theme is now installed, and PrestaShop asks you if you wish to install modules that were imported along with the theme, what you would rather do with the current modules configuration, and how you would like the images configuration to be taken into account.

Click "Next" one last time. A final confirmation page presents you with all the changes applied to your PrestaShop site. Click "Finish" to end the process.

Installing using the Theme Installator module

This works a lot like PrestaShop's own theme installer.

The "Import/export a theme" module is a native module, and should be installed by default. This is a special module that enables you to import a theme and install it (and its attached modules), or to export a theme and its modules from your shop in order to share it with the world.

Find this module in the module list (in the "Modules" page), install it if it is not already installed, and open its configuration screen. This screen presents you with 3 methods to install (or "import") a new module: from your computer, from a public website, or from your own FTP server. It also gives you a method to export your theme in a correct format.

The rest of the instructions are the same as for PrestaShop's theme installer above.

Installing using a FTP client

This method is not recommended, but is still available. Use with caution: your blocks might not have the expected position on their respective hooks.

To install a new PrestaShop theme via FTP:

1. Unzip (decompress) the theme archive file (.zip). This should result in at least one new local folder, /themes, containing your theme's folder(s).
2. Using your FTP client, place the theme's folder (as found in the local /themes folder) online in your PrestaShop /themes folder. Pay attention NOT to upload that folder in another theme's folder (which can happen when drag-and-dropping items). Upload the whole folder, not just the files it contains.
3. (optional) If the theme's archive contains a second /modules folder, it means your new theme comes bundled with modules that are specific to it, or necessary for it to run properly. Using your FTP client, place the folder(s) found in the local /modules folder online in your PrestaShop /modules folder. If your online PrestaShop install already has a module of the same name, try to only keep the most recent version of the two (the one with the most recent files). If unsure, keep the version bundled with the theme, as it is the most likely to work best with it.
4. Go to your back-office, in the "Themes" page under the "Preferences" menu.
5. Select the new theme in place of the current theme, by clicking on the radio button then clicking "Save".
6. Your theme is now in place.
7. (optional) If the theme came with modules, activate them on the back-office's "Modules" page, then configure them if need be.

Many themes come with an accompanying Install.txt file, which gives you instructions. Make sure to follow them in order to not forget anything.

Once configuration is complete, be sure to test the theme immediately, every page of it, to confirm that it works as planned. Do try to make a full order, from A to Z – you wouldn't want to miss orders just because you didn't notice the theme was incomplete!

Exporting a theme

Exporting a theme is very useful when you want either to back the theme up for safety, and create an archive of the theme for a friend or in order to make it available on the Addons marketplace (http://addons.prestashop.com/). Not only does it generate a complete Zip archive of your theme, but it also adds many information in an XML files, which is very useful both when uploading to Addons, and when importing to another PrestaShop site.

Just as for theme importation, there are two ways to export a theme: using PrestaShop's own exporter, or using the one from the Theme Installator module:

- PrestaShop's exporter: click on the "Export theme" button at the top of the "Themes" page (in the "Preferences" menu).
- Theme Installator's exporter: open the module's configuration page, then go to the "Export a theme" section.

Select a theme and click on "Export this theme". A configuration form appears where you can set the exported themes parameters: author, theme name, compatibility version, attached modules (if any), etc.

Once all the parameters are correctly set, click on "Generate the archive now". You will quickly get a file to download from your browser. Save it on your hard-drive, then give the save file a proper name. From there on, you can easily share this theme, and if it is your own creation, you can start selling it on PrestaShop's Addons website at http://addons.prestashop.com/.

PrestaShop's mobile template

The mobile template enables any PrestaShop merchant to have his or her shop be accessible to mobile devices: from the home page to the payment process, along with product pages and conversion funnel.

Installing the mobile template for your shop

Installing PrestaShop's mobile template is easy:

1. Connect to you PrestaShop's administration.
2. Go to the "Themes" page under the "Preferences" menu.

3. In the "Appearance" section, go to the "Enable mobile theme" part and choose one of the three options other than "I want to disable it".

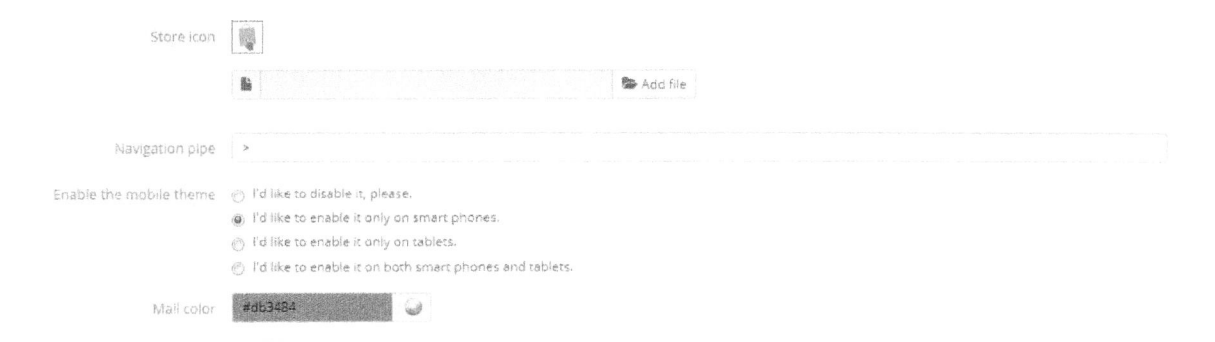

By default, the mobile template is only used for mobiles phones, tablet receiving the same theme as regular devices. With this option, you can choose to have the mobile template be used for tablets ("Both" option"), or even choose to only have it used for tablets (mobile phones receiving the regular theme).

Customizing the mobile template

The mobile template's files are located in the /mobile subfolder of the current theme's folder. This way, if you current theme is the default PrestaShop theme, the mobile template's files are in the /themes/default/mobile of your PrestaShop installation.

The template is made of HTML, CSS and JavaScript files: its structure is therefore the same as for the default theme, but its design is radically different, as it was built for the smaller screens of mobile devices.

Therefore, if you wish to change the colors or layout of the mobile template's pages, you must edit the CSS and/or HTML files in order to adapt them to your likings. You must have a good knowledge of web programming languages, or ask for help from a web developer.

Using the mobile template with another theme

The mobile template is only available if the current theme has a /mobile subfolder in its own folder. Hence, numerous PrestaShop themes do not have a proper mobile theme, and these themes' users cannot automatically offer a mobile version of their shop to their visitors

While the theme you are using is being updated with its own mobile template, you can use the default mobile template, thanks to a quick file manipulation: you just have to copy the /mobile subfolder from the /themes/default folder, and paste this subfolder (and all of its files) in your current theme's folder.

You will therefore use the default mobile template rather than a template with a design that is consistent with your main theme, but nothing is stopping you from editing the HTML, CSS or JavaScript files of the mobile template in order to get it closer to your own theme.

Front-office Positions

A modules can have to views: one on the back-office (its options, or even a configuration screen), and one on the front-office. The front-office view is how and where the module is displayed within your shop's theme.

The position of a module in your theme can be changed, because you might want one module's block to be placed much higher (or lower) in the page that others. In PrestaShop's parlance, this is called "transplanting", and is done using the tool available in the "Positions" page, under the "Modules" menu. In effect, this enables you to attach a module to one of the many available hooks in the current theme, without writing any code.

The "Positions" page displays all the available hooks, and their attached modules. Many are empty by default, but some of the most useful ones have a dozen of modules (the displayHeader hook has 33 modules by default).

displayHeader

This hook displays additional elements in the header of your pages.

33 Modules

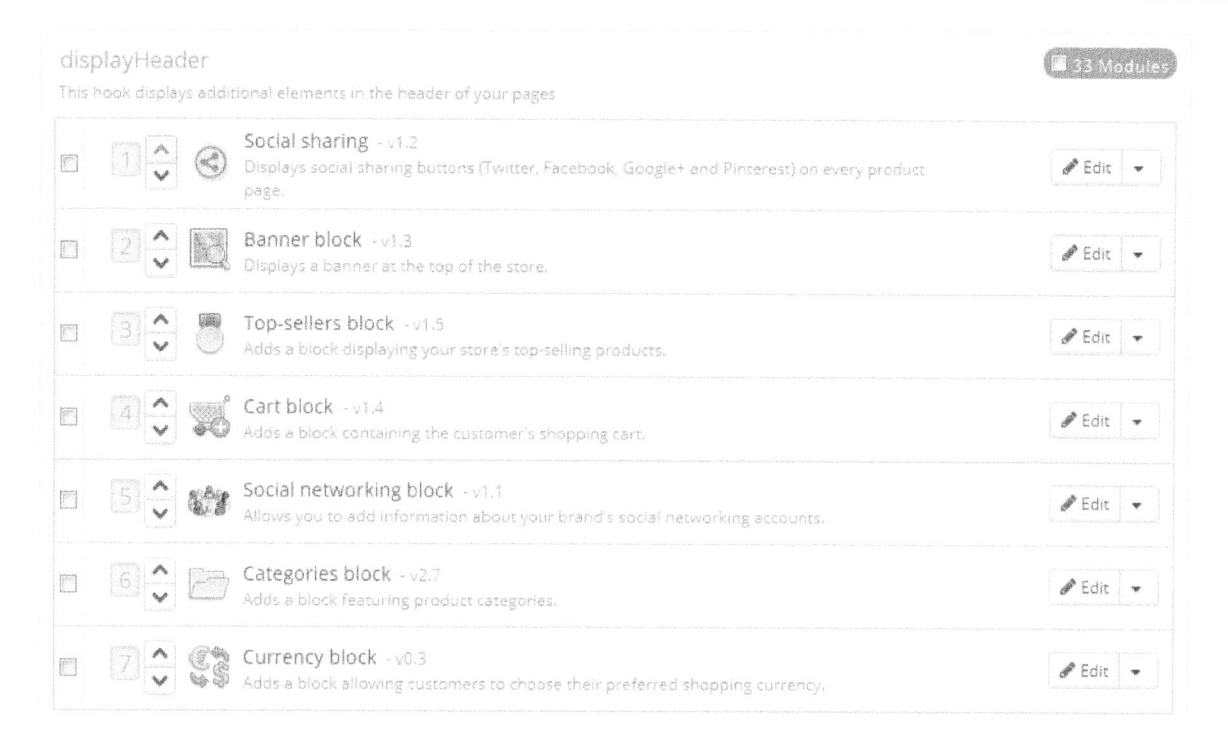

☐	1		**Social sharing** - v1.2 Displays social sharing buttons (Twitter, Facebook, Google+ and Pinterest) on every product page.	Edit	▼
☐	2		**Banner block** - v1.3 Displays a banner at the top of the store.	Edit	▼
☐	3		**Top-sellers block** - v1.5 Adds a block displaying your store's top-selling products.	Edit	▼
☐	4		**Cart block** - v1.4 Adds a block containing the customer's shopping cart.	Edit	▼
☐	5		**Social networking block** - v1.1 Allows you to add information about your brand's social networking accounts.	Edit	▼
☐	6		**Categories block** - v2.7 Adds a block featuring product categories.	Edit	▼
☐	7		**Currency block** - v0.3 Adds a block allowing customers to choose their preferred shopping currency.	Edit	▼

At the top of the page, a drop-down menu enables you to only display the hook in which you are interested.

By default, this page only displays the hooks on which you can position functions. Checking the "Display non-positionable hooks" box below displays all the hooks, even those where you cannot position something.

The header of the table for each hook displays the hook's name, its technical name (and for some, a quick description), and its number of attached modules. The table lists the modules that are attached to that hook.

The modules are displayed in the order in which they appear in the hook.

Moving a module within a hook

You have two ways of changing a module's position within a hook:

- Click the up or down arrow. The page will reload and display the new order.
- Drag and drop the module's row itself:

1. Place the mouse cursor on the position number to have it change into a "move item" cursor.
2. Click and hold while moving the cursor over the row/position where you want the module to be: the module's row changes position accordingly.
3. Release the mouse button: the current position for the module is saved.

For most modules, transplantation can easily be done directly via the back-office. Some modules require you to alter their code in order to transplant them.

Attaching a module to a hook: Transplanting

In PrestaShop, "transplanting" is the action of attaching a module to a hook. You can add a module to more than one hook.

Two things to know before transplanting a module:

- Some modules are written to only be attached to a given set of hooks.
- Some hooks are written to not accept some specific kinds of modules.

Therefore, be aware that you cannot always transplant any module to any hook.

Make sure to disable the cache when testing the effect of a new module on the front-end. You can do this in the "Preferences" page, under the "Advanced parameters" menu.

The transplanting process has its own interface:

1. Go to the "Modules" menu, and its "Positions" page.
2. Click the "Transplant a module" button at the top right. The transplanting interface appears.
3. In the "Module" drop-down list, select the module you want to transplant.
4. In the "Hook into" drop-down list, select where you want to transplant the module to. There are many available hooks. You can change your setting later if needed.

5. In the "Exceptions" field, type the name of the file(s) of the pages in which you do not want the module to appear.
   You can perform a multiple selection simply by clicking on the file names while keeping the Ctrl key pressed. You can deselect files in the same manner: Ctrl+click.
6. Do not forget to save your changes.

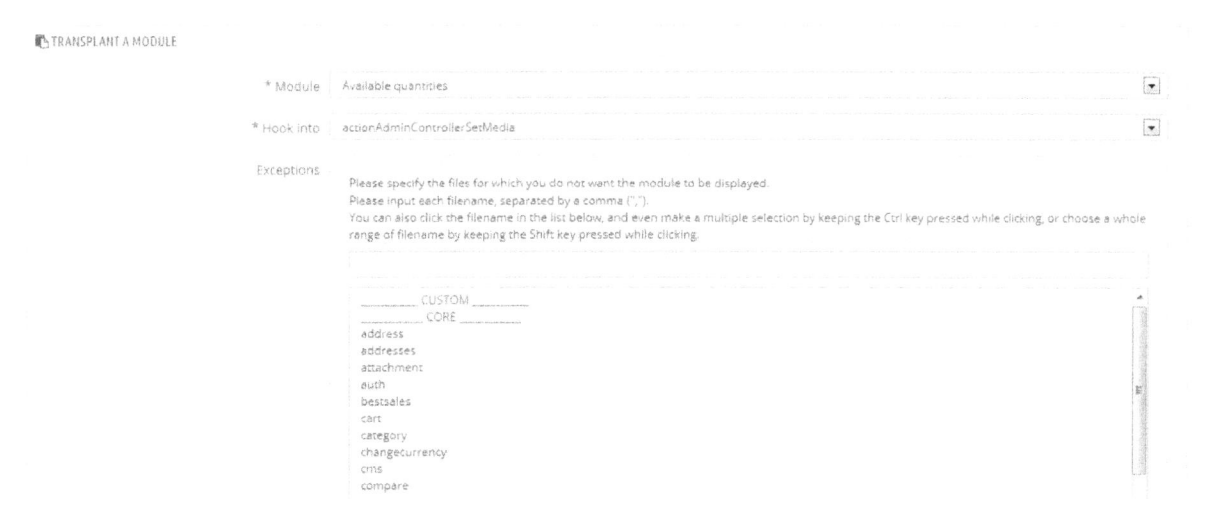

TRANSPLANT A MODULE

* Module	Available quantities
* Hook into	actionAdminControllerSetMedia
Exceptions	Please specify the files for which you do not want the module to be displayed.
	Please input each filename, separated by a comma (",").
	You can also click the filename in the list below, and even make a multiple selection by keeping the Ctrl key pressed while clicking, or choose a whole range of filename by keeping the Shift key pressed while clicking.

```
_____ CUSTOM _____
_____ CORE _____
address
addresses
attachment
auth
bestsales
cart
category
changecurrency
cms
compare
```

The "Hook into" drop-down menu gives you a good idea where module can be placed.

Even though the "Hook into" drop-down list gives a comprehensive overview of the available hooks, it might not always be clear which is the one to which you want to attach your module. Do not hesitate to try another hook if the result of your selection if not what you expect.
The list gives some detail: some hook have a description after the hook's name, for instance "Add fields to the form 'attribute value'" for displayAttributeForm. Peruse them all in order to choose your hook correctly.

Editing an attached module

Each module has two icons on the right side of its row: one to edit its settings, the other to delete the module.

Editing a module's setting uses the same interface as the one used for the transplanting a module. The major difference is that you cannot change the "Module" and "Hook into" settings, as they are disabled, and thus grayed out.

You can only edit the exception setting, which works just as described in the "Attaching a module to a hook" method above.

While you cannot edit the "Module" and "Hook into" settings, they can serve as a handy reminder of their current position, should you want to put them back there later on.

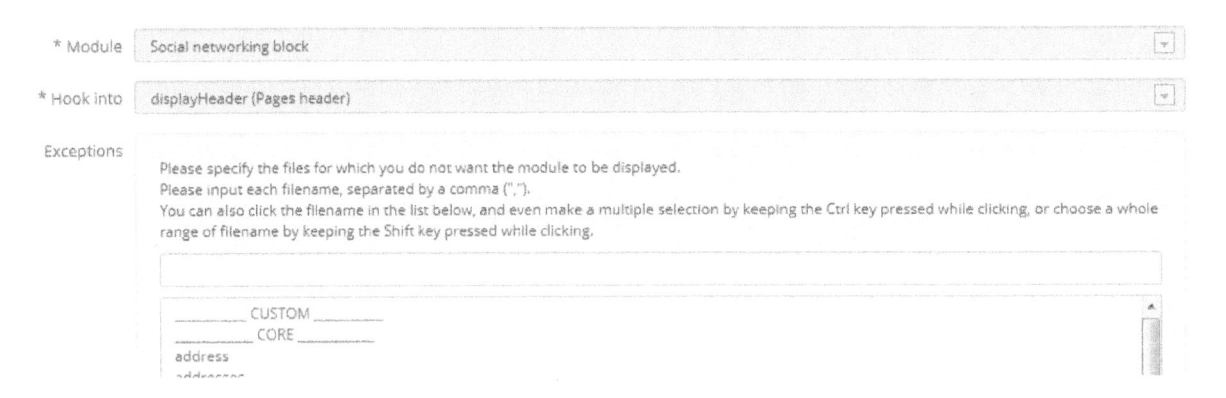

* Module	Social networking block
* Hook into	displayHeader (Pages header)
Exceptions	Please specify the files for which you do not want the module to be displayed. Please input each filename, separated by a comma (","). You can also click the filename in the list below, and even make a multiple selection by keeping the Ctrl key pressed while clicking, or choose a whole range of filename by keeping the Shift key pressed while clicking.

```
_____ CUSTOM _____
_____ CORE _____
address
addresses
```

If you want to move a module to another hook, you must use the transplanting interface:

1. Click the "Transplant a module" button at the top right. The transplanting interface appears.
2. In the "Module" drop-down list, select the module you want to move to another hook.
3. In the "Hook into" drop-down list, select where you want to transplant the module to.
4. In the "Exceptions" field, type the name of the file(s) of the pages in which you do not want the module to appear.
5. Save your changes. The hook list appears.
6. Go to the hook where you have transplanted the module: it should appear in there. Change its position if necessary.
7. Go to the hook where the module first was, and click the trashcan icon in order to remove it from that hook. This prevents you from having the same module appear twice.

Always check your front-office to make sure the module is indeed where you intended it to be.

Removing a module from a hook

There are two ways to remove a module from a hook:

- Removing a single module: click the trashcan icon on the right of the module's row.
- Removing a batch of modules: select the modules by checking the box on the right of their row, and then click the "Unhook" button, found at the top and the bottom of the list of hooks.

Moving a module visually: Live Edit

Another way to move modules around on the shop's homepage is the Live Edit mode, which embeds said homepage into a tool that lets you visually decide where to place your modules. You can access it from the "Position" page, by clicking the "Run Live Edit" button.

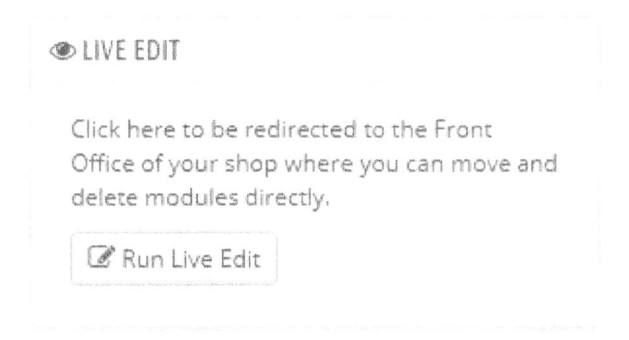

> **LIVE EDIT**
>
> Click here to be redirected to the Front Office of your shop where you can move and delete modules directly.
>
> [Run Live Edit]

When clicked, PrestaShop opens the homepage in a new browser windows/tab, with the Live Edit script on top:

- All module blocks have a dotted red border, enabling you to see which blocks you can move.
- At their top left side, a block-specific icon appears, along with the block's name, enabling you to always find your way among blocks.
- At their top right side, they have two icons:
    1. A "move" icon: click on it to start moving the module around.
    2. A "trash" icon: click it to remove the block from the home.

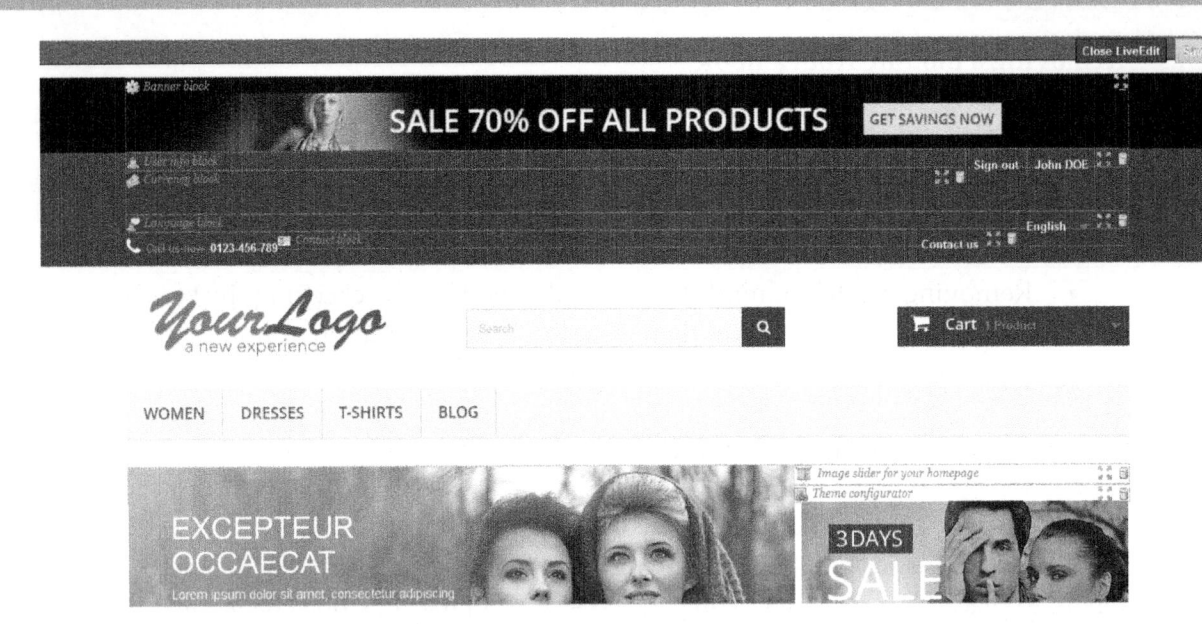

At the top of the Live Edit mode, a toolbar presents you with two buttons: "Close Live Edit" and "Save".

The first one is quite self-explanatory; the second one cancels all changes you might have made to your modules' position during this live-editing session.

> Once you have removed a module, if you want to bring it back, you will have to go to the "Positions" page and use the "Transplant a module" form.

Where to move modules?

Modules cannot be moved just about anywhere: it depends on both the theme's hooks, and each module's hook support (as seen in the above section). Therefore, you mostly can only move modules within their understood context: column modules can be moved within a column as well as from one column to the other (right to left, for instance), while regular homepage modules (the ones at the center) can only be moved within their specific column.

In order to give you a visual hint about where a given module can be moved, it will display an empty green block if the location is correct, and an empty red block if not.

Transplanting a module by modifying its code

This is for experts only: you must have a good knowledge of PHP and HTML before attempting anything with the code of a module.

Some modules cannot be transplanted into other sections of the front-office simply because they lack the necessary code.

For example, the "Quick Search" block (/blocksearch) contains templates for both column display and header display, whereas the "Currencies" block (/blockcurrencies) only has one template file which only works with the header section. Likewise, the default "Featured Products" block (/homefeatured) can only be placed in the center content section of the main page.

If you want to display simple modules such as the "Currencies" block in a position for which it was not built, you will have to edit its template files. More complex module, such as the "Featured" block, can also be made to be displayed in other sections of the page, but they might have to be partly rewritten in order to have their design work with that new location.

To customize the transplantation ability of a module, you must give it the correct PHP function for the new target hook. For example, the "Currency" block has this function:

```
function hookTop($params)

    {

    ...

    }
```

In order to transplant the "Currency" block into the right column, for instance, you need to add the hookRightColumn() function:

function hookRightColumn($params)

{

...

}

Afterwards, you must write the code that displays the content on the front page. At best, that means copy/pasting the content of the hookTop() function; at worst, you need to rework the content of hookTop() function into something that will work for the new location.

Payment settings

With PrestaShop, you can accept your customer's transactions using several different payment methods, such as checks, bank wire, cash on delivery, and through several partner modules such as PayPal, Moneybookers, Hipay, etc.

In the "Payment" page, you can see the following sections:

- **Modules list**. Basically, a shortcut to "Payments & Gateways" section of the module list, in the "Modules" page. You can install modules directly from this page.
- Three "restrictions" sections:
    - **Currency restrictions**. Choose with which currencies your installed payment modules should work.
    - **Group restrictions**. Choose with which user groups your installed payment modules should work.
    - **Country restrictions**. Choose with which countries your installed payment modules should work.

Installing a payment module

Installing a payment module is fundamentally no different from installing a regular module: simply click the "Install" button, and all that is left to do is to configure the module.

You should pay a lot of attention to the settings, and make sure they do point to your address or bank account. Configuring payment modules often means you must first be known by the payment service provider, meaning having an account on their service.

Let's install the "Cash on Delivery" module. Find the module in the list, and click on the "Install" button. PrestaShop will take care of everything, send you to the page with the list of all modules, and notifying you of the result. For instance, if a module needs to be configured before it can work, PrestaShop will display a notification box at the top of the page. In the case of the "Cash on delivery" module, there is nothing to configure.

Payments and Gateways
Cash on delivery (COD) v0.5 - by PrestaShop   ⏻ Disable ▼
Accept cash on delivery payments

Payment Module Restrictions on Currencies

Depending upon the payment, the customer's choice of currency can differ. You can limit the choice of available payment methods depending on the available currencies: you may want customers to be able to pay with any currency when using PayPal, but those paying Moneybookers should only pay using dollars, for instance.

CURRENCY RESTRICTIONS

Please mark each checkbox for the currency, or currencies, in which you want the payment module(s) to be available.

Currency restrictions	Authorize.net AIM (Advanced Integration Method)	Bank wire	Cash on delivery (COD)	Merchant Warehouse	Payment by check	PayPal USA, Canada
Dollar	☑	☑	--	☑	☑	☑
Customer currency	--	--	--	--	--	--
Shop default currency	--	--	--	--	--	--

Save restrictions

> By default, only your shop's default currency is available. If you need more, follow this process:
>
> 1. In the "Localization" page under the "Localization" menu, import the localization pack for the country which has the currency in which you are interested. For instance, USA for US Dollars, United Kingdom for UK Pound, etc.
> 2. In the "Currencies" page under the "Localization" menu, enabled the currencies you just imported.

If you need to restrict payment module usage according to the user's currency, simply check the boxes that apply and click on the "Save restrictions".

Note that currency restrictions work in different ways depending on the payment module:

- For some, such as Cash on delivery, you cannot change their default setting.
- For others, such as Bank wire, Payment by check, Skrill, Ogone, etc., you can change any of their currency settings, except for the "Customer currency" and "Shop default currency", which stay at their default state.
- Then, for other modules such as Hipay or PayPal, you can change any of their currency settings, but you can choose only one option between "Customer currency" and "Shop default currency", not both.

The customer can set his or her currency using the drop-down menu at the top of each front-office page.

You can set the shop's default currency in the "Localization" page, under the "Localization" menu.

> If you change the default currency *after* having configured some first products, you will have to reset the price of all these products. You should set the default currency once and for all before adding any product.

Payment Module Restrictions on Groups

You can limit the choice of available payment methods depending on the group of customers: you can have a set number of customer groups where people can have access to more payment methods then regular customers.

GROUP RESTRICTIONS

Please mark each checkbox for the customer group(s) in which you want the payment module(s) to be available.

Group restrictions	Authorize.net AIM (Advanced Integration Method)	Bank wire	Cash on delivery (COD)	Merchant Warehouse	Payment by check	PayPal USA Canada
Visitor	✓	✓	✓	✓	✓	✓
Guest	✓	✓	✓	✓	✓	✓
Customer	✓	✓	✓	✓	✓	✓

[Save restrictions]

For instance, you could choose to have regular customers pay with PayPal, Skrill and Hipay, while professionals would only be able to pay by bank wire. Depending on the type of customers and on your choices, customers will only pay using the methods that match with your decisions.

Payment Module Restrictions on Countries

You can limit the choice of payment methods according to your customer's country of origin. For instance, you could choose to accept all payment methods for customers from France, Spain and Germany, while customers from Italy, the United Kingdom and Switzerland would only be able to pay by bank wire.

COUNTRY RESTRICTIONS

Please mark each checkbox for the country, or countries, in which you want the payment module(s) to be available.

Country restrictions	Authorize.net AIM (Advanced Integration Method)	Bank wire	Cash on delivery (COD)	Merchant Warehouse	Payment by check	PayPal USA, Canada
Afghanistan	☐	☐	☐	☐	☐	☐
Åland Islands	☐	☐	☐	☐	☐	☐
Albania	☐	☐	☐	☐	☐	☐
Algeria	☐	☐	☐	☐	☐	☐
American Samoa	☐	☐	☐	☐	☐	☐

[Save restrictions]

The table lists all the known countries. If one is missing, you can add it using the "Countries" page, under the "Localization" menu.

Here again, just as with currency limitations, the available options vary depending on the payment module:

- For some, the only option is your own country.
- For others, the only options are the set of countries supported by the service: Austria, Belgium, France, etc.
- All the others native payment modules should work with all countries.

Find the country you are looking for in the alphabetical list, and check the boxes to select or unselect the payment methods you want to make available to customers from that country. Once all of your settings have been configured, click on the "Save restrictions" button, found at the bottom of the table.
By default, all installed payment methods are enabled for the shop's country.

Making the Native Modules Work

This chapter explores the configuration process of all the default modules in PrestaShop 1.6.

There are more than 130 native modules available in 25 sections. Module sections are only displayed if they actually contain at least one module.

Some modules have configuration pages, which give you access to a couple of tools and information pages.

In every configuration page, generic buttons are gathered at the top of the screen:

- **Disable**. Deactivates the module while keeping its current settings for later use.
- **Uninstall**. Deactivates the module end delete its current settings.
- **Reset**. Wipes the module's current settings to set them back to default.
- **Check and update**. Checks whether a new version of this module is available (either in the PrestaShop repository or in the Addons online store), and if so, updates the module.
- **Manage hooks**. This link is a shortcut to the "Positions" page, from the "Modules" menu. From there, you can change the location of the

> module's interface on the front-end of your shop, or launch the Live Edit tool. The "Positions" page is configured so that you only the hooks available to the current module are displayed.
> - **Back**. A link back to the module list.
>
> At the bottom of the screen, the **Manage translations** selector contains shortcuts to the "Translations" page for installed modules. From there, you can update the module's translation for the selected language. For instance, you might want to change the wording in order to better fit your use.

Some modules will not be installed from files on your server, but downloaded from the Addons website. It helps ensure that you always have the latest version of a module.

The "Must have" modules are also from the Addons website, but are not freely available. They are not listed in this chapter.

Administration modules

1-Click Upgrade - AutoUpgrade

This module makes it really easy to upgrade PrestaShop to its latest version.

See the "Automatic Update" chapter of the "Update PrestaShop" guide to learn more about this module:
http://doc.prestashop.com/display/PS16/Automatic+update.

Database Cleaner

This module is very useful when you are done exploring PrestaShop for the first time, and you are ready to start adding your own content: you must first remove all the demo data that was installed along with PrestaShop: products, categories, client, orders, etc.

The configuration page has three sections:

- **Catalog.** This will erase all the data from the current catalog, even the items that you added yourself. Check the box and click the "Delete catalog" button to start the process.
- **Orders and customers**. This will erase all the currently registered orders and clients, even the ones that you created yourself. Check the box and click the "Delete catalog" button to start the process.
- **Functional integrity constraints.** This will check your database and make sure that everything is correctly set, and will try to fix what is not.
- **Database cleaning**. This will help reduce storage space and improve disk access efficiency.

Be very careful: any action triggered by clicking on one of these buttons is irremediable. Be sure to have a fresh backup of your database available first.

Email alerts

PrestaShop enables you to alert you and your clients by e-mail in certain cases:

- Your clients: when a product is out of stock.
- You: when a new order is placed in your shop.
- You: when a product's stock is below a certain threshold.
- You: when a product's coverage is below a certain number of days.

Customer notifications

There is only one setting in this section:

- **Product Availability**. When you enable this setting, a field appears on the product page of your shop when the product is out of stock. It asks your customers to leave their contact information so that they may be contacted when you shop will have this product back in stock.

Merchant notifications

There are several settings for merchants:

- **New order**. Enable this setting if you wish to be alerted of each new order

- **Out of stock**. Enable this setting and set the "Threshold" field with the value at which you wish to be alerted (default is 3).
- **Coverage warning**. Enable this setting and set the "Coverage field with the value at which you wish to be alerted (default is 0).

Merchant mail alerts can be sent to multiple addresses at the same time. To do so, list each e-mail address that will receive the notification (one e-mail address per line).

Google Analytics API

This module enables you to tie your PrestaShop store with your Google Analytics account.

First, you must choose the API version you want to use:

- The 1.3 version will require you to enter your Google Analytics e-mail, password and profile.
- The 3.0 version will require you to enter your Google Analytics Client ID, Client Secret and profile.

We recommend the 3.0 one, since the 1.3 one is deprecated. In order to have the 3.0 version work, you must enable OAuth access by following these instructions:
https://developers.google.com/analytics/devguides/config/mgmt/v3/mgmtAuthorization

Image watermark

This module enables you to add a watermark to all the product images on your shop. This limits their circulation on the Internet – and hopefully deter people from stealing them.

> If you intend to export your products on Google Shopping, know that on this service, the usage of promotional text / logos and watermarks in the images is not allowed. You may only upload images which are free of any added watermarks / logos.
> Learn more about the Google Shopping policy here:

https://support.google.com/merchants/answer/2700371?hl=en&ref_topic=2701481

The configuration page notifies you right away of which settings are currently missing.

- **Watermark file**. The chosen image must be in GIF format.
- **Watermark transparency (0-100)**. 100 amounts to a non-transparent image, which means that your logo will be very visible, but it will also completely hide part of the whole picture. The default setting, 60, is usually a good compromise.
- **Watermark X align**. Select where your watermark should appear on each of your images, here on the horizontal axis.
- **Watermark Y align**. Select where your watermark should appear on each of your images, here on the vertical axis.
- **Choose image types for watermark protection**. The type of images to which the watermark should be applied. You really only need to choose the biggest sizes, as these are the ones most likely to be stolen.

Once you have saved your settings, the configuration is completed but the watermarks are not yet added to your shop's pictures. Go to the "Preferences" menu, and open the "Images" page. There, click the "Regenerate thumbnails" button, near the bottom of the page. PrestaShop will process all your pictures (as selected in the configuration), and your watermark image will appear on the types of pictures that you selected.

Incentivibe

Incentivibe is a cost-sharing program which pools businesses together so they can share the prize cost of big contest prizes with other businesses and motivate their individual visitors to become a lead, fan or follower for a chance to win that prize.

You must be signed up to their service in order to use it.

Merchant Expertise

This module was specifically designed to help PrestaShop users keep track of their progress as e-merchants, see how much they've grown and progressed over the days, months and years. It is installed by default.

This module adds a system of badges and points, broken down into three levels, all of which are integral to your success in the e-commerce world:

- **Features**. Tracks your use of key e-commerce features such as Site Performance, Catalog Size, Employees and SEO.
- **Achievements**. Tracks your completion of specific key e-commerce goals such as number of Customers, Orders and Revenue.
- **International**. Tracks your presence in key International markets such as the Americas, Oceania, Asia, Europe, Africa and Maghreb.

The more progress your store makes, the more badges and points you earn. There is no need to submit any information or fill out any forms. We know how busy you are; everything is done automatically. Use this tool to drive your business, view your progress and reflect on your great achievements.

Newsletters

This module was built to export a CSV file of the e-mail addresses that your customers registered in your system.

Your customers can give you their e-mail address either by entering it in the Newsletter block located on the homepage or by checking the "Yes" box to subscribe to the newsletter when they register. You need these e-mail addresses in order to do some marketing.
Upon registration, your customers have two choices related to the newsletter: The first one to subscribe to the newsletter, the second to receive offers from your partners (Opt-In).

Export Newsletter Subscribers

This first section enables you to export all the e-mail addresses recorded from the Newsletter block on your homepage. After clicking the "Export .CSV file" button, a notification appears, asking you to click on a link to download the file containing the addresses.

Four pieces of information will be present in this file: the customer id, e-mail address, the day of registration, and the IP address. If you use this data with software such as Microsoft Excel, you can sort the information as you wish.

Export Customers

This second section enables you to filter your customers' e-mail addresses before you export a CVS file of their data. For instance, filtering by country is particularly useful for sending newsletters in the right language and for adapting your offers.

You therefore take more information into account when exporting the e-mail addresses. Use the "Newsletter subscribers" selector to select one of the following three items:

- **All customers**. Enables you to select all the e-mail addresses of your customers who open an account on your shop. That is to say, those who do want to receive information from your part, as well as those who do not. Be careful what you did with it, then.
- **Subscribers**. Enables you to select only those customers who do want to receive a newsletter from you.
- **Non-subscribers**. Enables you to select only those customers who do not want receive a newsletter from you.

Next is the "Opted-in subscribers" selector, where you can filter the contacts based on their desire to register for messages from advertising partners. Similarly, three choices are available:

- **All customers**. Enables you to select all the e-mail addresses of your customers who open an account on your shop. That is to say, both those who do and do not wish to receive information from your part.
- **Subscribers**. Enables you to select only those customers who do want to receive a newsletter from your partners.
- **Non-subscribers**. Enables you to select only those customers who do not want receive a newsletter from your partners.

Once you have filtered the e-mail addresses to export, click the "Export .CSV File" button to retrieve all addresses. A notification appears, asking you to click and download the file. This file contains six types of information: the customer ID, last name, first name, e-mail address, IP address, and date of registration. You can then use this information to send your marketing campaigns.

NVD3 Charts

NVD3 (http://nvd3.org/) is JavaScript library that was built specifically to generate beautiful charts using D3.js (http://d3js.org/), a JavaScript library built to manipulate documents based on data.

This module enables the NVD3 charting code for your own uses, providing you with ever so useful graphs.

Zingaya

Zingaya enables online calls - right from a webpage (your website, your social media page, your banner or email message). No downloads. No phone.

You must be signed up to their service in order to use it.

Advertising and Marketing modules

AddShoppers Social Commerce Platform

This module requires the cURL PHP extension enabled.

This module adds social sharing buttons to your site that help your products get shared more, along with detailed analytics that reveal the ROI of social sharing.

You must have an AddShoppers account in order to use this module. You can create one directly within the module.

Once you have an account, you can connect to the service through the module, and follow the instructions.

Advertising block

This module will display a block on the front office of your shop, containing the image of your choice, with a link to any URL you choose. This is a very easy way to promote another site: your blog, another store of yours, a friend or partner site, etc.

In the configuration page, you can load an image, set the target URL, and add a title to the image. Save and the image will appear to all your visitors.

Customer follow-up

This module enables you to create e-mail alerts for your customers. It gives you a way to automatically send discount vouchers to some of your customers.

There are four types of event that can trigger the sending of a voucher:

- Canceled cart: generate a discount when a cart does not become an order.
- Validated order: generate a discount when an order is validated.
- Frequent customer: generate a discount when the customer reaches a certain number of orders.
- Lost customer: generate a discount when a customer, who has already ordered once, has not come back to your site since.

Please note that the "Canceled cart" and "Validated order" options can dangerous. For instance, a customer might quickly notice he receives a discount every time he abandons a cart, and thus choose to frequently abandon his carts in order to receive a voucher...

> This module will only work if you put a new cron task in place: it should daily call the URL that is indicated at the top of the screen.
>
> Alternatively, you could call that URL manually every day – but this would quickly get tedious.

At the bottom of the screen, you will find two sections:

- **General**: has a single option, "Delete outdated discounts during each launch to clean database". If enabled, its action is triggered every time the URL is called.
- **Statistics**: displays the number of discounts set during the last 30 days.

Feedaty

Feedaty is the tool to professionally collect and manage Customer Feedback. Feedaty collects ratings and reviews from real customers of your ecommerce and, after moderating them, it publishes them on your website and on other channels throughout the web, growing trust in customers and helping your sales increase immediately.

Google AdWords

France only.

Google AdWords is Google's contextual advertising solution.

This module promotes the partnership between PrestaShop and Google, giving 75€ of ads for your first 25€ spent.

Referral program

This module gives you all the tools to turn your current customers into promoters of your brand among their friends. Using a referral system, you can win new customers while making your customers happier.

The configuration screen has two sections. Here are the options in the "Settings" section:

- **Minimum number of orders a sponsored friend must place to get their voucher**. Fill in the field with the value of your choice. Until this number is reached, your clients cannot take advantage of the discount.
- **Number of friends in the referral program invitation form**. Fill in the value of your choice.
- **Voucher type**. You can give two types of reduction, either in percentage or amount. Select the one you prefer, then specify the value of the

discount you want to apply in the various currencies supported by your shop.
- ○ **Percentage**. Default voucher is 5% of the order.
- ○ **Voucher amount**. Default voucher is 5 of every currency.
- **Voucher description**. Enter the name for the coupon, in all the supported languages.

Once the setup is complete, click the "Save" button.

The "conditions of the referral program" is where you enter the rules of your referral program, which is a new CMS page where you can set some limits to the voucher, such as "The voucher is valid for 1 year".

Understanding the referral process

To fully explain how the referral program works, you can write a description in the "Referral Program Rules." Once the conditions are completed, click the "Update text" button.

When your customers register and want to view the benefits they can reap from this program, they must go to the "Referral" section of their account. A new screen will appear.

Your customer can then enter the name and email address of the person he wishes to refer to your site. After he clicks "Confirm," the persons he entered will receive an email.

In "Pending Friends", the referral tool displays to the customer which of his referrals did not make a purchase after the email was sent. They may choose to resend an email by selecting the name and clicking "Refer my friends". Friends will then receive an email inviting them to register and submit an order.

The last tab in "my referrals", named "Friends I have sponsored", enables customers to see who among those to whom they sent a referral message, did accept the invitation and ordered an item on the shop. When registering, the referees must indicate the email address of the person who referred them, so that they in turn may benefit from the discount.

Search & Merchandising Prediggo

Prediggo increases your conversion rate and average basket value thanks to their innovative eMerchandising solution. Using an exclusive technology, Prediggo builds a profile for every visitor to your webshop and then recommends the appropriate product in real time.

SendinBlue (formerly MailinBlue)

France only.

Easily manage your Marketing campaigns, Transactional Emails, and SMS messages all in one simple and powerful platform.

Once you have an account, you can connect to the service through the module, and follow the instructions.

Trustpilot - Review and online reputation

Trustpilot is the global standard for online trust. Trustpilot enables customer centric businesses like yours to collect reviews, engage with consumers and share your most powerful marketing asset – real customers' positive experiences.

Once you have an account, you can connect to the service through the module, and follow the instructions.

Yotpo Social Reviews

Yotpo is a plug and play social reviews solution for e-commerce websites. Yotpo is focused on providing the best social.

Once you have an account, you can connect to the service through the module, and follow the instructions.

Analytics and Stats modules

Most of these create a new section in the "Stats" page of your PrestaShop installation. Many are installed by default. Therefore, if some of PrestaShop's statistics are not useful to you, you can disable them here. Note that stats are also resource-consuming tools; therefore, if your server is slow or has little disk space, you should limit your stats options to the bare essentials.

Many of these modules are described in detail in the "Understanding Statistics" of this user-guide. In this section, we will only describe the ones that are not enabled by default (that is, two modules among the 25 in this section).

Best manufacturers

This module adds a "Best Manufacturers" option to the list of available statistics.

In effect, the module enables you to have a better view of which manufacturer's product are the best-selling on your shop. In return, you might want to more frequently restock with the products from the best manufacturers.

Google Analytics (ganalytics)

This module makes it easy for you to install a Google Analytics script on your shop. You will then be able to enjoy the statistics tools offered by Google.

You must have a Google Analytics account to make this module work. You can create one on http://www.google.com/analytics/.
Once you have one, follow the Analytics instructions to create a profile for your shop. You will receive a unique identifier. Use it in the module's "username" field and save it. Google Analytics will start gathering statistics about your visitors.

Do read all the instructions provided by the module.

Billing & Invoicing modules

Avalara - AvaTax

Sales Tax is complicated. AvaTax makes it easy.

Doing sales tax right is simple with Avalara. They do all of the research and automate the process for you, ensuring that the system is up-to-date with the most recent sales tax and VAT rates and rules in every state and country, so you don't have to. As a cloud-based service, AvaTax eliminates ongoing maintenance and support. It provides you with a complete solution to manage your sales tax needs.

European VAT Number

This module enables your customers to fill in their VAT number in their details. The VAT can be fetched through a web service, based on your country.

The configuration screen is therefore quite straightforward:

- **Your country**. Choose your shop's country.
- **Enable checking of the VAT number with the WebService**. Tell PrestaShop that you want to retrieve the VAT for your country.

The VAT field appears only when the customer enters his or her company name in the address field.

Drop Shipping modules

Ecopresto Dropshipping

Ecopresto dropshipping is a platform that allows you to integrate many products in your shop in a few click.

Front Office Features modules

Many of these are installed by default. Therefore, if some of PrestaShop's functionalities are not useful to you, you can disable them here.

Banner block

Displays a banner at the top of your store's home page (depending on your store's settings).

Make the banner very wide while keeping the content centered, so that the banner can adapt to all device sizes.

Add Sharethis

Adds social count buttons on the home page, for the following social networks: Twitter, Facebook, Google+ and Pinterest.

You must have a Sharethis button in order to use this module: http://www.sharethis.com/.

Once you have an account, enter your Publisher Pub Key in the module's configuration page, validate, and the buttons will appear on your homepage.

Cart block

Displays the products that your customers added to their carts; on all the pages. Visitors can then see their choices while shopping, change the quantity of product they are ordering, and delete or add a coupon. By clicking on "Shopping Cart", they see the "Shopping cart summary" of all products added to their cart, and their quantity.

You can configure the cart to use Ajax, which means that any change that the uses makes to his shopping list will apply immediately instead of reloading the page. The Ajax setting is not compatible with all themes, be sure to test it thoroughly with your own theme.

You can also set the maximum number of products that your cart should display.

Categories block

Displays a list of your product categories on your shop.

You have a few configuration possibilities:

- **Maximum depth**. If you have a great number of categories, or with long names, you might prefer to not break your design and limit the number of sub-levels that should be displayed.
- **Dynamic**. When enabled, sub-categories are hidden by default, and the customer can choose to display them. This is great for preserving space

and avoiding clutter: if disabled, this module displays all categories and all their sub-categories.
- **Sort**. Most of the time, you should keep the category sort to alphabetical, for easier perusing. But the "By position" sort enables you to choose which categories should be at the top, and thus promote these.
- **How many footer columns would you like?**. Enables you to choose the number of columns in the "Category" block of your footer.

CMS Block

Adds a block with several CMS links.

The first section, "CMS Block configuration", has one option:

- **CMS blocks**. You can have your CMS content be displayed either in the left column of your shop, or the right column. You can edit the content of the existing page by clicking on the 'edit' icon on the right of its name, or add new blocks of content on either side by clicking on the "Add new" button.

The second section, "Footer's various links configuration", has four options:

- **Display various links and information in the Footer**. You can choose to not display any CMS page in the footer, simply by unchecking this setting.
- **Footer links**. The CMS pages linked from this section appear at the bottom of the site. This is where shop owners tend to place informational pages: legal notice, terms & conditions, etc.
- **Footer text**. You can add one line or paragraph of text below the list of CMS pages in the footer. Write it in as many languages as needed.
- **Display "Powered by PrestaShop"**. Adds a line with a link to prestashop.com. Note that this line is located between the links and the footer text.

> When you delete the footer text, PrestaShop might give you this error: "Please provide footer text for the default language".

> This is because when you first enter a footer text, PrestaShop replicates it in all the available languages. When you delete the text, you must therefore delete it from all the available languages: first delete the text from the default language, then click on the language selector next to the text field, choose another language, and delete the content of the field again. Do this for every language. You can then save your changes, and PrestaShop will not display the error anymore.

When you delete the footer text, PrestaShop might give you this error: "Please provide footer text for the default language".

This is because when you first enter a footer text, PrestaShop replicates it in all the available languages. When you delete the text, you must therefore delete it from all the available languages: first delete the text from the default language, then click on the language selector next to the text field, choose another language, and delete the content of the field again. Do this for every language. You can then save your changes, and PrestaShop will not display the error anymore.

Contact block

Allows you to display extra information about customer service:

- **Phone number.** This should be a dedicated customer service/support number, not a way to contact the sales section or the partnership program (if any). If you do not provide customer service by phone, leave this field empty.
- **E-mail.** Again, this should be a dedicated customer service/support e-mail address.

This information appears in the footer by default.

Contact information block

Adds a block to add some information about contacting the shop:

- **Company name.** Your company's name might be different from your shop's name. Indicating the full name brings trust to your brand.

- **Address**. Your headquarters' address, or if it applies, your main shop address. Do not give your own personal address, as you certainly do not want customers to come knock at your door. If you do not want people visiting or sending your letters, leave this field empty.
- **Phone number**. Your business phone line. Again, do not give your personal number here. If you do not have a dedicated business line, leave the field empty.
- **Email**. Your business e-mail address, where you want to receive any correspondence (often including support requests).

This information appears in the footer by default.

Cross-Selling

Displays a "Customers who bought this product also bought..." block on each product page. You can set the number of products to be displayed (default is 10).

Currency block

Adds a little interface feature where customers can choose which currency will be used to display prices, as well as how the customers will pay for their orders. The block appears in the header (top part) of your shop, and only displays the installed currencies. To add a currency or configure the existing ones, go to the "Currencies" page, under the "Localization" menu.

Custom CMS information block

Adds a block containing information for your customer, retrieved from your CMS pages.

You have two custom blocks by default, each with an edit button. Click that button will give tou access to and a text editor, where you can enter the basic information for your home page. That editor features an "HTML" button, which makes it possible to enter specific HTML tags, and using custom classes and such, which you can then style with CSS.

Customer data privacy block

Adds a block to display a message about customer data privacy. The configuration screen simply presents you with a big text area. It is up to you to fill it up with your data privacy policy.

This is an important text, as people online are more and more worried about privacy. Providing a clear policy of how you handle their private information brings trust to your brand – and also ties you legally to respect it. You should never copy/paste a policy from another site, but write your own, based on your country's privacy laws.

Customer reassurance block

Adds a block to display more information to reassure your customers. This block appears in the footer of the default theme. It was previously called "Bloc reinsurance".

The default sample pages are:

- **Money back guarantee**. Says Wikipedia, "A money-back guarantee is essentially a simple guarantee that, if a buyer is not satisfied with a product or service, a refund will be made."
- **In-store exchange.** The text should explain that the customer can bring any unwanted product to your physical store in order to make an exchange with another model, or get a refund. If you do not have a store, you certainly should delete this page.
- **Payment upon shipment**. The customer only pays for the order once it has been shipped. It is not recommended for smaller shops.
- **Free shipping**. This is where you indicate your shipping policy. All shipping can be free, or you can choose to have it be free starting with a certain amount, for instance.
- **100% secured payment processing**. Typically, because you rely on third-party payment services such as PayPal or Moneybookers, you trust them with your money exchanges, and so should your customers. You can paste information about each payment service in this page.

These are only sample pages: they do not have any content by default. It is therefore up to you (and your legal team) to fill it with the proper text. If some

of the sample policies do reflect your business, you should delete them.
Click on the 'edit' icon at the right in order to add text that fits your shop's trust features. You can remove or add pages as you see fit.

Facebook block

Displays a new block on your home page with a link to your store's Facebook page, a Like button, and photos of people who liked your page.

Facebook sharing block

Adds a block to display a link "Share on Facebook" on product pages. Clicking the link directs the customer to his or her Facebook page, with a pre-filled link to the product.

Favorite Products

Adds an "Add this product to my favorites" link on each product page, only visible to logged-in customers. They can then access their list of favorite products by going to their account page and clicking the "My favorite products" link.

Featured Products on the homepage

With this module, you can choose which products to highlight by placing them on your homepage.

In the configuration page, you can set the number of products you want to show. Once this value is saved, go into the configuration page of a product of your choice ("Catalog" menu). Select "Home" as the category into which the product appears, in addition to its current categories (do not remove its original category). Save your change, and you product will appear on your shop's home page.
Repeat for all of the products that you want to place on the home page.

FIA-NET Sceau de Confiance

France only.

Turn your visitors into buyers by promoting trust in your site.

FIA-NET is a French third-party e-commerce trust partner: it protects both customers and online shops against credit card frauds and other malevolent activities.

You have to be a FIA-NET partner in order to use the module. Ask for more information here: http://www.fia-net-group.com/form_partenaires_fianet.php?p=185. Once you have your account details, you can configure the module with them, and the FIA-NET logo will be displayed on your front page. This logo is well known in France, and lets visitors know that your shop is trustworthy.

When configuring the module, you can choose to use the Test mode or the Production mode. The Test mode enables you to perform some test purchases and see how the FIA-NET system reacts.

Home Editorial

Adds a block to the central column of your homepage, with an image above a text, both of which you can edit by configuring the module.

You can move the block around in your design using the Live Edit tool.

The homepage is the first thing your visitors experience when they discover your shop. Therefore, be sure to make it pleasant and efficient, and to update it regularly. Make sure to translate the text in as many languages as your shop supports.

Image slider for your homepage

Adds a slider block on your homepage's central column, where you can define a set of images that will be displayed one after the other, with a sliding motion.

The module's configuration screen presents you with two sections:

- **Settings**. You can set the size of the block, the time to wait between two images, and whether the slide should loop or not.

- **Slides list**. You can visually arrange the images' order by drag-and-dropping their individual blocks.
  Three icons at the right of each block enables you to enable/disable the image, edit its settings, or remove it from the set altogether.

Adding/editing an image

> Make sure that all the images have the exact same size, and that this size is reflected in the block's own size (in the "Slider configuration" section).

Clicking the "Add Slide" link brings you to a new screen.

- **Select a file**. Note that you can have text on the image, and indicate the language of that text using the language selector.
  Additionally, this means you can have a different image for each language. But be aware they these images will be tied: same position, inability to delete one without deleting the others, etc.
- **Title**. The title appears in the "Slides configuration" section, and helps you sort the images.
- **URL**. You can choose to send the customer to a given page of your shop when he or she clicks the image. This is useful when the image promotes a certain product, category or manufacturer.
- **Legend**. The alternate text to be used if somehow the image cannot be loaded. This is essential for accessibility.
- **Description**. The text appears when the mouse pointer hovers over the image.
- **Active**. You can disable an image whenever needed, for instance when the discount it promotes ends.

Language block

Displays a block of the available languages at the top of the homepage. This block enables the customer to choose the language in which he or she wants the shop to appear. If you do not want the customers to be able to change the shop's languages, then uninstall this block.

Layered navigation block

Displays a block with layered navigation filters. Layered navigation enables the customer to define cumulative criteria to filter category products, little by little providing more details in order to reduce the number of displayed products. This is a great tool for customers who know the details of what they want (color, condition, price range...), but are unsure how to find it.

When configuring the module, you are presented with 4 sections:

- **Indexes and caches**. This module heavily relies on database index and its own content cache.
- **Existing filter templates**. A filter template is the kind of navigation to which the customer has access to.
- **Build your own filter template**. You can build various templates, which will serve as the basis for what the customer sees.
- **Configuration**. You can further detail the way this module operates.

Indexes and caches

In order to work properly, layered navigation needs to be kept up-to-date with your latest products, product attributes and product prices – unless these never change. You should therefore regularly re-index the data, using the buttons provided here. They each have specific actions:

- **Index all missing prices**. Only adds to the index the prices that were not indexed before. Much faster than the next button.
- **Rebuild entire price index**. Adds to the index all the prices, whether they were already indexed before or not. Much slower than the previous button when you have many products.
- **Build attribute index**. Adds to the index all the product attributes.
- **Build url index**. Adds to the index the URLs for all the products.

You should update your indexes every time your products' data changes. As this can prove pretty painstaking or even boring, PrestaShop enables you to trigger the indexing automatically, using cron tasks. Add the provided URLs to your crontab, and you will not have to handle this yourself anymore. If you do not know about cron and crontab, ask your webhost about it.

Existing filters templates

Layered navigation is based on templates, or groups of criteria. There is one by default, named "My template", which makes use of all the available filters. You should create templates more adapted to your content or needs.

You can have as many templates as needed. This section enables you to edit and delete them when necessary.

Build your own filters template

The template builder enables you to specify what kind of filters your customers should have access to.

Creating a new template requires only three easy steps:

1. **Select categories**. You can either create filter for the whole site, or on a per-category basis.
   You could for instance have the whole site display the price filter, while some categories can have additional filters.
   When choosing "Specific categories", a small window opens where you can choose in which categories this filter should be available.
   Note that filters do not automatically apply to sub-categories of the selected category: if there is no product on your "Home" category, then the layered navigation will not appear there.
2. **Selected filters**. The number of available filters depends on the content of your shop. Six default filters will appear here: price, weight, condition, manufacturer, available stock and sub-categories. Along with these are the attribute groups for all products in the selected categories (with the number of products). Check a filter's box to move if from the "Available" section to the "Selected" one. You can move the filters up and down with your mouse cursor, which will influence their display in the front-page.
   Each filter has a two drop-down menu included:
   - **Type of display**. You can choose how the filter is displayed to the customer. The visualization depends on the type of the filter.
     - Numerical (price & weight): check-box, radio button, drop-down list. Note that only the check-box setting allows for multiple selection.

- Alphabetical (all others): slider, inputs area, list of values.
    - **Limit**. If some of your categories have too many choices for a given filters, you can limit the number of displayed items using this selector.
3. **Name your template**. Customers will not see the name, but it will prove very useful to you when you have to edit one template among the dozen or hundred you may create in the lifespan of your shop.

Note that saving the filter will not save the whole configuration: you have to save the filter first, then click on "Save configuration".

Configuration

Two options are available:

- **Hide filter values with no product is matching**. If disabled, you will still see filters, even if they are useless because of the lack of matching product (which can make the layered navigation over-crowded with options).
- **Show the number of matching products**. Displays the number after the name of the filter, between brackets. If there is no matching product, it will display "(0)".
- **Show products from subcategories**. The filter applies to more than just the current category.
- **Category filter depth (0 for no limits, 1 by default)**. If the above option is enabled, you risk having too many products taken into account, and lose the interest of layered navigation. The depth is of 1 by default, but you can use even deeper sub-categories.
- **Use tax to filter price**.
- **Allow indexing robots (google, yahoo, bing, ...) to use condition/availability/manufacturer filter**. These four filters help you define whether search bots should be able to browse your navigation and index it. This can prove beneficial for SEO (search engine optimization).

These options apply to all templates and filters.

Link block

With this module, you can add links to the sites you want, or to pages of your shop.

The configuration page is divided in three sections:

- **Add a new link**. Enables you to specify the link's name and URL, and whether it should open in a new page or not.
  When adding a link, do not forget the "http://" part. For instance, http://www.myprestashop.com.
  Note that it is often said that opening a link in a new page is bad practice. At the very least, you should keep your shop's own page in the same window.
- **Block title**. Enables you to rename the link block itself, and even link to a page from the block's title.
- **Settings**. Enables you to sort the links. By default the links are ordered by most recently added link. If you want to invert this setting, select instead "by oldest links" from the drop-down list.

At the bottom of the page, you will find all of the links that you have entered. If you would like to modify the links, click the edit icon. To delete a link, click the trashcan icon.

Manufacturers block

Displays a block of manufacturers/brands.

The block's content can be displayed in two ways: either as a list of links, or as a drop-down list. It can even display both, with the text links being limited in number, whereas the drop-down list gives access to all the manufacturers. Manufacturers are displayed alphabetically.

My Account block

Displays a block containing links to the logged customer's various account pages: previous orders, package tracking, product returns, registered addresses, available coupons, etc. Once the client is connected, this block is displayed.

My Account block for your website's footer

This is the equivalent to the "My Account block" module (see above), but specifically designed to be used in the theme's footer.

New products block

Displays a block presenting the recently added products, in order to make them more visible. With this block, you can drive more traffic to your new products. You can set the number of visible links by configuring this module.

By default, a product is considered as new if it has been added to the shop's catalog in the last 20 days. You can change that setting in the "Products" page under the "Preferences" menu.
If you do not have recent product, displaying this block will hint that you do not renew your catalog much. Therefore, it is not recommended to enable the "Always display block" option for this module.

Newsletter block

Displays a block which invites your shop's visitors to subscribe to your newsletter.

In the configuration screen, you can set several options:

- **Would you like to send a verification email after subscription?**. This is important, as it prevents unsuspecting people to be subscribed without their knowledge.
- **Would you like to send a confirmation email after subscription?**. Likewise, a customer should always confirm they he or she chose to be subscribed to your newsletter. This way they cannot say you are sending them spam without their consent.
- **Welcome voucher code.** You can thank new subscribers with a voucher code. For instance, you can offer them 10% off their next order.
  To create a new voucher code, go to the "Cart rules" page under the "Price rules" menu. See how to create a voucher in the "Creating Price Rules and Vouchers" chapter.

Payment logos block

Adds a block to display all payment logos.

The module's configuration page enables you to choose where to display these logos. Therefore, you should first create a CMS page where you would put the payment logos and descriptions for all the payment services you support, then link to that page from the module's configuration page.

Permanent links block

Adds a block on the front-end which displays permanent links to your CMS pages, such as sitemap, contact, etc.

Product Comments

Enables logged-in customers or visitors to leave a message on your product page. Comments will appear in a new tab right on the product page, next to the "More info" section. They can also rate your products, between 0 and 5 stars. You can also manage comments from this module, such as moderate them or delete them.

Logged-in customers can also report spam or useless comments to you: when a comment is displayed on a product page, it has two options:

- "Was this comment useful to you?" If the customer clicks "No", other visitors will see this.
- "Report abuse". If the customer clicks this button, the comment goes to the "Reported comments" queue.

The configuration screen gives you access to several sections:

- **Configuration**.
  - **All comments must be validated by an employee**. This makes sure that no spam or insult ever appears on your live site, which could ruin your content. Note that in some countries, validating content is akin to publishing them yourself, and therefore can make you responsible for their content.

- o **Allow guest comments**. You can allow non-logged visitors to publish comments too. Be careful, as this can greatly increase spam comments.
- o **Minimum time between 2 comments from the same user**. This prevents spam bot to fill your inbox with comments – or at least limits the impact.
- **Moderate Comments**. If you chose to have comments validated by your staff before they are public, they will be displayed in this section, and can choose to put them offline if you feel they are detrimental.
- **Reported Comments**. Customers can click a "Report abuse" link on any comment, which will bring it to your attention here. You can choose to dismiss the report and accept the comment, or remove the comment altogether.
- **Add a new comment criterion**. You can motive your customers to leave comments by providing them with criteria, or "themes": text fields with a title indicating what the comment should be about, such as "scent", "taste", "robustness". This helps your customers come up with ideas for their comment.
  - o **Name**. The name is visible to your customers, so choose a short and specific one.
  - o **Apply to**. You can choose to have the chosen criterion field appear on all products ("Valid for the entire catalog"), or on a set of products.
    If you choose to restrict the criterion to a subset of your catalog (either some categories or some products), a new section will appear after saving your criterion: "Manage criterions scope". See below.
  - o **Active**. You can disable a criterion at any time.
- **Manage criterions scope**. This section only appears when you have at least one criterion that is restricted to a subset of your catalog.
  In the drop-down list, choose the criterion for which you want to set the scope. The page will reload with a table of all your categories or products (depending on the scope choice). Check the boxes for all the items that apply, and validate.
- **Manage Comments**. This is where all the public comments appear. You can choose to delete them by clicking on the Delete icon, either one by one or in batch.

Product Payment logos block

Displays payment logos right on the product page. The configuration page makes you choose an image – which you have to build yourself by combining the logos of the payment methods you accept.

Products category

On each product page, displays suggestions of other products that are in the same category. This module is particularly useful for discovering what your shop has to offer.

In the configuration page, you can choose whether to display the other products' prices or not.

Product tooltips

Displays live notifications on your shop. This module helps the visitors know what is happening on your shop in real time. Whenever a visitor visits a product's page, three kinds of notification can be displayed over the content at the top right of the page:

- The number of people who are currently also watching this page. In effect, it displays the number of people who have been on this page in the last 30 minutes, 30 being the default value, which you can change using the "Lifetime" option.
- The last time this product has been bought.
- The last time this product has been added to a cart.

The first option is always a nice thing to have. The other two are a bit trickier: on a successful product, it can be nice to see it has been recently bought; on the other hand, less-successful products will be seen as failures if they have not been bought for a long period of time.
This is why the "Do not display events older than" option is important: make sure not to change it to double-digit number, or you will without doubt make fewer sales of already-disappointing products.

RSS feed block

Adds a block displaying an RSS feed. A RSS feed is a website content syndication format, which enables anyone to display the latest content from a website on another.
With this module, your visitors can stay informed about news from a site that you specify in the field provided in the module configuration. The RSS feed will then appear on the front of your shop in a block. Visitors can sign up for the RSS feed in this block.

This module has three configuration options:

- **Block title**. Give the block a comprehensible name: you might not want your visitors to think that the content displayed is from your own website.
- **Add a feed URL**. Do not put your shop's address in this field, as it could create an error.
- **Number of threads displayed**. Usually, a RSS feed contains 10 to 20 of the latest articles from the source website. You could limit that to 5 or fewer, in order to not clutter your homepage with content other than your products.

RSS products feed (RSS Feed)

Enables you to generate a RSS Product feed for your shop's catalog. A RSS feed is a website content syndication format, which enables anyone to display the latest content from a website on another.
With this module, loyal customers will be able to get regular updates about products added to your catalog, by adding this feed to their own feed reader, without the need to subscribe to your newsletter. Also, other websites will be able to display your new products on their page. Finally, search engines may use it to discover your new content.

> In case of a multistore installation, you can display the new products from one shop, right in the sidebar of another of your shop using its RSS Feed Block module.

If you would rather not have your content be available to anyone online, disable this module.

Send to a Friend module

Displays a "Send to a friend" link at the bottom of every product pages. Clicking it opens a window where the customer can enter the name and e-mail of the person who he wants to tell about this product. The e-mail sent contains a simple link to the product's page.

This module can be important, because as a shop owner, you want to give your customers the opportunity to spread knowledge of your products and your shop.

Social networking block

Allows you to add extra information about social networks where your customers can find you. Specifically, you can indicate your account URLs for:

- **Facebook**. Avoid using your own userpage! Try to create a page for your shop/company instead.
- **Twitter**. Likewise, use your company's user account, not your CEO's.
- **Your RSS feed**. A RSS feed is a special file that is generated automatically by your shop, and can be used by RSS readers tools (such as Google Reader) to send your latest news to your customers. While it is not a social network, it is an important aspect of sending regular news out there. Note: you must have the "RSS products feed" module installed in order for this to work.

Store locator block

Displays a block with a link to the store locator. If you do not have any physical location where customers can buy or at least retrieve products, then be sure to disable this module.

Your list of physical stores is available in the "Store Contacts" page, under the "Preferences" menu. By default, there are a handful of sample stores lists, which you should delete in order to replace them with your own.

The configuration page simply enables you to choose a picture to display as the link to the store locator.

Suppliers block

Displays a block of suppliers.

The block can display two types of content: either as a list of links, or as a drop-down list. It can even display both, with the text links being limited in number, whereas the drop-down list gives access to all the suppliers.
Suppliers are displayed alphabetically.

Tags block

Each of your products can have tags added to its description page. Basically, they help create on-the-fly categories of products which have the same tags, but this module makes tags even more useful by adding a block in one of the theme's columns, where the most popular tags are displayed in order of importance, with the most prominent ones using a bigger font.

In the configuration page, indicate how many keywords should appear.

Top horizontal menu

This is an important module: it adds a whole new block at the bottom of the header, where you can display links to the various categories and pages of your shop.
This is very useful, as it helps your customer quickly find their way through your shop. You can have simple links or menus with sub-menus, thus enabling customers to have a good bird's eye view of your content.

Theme configurator

Helps you configure some aspects of your theme.

The configuration page for this module serves two purposes.

First, it gives you direct links to the most usual front-office settings: from this module, you can enable and disable a dozen of features, such displaying social buttons or the Facebook block. You can also access the Live Configurator (Live Edit) from here.

Second, the Theme Configurator itself makes it possible for you to easily attach images with links on specific home page hooks: home, top, left, right, footer. Each available language has its own tab with its own hooks that you can edit from here.

Top-sellers block

Adds a block displaying the shop's top selling products.

The configuration page enables you to set if the block should be displayed even when there is no product or even no product sale yet.

> The block is not present in the default theme at first. You will have to hook it to a location, for instance the right column.
>
> To hook the module to the right column, go to the module's configuration page, then:
>
> 1. Click the "Manage hooks" link at the top. You are taken to the "Positions" page.
> 2. As you can see in the "Positions" page, the module does not appear in any hook. Click the "Transplant a module" button at the top right to hook the module.
> 3. In the hooking tool, select "Right column blocks" from the "Hook into" drop-down list.
> 4. Save your change, then reload the homepage to see the module's block appear. You can then change the module's location by using the Live Edit tool.

Top horizontal menu

Adds a new horizontal menu to the top of your store.

The "Menu top links" section of this module helps you build your menu with links to a selection of pages, categories or to individual products.

User info block

Adds a block that displays information about the customer:

- Link to his or her cart, with a quick view of its content.
- Link to the customer's account.
- Link to log out of the shop.

Viewed products block

Displays the latest products that a customer has recently consulted. You can set the number of products shown using the "Products to display" field.

Wishlist block

Adds an "Add to my wishlist" link on all product pages. Logged-in customers can then build a wishlist of products from your shop, and send it as a link to their friends. A customer can have many wishlists.

The module also adds a "Wishlist" block on every pages of the shop, which only the customer can see. The block is there so that the customer knows exactly what is in it, and can review it regularly. The block features a "My wishlists" link to access the wishlists management tool.

The module's configuration page enables you to view your customers' lists: simply select a customer in the drop-down list to have the page reload with the chosen customer's lists, then choose a list to display.

Marketplace modules

eBay Marketplace

This module enables you to easily bring your product catalog on eBay.

You must have an eBay account to make this module work. Create one on http://www.ebay.com/.
Then, configure your module with eBay login and click on the "Register the module on eBay". This will link your shop to eBay, using a specific token. From there on, follow the module's instructions.

Neteven Marketplaces

Neteven and PrestaShop have set up a European partnership in order to help you to manage your catalogue on the marketplaces of your choice. Developed in close collaboration with the technical teams at PrestaShop, Neteven can now offer you the most complete marketplace management module:

- Free installation
- Quick configuration
- Automatic stock update
- Define product assortment by marketplace
- Define shipping costs by marketplace
- Detailed vision of listings online by marketplace
- Auto repricing tool
- End of transaction management (tracking number, cancellation and refund management...)
- Permanent synchronization of stock and orders between Prestashop, Neteven and the marketplaces

Neteven is fully integrated into your Prestashop account. The module is free and the business model is based on success. Install the Neteven module for PrestaShop for free and enjoy personalized support for efficient marketplace distribution.

Mobile modules

Brow.si

This module seamlessly adds powerful features to your online store when accessed from a mobile device to help your customers easily search, discover, share and purchase your products wherever they are on your site.

You must have a Brow.si account in order to use this module.

Shopgate M-Commerce

Shopgate is the world leader of mobile shopping solutions. We create a mobile optimized website for your store and shopping apps for iOS and Android.

Shopgate connects your offline marketing strategy to mobile commerce by connecting your advertising to your mobile device.

Payment Security modules

Certissim

FIA-Net is a **French** third-party e-commerce trust partner: it protects both customers and online shops against credit card frauds and other malevolent activities.

You must already have a FIA-Net account in order to use the module. You can ask for one here: https://www.fia-net.com/marchands/devispartenaire.php?p=185.
Then, configure the module with your login, your password, and your Site ID, and finally choose whether you want to use the module in Production mode or not. You must also indicate the global business type of your shop. Additionally, you should indicate the business type of each of your categories, the carrier type of each of your carriers, and what kind is your default carrier.

Once the settings are in place, a FIA-Net logo will appear on your homepage, and your orders will be analyzed by FIA-Net to make sure no fraud is happening.

PrestaShop Security (prestafraud)

PrestaShop Security is a service provided by PrestaShop in order to protect the security of your shop against fraudulent payments.

If you do not have an account, you can create one directly from the module: fill in the first field with your e-mail, and check that the second one does contain the correct URL for your shop, then click "Create Account". You will have to agree with the terms and conditions of the module.

If you do already have an account, change the top selector accordingly in order to make the full configuration form appear. Fill the various fields with the exact details of your shop, along with your Shop ID and Shop KEY (as provided by PrestaShop Security).

Once the settings are in place, orders will be analyzed by the module to make sure no fraud is happening.

Payments and Gateways modules

With PrestaShop, you can accept your customer's transactions through several different payment methods, such as checks, bank wire, cash on delivery, and some partner modules such as Hipay, Moneybookers, PayPal and others. They are already included in your store and are ready to be used. However, it is necessary to configure them.

PrestaShop has three basic payment modules, that you can use out-of-the-box, without any 3rd-party service registration:

- Bank wire
- Cash on delivery
- Payment by check

Additionally, several modules for 3rd-party payment services are available by default:

- Adyen
- Hipay
- Kwixo
- Ogone
- PayPal Europe
- Skrill

Many are developed by the PrestaShop developers themselves, in close collaboration with the services' developers. All are safe to use.

Note that you can find many other payment modules on Addons: http://addons.prestashop.com/en/4-payments-gateways.

Adyen

Adyen is a global payment company leading the way in defining a new generation of payment services. Built from the ground up on cutting-edge technology, its global payment platform enables businesses to accept payments from anywhere in the world using the same technical platform and administrative back office interface. It supports all relevant sales channels, including online, mobile and Point-of-Sale (POS), and can process 224 different payment methods and 187 transaction currencies used across six continents. Meeting the highest standards of security and stability, the Adyen payment platform is certified PCI Level 1.

The Adyen module makes it possible for your shop to accept payments by credit card.

You must have an Adyen account in order to use this module.
Then, configure the module with your Merchant Account, your Notification username password, your country code ISO and your language locale.

Finally, you can choose the payment modules.

Once the settings are in place, your customers will see the payment options that you chose appear in the shop's front-office as part of the available payment methods.

Bank wire

This module makes it possible for your customers to pay by bank wire transfer.

In order for the module to accept bank wires, you need to fill out the address of the bank that your store uses, along with the name of the account owner and the other account details (bank branch, IBAN number, BIC, etc.). This is done in the module's configuration page.

Once the settings are in place, your customers will see the "Pay by bank wire" option appear in the shop's front-office as part of the available payment methods. After they have selected it and indicated their choice of currency, your bank information will appear.
Note that when receiving the customer's bank wire, you **must** manually change the payment status of the order to "Payment accepted" in your back-office. This is different from a credit card order, where the payment is carried out automatically. You can find the order and change its status in the "Orders" page, under the "Orders" menu.

Cash on Delivery (COD)

This module makes it possible for your customers to tell you that they will pay for the product directly to the one who delivers it. This could be in-store, or you could have your own employees bring the product to your customers. This is mostly useful for local deliveries.

There is no configuration page: your customer can simply choose to pick up their products at your store.

FerBuy

Thanks to FerBuy's new All-In-One payment service your customers can enjoy new level of simplicity, security and flexibility. FerBuy offers instant credit to Customers up to 500€ per purchase and total credit up to 1500€. Merchants will enjoy growing revenue due to maximized conversion rate, and full security as FerBuy will cover full credit and fraud risk.
FerBuy is a payment method allowing merchants to offer risk free payments by invoice and in installments.

Hipay

The Hipay module makes it possible for your shop to accept payments by credit card.

You must have a Hipay account in order to use this module. Click on the "Create an account" button to do so.
Then, configure the module with your Account number, your Merchant password, and your Site ID.
Finally, you can choose the authorized age group, pick the payment methods you want to accept, and restrict the module to certain zones.

Once the settings are in place, your customers will see the "Hipay" option appear in the shop's front-office as part of the available payment methods.

Kwixo

The Kwixo module makes it possible for your shop to accept payments through Kwixo's own payment service. Kwixo is part of FIA-Net, the French e-commerce trust seal, and two major French banks, Crédit Agricole and LCL. Customers need to have a Kwixo account, and to have registered a credit card on their service.

You must have a Kwixo account in order to use this module. You can reach the sign-up form by clicking on the link in the configuration page.
Once you have an account, configure the module with your Login, Password, Site ID and Key, and indicate whether you want to work in Test or Prod mode, your delay for delivery, the type of payment you want to accept.
From there on, complete the configuration information by indicating your main product types in the "Categories settings" section, and your carrier types in the "Carrier settings" section.

Once the settings are in place, your customers will see the "Kwixo" option appear in the shop's front-office as part of the available payment methods.

As a merchant, you have access to a Kwixo-specific back-office at the URL located in the "Manage your payments in your Kwixo administration interface" section.

Ogone

The Ogone module makes it possible for your shop to accept payments by credit card.

You must have an Ogone account in order to use this module. You can reach the sign-up form by clicking on the "Create your free Test account!" button in the configuration page.
Then, configure the module with your PSPID, your SHA-in signature, your SHA-out signature, and finally choose whether you want to use the module in Test mode or in Production mode.

Once the settings are in place, your customers will see the "Ogone" option appear in the shop's front-office as part of the available payment methods.

Payment by check

This module makes it possible for your customers to pay by sending a check (or "cheque" in UK English) to you.

To configure payment by check, open the module's configuration page and indicate the order to which your customer must make the check payable – most of the time, your name or your company's name and your address. You can also add details about the transaction.
This information will then appear to the user at the end of the ordering process, after clicking the "Pay by check" option, and validating with a click on the "I confirm my order" button.

Note that when receiving the customer's bank wire, you **must** manually change the payment status of the order to "Payment accepted" in your back-office. This is different from a credit card order, where the payment is carried out automatically. You can find the order and change its status in the "Orders" page, under the "Orders" menu.

PayPal Europe

Europe only.

The PayPal module makes it possible for your shop to accept payments by credit card or PayPal's own payment service.

You must have a PayPal account in order to use this module. You can reach the sign-up form by clicking on the "Sign Up" button in the configuration page. Then, configure the module and enter your API Username, your API Password and your API Signature. You should also make sure the other settings fit your needs.

Once the settings are in place, your customers will see the "PayPal" option appear in the shop's front-office as part of the available payment methods.

Realex

Realex Payments processes payments in excess of £18 billion per annum for over 12,500 online retailers, including some of the world's leading brands –

Vodafone, Aer Lingus, Virgin Atlantic, Paddy Power, Chain Reaction Cycles, AA, 32Red, notonthehighstreet.com to name a few.

Skrill

Skrill has been moving money digitally since 2001, offering online payment solutions for businesses and consumers, allowing them to pay and get paid globally. Over 36 million account holders and 158,000 merchants already trust Skrill.

The Skrill module by Moneybookers makes it possible for your shop to accept payments by credit card.

You must have a Moneybookers account in order to use this module. You can reach the sign-up form by clicking on the image in the "Open Account" section. Then, click on the "I already have a Moneybookers account" button to continue configuring the module.

Once the settings are in place, your customers will see the "Moneybookers Skrill" option appear in the shop's front-office as part of the available payment methods.

Sofort

Sofort Banking: The attractive payment method for you.

Your customers simply pay in your online shop just as they are used to: By entering their familiar online banking login details and confirmation codes ensuring a maximum level of security. You will receive a real-time transaction confirmation immediately after the transfer has been listed. And all this at unbeatable low fees!

Trustly

Allow your customers to pay from their online bank account directly in your web-shop. The only payment method in Spain with 90% bank coverage.

Pricing and Promotions modules

Loyalty Program

PrestaShop's loyalty module offers an advanced tool for building automatic vouchers depending on your customers' purchases and reward points.
Your customers get a certain amount of loyalty points depending on the amount they spend at your shop.

The configuration screen enables you to be very specific about the generation of vouchers:

- **Ratio** and **1 point =**. Basically, the conversion rate of money spent in reward points, and of reward points in money won. The module uses the default currency of the shop.
  The **Ratio** field indicates how much money the customer should spend in order to get 1 reward point.
  The **1 point =** field indicates how much money the customer gets for each reward point.
  By default, the settings are 10 and 0.20, which means that the customer wins $2 for each $100 spent on your shop.
- **Voucher details**. This is simply the name of the voucher. It will appear in the customer's account page.
- **Minimum amount in which the voucher can be used**. You can set a limit in order to keep customers from using vouchers as soon as there is the smallest sum of money on it. By default, it is set to 0, which mean that they can use the voucher whenever they want.
- **Apply taxes on voucher**. You can choose to have the voucher be part of the tax calculation in the invoice, or exclude it from that calculation.
- **Points are awarded when the order is**. By default, the reward points are awarded only when the product is delivered. But you might prefer to have them awarded at any other order status, for instance as soon as it is paid.
- **Points are canceled when the order is**. Points can be canceled if the order reach a given status, for instance if it is canceled.
- **Give points on discounted products**. Choose whether or not the customer get points when buying discounted products.

- **Categories**. You might want the awarded vouchers to not work in some specific categories. Choose which ones are okay using this form.

Loyalty points progression. This section contains the messages that are displayed to the customer. You might want to change the phrases to better fit your shop's "attitude". Also, make sure to translate the phrases in all your supported languages.

Specials block

This module adds a block to your shop's home-page, where the customer can discover the current specials, as configured in your catalog.

You can add more products to the "Specials" by giving them a discount: go to the product's catalog page, open its "Prices" tab on the left, and in the "Specific prices" section, click the "Add a new specific price" button to open the creation form.

SEO modules

Google Sitemap

This module helps you build a sitemap for your shop, and keep it up to date.

In order to optimize your SEO, it is essential to have a sitemap, which is a XML file that lists all the products and pages on your shop. This file will enable search engines to index all pages easily and efficiently. Your products will then appear perfectly in the search engines when a visitor conducts a search. You can create a sitemap for PrestaShop, and be indexed by all the search engines that support the file format (Google, Yahoo, Bing...), using tools such as Google's Webmaster Tools.

The configuration page has few options: indicate how often your store (including the catalog and the CMS page) is updated on average, check the boxes of the page you do not want to include in the sitemap, and click the "Generate Sitemap" button.

Once you have finished configuring the module, click on "Update sitemap file". You are then given the Sitemap's address (e.g., myprestashop.com/sitemap.xml).

Copy this URL to save it to your Google Webmaster Tools account. The module will then show you the file size and the number of pages indexed. Remember to update it regularly so that search engines index your content perfectly.

The last part of the configuration page gives a cron link. A good sitemap is an updated one, and unless you are willing to click on the "Update sitemap file" button every time there is a change on your shop, you might want to have your server do the work for you. Create a cron task with the given URL, and never worry about this again.
If you do not know what a cron task is, ask your web host.

Search and Filter modules

Quick search block

This module installs a block with search field in your shop front-end. The search block can display results as soon as the first letters are typed.

The module is installed and enabled by default, and you should leave it enabled to facilitate visitor's navigation.

Shipping and Logistics modules

Carrier Compare

This module enables the customer to compare carrier possibilities before continuing with the checkout process.

This module is very straightforward: just install it to display its option on your front-office.

> All the available carriers must have their fees properly set. This is done at the bottom "Shipping" page, in the "Fees by carrier, geographical zone, and ranges".

The module configuration page only has one option, "Refresh carrier list method". This enables you to display a carrier either only when all the information is set, or at any time.

Date of Delivery

This module displays an approximate date of delivery during the checkout process.

The configuration page has two sections:

- **Carrier configuration**. The module relies on indications from your carriers. You must therefore add rules for each of your carriers, by clicking on the "Add a new carrier rule" link.
- **Settings**:
    - **Extra time when a product is out of stock**. Estimate the time it might take for your team to re-stock products. This is only useful if customers can order out-of-stock products (the option for this is in the "Products" preference page, in the "Products stock" section).
    - **Extra time for preparation of the order**. Estimate the time it might take for your team to prepare an order.
    - **Preparation option**. If your packaging team also works on weekends, indicate it, as the module takes this into account.
    - **Date format**. The format in which the expected delivery date is displayed. It uses PHP date() format: each letter has a meaning, as explained in the indicated link. The default, "l j F Y", means the date will be displayed in the format "Saturday 21 January 2012". There are many more parameters that you can use to build the date format as you see fit: see http://www.php.net/manual/en/function.date.php.

Adding a new carrier rule is pretty straightforward:

- **Carrier**. Choose the carrier for which you want to add the rule. If the wanted carrier is not there, you must create it in the Shipping > Carriers page.
- **Delivery between**. Set the timeframe in which the chosen carrier promises to deliver products. You have to gather this information from the carrier itself.
- **Preparation options**. Some carriers also prepare their packages on weekend days, so as to send them first thing on Monday morning. Be sure to indicate it if so.

You should create as many carrier rules as necessary.

Globkurier

Poland only.

GlobKurier.pl is one of the biggest national leaders in delivering shipments. We provide domestic and international services to more than 200 countries. Our main aims are competitive price, speed and security. With GlobKurier.pl you can be sure that your shipments always come on time. Moreover we offer convenience of using our services.

GoInterpay

Bring over 200 payment methods to your checkout with one simple integration.

Kiala Advanced (Kiala contract holders only)

This module makes it possible for your customers to have their parcels delivered in a Kiala collection point. Kiala points are widely available in France, and also in other select European countries.

You must have a Kiala account in order to use this module. You can reach the sign-up form here: http://www.kiala.com/.
Then, configure the module with all the information about you and your shop in the form in the "Kiala Module Status" section.
The "Country settings" section further down helps you indicate in which countries you want to make Kiala delivery available for your customers.
Finally, the "Kiala advanced settings" section adds a few more options:

- **Export folder**. The local folder where the module will save its export, containing a lot of useful information.
- **Prefix for order and parcel number**. You can have a shop-specific prefix for your shop, which make it look more personalized for your customers.
- **Export on each order?**. You may prefer to have several order-specific export files rather than a big one.
- **Parcel tracking criterion?**. Should the parcel be tracked on a per-customer or a per-order basis? If you are unsure, keep it to per-order.

Once the settings are in place, your customers will see the "Kiala" option appear in the shop's front-office as part of the available delivery methods.

Mondial Relay

This module enables you to display rates for delivering in Mondial Relay points. This service is available in France, Luxembourg, Spain and Belgium.

You must have a Mondial Relay account in order to use this service. You can reach the sign-up form here: http://www.mondialrelay.com/.
Then, from the module's configuration page, click on the "Account details" icon and enter the necessary information, as provided by Mondial Relay: Webservice Enseigne, Code marque, Webservice Key, Etiquette's Language and Weight Coefficient. The Etiquette's Language can only use the languages that are enabled on your shop; you can enable more language from the "Languages" page, under the "Localization" menu. Click "Update Settings" in order to connect your shop to the Mondial Relay webservice, and from there on, follow the module's instructions in the "Shipping" and "Advanced settings" screens.

Once the settings are in place, your customers will see the "Mondial Relay" option appear in the shop's front-office as part of the available delivery methods.

So Colissimo

This module enables you to display rates for deliveries via SoColissimo, a service by La Poste, France's historical postal service. This service is available mainly in France.

You must have a SoColissimo account in order to use this module. This is done by calling La Poste from a French phone, using this number: **3634**.
Then, configure the module with your SoColissimo information: ID So, key, preparation time, overcost, URL So, Fancybox, Supervision and Supervision URL.
A full documentation is available (in French) as a PDF file, which you can find under the "Documentation" link on the configuration page.

In order to finalize the installation, copy/paste the two final URLs in your SoColissimo back-office.

Once the settings are in place, your customers will see the "SoColissimo" option appear in the shop's front-office as part of the available delivery methods.

TNT Express France

France only.

This module enables you to display rates for deliveries via TNT express services. This service is available worldwide.

You must have a TNT account in order to use this module. You can reach the sign-up form here: http://www.tnt.com.
Then, configure the module with your TNT login, password and account number, all in the "Account settings" tab.
From there on, you can keep configuring the module using the "Shipping Settings" and "Service Settings" tabs. This last tab enables you to be very specific about the delivery service you want to make available for your customers, as well as any additional charge you might require depending on the package's weight.

Once the settings are in place, your customers will see the "TNT Express France" option appear in the shop's front-office as part of the available delivery methods.

Tracking - Front office

This module completes PrestaShop with an integrated affiliate program feature, which enables your affiliates to access their own statistics.

The affiliate program tool is located in the "Referrers" page, under the "Stats" menu. Once you have installed the "Tracking - Front office" module, these affiliates can access their statistics by going to http://www.example.com/modules/trackingfront/stats.php.

To create a new affiliate, click the "Add new" button, and in the creation form, add the affiliate account username and password, then specify the fee they receive per click, per order and per percentage of sales.

Click on the header of the "Help" section to display instructions on how to set up the referrer URLs.

The "Technical information - Expert mode" enables you to use regular expression instead of plain text URLs.

Smart Shopping modules

Shopping Feed

This module makes it possible to list your shop and its products on hundreds of price comparison sites and marketplaces (mostly French), through the Shopping Flux service (http://www.shopping-flux.com/).

You must have a Shopping Flux account to make this module work. You can request one using the form at the bottom of the module.
Then, configure the module with your login and token, and set the various options to your likings.

You can find more information about this module on the Shopping Flux website: http://www.shopping-flux.com/module-prestashop-shopping-flux/.

Twenga Price Comparison

This module makes it possible to list your shop and its products on Twenga. Twenga is an online open shopping platform that aims to bring together "all online products and shops in one place". This module exports your list of products to their service, and helps you track your sales through them.

You must have a Twenga account to make this module work. You can reach the sign-up form here by clicking the "List my website on Twenga" button.
Then, configure the module with your hashkey, login and password. The module will take care of sending your catalog to Twenga, and you should be listed within 72 hours.

> Each visitor who comes to your website from Twenga will cost a few cents. You can view the pricing grid by clicking on the "Twenga Prices" link at the bottom of the configuration page.

Translation modules

Textmaster

Adds support for Textmaster's translation features, which provides you with translation for the content of your store (CMS pages, product description, category names, etc.)

You must have a Textmaster account in order make this module work. Note that translations are not free.

Other modules

Dashboard Activity

Adds a block on PrestaShop's Dashboard, with an overview of the current activity on your store.

Dashboard Goals

Adds a block on PrestaShop's Dashboard, with your store's forecast.

Dashboard Products

Adds a block on PrestaShop's Dashboard, with a table of your latest orders and a ranking of your products.

Dashboard Trends

Adds a block on PrestaShop's Dashboard, with the evolution of your stores main numbers (along with a graphic).

Managing Shipping

How you choose to ship your products is a key element to the management and success of your store. You must account for the great variety of available methods, which can mix carriers, regional and international taxes, package weight and the price of a product itself. Luckily, PrestaShop makes it easy for you to handle it all in just a few screens.

A product's shipping price is basically calculated using either of two methods: the total price of the order, or the total weight of the order. This is how most carriers calculate their shipping fees, and this is why you should fill-in the weight setting when creating a product in the catalog, and also why you absolutely must indicate the per-weight and per-price costs for each carrier in the "Carriers" page.

> PrestaShop computes shipping price according to a system of either weight ranges or price ranges. That system can only work for one or the other of these types of range.

The shipping settings work closely with the local settings of your PrestaShop installation. While in PrestaShop 1.4 some of these settings were also found in the "Shipping" menu, since version 1.5 all local settings have been moved in a new menu, named "Localization". This is where you will be able to edit geographical zones, countries, currencies, etc. Therefore, make sure to have a serious look at the "Localization" menu, which is explained in the next chapter of this guide, "Understanding Local Settings". For instance, in order to create a complete carrier in PrestaShop, you must have clearly defined your geographical zones before; this is done in the "Zones" page under the "Localization" menu.

The way carriers are created in PrestaShop was completed reworked in version 1.5.5.0: you now build new carriers using the Carrier Wizard.

Managing Carriers

You must have carriers added to your PrestaShop installation – that is, a clear indicator of who will deliver your products. It might be just yourself or your shop (for instance if you are selling downloadable products, or only work locally), but as soon as you are actually sending packages using stamps and a 3rd-party delivery such as your local postal service, or FedEx, UPS and such, then you must have their details added to your shop's database. This will enable your customers to better choose which carrier to use, based on their delivery ranges, fees and dates.

The "Carrier" page presents you with a list of all your current carriers. From there, you can directly change their status, indicate that why of shipping is free or not, and change their position when presented to customers.

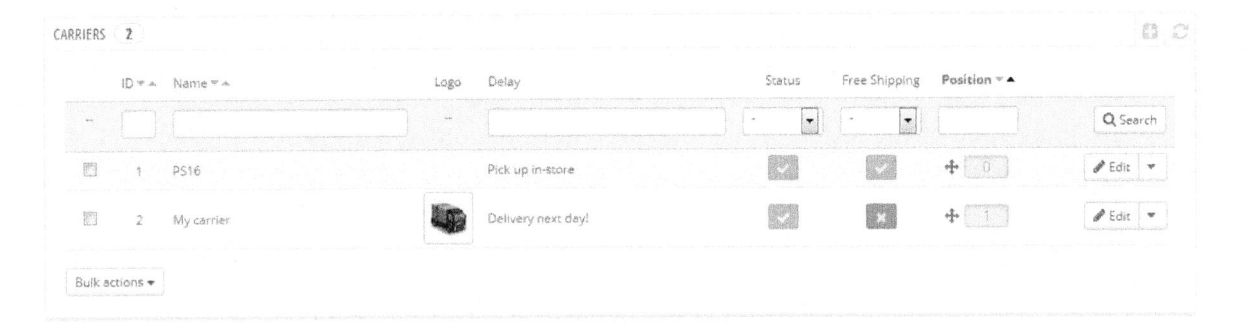

By default, you have two carriers in your database:

- Your own shop: This represents your physical store, where customers can supposedly come and pick up their products themselves. It has no price range or weight range set.
- "My carrier": This is a sample carrier and should not be used in production. It has one price range (from $0 to $10,000) and one weight range (from 0 kg to 10,000 kg).

It is up to you to remove these default carriers and add new ones for your customers. At the very least, you should edit the "My carrier" carrier and replace its data with that of a real carrier: name, details, and ranges.

Creating a New Carrier

In this section, we are going to create a complete carrier, from A to Z, using the Carrier Wizard. You can create as many carriers as you wish.
If one carrier has different shipping services, you should create as many carriers in PrestaShop, and differentiate them with their names.

Many of the details asked by PrestaShop's forms should be provided by your carriers once you have set up an account or are under contract with them directly. Check with them in order to make sure everything is configured correctly.

To create a new carrier, click on the "Add new" button in the "Carriers" page. This will open the Carrier Wizard on the first of its four panels.

Panel 1: General settings

This is where you describe the carrier, giving information that the customer will need in order to recognize and choose the carrier he prefers.

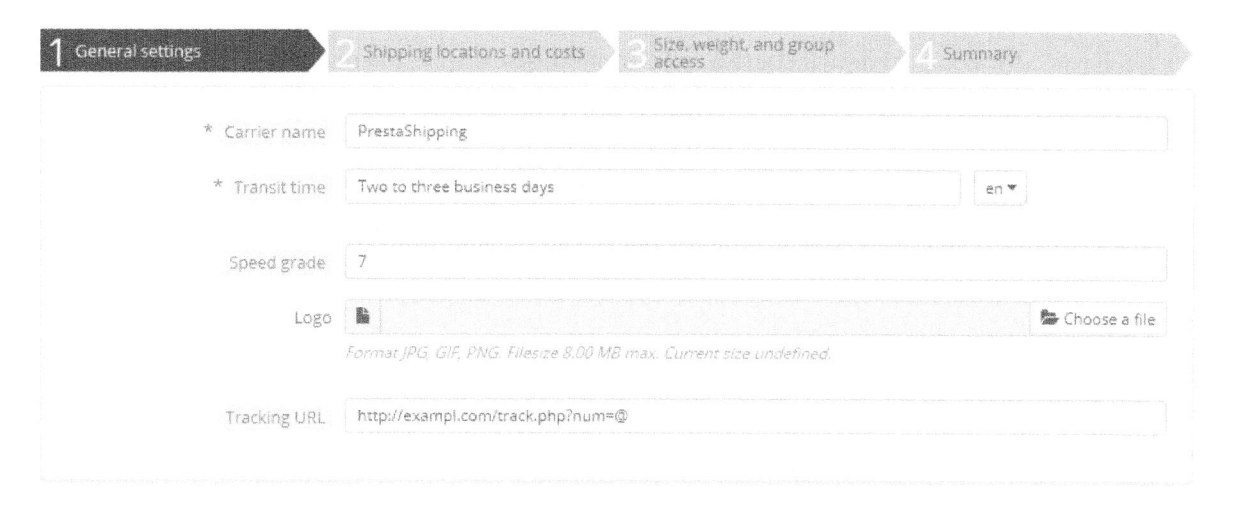

Let's examine all of the information you need to enter:

- **Carrier name**. The name is public, so you should use the official name. If you have create one PrestaShop carrier per shipping services from a single carrier, the name will help you differentiate them.
  You could also add a description of the service. For instance, you could

fill in "PrestaShipping – 500 lbs and over".
You must add a name in order to
- **Transit time**. The estimated time it takes this carrier to deliver your products, written in plain language. This is displayed to customers during checkout. It will help them select their carrier according to the amount of time they are willing to wait to receive their shipment. Customers can often accept to pay more for a faster carrier.
  You must fill this field in all the available languages, especially the default one.
- **Speed grade**. Since the "Transit time" field can contain any text, it cannot be used to compare the carriers' transit times. The "Speed grade" setting enables you to give the carrier a grade, from 0 (very slow) to 9 (very fast). This is then used to sort carriers by their speed grade, and help customers choose the one they prefer.
- **Logo**. Having a logo helps customers choose between different carriers more easily. PrestaShop will resize your image in order to fit in the order form.
  The logo will appear in each panel of the Carrier Wizard, as a reminder of which carrier you are editing/creating.
- **Tracking URL**. This field must be filled with the tracking URL provided by your carrier (if there exists one). For example, France's postal service (La Poste) offers this URL: http://www.colissimo.fr/portail_colissimo/suivreResultat.do?parcelnumber=@.
  When customers finish their purchase, they will receive that URL with the "@" replaced by the tracking number provided by the carrier, making it possible to click that link and see where the delivery process is at.

Click "Next" to reach the second panel.

Panel 2: Shipping locations and costs

Will be applied when the weight is >=	lb 0.000000	lb 5	lb 10
Will be applied when the weight is <	lb 5	lb 10	lb 20
All	$	$	$
Africa	$	$	$
Asia	$	$	$
Central America/Antilla	$	$	$
Europe	$ 5	$ 10	$ 20
Europe (non-EU)	$	$	$
North America	$ 2	$ 4	$ 8
Oceania	$	$	$
South America	$	$	$

Settings shown:
- Add handling costs: NO
- Free shipping: NO
- Billing: According to total weight.
- Tax: No tax
- Out-of-range behavior: Apply the cost of the highest

First, this panel presents a handful of settings:

- **Add handling costs**. Include or exclude shipping & handling costs in this carrier's price, as set in the "Shipping" page.
- **Free shipping**. If enabled, you will not be able to indicate shipping prices.
  If disabled, you will be able to edit the ranges and per-country costs in the form below.

- **Billing**. When billing the customer, PrestaShop can apply one of two behaviors, which you have to set depending on how you carrier handles billing (so make sure to check their documentation about this):
    - **According to total price**. Billing depends on the total price of the order.
    - **According to total weight**. Billing depends on the total weight of the order.
- **Tax**. Indicates if this carrier requires a local tax in order to deliver, and if so, which one. The tax must already exist in PrestaShop (which can be done in the "Taxes" page of the "Localization" menu).
- **Out-of-range behavior**. In case the chosen carrier has not set shipping cost for the required zone or weight, you can indicate how PrestaShop should react. You have two options:
    - **Apply the cost of the highest defined range**. PrestaShop will take the most costly range and apply its conditions.
    - **Disable carrier**. PrestaShop will not suggest this carrier, since it probably cannot deliver this order.

Then comes the important part: the creation of the carrier's range. This is a very important step, as PrestaShop needs this information to present the customer with carriers which can actually deliver the ordered package. Indeed, depending on the order's total price or total weight, some carrier options will not be available while others will only appear at a certain value. You must be very precise when filling these values, and preferably those suggested by each carrier's documentation.

This is where the whole Carrier Wizard takes its name. Here, you will build your carrier's price or weight ranges (depend on your choice for the "Billing" option above), one range after the other, applying your prices for each zone along the way.

For each range, you only need a couple of steps:

1. **Fix the lower and upper limits of the range you are creating**.
   Depending on the "Billing" choice, it will display either "Will be applied when the price is" or "Will be applied when the weight is" for the lower limit, and either "Will be applied when the price is" or "Will be applied when the weight is" for the upper limit.
2.

> Note that the lower limit inclusive (>=) whereas the upper limit is exclusive (<). This means that a range's upper limit can have the same value as the next range's lower value, as the two will not overlap.

3. **Fill in the prices**. As soon as both lower and upper limits are filled, PrestaShop makes the "All" field available to edit. This is a special field: any value you enter in it will be copied into the field for all the available geographical zones, without any action on your part. You can then edit the value of each zone field separately.
   Check the checkbox for each zone the carrier delivers to at this range. If this carrier does not make deliveries in a given geographical zone for this current range, make sure to uncheck its checkbox.
4. **Create the range**. Click the "Add new range" button. PrestaShop will add a new column of zone fields. Start again by fixing the lower and upper limits of this range, then filling the prices per zone.

> The weight and price units are the default ones for your PrestaShop installation, and the ones your products use. You can change these units "Localization" page of the "Localization" menu.

Click "Next" to reach the third panel.

Panel 3: Size, weight and group access

Maximum package height (in)	200
Maximum package width (in)	200
Maximum package depth (in)	200
Maximum package weight (lb)	500

Group access:

	ID	Group name
☑	1	Visitor
☑	2	Guest
☑	3	Customer

This panel presents two sets of options:

- **Maximum package height/width/depth/weight**. You can now indicate the minimum and maximum package height and weight, which are an essential part of choosing a package carrier. The value is to use the default weight and dimension units, as set in the "Localization" page of the "Localization" menu.
- **Group access**. You might want only some user groups to be able to use a carrier. This option serves this purpose.

Click "Next" to reach the fourth and final panel.

Panel 4: Summary

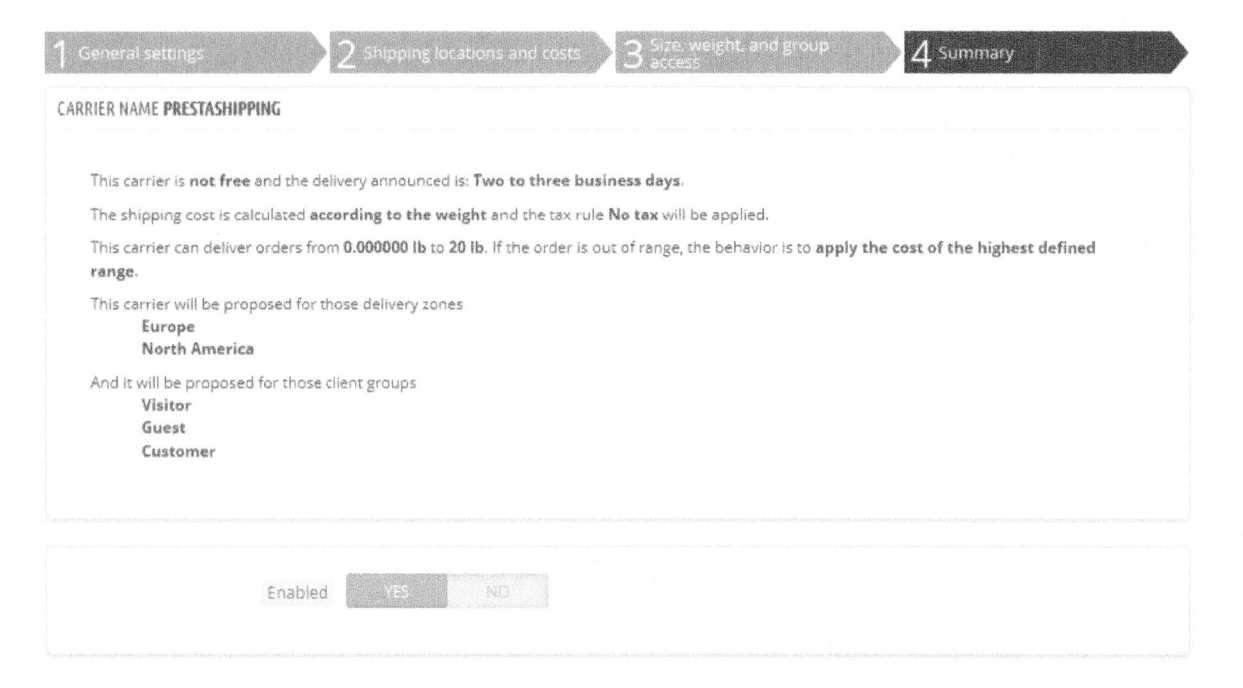

```
1 General settings    2 Shipping locations and costs    3 Size, weight, and group access    4 Summary
```

CARRIER NAME **PRESTASHIPPING**

This carrier is **not free** and the delivery announced is: **Two to three business days**.

The shipping cost is calculated **according to the weight** and the tax rule **No tax** will be applied.

This carrier can deliver orders from **0.000000 lb** to **20 lb**. If the order is out of range, the behavior is to **apply the cost of the highest defined range**.

This carrier will be proposed for those delivery zones
    Europe
    North America

And it will be proposed for those client groups
    Visitor
    Guest
    Customer

Enabled   YES   NO

This last panel gives you an overview of your settings for this carrier.

If some settings are wrong, you can go back to any previous panel by either using the "Previous" button, or directly clicking on the panel's tab.
If you want to save this carrier as a draft for now then come back to it later, disable the carrier using the "Enabled" option at the bottom of this final panel.

Either way, click on the "Finish" button to save your work, and create the carrier.

> When using PrestaShop in multistore mode, another panel is available, and the panel order changes slightly:
>
> 1. General settings
> 2. **MultiStore**
> 3. Shipping locations and costs
> 4. Size, weight, and group access
> 5. Summary
>
> All the panels are as described above. The new one, "MultiStore", makes it possible for you to limit this carrier to a selection of your stores.

Shipping Preferences

The more general settings of you shop's shipping configuration are found in the "Shipping" page, under the "Shipping" menu.

This page provides handling charges settings:

![Handling settings screenshot showing Handling charges: 2, Free shipping starts at: 0 ($), Free shipping starts at: 0 (lb)]

- **Handling charges**. Enter the per-order handling expenses, which will be added to the final purchase price. This is separate from your shipping costs: it is really the cost of you or your employee having to fetch the products, package them and have them shipped. If there is no such cost, leave it at 0.

- **Free shipping starts at (currency)** and **Free shipping starts at (weight)**. Enter the price or weight after which your customers will receive free shipping. For instance, you might choose to offer free shipping when the order exceeds $250. A message will appear to your customers indicating how much more money they need to spend in order to receive free shipping.
  If you do not want to offer free shipping and you do not want this message to appear, leave these values at 0.

The "Carrier options" section gives you access to 3 settings, which impact the front-office in order to help the customer make a choice:

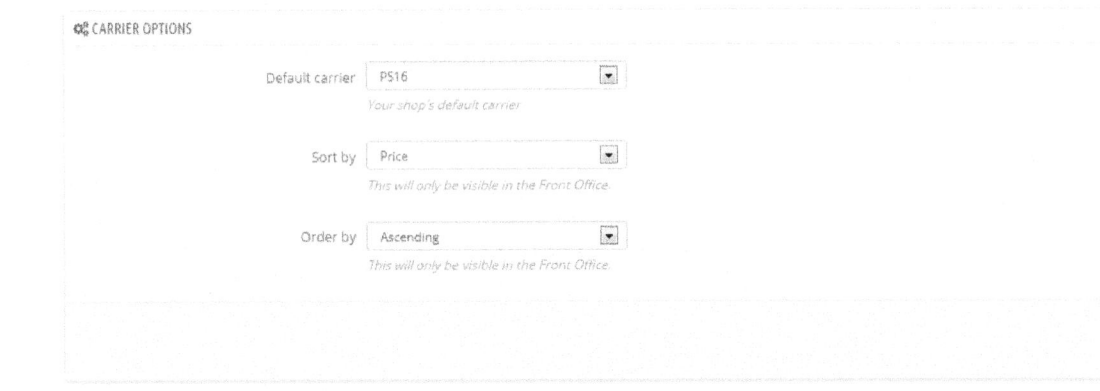

- **Default carrier**. If you have more than one carrier in your system, you might want to promote one to your customers. Besides the carriers themselves, this drop-down list has two contextual options:
  - **Best price**. Depending on the amount of the order, on its weight and its delivery zone, PrestaShop will choose the cheapest price for the customer.
  - **Best grade**. Speed grades make it easier to identify the fasted carriers. PrestaShop will display the carrier which, within the context of the order, will have the shortest shipping delay.
- **Sort by**. When customers are presented with a choice of carriers, you can choose to either sort the list by shipping price or by their position, as set in the carrier list on the "Carriers" page.
- **Order by**. This enables to set the order in which the carriers are sorted:
  - If sorted by shipping fee and with an ascending order, then carriers will be displayed from the cheapest to the most expensive.

- If sorted by position and with a descending order, then carriers will be displayed from the top position of the list, to the bottom position.

Understanding Local Settings

As obvious as it might seem, this is the Internet, and people from all over the world will certainly visit your shop, and order your products. As a shop owner, you must cater for as many customers as possible. This means having your website fully translated in as many languages as necessary, with local taxes, weights and currency units, local geographical zones, etc.

The "Localization" menu appeared with PrestaShop 1.5, and brings together many local settings and tools that used to be scattered in other menus in previous versions.

Localization

The main page under the "Localization" menu enables you to configure the units used for your products.

Import Localization Pack

This section provides you with an extensive list of existing localization packs which you can import. Not only does it set your PrestaShop install with your proper local units, but it also adds many other data:

- **States**. When shipping product to a country, knowing which state it is sent to can prove important, as this might have an impact on local customs and taxes. The added states can be viewed and edited in the "States" page under the "Localization" menu.
- **Taxes**. The real importance of localization is local taxes, and they can be numerous and varied depending on the country or the state. PrestaShop provides you with a basic support for the major taxes and tax rules. The added taxes and tax rules can be viewed and edited in the "Tax" and "Tax rules" pages under the "Localization" menu.
- **Currencies**. Foreign customers will appreciate to be able to convert the prices on your shop into their own currency. You should at least have US dollars and Euros available along of your country's own currency (if not one of those two). Once added, you must activate a new currency using the "Currencies" page under the "Localization" menu, and make sure the conversion rate is correct. The added currencies can be viewed and edited in that "Currencies" page.
- **Languages**. All the public fields on your shop can be created in multiple languages, and it is important you do so for your products name and description, at the very least. Note that importing a language also imports its date format (d/m/Y, m/d/Y, d.m.Y, etc.), among other things. The added languages can be viewed and edited in that "Languages" page under the "Localization" menu.
- **Units**. Weight, dimension, volume, distance: these units are essential in order to correctly describe a product to your customer, and for your own packaging information. They can be viewed and edited on this very page, in the "Localization" section.
- **Change the behavior of the taxes display for the groups**. This is not data to import but a setting that you can change when doing the importation.

As you can see, these additional data are optional: you can choose to import the currency and language for a given country, and not its taxes, for instance.

While you should not add too many local data for fear of overwhelming both yourself and your customers with it, it may be useful to import the localization pack for your most visited countries (according to your stats).

Apart from the default units, **you cannot automatically remove all the data for a given country**; if you need to remove data, you will have to do so manually, in their respective pages under the "Localization" menu.

Configuration

This section groups four default local settings, of prime importance:

- **Default language**. This is the main language for your shop. This setting will influence your back-office's language (including the main language for your products), as well as the front-office. Note that the front-office's language might adapt to the setting of the customer's browser.
- **Default country**. The location of your business. If you have headquarters in many countries, use your main or original country.
- **Default currency**. The currency in which your product's prices are first set. Currencies are added by importing and activating a country's currency. Note that if you change currency after having already set a few product prices, you will have to manually update all the existing prices. Make sure to set that value once and for all.

- **Time zone**. You own time zone. This is useful for daily discount for instance: you know exactly when it starts and ends.

Localization

The physical units presented in this section (weight, distance, volume, dimension) are used both in your product sheets and for your own packaging needs – and ultimately, is essential in your relationship with your carrier.

These values can be set when you import the localization package for a country, but you can edit manually them afterwards. For instance, if you would rather have centiliters instead of liters for the volume unit, change the default "L" to "cL".

The values should be unit symbols from the International System of Units (http://en.wikipedia.org/wiki/International_System_of_Units).

Advanced

This last section asks you to set your server's local language and country, as ISO code:

- For the language: ISO 639-1 code (http://en.wikipedia.org/wiki/List_of_ISO_639-1_codes).
- For the country: ISO 3166-1 Alpha 2 code (http://en.wikipedia.org/wiki/ISO_3166-1_alpha-2).

ADVANCED

| Language locale | en |
| Country locale | us |

These values can be set when you import the localization package for a country, but you can edit manually them afterwards.

Languages

PrestaShop comes multilingual out of the box: there is one default language (the one you used to install it), and many more are available to download.

The "Languages" page manages the languages you will see in your back office and your shop.

The page displays the languages already installed on your shop, along with some information: ISO code, language code, date format (short and full). You can enable or disable a language by clicking on the icon in the "Enabled" column.

Adding a new language is simply a question of importing the localization pack from a country which uses that language (in the "Localization" page). If it turns out this does not work, or that you need something customized, you can add a new language manually, using the form behind the "Add new" button.

Creating a New Language

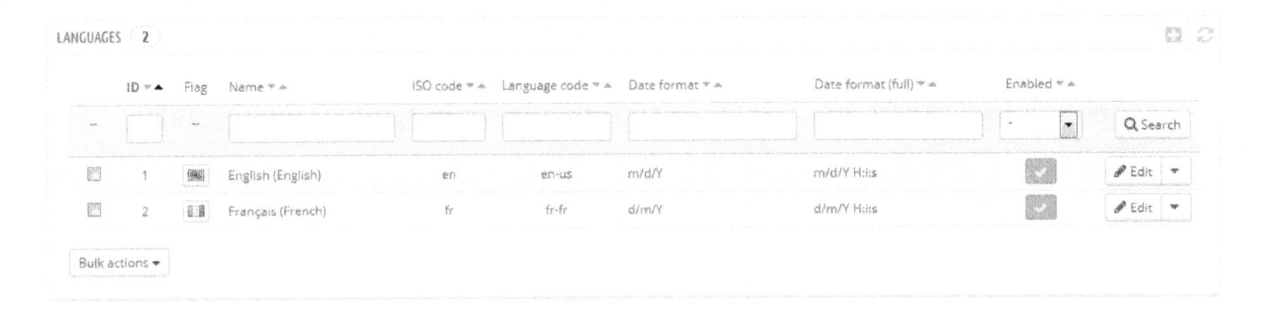

Creating a new language means you will have to translate all of the text for PrestaShop's front-end, back-end, modules, etc., or risk using the default English strings. Translation is made using the tool in the "Translations" page, under the "Localization" menu.

You can also create a new language in order to cater for a language pack that you would have downloaded from the PrestaShop site.

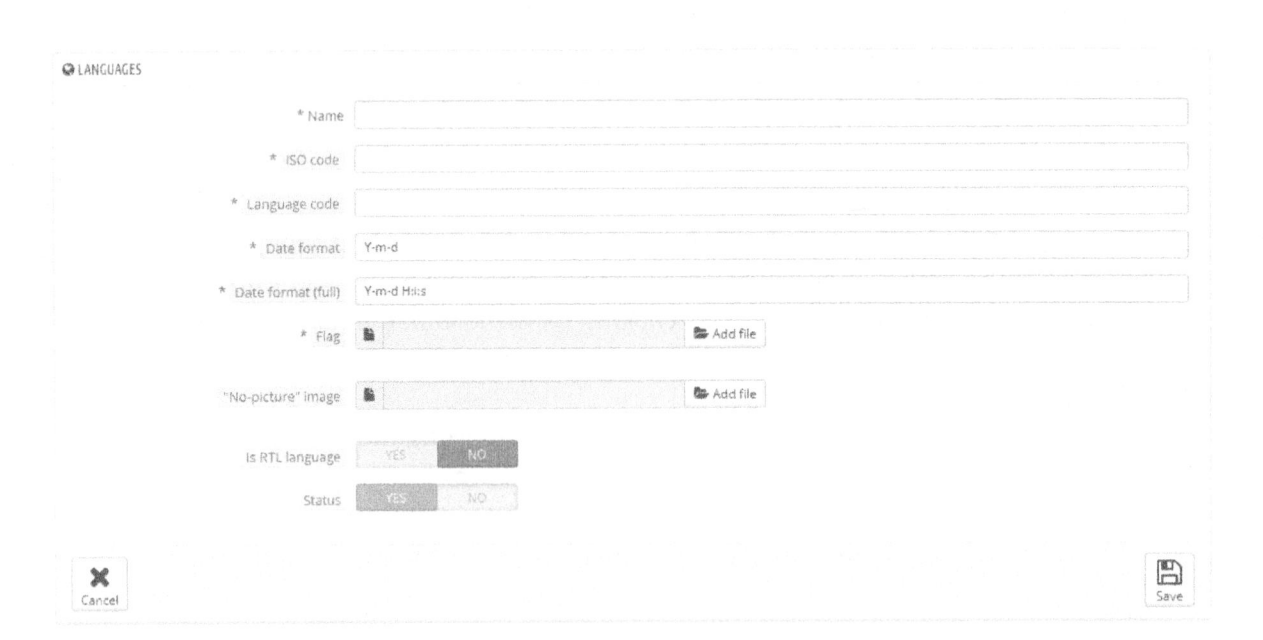

In order to create a new language, you must fill as many of the form's field as possible:

- **Name**. The name is public. If you are creating that language for regional purpose, you may indicate that in the name: "French (Quebec)", for instance.
- **ISO code**. Enter the adequate 2-letter ISO 639-1 code. See http://en.wikipedia.org/wiki/List_of_ISO_639-1_codes for more information.
  If you are importing a language pack, this code should exactly match the one for the pack.
- **Language code**. Enter the adequate 4-letter language code, in the form xx-yy, xx being the language ISO code (same as above), and yy the country ISO code, using ISO 3166-1 alpha-2 (http://en.wikipedia.org/wiki/ISO_3166-1_alpha-2). See http://en.wikipedia.org/wiki/IETF_language_tag for more information.
- **Date format**. Countries do not always share the same date representation (See http://en.wikipedia.org/wiki/Date_format_by_country). Hence, when your shop display 02/08/12, a customer from France will understand "August 2nd, 2012" whereas one from the US will understand "February 8th, 2012" – and a japan customer might even read it as "August 12th, 2002". This is why it is important to indicate the date format tied to your language. The letters used should be that of PHP's date() function: http://php.net/manual/en/function.date.php.
- **Date format (full)**. Same as the date format above, but including the hour-minute format.
- **Flag**. Upload an image of the flag which best matches the language you want to add. It should be 16*11 pixels. You recommend you use the free FamFamFam Flags image set: http://www.famfamfam.com/lab/icons/flags/.
- **No-picture" image**. Upload an image which will be displayed when a product does not yet have a picture. That image is simply a blank image, with "No image" or "No image available" in this language. The picture should be 250*250 pixels. You can find existing "No-picture" images in the /img/l directory of your PrestaShop installation.
- **Is RTL language**. Some languages are written from right to left, most notably those using Arabic script or the Hebrew alphabet

(http://en.wikipedia.org/wiki/Right-to-left). When a PrestaShop theme is well coded, it is able to handle RTL languages - provided it is clearly set as such.
- **Status**. You may disable a new language until you are ready to translate everything.
- **Shop association**. You can make the language only available to a selection of your shops, for instance shops that target a specific locale.

Once your language is saved and enabled, you can import its language pack. This is done in the "Translations" page, under the "Localization" menu. Use the "Import a language pack manually" tool.

Finally, make sure everything works: go to your shop's front-office and click on the flags at the top. Similarly, customers can now select an additional language by using these icons.

Zones

PrestaShop's zones are a list of the world's subregions (http://en.wikipedia.org/wiki/Subregion). It helps categorize countries.

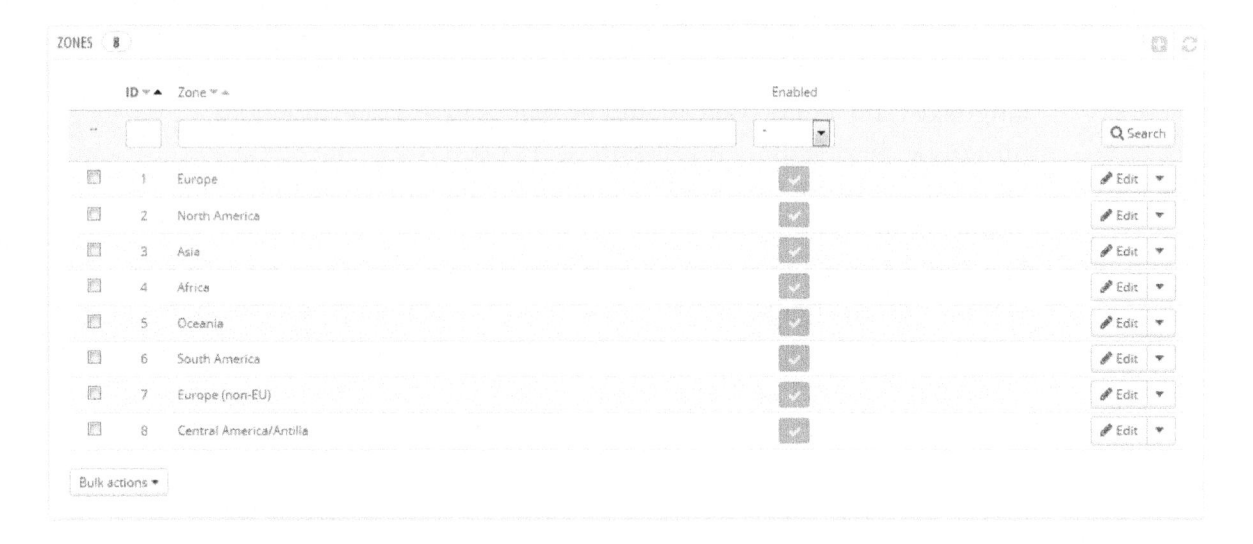

ID	Zone	Enabled	
1	Europe	✓	Edit
2	North America	✓	Edit
3	Asia	✓	Edit
4	Africa	✓	Edit
5	Oceania	✓	Edit
6	South America	✓	Edit
7	Europe (non-EU)	✓	Edit
8	Central America/Antilla	✓	Edit

If needed, you can create more zones: click on "Add New" to display the creation form.

All you need is a name and a status, for instance indicating that you do not allow deliveries in Oceania.

When in multistore mode, you can also associate a zone with a selection of stores.

Countries

Your PrestaShop installation must know all existing countries in order for your customers to clearly indicate where in the world they live.

There are roughly 200 countries in the World, but PrestaShop has 244 registered. This is because some countries include overseas regions are part of the country proper.

For instance, the French departments formerly known as DOM (Guadeloupe, Martinique, Mayotte, Reunion, and French Guiana) nowadays have equals status as the French metropolitan region. Likewise, Alaska and Hawaii are US States proper.

Still, sending a package to Guadeloupe does not mean sending it to France, if only for the shipping fees. Therefore, the list of countries in PrestaShop actually separates the country from the mainland.

Be default, only your own country is enabled. You should enable them one by one, as needed for your customers. If you are unsure which to enable, check your stats to see the countries with most visitors.

At the bottom of the list, the "Country options" section to only display on your front-office the countries that your carriers cover. We recommend that you enable this setting, as it prevents customers from having to scroll through all the country names to find their own.

Adding a New Country

Normally, PrestaShop comes with all current countries in the database. But in the case new ones are created, you would need to add a new country.

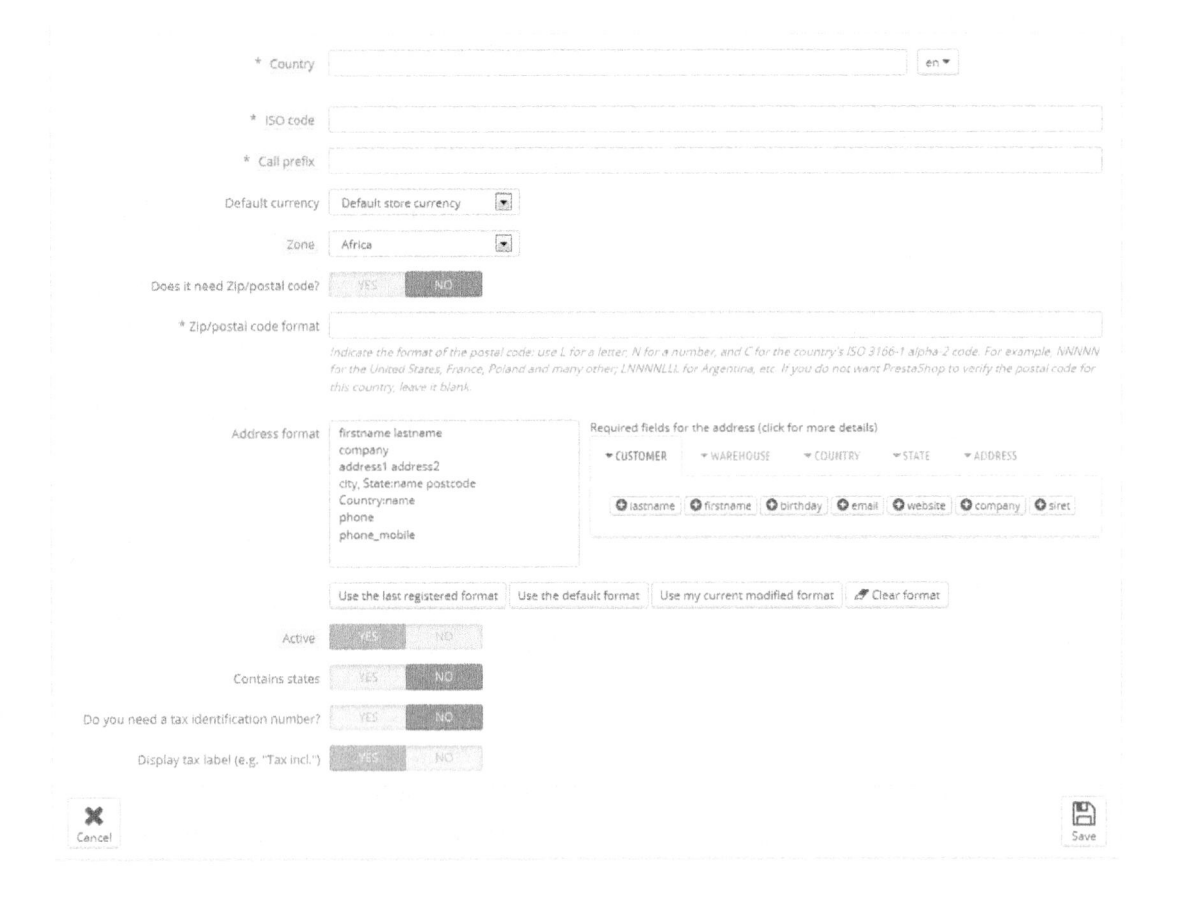

- **Country**. The official name of the country that you would like to add, in all supported languages. Check the country's Wikipedia page if unsure about the name.
- **ISO code**. The country's ISO-3166 code, which you can find on the official ISO page: http://www.iso.org/iso/country_codes/iso_3166_code_lists/country_names_and_code_elements.htm.
- **Call prefix**. Its international call code, which you can find on this Wikipedia page: http://en.wikipedia.org/wiki/List_of_country_calling_codes.
- **Default currency**. You can use your shop's default currency (as set in the "Localization" page, under the "Localization" menu), or one of the other installed currencies. Remember that if needed, you can add a new currency to your shop using the "Currencies" page.
- **Zone**. The world's subregion to which this country is attached. If necessary, you can add new zones using the "Zones" page, under the "Localization" menu.
- **Does it need zip/postal code?**. Indicates whether a user living in this country must give a zip code or not when signing up to your shop.
- **Zip/post code format**. You may also give more detail on the format of the postal code (or zip code). If you do not put anything, PrestaShop will not verify the validity of the zip code when given a new address for this country.
  Use the following codes for the postal code: "L" for one letter, "N" for one number and "C" for the country's ISO code (the one which you entered in the ISO field above).
  If you do not know the country's postal code format, you can rely on this Wikipedia page http://en.wikipedia.org/wiki/List_of_postal_codes. Make sure you do NOT copy/paste the notation from Wikipedia, but to adapt it! For instance, Wikipedia indicates "AAA 9999*" for Malta, so the notation for PrestaShop becomes "LLL NNNN" (without the final *).
- **Address format**. Give details about the address layout, when displaying it to customers. You can click on the various helper links on the side of the text-field in order to add more fields. In live usage, they are automatically replaced by PrestaShop with the data from the customer's account.

Your changes are only saved when you save the whole page. If you have

made a mistake, you can make use of one of the four helper buttons at the bottom of the form, depending on your situation.
- **Active**. A disabled country will not be suggested as an option when a visitor wants to register and create a new account.
- **Contains states**. Indicates whether the country has "states" or not. This adds a new field to the PrestaShop address form. Note that "states" can be regions, provinces, departments... anything that makes sense to that country's postal service.
- **Do you need a tax identification number?** and **Display tax label (e.g. "Tax incl.")**. A Tax Identification Number is an identification number used by the country's revenue service in the administration of tax laws. Not every country needs of even has such a number for business. Inquire about this with the country's revenue service.
- **Shop association**. You can make the country only available to a selection of your shops, for instance shops that target a specific locale.

States

By "States", PrestaShop calls first-level administrative divisions of a country. In the United-States, they are called *states*; in Italy, it is *regioni* (singular: *regione*); in France, it is *régions*; in the United-Kingdom, it is *regions*.
By default, PrestaShop provides you with a set of states: 54 US states and territories, 31 Mexican *estados*, 13 Canadian provinces and territories, 34 Indonesian *provinsi*, 24 Argentinian *provincias*, 47 Japanese *todōfuken*, and 110 Italian *province* (singular: *provincia*).

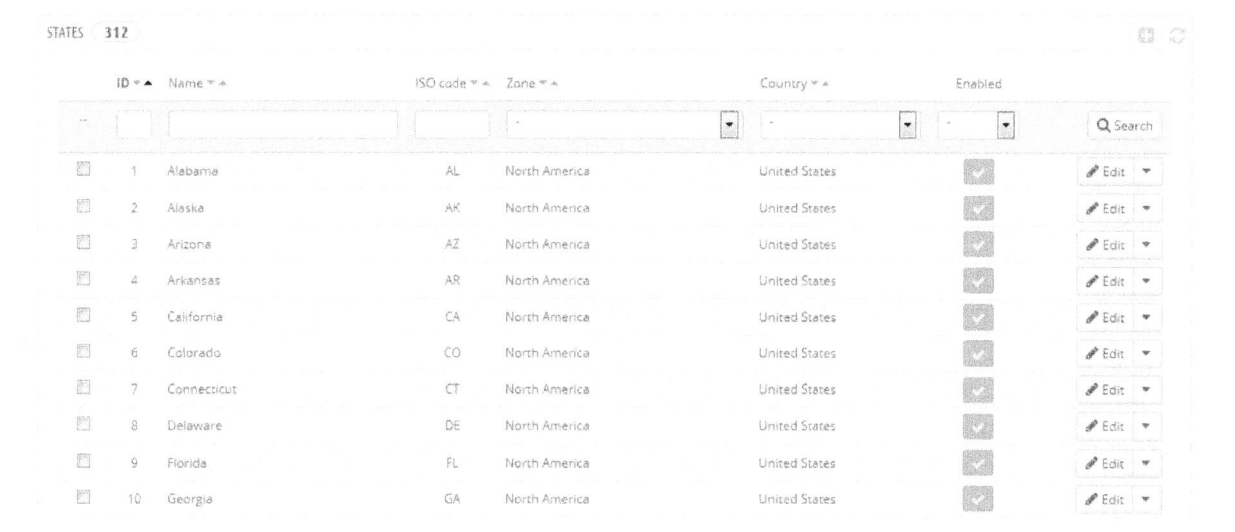

	ID	Name	ISO code	Zone	Country	Enabled	
	1	Alabama	AL	North America	United States	✓	Edit ▼
	2	Alaska	AK	North America	United States	✓	Edit ▼
	3	Arizona	AZ	North America	United States	✓	Edit ▼
	4	Arkansas	AR	North America	United States	✓	Edit ▼
	5	California	CA	North America	United States	✓	Edit ▼
	6	Colorado	CO	North America	United States	✓	Edit ▼
	7	Connecticut	CT	North America	United States	✓	Edit ▼
	8	Delaware	DE	North America	United States	✓	Edit ▼
	9	Florida	FL	North America	United States	✓	Edit ▼
	10	Georgia	GA	North America	United States	✓	Edit ▼

Having states properly defined in your database helps better represent the delivery possibilities of your carriers. These states can also be essential for tax rates calculation, depending on the country. It is therefore important to enter all of a given country's administrative divisions if they are important to your carriers. You can find a list of such divisions on this Wikipedia page: http://en.wikipedia.org/wiki/Table_of_administrative_divisions_by_country.

> The PrestaShop address form currently only lists states which are available for the customer to choose. Therefore, make sure to use a sensible list when adding content to your states list. That is the reason why, for instance, the list contains Italian *province* (second-level administrative divisions) rather than *regioni* (first-level administrative divisions).

Adding a New State

Let's create a new state. Click the "Add New" button to get to the creation form.

- **Name**. The name of the state, as it should be displayed on invoices and the package. It should therefore be in the language of the state's country.
- **ISO code**. The state's ISO-3166-2 code:
  1. Go to this Wikipedia page: http://en.wikipedia.org/wiki/ISO_3166-2,
  2. Click the state's country two-letter code (in the "Entry" column of the main table),
  3. On that page, find the state's code (it should be in a list on the page, or in the text for the smallest countries),
  4. If there is one, remove the country's prefix in order to keep the code under 4 characters. For instance, the full ISO 3166-2 for Devon, in the United Kingdom, is "GB-DEV". Simply use "DEV" as the state's ISO code – it already is attached to the country using PrestaShop's "Country" drop-down list (see next step).
- **Country**. Indicate its country using the drop-down list.
- **Zone**. Indicate its geographical zone using the drop down list. Pay attention not to use the wrong zone, as this can mix up PrestaShop's country and zone settings.
- **Status**. A disabled state will not be suggested as an option when a visitor wants to register and create a new account.

Currencies

PrestaShop can accept a large number of currencies. By default, there is only one standard currency: the one for your country. However, you must add and configure new currencies depending on your customers' needs. Indeed, customers will appreciate the ability to display your shop's prices in their country's currency.

ID	Currency	ISO code	ISO code number	Symbol	Exchange rate	Enabled	
1	Dollar	USD	840	$	1	✓	Edit ▼

The two sections at the bottom of the "Currencies" page are very simple yet essential, as relate to your currencies exchange rates (or "conversion rates"). To quote Wikipedia, "In finance, an exchange rate between two currencies is the rate at which one currency will be exchanged for another. It is also regarded as the value of one country's currency in terms of another currency." Rates change daily, sometimes drastically depending on current events, and your shop should always be updated to the latest values.

> In order to change the default currency, you must go to the "Localization" page of the "Localization" menu, and use the "Default currency" option from the "Configuration" section.
> If the currency you want to use is not available in this option, you must import the currency from one of the countries which use it, using the "Import a localization pack" section of the "Localization" page.

Updating the Currency Rates

In PrestaShop, there are two ways to update your conversion rates:

- **Manually**. In the "Currency rates" section, click on the "Update currency rates" button. This will download the update file from the PrestaShop.com servers using PrestaShop web-service.
- **Automatically**. This is the recommended way. Instead of having to click on the "Update currency rates" button once or thrice a day, you can create a cron task that will trigger the rate file download as often as you feel necessary. Add the provided URL to your crontab file in order to activate automatic update. If you do not know what a cron task or a crontab file is, contact your hosting provider.

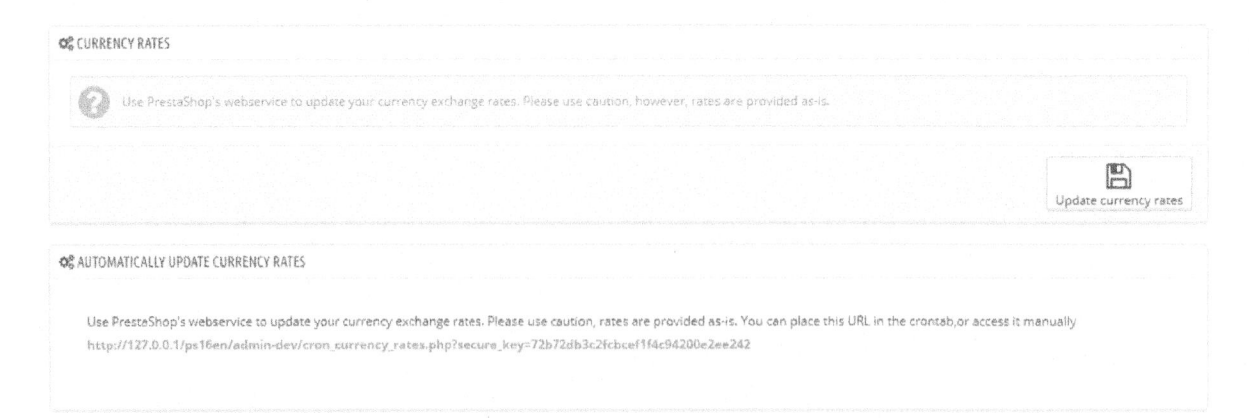

> You can start adding products with minimal information and edit them at will, but before launching your shop, you should at least have this information written down.

Note that the rates are provided as-is: the PrestaShop team does pay attention to have correct rates in these file, but might slightly differ from the actual ones, if only because these rates can fluctuate greatly in a short time.

Adding a New Currency

The easiest way to add a country's currency is to import its localization package. This is done in the "Localization" page, under the "Localization" menu. Once import, you must go the "Currencies" page to enable it.

You might need to add a currency not featured in any the localization packages. In that case, you can use the creation form.

- **Currency**. The name of the currency, preferably in English that as many customers as possible can read it.
- **ISO code**. The currency's three-letter ISO 4217 code. See this Wikipedia page: http://en.wikipedia.org/wiki/ISO_4217.
- **Numeric ISO code**. Its three-digit code ISO 4217 code. Same Wikipedia page as above.
- **Symbol**. The currency's symbol, if any. See this Wikipedia page: http://en.wikipedia.org/wiki/Currency_sign.
- **Exchange rate** (or **Conversion rate** in earlier version). This rate is to be defined according to your shop's default currency. For example, if the default currency is the Euro and this currency is dollars, type "1.31", since 1€ usually is worth $1.31 (at the time of this writing). Use the converter here for help: http://www.xe.com/ucc/.
- **Formatting**. Set up how you want your price to be displayed. The X corresponds to the currency's symbol. You have five possibilities.
- **Decimals**. You can indicate whether your shop should display decimals. While you may choose to have all your prices be a round number, discounts and other price variations might warrant decimals. You can prevent them with this option.
- **Spacing**. Once you have chosen the currency's formatting, you can choose whether to have a space character between the symbol and the price itself. Some languages require this. For instance, Spanish people would use "50€" whereas French people would use "50 €". Choose whichever you feel is best.

- **Enable**. Any currency can be disabled at any time, both from its own edit page, and the currencies table on the "Currencies" page.
- **Shop association**. You can make the currency only available to a selection of your shops, for instance shops that target a specific locale.

Taxes

> Taxes are a complex subject, which should be fully understood as it can have a significant impact on your product prices or your shipping fees. While this user-guide is not meant to teach all the ins-and-outs of taxes, we will try our best to give you pointers.
>
> Taxes are "compulsory contribution to state revenue, levied by the government on workers' income and business profits or added to the cost of some goods, services, and transactions". In short, every product you sell is subject to sales taxes, which depend on your state's tax laws. In effect, you contribute to your state or government functioning (public goods and services) with a percentage of all your sales, as defined by local tax rates.
>
> There are hosts of tax rates in the World, and they vary considerably from one country to another, and even within a single country if it has federal states (USA, Germany, Spain, Russia...). You should therefore make sure to strictly conform to your country's tax laws, and even those of your state or town if they apply to you. Check with your local tax representative as soon as possible in order to get all the official details.

By default in PrestaShop, a tax applies to all countries/states/zones. If order to apply a specific tax rate for a single country or a set of countries (and not some others), you must create a tax rule. The tax rule is then applied on a per-product basis, during the creation of the product ("Prices" tab).

You cannot directly apply a tax to a product; you can only apply tax rules. Therefore, you must first register all relevant taxes, and then create a tax rule for that tax in order to specify the countries the tax applies, and finally set the tax rule to the product.

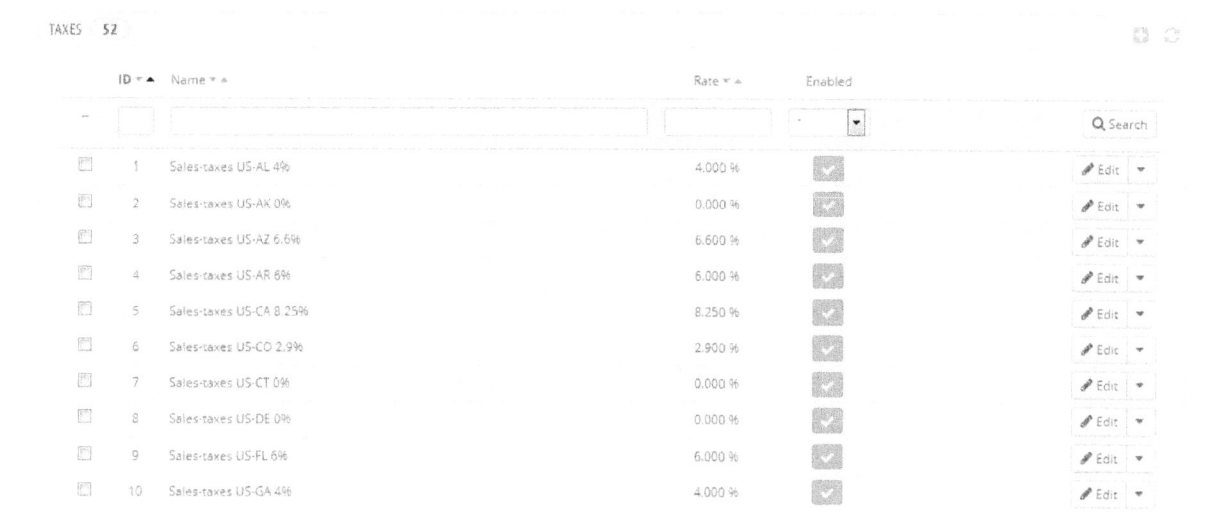

Tax Options

At the bottom of the page is the "Tax options" section. These options apply to the whole shop, and all of the orders.

- **Enable tax**. Whether or not taxes are included in each purchase.
- **Display tax in shopping cart**. You might prefer the customer not to be aware of the taxes that are applied to the order. In that case, disable this option.
- **Based on**. The customer can choose to have the product not delivered at the same address as the one the order invoice should be sent to. This can have a great impact on taxes. By default, PrestaShop bases its tax rates on the delivery address, but you can choose to have them based on the billing address.

- **Use ecotax**. The ecotax refers to "taxes intended to promote ecologically sustainable activities via economic incentives". It is a tax that shop owners pay in order to "feel the social burden of their actions". Learn more about ecotax on this Wikipedia page: http://en.wikipedia.org/wiki/Ecotax.
  Once you have enabled the use of ecotax, all your products' back-office page will feature an "Eco-tax (tax incl.)" field in their "Prices" tab. You should fill that field with the exact value of the tax, which depends on your country's tax laws (it is probably based on the product's price).

If you decide to enable the ecotax after having added products, you will have to edit them all in order to set the tax properly for each product.
Note that if you have set ecotaxes for your products already, and that you choose to disable ecotax, then all your products will lose their ecotax settings. Re-enabling the ecotaxe will mean having to set all your products' ecotaxes again.
The ecotax will also appear to the customer, on the product's page.

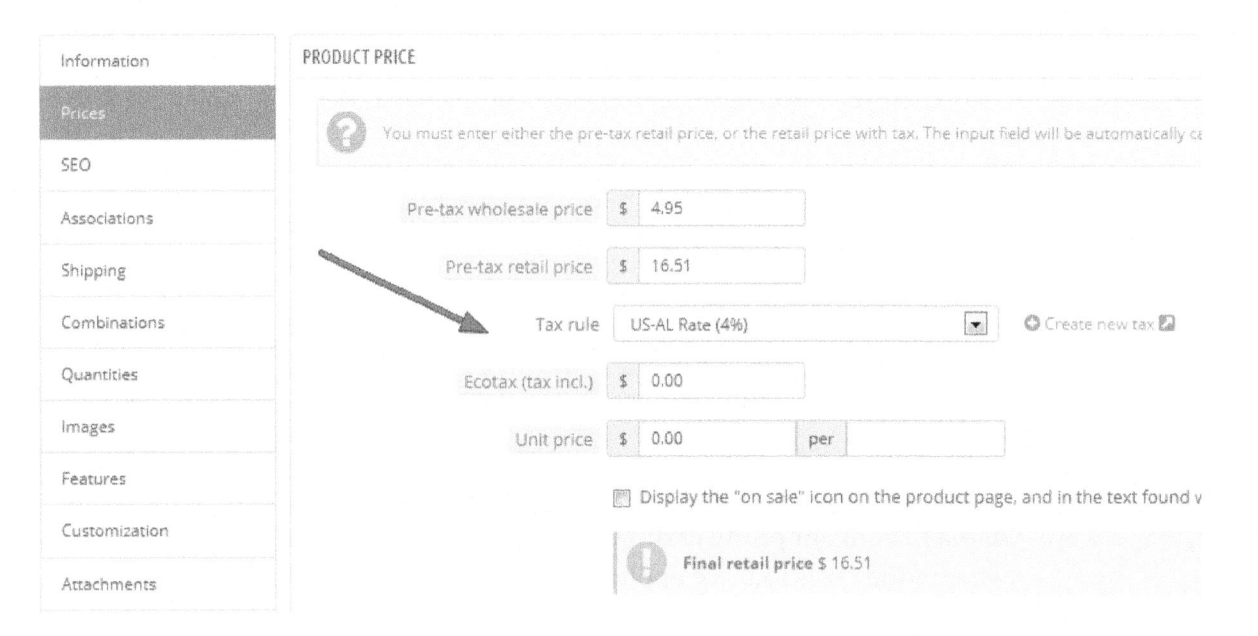

Adding a New Tax

Adding a new tax is very easy, because tax rules take out all the burden of having to specify the countries where the tax applies. The tax creation form is therefore very short:

- **Name**. Be very specific, as this will help you build tax rules faster. It is a recommended to add reminders within the name, such as the country/group/zone the tax applies to, and its rate. This greatly helps you remember which tax is to be used in a tax rule.
- **Rate**. The exact rate, in the XX.XX format.
- **Enable**. You can disable and re-enable a tax at any time.

Tax Rules

Tax rules make it so that taxes are only applied to select countries.

By default in PrestaShop, a tax applies to all countries/states/zones. In order to apply a specific tax rate for a single country or a set of countries (and not some others), you must create a tax rule. The tax rule is then applied on a per-product basis, during the creation of the product ("Prices" tab).

You cannot directly apply a tax to a product; you can only apply tax rules. Therefore, you must first register all relevant taxes, then create a tax rule for that tax in order to specify the countries the tax applies, and finally set the tax rule to the product.

A few sample taxes rules are already in place, which depend on the country you chose for your shop during the installation of PrestaShop. The tax rules are set for each tax: the rules actually serve as a kind of country filter, limiting the use of that tax to a specific set of countries.

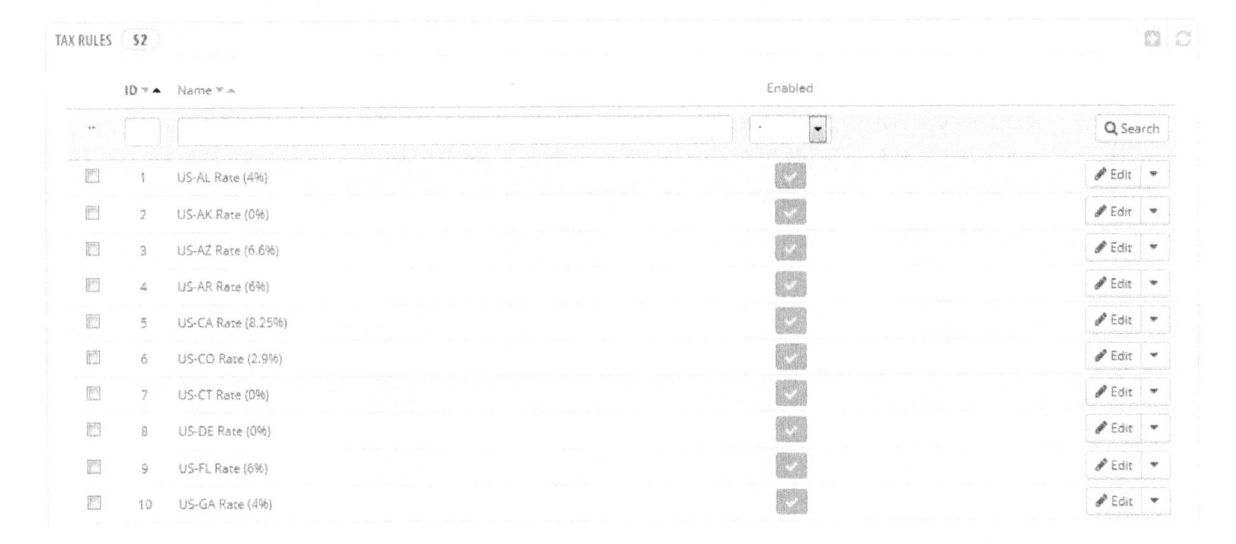

ID	Name	Enabled	
1	US-AL Rate (4%)	✓	Edit
2	US-AK Rate (0%)	✓	Edit
3	US-AZ Rate (6.6%)	✓	Edit
4	US-AR Rate (6%)	✓	Edit
5	US-CA Rate (8.25%)	✓	Edit
6	US-CO Rate (2.9%)	✓	Edit
7	US-CT Rate (0%)	✓	Edit
8	US-DE Rate (0%)	✓	Edit
9	US-FL Rate (6%)	✓	Edit
10	US-GA Rate (4%)	✓	Edit

You should edit a couple of the presented rules in order to get a better grasp of how tax rules can be set.

Adding a New Tax Rule

You can add as many tax rules as needed to your PrestaShop installation. Not only that, but you should make sure that all of the needed tax rules are registered in your shop.

Creating a new tax rule is done in two steps:

1. Create the tax rule:
   - Click on the "Add new" button.
   - In the form that appears, name the rule. Use a telling name: use the tax rule's country code, its name, maybe even its rate, so as to find it again easily. If PrestaShop already has tax rules for the target country, use their name as inspiration so as to have some consistency.
   - Select whether the rule should be enabled from the get-go or not. You can enable it later if needed.

- Click the "Save and stay" button. The page reloads, with a table header at the bottom.
2. Specify the country and behaviors:
    - Click on the "Add new tax rule" button.
        - A new form appears. Fill in the fields:

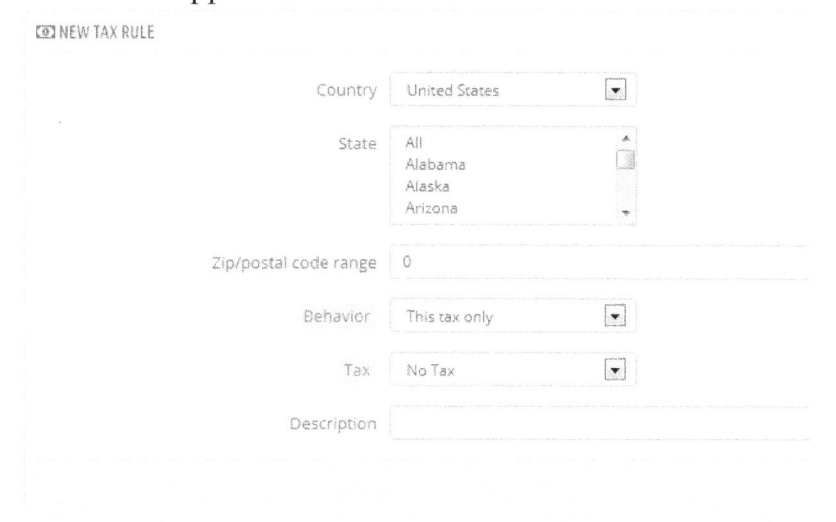

        NEW TAX RULE

Country	United States
State	All / Alabama / Alaska / Arizona
Zip/postal code range	0
Behavior	This tax only
Tax	No Tax
Description	

        - **Country**. The target country for the rule you are creating.
            - **State**. Some countries have federal states registered in PrestaShop (see the "States" page, under the "Localization" menu). In that case, you can make the tax even more specific, or choose to have it applied to the whole country. You can select more than one state by pressing the Ctrl key when clicking on state names.
        - **Zip Code range**. Whether the country has registered states or not, you can further specify the tax application using the customer's zip code. This field enables you to define zip codes in which the tax should be applied: either enter a single zip code, or define a range using the dash. For instance, use "75000-75012" to create a range for all zip codes between these two.
        - **Behavior**. Some customers might have an address that matches more than one of your tax rules. In that case, you can choose how this tax rule should behave:

- **This Tax Only**. Will apply only this tax, not any of the other matching taxes.
- **Combine**. Combine taxes. For instance: 100€ + (10% + 5% => 15%) => 115€.
- **One After Another**. Apply taxes one after another. For instance: 100€ + 10% => 110€ + 5% => 115.5€.
    - **Tax**. The tax to be used for this tax rule. That tax must already be registered in PrestaShop. If not: choose "Not tax", disable the tax rule, save it, go create a tax in the "Taxes" page, then come back to edit the tax rule.
    - **Description**. You may add a short text as a reminder of why this tax rule exists for this country.
  - Click on "Save and stay". The country is added to the table below, and you can start adding another country using the new-empty fields.

Note that the default rate applied to your products will be based on your store's default country.

Translations

PrestaShop provides you with full translation tool for your shop. This helps you add and edit your pages translations. This way, you are the master of your shop, and can handle your translated strings without having to wait for official translators to publish their corrections.

Even if you do not want to correct the translators' work, you might want to change the wording they chose to use (less formal, less wordy, etc.), and customize the various available text, thus tailoring your website to your audience; for instance, a hip-hop clothing shop might be better off using different expressions from that of a luxury watches shop.

> The process of adapting a program to foreign languages is called *internationalization and localization*, or i18n and L10n for short.
> Internationalization is the first step, where developers choose a mechanism for the translation of the software. All the strings of the software are then converted to make use of this mechanism.
> Localization is the second step, where bi- or multi-lingual users of the software

> actually translate the original strings into their own language. Localization may also include providing local data in order to further improve the software for local users.
> You can learn more about i18n and L10n at this Wikipedia page:
> http://en.wikipedia.org/wiki/Internationalization_and_localization
>
> The PrestaShop team has chosen to use its own built-in translation tool, so that anyone with a PrestaShop installation may customize their shop to their needs. The community translation is done with an online tool, located at https://crowdin.net/project/prestashop-official.
>
> The official translation packs can be downloaded manually from this address: http://www.prestashop.com/en/translations.

Modifying a Translation

The most important tool of the "Translation" page is in the "Modify translations" section. This is where you can choose to edit a translation, and completely customize each and every sentence if you wish so.

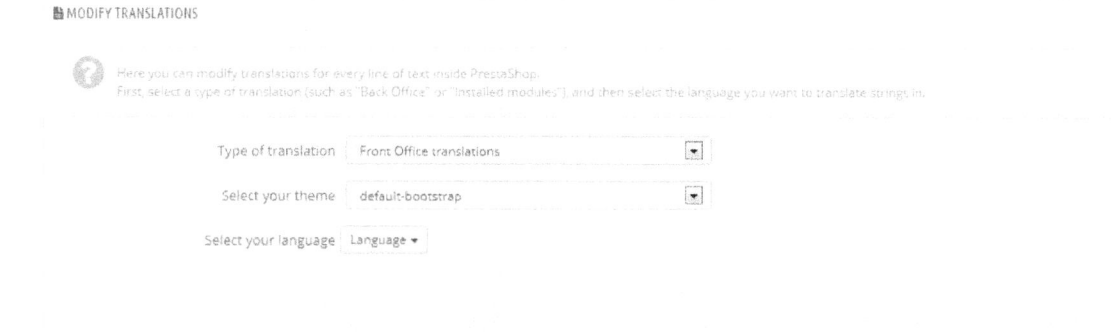

MODIFY TRANSLATIONS

Here you can modify translations for every line of text inside PrestaShop.
First, select a type of translation (such as "Back Office" or "Installed modules"), and then select the language you want to translate strings in.

Type of translation: Front Office translations
Select your theme: default-bootstrap
Select your language: Language ▼

Modify

Select the part of the current translation that you wish to edit:

- **Front Office translations**. The text visible to your customers when browsing your store.
- **Back Office translations**. The text to you and your team from your store's administration panel.
- **Error message translations**. The error messages that may appear on the front-office.

- **Fields Names translations**. The name of the fields in both the front-office and back-office.
- **Module translations**. The terms used by the installed modules. Note that modules which are available but not installed will not appear in the tool.
- **PDF translations**. The terms used in the generated PDF files: invoices, delivery slips, etc.
- **E-mail template translations**. The terms used in the default e-mail templates.

Some categories have a second drop-down list, which lists the available themes. PrestaShop themes have their own strings, but can also have their own modules, PDF templates and e-mail templates. The drop-down list therefore enables you to choose which theme you want to work with.

Once your selection is done, click the language code of the language in which you wish to edit that category of translation.

A long page then appears. It contains the hundreds of available strings for that category, sometimes split in tens of fieldsets.

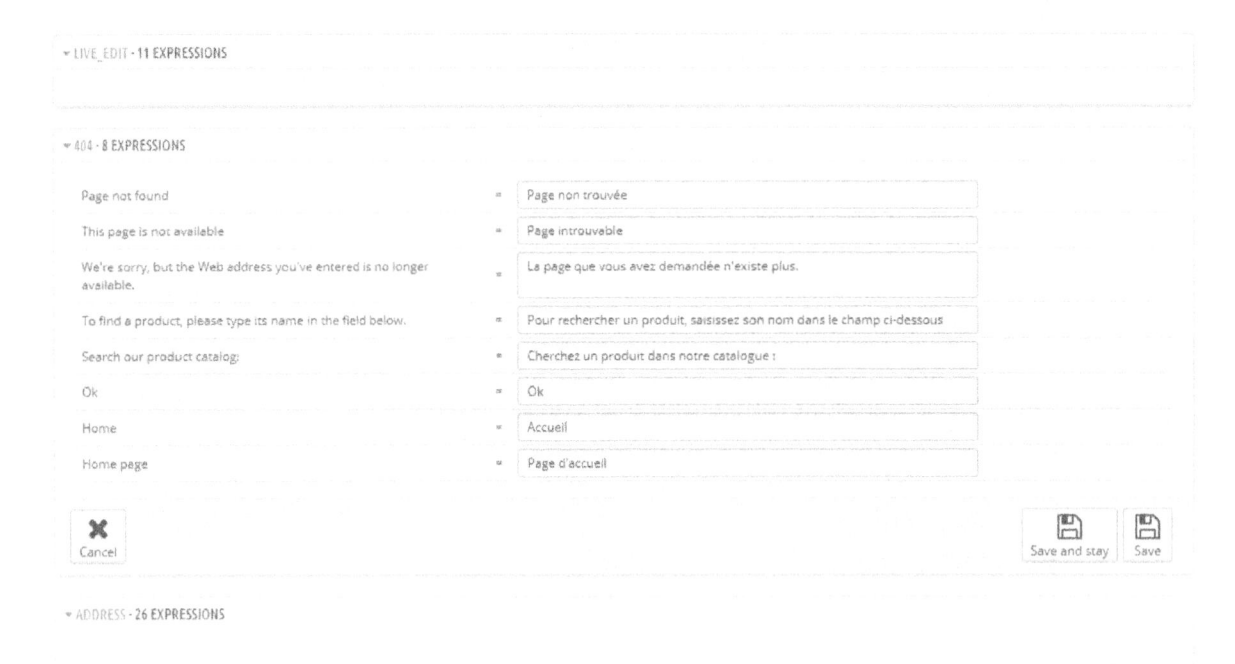

By default, only the fieldsets which have untranslated strings are open. If you wish to open them all, click on the button on the top left twice: once to close all of them, once more to expand them all. You can open and close fieldsets one by one by clicking on its title.

Editing a translation is easy:

- Open a fieldset,
- Edit its content,
- Click on either the "Update Translations and stay" button to save while and keep translating more for this category, or on the "Update translation" button to save and return to the main "Translations" page.

> PrestaShop 1.5 introduced a new syntax where strings can contain placeholders, such as %s, %d, %1$s, %2$d, etc.
>
> When you find a string with such placeholder, it means that PrestaShop will replace it with an actual dynamic value before displaying the translated string. For instance, in the string "Your order on %s is complete", %s will be replaced by the shop's name. Therefore you should keep it in your final translation; for instance, in French, the translation would be "Votre commande sur %s a bien été enregistrée."
>
> Technically, having placeholders prevents strings from being split in parts. Thereby, in previous version of PrestaShop, "Your order on %s is complete." would have been split in two: "Your order on" and "is complete.". While the literal translation of these worked for some language, it made translation nearly impossible for many other languages, none the less RTL languages such as Arabic or Hebrew. Thanks to the placeholders added in PrestaShop 1.5, such strings are now fully translatable in any language.

Some strings might have a warning icon to their right. This indicates strings with placeholders. You can click on the icon to get more information.
In case of a string with a placeholder, you should make sure that the content of that placeholder will be placed in the correct flow of the sentence, and avoid literal translation.
Numbered placeholders (%1$s, %2$d, etc.) enable translators to rearrange the order of the placeholders in the string while maintaining the information each is

replaced with. This way, a French translator could choose to translate "Order #%1$d from %2$s" into "Commande n°%1$s du %2$s" or "Le %2$s, commande n°%1$s".

Next	=	Suivant	
Showing %1$d - %2$d of %3$d items	=	Résultats %1$d - %2$d sur %3$d.	⚠
Showing %1$d - %2$d of 1 item	=	Résultats %1$d - %2$d sur 1.	⚠

Specific features

Most translation categories present their strings in the same way: the category's strings are grouped into fieldsets that you can close or expand by clicking on their title. The title indicates the number of expressions that the fieldset contains, and when needed, the number of missing expressions, in brackets and in red.

This is true for most categories, except three:

- **Error messages**. Strings are not group into many fieldset, they are all presented together.
- **PDF templates**. There is only one fieldset, "PDF".
- **E-mail templates**. Strings are split into fieldsets, but they are not simple text fields anymore. Each e-mail has two templates: a HTML one, which is styled and colored, and a text one, when is plain and simple. While the plain text one can be edited directly in the textfield, the HTML one can only be edited by clicking on the "Edit this e-mail template" button at the bottom of the preview. That click turns the preview into a WYSIWYG textfield (what you see is what you get), with a complete editor at the top (based on TinyMCE: http://www.tinymce.com/). In addition to editing the text, you can change the design as you see fit, for instance you can change the colors in order to adhere to your shop's design. Note that the e-mail templates feature placeholders, such as {lastname} or {shop_name}, which PrestaShop replaces with the actual values when sending the e-mail. Make sure to keep them in both your translation.

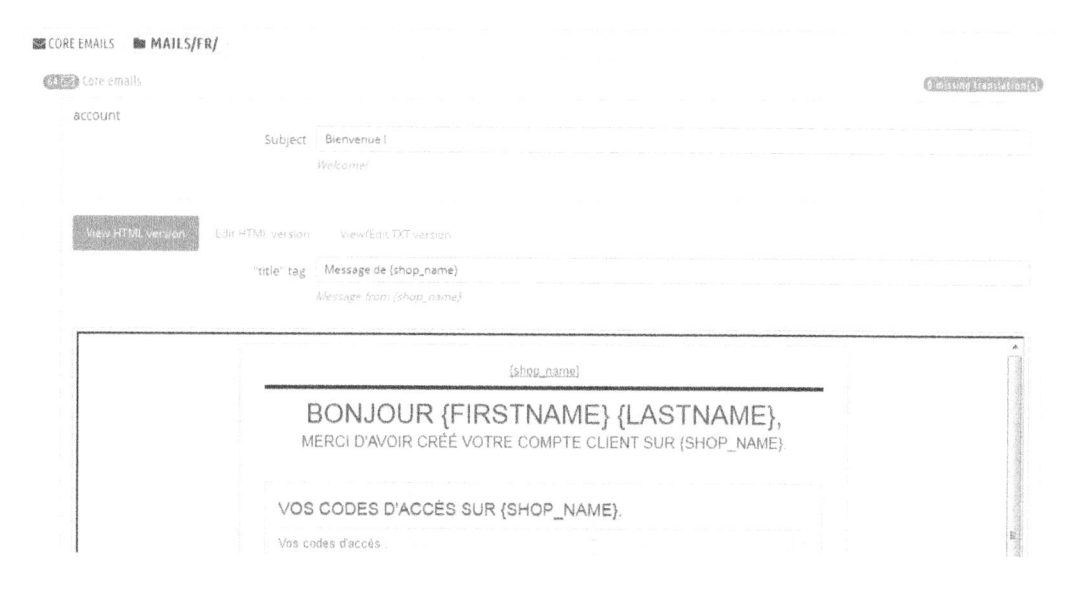

Add / Update a Language

PrestaShop translations are available in packs, which combine all the different translation categories into a zip file. Many language packs are available freely for you to download and install, directly from the PrestaShop.com servers. PrestaShop will take care of downloading the language pack, unpacking it and creating the correct sub-folder in your installation's /translation folder.

You can also update the currently installed languages, likewise directly from the PrestaShop.com servers, but be reminded that any change that you might have made to your own translations will be lost once you update it.

Import a Language Pack Manually

In the case where you do not want to use an official PrestaShop translation pack, but rather a custom one (either provided by someone you know, or one that you exported from another PrestaShop installation), then this tool is for you.

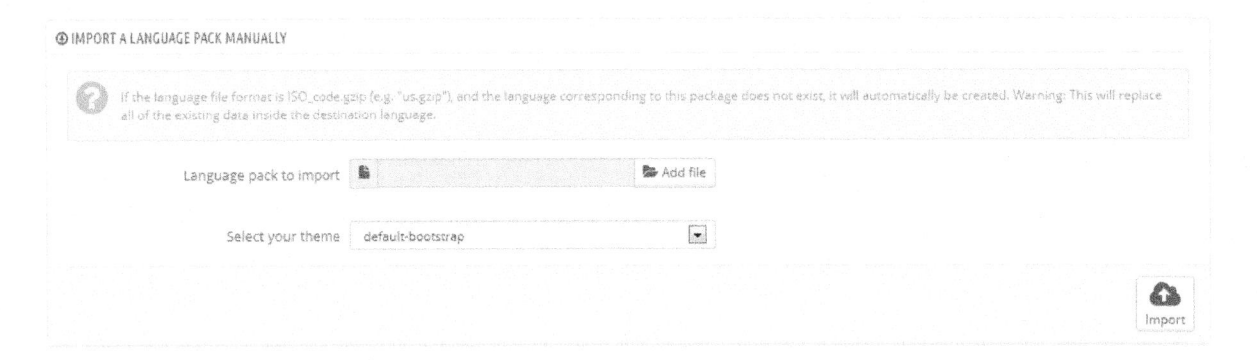

Select the Zip file, select the theme to which you want that pack to be applied to, then click the "Import" button, and it will install the pack in the /translation folder.

> If there is already a language folder with the same ISO 639-1 code, it will be replaced by the files from the pack you are importing.

Export a Language

You can create your own language pack using this tool, either as a way of making a backup of your customizations, or in order to share your translations with other PrestaShop installation – your own or someone else's.

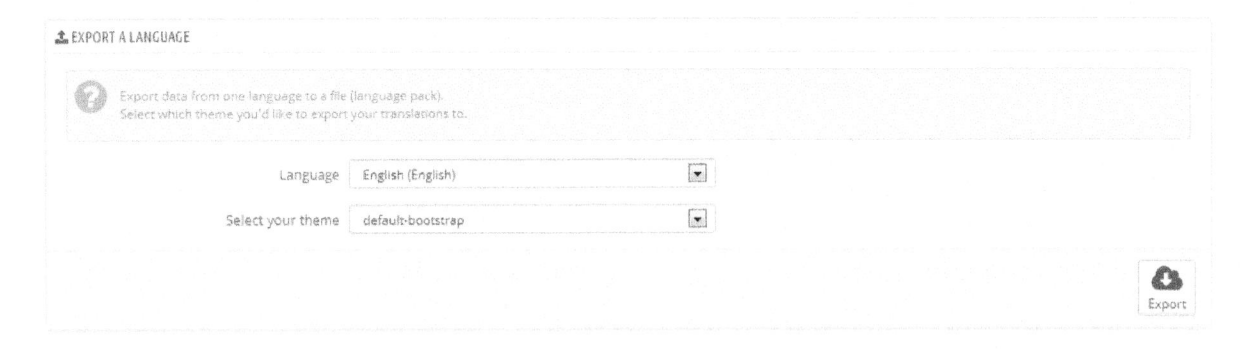

Simple choose the language and the theme of the translation you wish to export, and click the "Export button.

Note that the pack will contain the theme that your translation is supposed to support.

Copy

You can copy the content of one language to another. This is especially useful when you wish to replace a theme's language with the same language from another theme.

Choose the source language and theme, then the destination language and theme, then click the "Copy" button. In most case, the language should remain the same in both drop-down lists.

> If there is already a language folder for this language in the destination theme, it will be replaced by the files from the language and theme you are copying.

You might prefer to first create a new language for the destination theme before copying the source language to it.

Understanding the Preferences

The "Preferences" menu enables you to configure and fine-tune some of your shop's details. These include a lot of different aspects of the shop, from technical settings to the customer's shopping experience. Therefore, all of the Preferences options should be carefully examined, and you should consider each option, as enabling or disabling any of them can have a real impact on your shop, and ultimately, your sales.

General Preferences

The "General" preference page features a handful of specific settings that could not fit in the other menus. They are nonetheless essential:

- **Enable SSL**. SSL means "Secure Sockets Layer", and includes TSL (for "Transport Layer Security"). Both are cryptographic Internet protocols which secure Web communications. You can read more about these protocols on Wikipedia:
  http://en.wikipedia.org/wiki/Secure_Sockets_Layer.
  Providing an SSL connection to your shop is not only excellent for any Internet exchanges, but also a great way to reassure your customers about the safety of their own data (authentication, credit card, etc.) on your shop, as modern browsers now display visual cues showing that

the connection is secured. If your hosting provider does support SSL, make sure to activate PrestaShop's SSL support, by clicking on the link. This will reveal a selector, where you should choose "Yes".
- **Increase Front Office security**. This adds security tokens to your shop in order to improve its security. In effect, each URL is specific to a customer's session, and cannot be used as-is on another browser, thus protecting whatever information they might have stored during that session.
- **Allow iframes on HTML fields**. The option enables you to put iframes in text fields, such as product description. Iframes are HTML elements that make it possible to load an external content into the page's own content. We recommend that you leave this option disabled unless necessary.
- **Round mode**. Once taxes and discount are applied, a price can feature too many decimals, such as $42.333333333. The round mode is used during the price calculation process (taxes, discount, etc.). There are three modes:
    - **Superior**. Rounding up: 42.333333333 becomes 42.34.
    - **Inferior**. Rounding down: 42.333333333 becomes 42.33.
    - **Classical**. It rounds the value up of down depending on the value: up when above .5, down when below .5.
- **Display suppliers and manufacturers**. Enable suppliers and manufacturers pages on your front-office even when their respective modules are disabled.
- **Enable Multistore**. This little option has major implications: it turns your single-shop installation of PrestaShop into a multiple stores installation. This gives you access to the new "Multistore" page in the "Advanced parameters" menu, and every administration page can be contextualized to apply its settings to either all stores, a specific group of stores, or a single store.
You can read more about PrestaShop's multistore feature by reading the "Managing multiple shops" chapter of this guide.
- **Main Shop Activity**. You might have set the wrong shop activity when installing PrestaShop. You can choose the correct activity here.

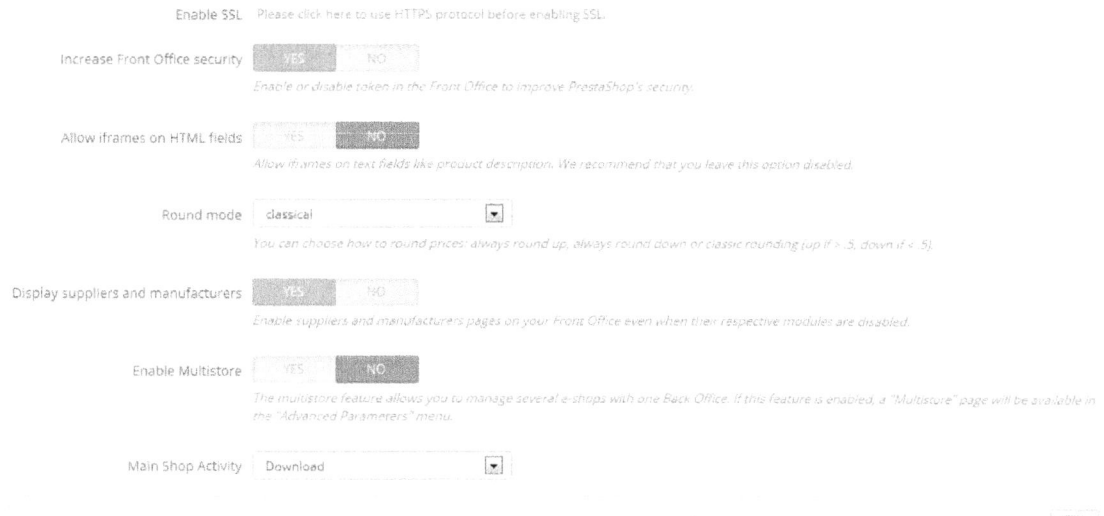

GENERAL

- **Enable SSL**: Please click here to use HTTPS protocol before enabling SSL.
- **Increase Front Office security**: YES / **NO**
  Enable or disable token in the Front Office to improve PrestaShop's security.
- **Allow iframes on HTML fields**: YES / **NO**
  Allow iframes on text fields like product description. We recommend that you leave this option disabled.
- **Round mode**: classical
  You can choose how to round prices: always round up, always round down or classic rounding (up if > .5, down if < .5).
- **Display suppliers and manufacturers**: **YES** / NO
  Enable suppliers and manufacturers pages on your Front Office even when their respective modules are disabled.
- **Enable Multistore**: YES / **NO**
  The multistore feature allows you to manage several e-shops with one Back Office. If this feature is enabled, a "Multistore" page will be available in the "Advanced Parameters" menu.
- **Main Shop Activity**: Download

Save

Orders Preferences

The settings from the "Orders" preference page apply to the orders that your customers make, but also to some other details, such as gifting.

General preferences

GENERAL

- **Order process type**: Standard (Five steps)
- **Enable guest checkout**: YES / **NO**
- **Minimum purchase total required in order to validate the order**: $ (tax excl.) 0
- **Delayed shipping**: YES / **NO**
- **Terms of service**: **YES** / NO
- **CMS page for the Conditions of use**: Terms and conditions of use

Save

- **Order process type**. By default, the customer has to go through 5 steps in order to complete the checkout process, each on a different page.

However, you can choose to have it all done in a single page. The page will be longer, but some customers might prefer this approach.
- **Enable guest checkout**. Allows non-registered visitors to place an order, without having to create an account.
- **Minimum purchase total required in order to validate order**. Indicates the minimum amount that must be in the shopping cart to submit an order. If the amount in this field is not reached, your customer cannot complete their purchase. If you do not want to set a minimum amount, enter "0" in the field.
- **Delayed shipping**. If you enable the "Allow ordering of out-of-stock products" option (in the "Products" preference page), you can allow order items to be dispatched as they become available, in as many shipment as needed (depending on how you team sees it fit). Initially, PrestaShop will split the order in two: the available items are sent right away, while the other items become a second order, waiting to be validated.
- **Terms of service**. Makes your customers have to accept your terms of service before they can validate an order.
- **CMS page for the Conditions of use**. Your shop's "conditions of use" are to be stored in a static page (a "CMS page"). Select which page to use so that PrestaShop can point to it correctly.

Gift options

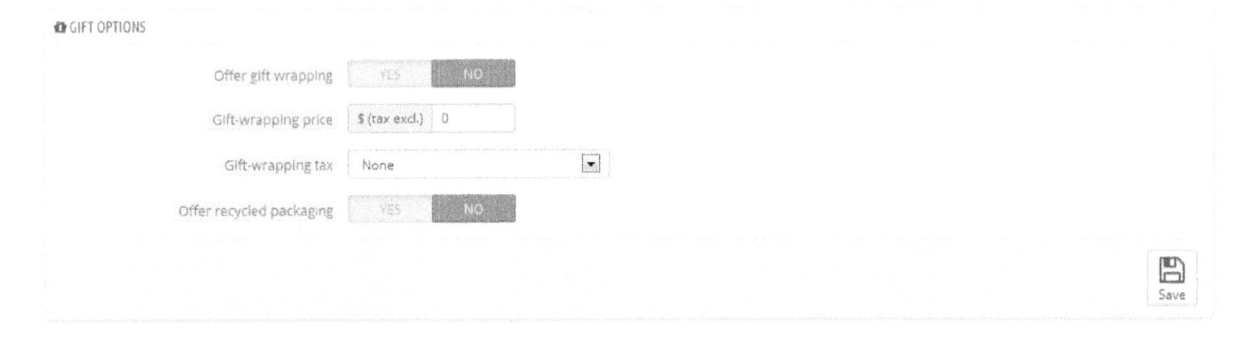

- **Offer gift wrapping**. Have PrestaShop suggest gift-wrapping to customer, and the possibility of adding a printed a message. It is always a nice feature for people who want to send gifts through your shop.
- **Gift-wrapping price**. Sets the price of your gift-wrapping service.

- **Gift-wrapping tax.** If needed, indicates to which local tax the gift-wrapping is tied. You can add more taxes in the "Taxes" page, in the "Localization" menu.
- **Offer recycled packaging.** If you can offer this service, many customers will appreciate it.

Products Preferences

This page contains a few preferences pertaining to how your products are to be handled and displayed by PrestaShop.

General preferences

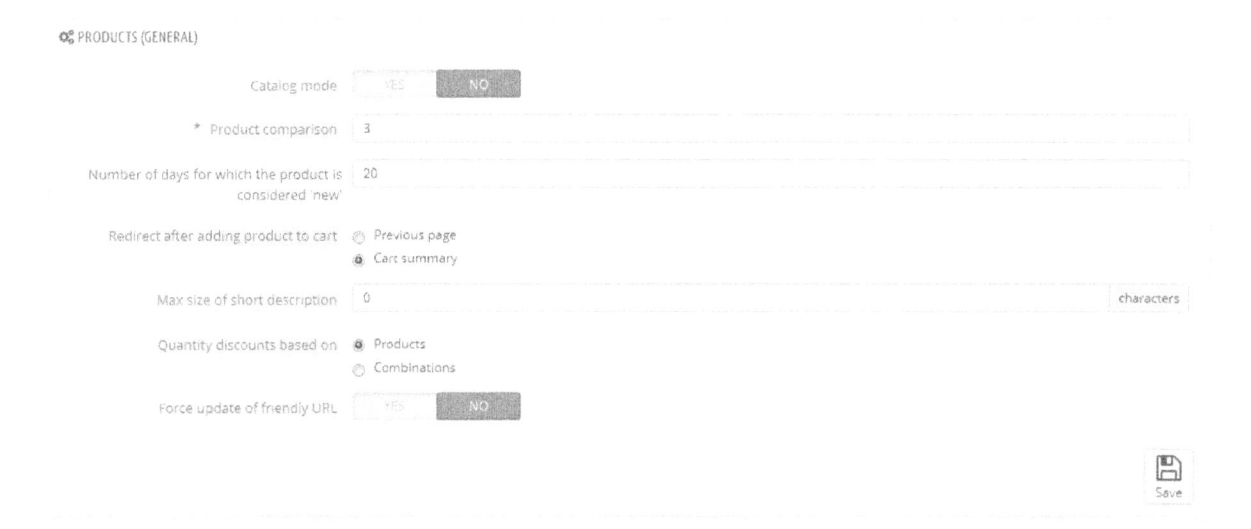

[Screenshot: PRODUCTS (GENERAL) settings panel showing: Catalog mode: NO; Product comparison: 3; Number of days for which the product is considered 'new': 20; Redirect after adding product to cart: Cart summary; Max size of short description: 0 characters; Quantity discounts based on: Products; Force update of friendly URL: NO]

- **Catalog mode.** Enabling catalog mode turns your shop into a simple gallery of products, with no way to buy the items whatsoever.
- **Product comparison.** Set the maximum number of products that can be selected for comparison.
- **Number of days for which the product is considered 'new'.** When you add a product in your shop, it is considered new and it is reported back through the "New products" block and the "New products" page. The field allows you to specify how many days the product will remain visible on the block and page. With this feature, you choose how to display and updated your shop's news. The "New products" page is usually most accessed by your regular customers.

- **Redirect after adding product to cart**. You can either redirect the customer to the previous page, or to the cart summary.
- **Max size of short description**. Your product has two descriptions: a "short description" one and a regular one. The short description, which appears in search engines and in the category description for your product, is limited to 400 characters by default, but this option enables you to change that limit. 0 means that there is no limit.
- **Quantity discount based on**. This settings indicates upon what PrestaShop should base quantity discounts: per-product, or per-combination (which can feature multiple products).
- **Force update of friendly URL**. By default, the friendly URL of a product page is generated from the product title, and it stays the same even though the product title changes – because in order to be well referenced, your URLs should be stable. By enabling this option, PrestaShop will update the friendly URL every time you change the product's name or page's title.

Pagination preferences

- **Products per page**. Indicate how many products are displayed on the pages of your categories.
- **Default order by**. Indicate the order of products in your shop's categories. 6 choices are available:
    - **Product name**. Displays your products based on the alphabetical order.
    - **Product price**. Displays your products according to their prices.
    - **Product add date**. Displays your products according to the date it was added to your shop.

- o **Product modified date**. When you edit a product, its modification date is changed. This option makes them appear in the order of modification date.
  - o **Position inside category**. Displays your products as they are positioned in the categories in your catalog. The position of the products can be modified directly in the catalog of your shop using the position arrows. This way you have your product in the most attractive fashion for your customers.
  - o **Manufacturer**. Displays your products in alphabetical order of their manufacturers' names.
  - o **Product quantity**. Displays your products based on their available quantity.
  - o **Product reference**. Displays your products based on their reference number.
- **Default order method**. The above options can be sorted by ascending or descending order.

Product page preferences

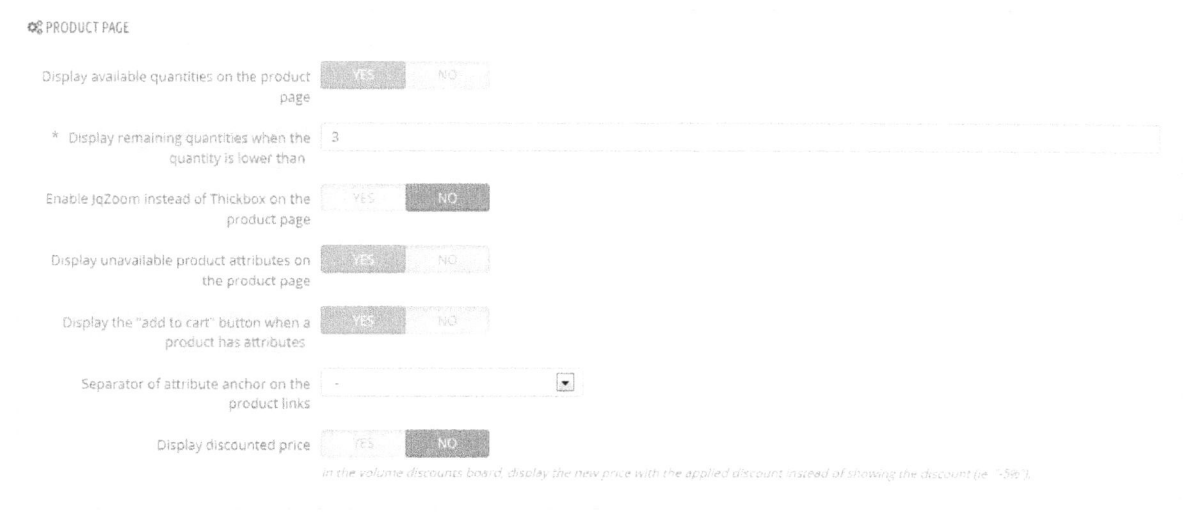

- **Display available quantities on the product page**. By enabling this feature, your visitors can see the quantities of each product available in stock. Displaying this information can be used to stimulate sales in the

case where the quantity in stock is low. The quantities displayed are the selected attributes and combination.
- **Display remaining quantities when quantity is lower than**. You can choose to display an alert when the remaining available stock for a product gets below a certain level. This option is particularly useful for promoting purchases. The text and placement of the alert depend on the theme; in the default theme, it is "Warning: Last items in stock!", and is placed directly below the "Quantity" field.
- **Enable JqZoom instead of Thickbox on product page**. By default, at the click of the mouse, a bigger version of the product image is displayed as an overlay of the page. Once you activate this feature, visitors will still be able to click on the image in order to get the zoom, but a zoom will also appears whenever the mouse hovers over the product's image.
- **Display unavailable product attributes on product page**. Your products can be composed of many different combinations or attributes: color, size, capacity, etc. Attributes can be edited in the "Attributes" page of the "Catalog" menu. Read the chapter titled "A Look Inside the Catalog" to learn more about attributes, and how to use them.
  When one or several attributes are not available anymore, you have two possibilities:
    o First possibility: Leave this preference active. Example: The "iPod Shuffle" is no longer available in "Blue" in our shop. By keeping this option enabled, the product's combination will remain visible in the shop. A message will indicate that the product is no longer available in the chosen option, and invite customers to choose another combination. If you enabled the "Allow ordering of out-of-stock products" option (see below), then they will be able to add the unavailable combination to their carts.
    o Second possibility: Disable this preference. If the "Blue" combination of the "iPod Shuffle" product is no longer available, that selection is not displayed the front-office and the customer cannot select it. This feature helps to clearly display the availability of your products.
- **Display the "add to cart" button when product has attributes**. This option prevents customers from adding a product to their cart directly from the category page, if that product has combinations. This forces customers to visit the product's page and pick a combination, instead of

only adding the default one to the cart. Note that products with no combination will still have an "Add to cart" button in the category page.
- **Separator of attribute anchor on the product links**. Choose the separator, between "," and "-".
- **Display discounted price**. When using the volume discount board, show the discounted price rather than the discount percentage.

Products stock preferences

- **Allow ordering of out-of-stock products**. If a product does not have any available stock anymore, the customer can still order it.
- **Enable stock management**. This option gives you access to basic stock management options and features: you can set the current quantity of product, and have PrestaShop lower it for each order, and "re-stock" for each canceled or returned order.
  By default you should leave this feature enabled, as disabling it affects the entire inventory management of your shop. Only if you do not have any physical inventory should you disable it – for instance, if you only have virtual products.
- **Enable advanced stock management**. Another little option which has major implications: it adds a new menu called "Stocks", which makes it possible to manage very precisely your stock, on a per-warehouse basis if necessary. You can see all the details about your stock: movement, coverage, re-stocking orders, etc.
  You can read more about PrestaShop's advanced stock management feature by reading the "Managing Stock" chapter of this guide.
- **New products use advanced stock management**.
- **Default warehouse on new product**.

Customers Preferences

The "Customers" page bring together specifically customer-related options, most notably the B2B mode.

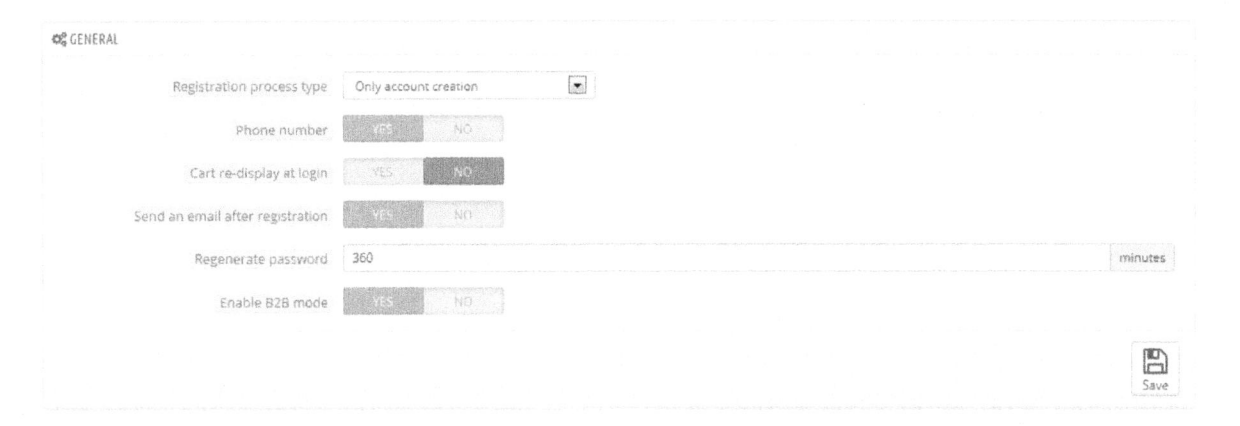

- **Registration process type**. You can let visitors create a new account without any immediate obligation to register an address, or force them to register an address as soon as they create their account.
  The first option makes it quicker to create account, which is great, but this will add a new mandatory screen once they want to validate an order, which can turn them off.
  On the other end, the second option makes account creation longer, but at least they will already have an address registered when they want to validate an order.
- **Phone number**. Likewise, you can require your client to register a phone number, or not. Having a phone number can prove invaluable to you, as this makes it possible to contact a client directly, but some client resent giving this kind of information. If you select "No", the "Phone number" fields will still appear in the address creation form, but they will no longer be mandatory.
- **Cart re-display at login**. If the customer had a cart that was not checked-out, display it once he or she logs back in.
- **Send an email after registration**. You can have PrestaShop send an e-mail to any newly-created customer with a summary of his account information (email, password) after registration.

- **Regenerate password**. You can choose to limit the frequency at which a customer can generate a new password for his or her account. By default, it is set at 360 minutes – 6 hours.
- **Enable B2B mode**. The B2B mode brings a handful of new features to your store. Customers are no longer considered as individuals but as companies, and therefore some new options appear:
    - The customer profile has new fields related to professional information (Duns number in the USA, SIRET number in France, CNPJ number in Brazil, etc.),
    - Prices can be masked to specific groups,
    - Prices can be managed on a per-customer basis for the whole catalog or per category,
    - Invoices can be generated manually,
    - etc.

Themes Preferences

The "Themes" page enables you to efficiently manage your themes.

Your current theme

The first section of the page serves as a reminder of which theme you are currently using, with its details:

- Theme name.
- Theme version.
- Theme author's name, website and email address.
- Thumbnail for the theme.

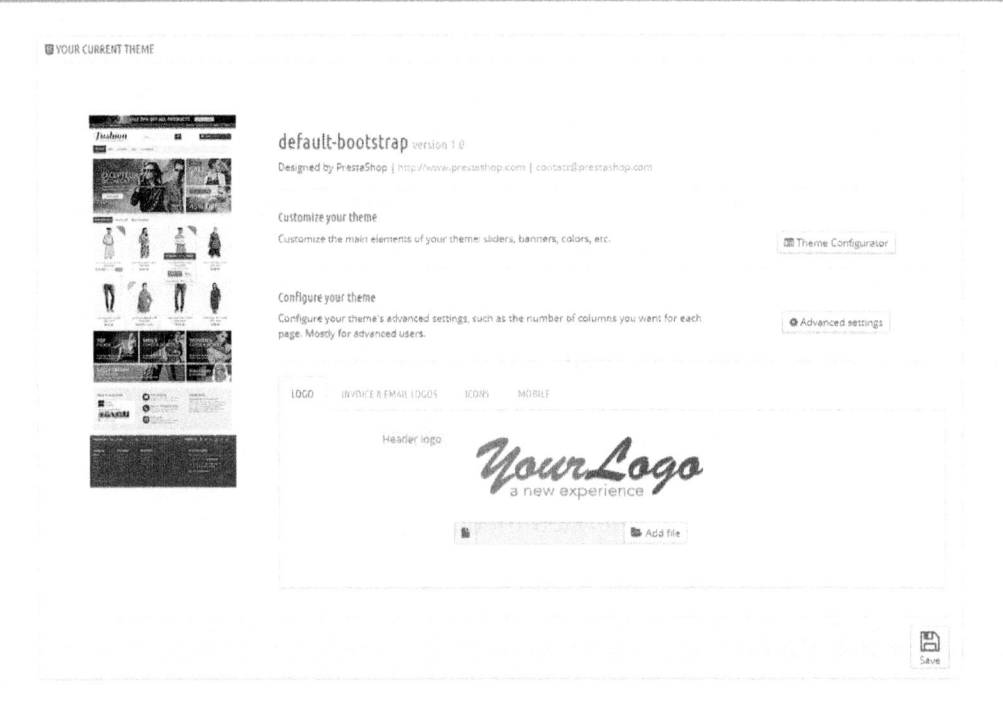

This section also gives you access to a handful of tools, which helps you to quickly customize the current theme: header logo, mail logo, invoice logo, favicon, store icon and even the navigation pipe can be easily modified from there. This section features:

- **Customize your theme**. A link to the Theme Configurator (provided that the Theme Configurator module is indeed installed and enabled).
- **Configure your theme**. A link to the theme's advanced settings.
- 4 tabs with the theme's appearance options:
    - **Logo**. The logo that will appear on all the pages of your shop.
    - **Invoice & email logos**. The logos that will respectively appear in your shop's invoices, and its email notifications.
    - **Icons**. Your shop's favicon (displayed in the web browser's address bar) and your Store icon (for use on the Store map as an indicator of where a store is).
    - **Mobile**. The logo that will appear on all the pages of your shop, when accessed through a mobile device. You can also choose to selectively enable or disable your theme's mobile version (if it does exist) for smartphones, tablets, or both.

The default theme uses a "YourLogo" logo. It is strongly recommended to change all of the instances of the logo and use yours!

In multistore mode, you can apply these changes to all your stores or to a group of stores at one time, using the multistore menu.

The "Enable the mobile theme" makes it possible for you to use the default mobile theme. With this theme, any PrestaShop merchant can have his or her shop be accessible to mobile devices: from the home page to the payment process, along with product pages and conversion funnel.

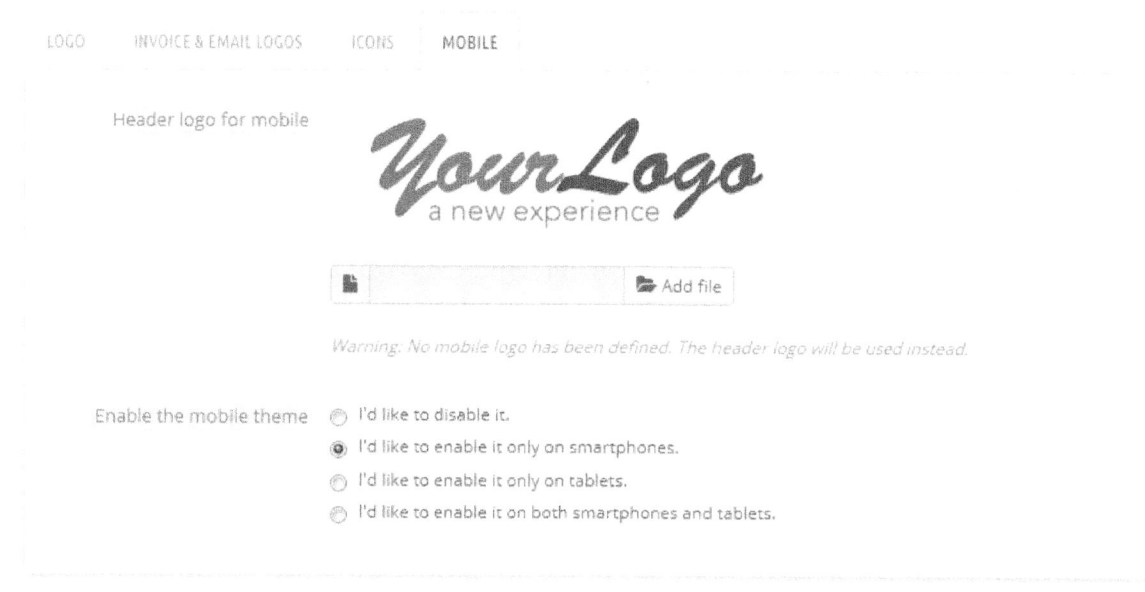

The mobile theme only works for PrestaShop's default theme, since it is included in its folder: /themes/default/mobile. Therefore, it will not work if you use another theme which does not have its own mobile theme.

Nonetheless, you can easily use the default mobile theme with any other theme, at least temporarily: simply copy the mobile theme's folder from the default theme's folder to the new theme's folder, and you should be good to go. For instance, if your new theme's folder is /themes/magnolia, copy the /themes/default/mobile folder to the new theme's folder: /themes/magnolia/mobile.

> This is particularly useful if the new theme does not feature a responsive design: this way, your shop can still look good on mobile devices – albeit with the default PrestaShop look.

The Theme Configurator

The Theme Configurator module helps you configure some aspects of your theme.

Clicking on the link from the "Themes" preferences page opens its configuration page. That page gives you direct links to the most usual front-office modules: you can enable and disable a dozen of features, such as displaying social buttons or the Facebook block (provided their respective modules are enabled), and get direct access to their configuration page. You can also enable and access the Live Configurator from there, which makes it possible to easily change your theme's main color and font.

In a second section, the Theme Configurator makes it possible for you to easily attach images with links on specific home page hooks: home, top, left, right, footer. Each available language has its own tab with its own hooks that you can edit from here: this is essential as images often contain text directly on them, making it necessary to have as many versions of the image per available languages.

The module is explained in more details in the "Making the Native Modules Work" chapter of this guide.

The theme's advanced settings

Clicking on the "Advanced settings" button displays the main information about the theme (see the "Creating a brand new theme" section below to find an explanation of the fields).

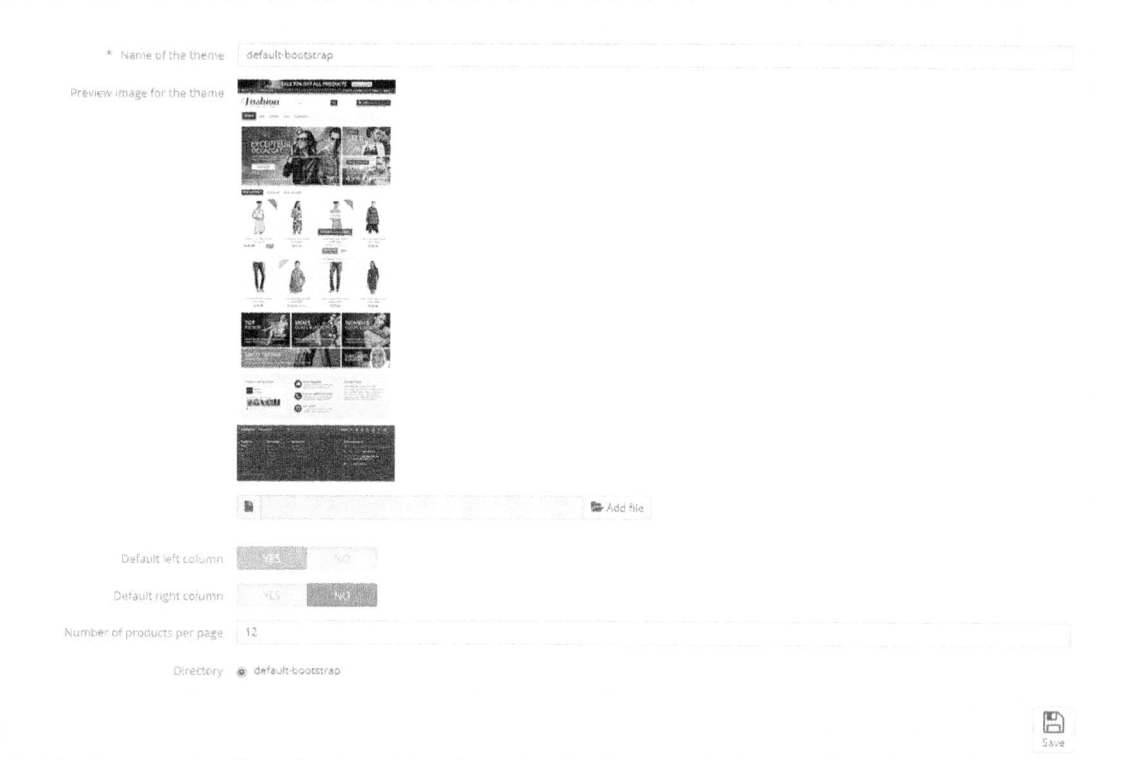

Below the main section, the "Appearance of columns" section displays a lot of information about the way the left and right columns appear, depending on the page:

- If the box is checked, the column appears in the page (for instance, the Category page).
- If it is left unchecked, it will not appear on that page.

Note that even if you can click on the buttons at will, these settings are only informational, and the theme will not necessarily be able to adapt to your changes!

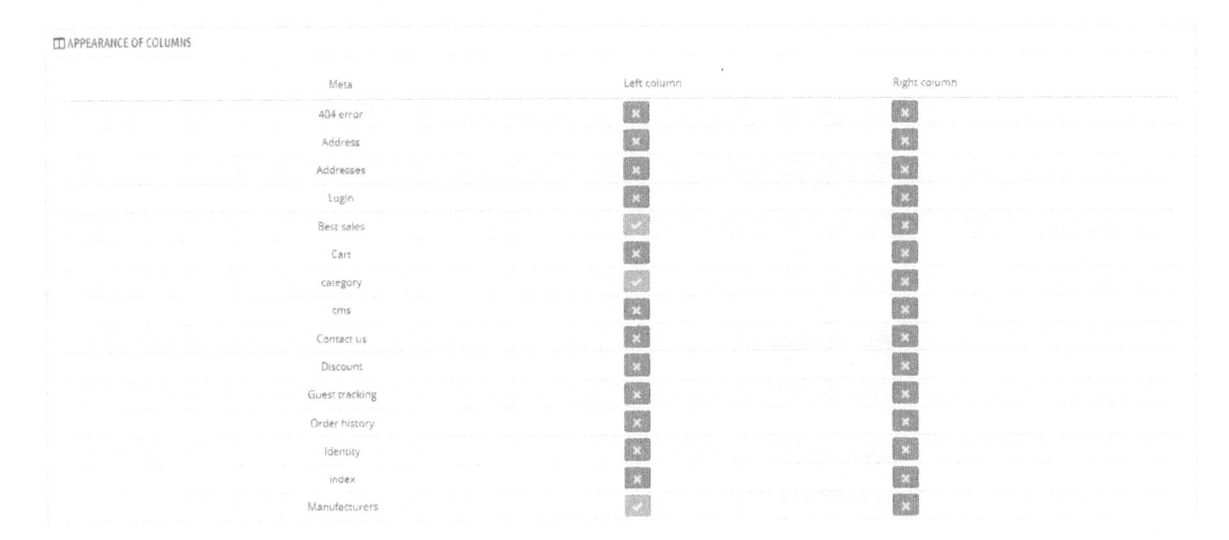

Select a theme for your "[name]" shop

This section is only display if you have at least two themes installed. It presents you with the other available themes on your PrestaShop installation beside the already-enabled one.

This section simply shows the thumbnails of the available themes, with their names.

Move your mouse cursor over the thumbnail to display a menu with two options:

- **Use this theme**. This will replace your current theme with this theme.
- **Delete this theme**. This will delete this theme's files from your web server.

At the top right, the "Visit the theme store" opens a new page to the PrestaShop Addons marketplace, where you can find more themes.

> In multistore mode, you cannot apply a theme to all your stores or a group of stores; you must select a single store in the multistore menu, then pick a theme.

Adding and exporting a theme

Two buttons at the top of the screen enable you to import a theme and install it (and its attached modules), or to export a theme and its modules from your shop in order to share it with the world.

Importing a theme: the "Add new theme" button

This screen presents you with 3 methods to install a new theme: from your computer, from a public website, or from your own FTP server. A final button leads you to the theme creation form, presented in the next section.

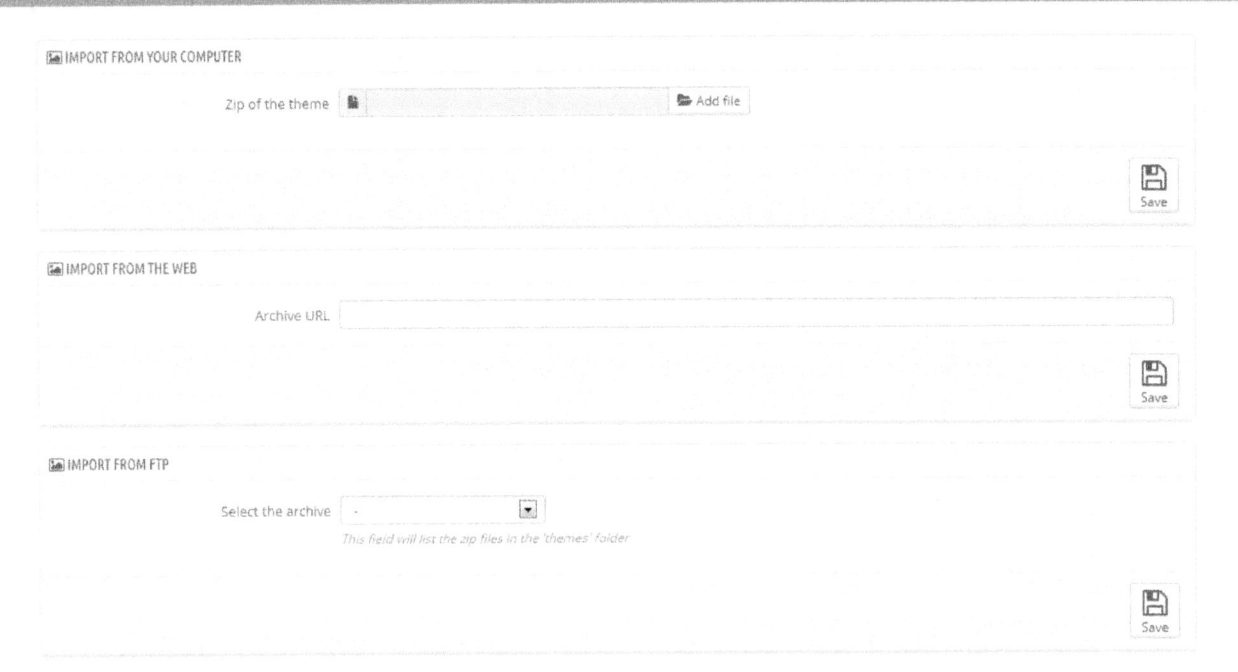

Whatever the method, the process remains the same: indicate the location of the theme's Zip archive, then click "Save". The only thing that changes is the source of the Zip file:

- **Import from your computer**. Use the file explorer to find the archive.
- **Import from the web**. Indicate the direct public URL to the archive.
- **Import from FTP**. Using your FTP client, upload the archive in the following folder: /modules/themeinstallator/import/ .

Click "Save" to validate your choice. The theme is now installed, and PrestaShop asks you if you wish to install modules that were imported along with the theme, what you would rather do with the current modules configuration, and how you would like the images configuration to be taken into account.

Click "Save" one last time. A final confirmation page presents you with all the changes applied to your PrestaShop install. Click "Finish" to end the process.

Creating a brand new theme

The best way to create a new theme for PrestaShop is to copy the files from the default theme, and start modifying its TPL and CSS files to make them your own. The reason is that a PrestaShop theme requires many files to be present: by starting from an existing theme instead of from scratch, you make sure that your own theme will not be missing any part.

You can do this directly on the web server, but PrestaShop makes it easy to copy the files from an installed theme and register your new theme in its system (a step you would have to do in any case).

All of this is done by clicking on the "Create new theme" button from the "Add new theme" button at the top of screen. It displays a creation form.

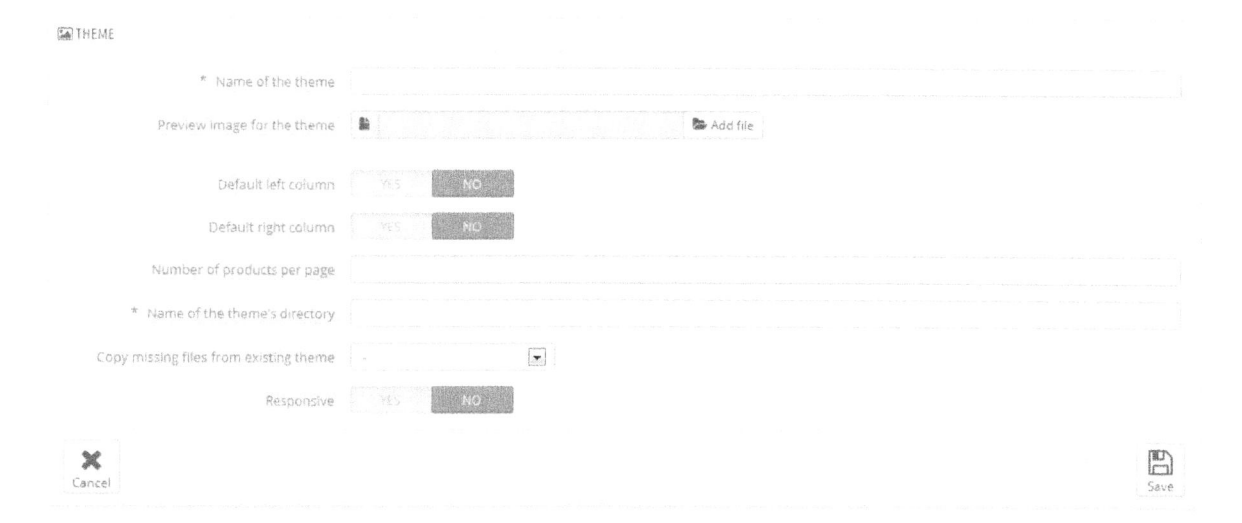

Fill-in its fields:

- **Name of the theme**. Make sure the name is not already used by another theme (check on the Addons website).
- **Preview image for the theme**. You should always add a preview image, as it is a clear reminder of what the theme looks like. If you do not have one yet, leave that for later, when the time will come to release the theme.
- **Default left column** and **Default right column**. Indicate if your theme has a column (or even two columns), and if so, on which side of the screen. This is purely informational, and can be changed at any time.
- **Name of the theme's directory**. Try to keep it close to your theme's name. If you have not already created a theme folder, PrestaShop will create one for you.

- **Copy missing files from existing theme**. This is the cleanest method to start a new theme from another theme's files. Choose "default-bootstrap", or any other theme that you would like to base your foundation on.
- **Responsive**. Indicate if your theme has a responsive design or not (if you do not know what a responsive design is, then you probably should choose "No"). This is purely informational, and can be changed at any time.

Click save, and PrestaShop will register this information for you: the theme is ready to be enabled, and its preview image appears in the theme selector.

It is now up to you to change your theme's files in order to make it unique! On your local installation (not a production one!), select your new theme, and start working!
Once you are done with your designing and code it, go back to this setting page and change it accordingly: definitive preview image, default column, number of products, and responsiveness.

> Is your theme so good that other merchants could pay money for it? You can sell it on Addons, PrestaShop's official theme & module marketplace: http://addons.prestashop.com/.

Exporting a theme

This section is only available when there is at least one theme installed on your PrestaShop site. It gives you a method to export your module in the correct format (most notably with a working configuration file).

Exporting a theme is very useful when you want either to back the theme up for safety, and create an archive of the theme for a friend or in order to make it available on the Addons marketplace (http://addons.prestashop.com/). Not only does it generate a complete Zip archive of your theme, but it also adds many information in an XML files, which is very useful both when uploading to Addons, and when important to another PrestaShop site.

THEME

Choose the theme you want to export: default-bootstrap

Select a theme and click on "Export". A configuration form appears where you can set the exported themes parameters: author name, modules to export along, theme name, version compatibility, etc.

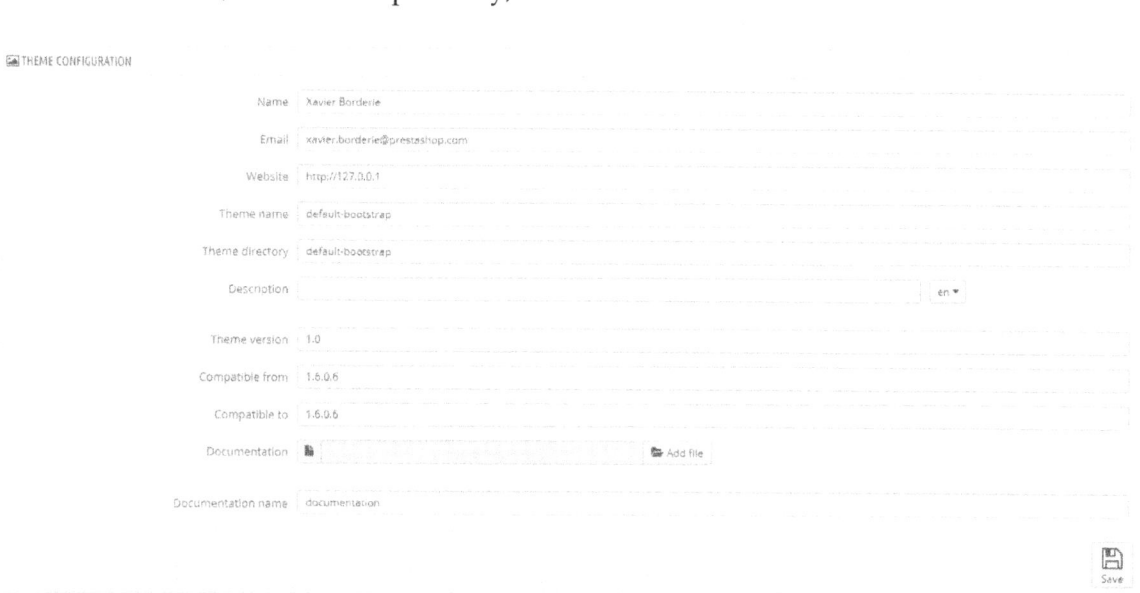

THEME CONFIGURATION

Name	Xavier Borderie
Email	xavier.borderie@prestashop.com
Website	http://127.0.0.1
Theme name	default-bootstrap
Theme directory	default-bootstrap
Description	en
Theme version	1.0
Compatible from	1.6.0.6
Compatible to	1.6.0.6
Documentation	Add file
Documentation name	documentation

Once all the parameters are correctly set, click on "Save". You will quickly get a file to download from your browser. Save it on your hard-drive, then give the saved file a proper name instead of the random one it currently has. From there on, you can easily share this theme, and if it is your own creation, you can start selling it on PrestaShop's Addons marketplace at http://addons.prestashop.com/.

Live from PrestaShop Addons!

This final section presents you with 12 of the latest themes from PrestaShop's Addons marketplace. You can click on each image to reach the theme's individual Addons page and get a better view of it, and possibly buy it.

SEO & URLs Preferences

The tools on this page help you improve the presence of your PrestaShop site on web searches, and therefore reach more potential customers.

> SEO means "search engine optimization". It represents a set of techniques and best practices aimed at improving the visibility of a website on search engines. You can read more about this at Wikipedia: http://en.wikipedia.org/wiki/Search_engine_optimization.
>
> URL is short for "uniform resource locator", or simply put, the online address of a web page. You can read more about what a URL is at Wikipedia: http://en.wikipedia.org/wiki/URL

By default, PrestaShop's deep URLs (that is, specific pages rather than online the domain name) are rather uninformative to both the customer and search engines: an URL such as http://www.myprestashop.com/product.php?id_product=27 does not help visitors know what product is on that page. Friendly URLs are the way to achieve that, and get for instance http://www.myprestashop.com/2-music-players/27-ipod-nano-green.

As you can see in the second example above, both categories and products can have a friendly URL: in the example above, id_category=2 becomes 2-music-players, and id_product=27 becomes 27-ipod-nano-green. While the ID number cannot be removed by default, the words can be either generated from the category/product name, or written by hand. This is done directly in the configuration page for the product or the category (in the Catalog menu): the "Friendly URL" field can be found directly in the main configuration page of a category, and under the "SEO" tab of the configuration page of a product.

There are other individual pages in your PrestaShop install that would certainly benefit from friendly URLs: CMS pages, user account pages, pages with automatically generated content... The "SEO & URLs" page presents you with a list of these pages, and enables you to edit their friendly URLs as well as their meta tags (title, description, keyword).

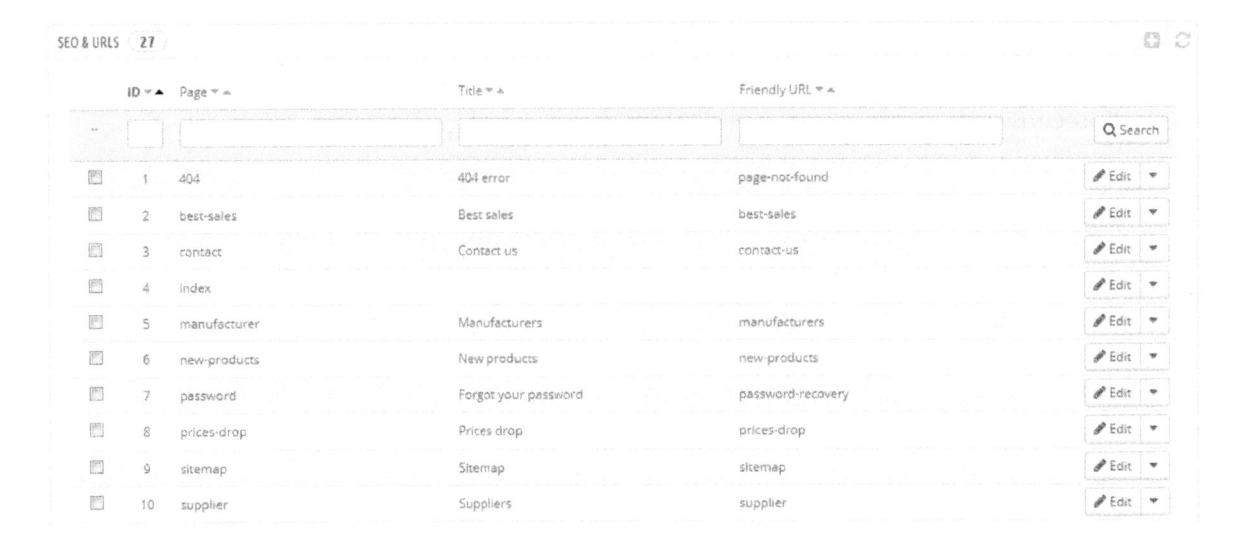

	ID	Page	Title	Friendly URL		
	1	404	404 error	page-not-found	Edit	
	2	best-sales	Best sales	best-sales	Edit	
	3	contact	Contact us	contact-us	Edit	
	4	index			Edit	
	5	manufacturer	Manufacturers	manufacturers	Edit	
	6	new-products	New products	new-products	Edit	
	7	password	Forgot your password	password-recovery	Edit	
	8	prices-drop	Prices drop	prices-drop	Edit	
	9	sitemap	Sitemap	sitemap	Edit	
	10	supplier	Suppliers	supplier	Edit	

Homepage SEO settings

In order to change the homepage meta tags, you simply need to open the "SEO & URLs" page, open the "index" page's settings, and there you can freely edit some important SEO information.

A few tips:

- The default homepage title is the name of the store, and therefore the index' title field is empty. If you put content in the field, the homepage's full title will be "<your content> – <the name of the store>".
  The name of the store itself is set during the installation of PrestaShop,

> and can be changed from the "Store Contacts" preference page, using the "Shop name" option of the "Contact details" section.
> - Keep your description short: a paragraph of text is enough.
> - To add a tag, click in the "Add tag" field and validate by pressing return. You can remove tags by clicking the cross.
> - You do not have to add a rewritten URL if there is not already one.
>
> Note that if your store has already been indexed by Google or any other search engine, it might take a while for your changes to appear in the search results. Please be patient.

Friendly URLs only work with a server setup that supports URL rewriting (through the Apache Web Server mod_rewrite feature, for instance). Make sure to check that your server does (ask your hosting provider!), as it can make your shop completely unavailable to customers if you enable friendly URLs and the server does not support it!

At the bottom of the "SEO & URLs" page are three sections with additional options: Set up URLs, Set shop URL and Robots file generation. See below for an explanation of these.

Adding a New Friendly URL

Friendly URLs are to be set in the configuration page of each product, category, CMS page... This creation page is only useful for some automatic pages, and most of the time you won't have to worry about these.

> Make sure to fill the fields for all the available languages on your shop: not only is it immensely useful to local users, but some search engines can even make use of this local information.

META TAGS

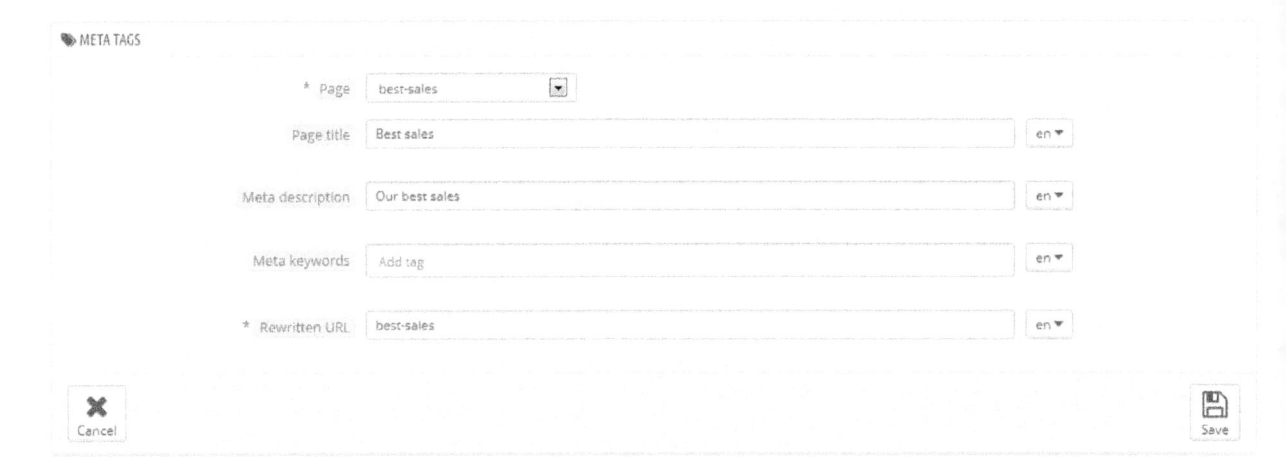

* Page	best-sales
Page title	Best sales en ▼
Meta description	Our best sales en ▼
Meta keywords	Add tag en ▼
* Rewritten URL	best-sales en ▼

[Cancel] [Save]

Click the "Add New" button to reach the friendly URL creation form. It has a handful of fields:

- **Page**. The drop-down list gives you all the pages that can benefit from a friendly URL.
- **Page title**. The title that will appear in search engines when a request is made.
- **Meta description**. A presentation of the page in just a few words, intended to capture a customer's interest. It will appear in search results.
- **Meta Keywords**. Keywords that you must define in order to have your site referenced by search engines. You can enter several of them: type the words, press the Return key, and see how the tag gets encapsulated in a yellow block, with a tiny cross icon to delete it.
- **Rewritten URL**. This is where you set the friendly URL. Make it short and descriptive, use only letters and numbers, and replace spaces (" ") by hyphens ("-").

Set up URLs

The main options for friendly URLs:

- **Friendly URL**. Change this option **if you know that your server** can support URL rewriting. If not, leave it at "No".
-

> You may see a message such as "*URL rewriting (mod_rewrite) is not active on your server or it is not possible to check your server configuration. If you want to use Friendly URLs you must activate this mod*". In this case, PrestaShop cannot detect your server settings, but that does not mean the feature will not work. You must test it yourself.

- **Accented URL**. PrestaShop is now able to produce URL with special characters, for products with non ASCII names. You can disable that option here.
- **Redirect to Canonical URL**. Canonical URLs are a way to eliminate self-created duplicate content – which can dramatically bring your search engine rank down, as this is considered spam. To avoid search engines thinking you are spamming their index, PrestaShop uses standard rel="canonical" link tag to indicate which is the one base URL for a given content.
  While it is highly recommended to enable this option, it also depends on your theme actually implementing correctly the <link> header tag. Ask the theme designer for more information.
- **Disable apache multiviews**. Apache is the most popular web server, and is most likely the one your web host uses for your site (although you should check this for yourself). Multiviews is a content negotiation system: when enabled, the web server tries to serve the user a page in what it thinks is the best matching language version, under the same URL. Unfortunately, this might bring trouble to PrestaShop's friendly URLs feature. If this is the case, you can try to disable multiviews with this option.
- **Disable apache mod security**. mod_security is an Apache server module which acts as a firewall, protecting your server from intrusions. It can however block some key features, or even produce errors in some configuration. In such case, disable that firewall here.

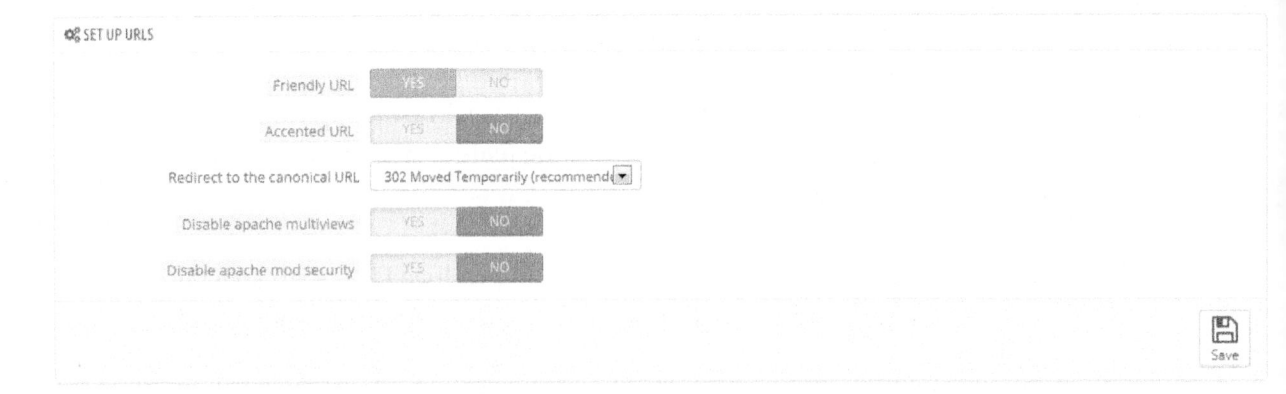

> In previous version of PrestaShop, you had to manually generate a new .htaccess file after having enabled friendly URLs. This is no longer the case since version 1.5: the .htaccess file is now silently managed by PrestaShop, and you do not have to worry about it.

Set shop URL

In this section, you can view and edit some of the default server settings:

- **Shop domain**. Your store's main domain name or IP address.
- **SSL domain**. Your store's secure domain name (https://) or IP address.
- **Base URI**. The folder where you installed PrestaShop. If it is at the root of the domain, use "/".

Most of the time, you should not touch these fields without knowing exactly what you are doing. One mistake could break your shop.

Schema of URLs

New in 1.6.

You can change the way friendly URLs are generated, by changing the route to a resource on your shop.

For instance, the default route to display a product's page is {category:/}{id}-{rewrite}{-:ean13}.html, which results in /summer-dresses/7-printed-chiffon-dress.html
You could change that route to {manufacturer:/}{id}-{rewrite:/} to obtain /fashion-manufacturer//7-printed-chiffon-dress/

8 fields are available by default, and each is accompanied with a list of available keywords. Some keywords are mandatory, and are indicated with a *.

SCHEMA OF URLS

Change the pattern of your links. There are some available keywords for each route listed below, keywords with * are required. To add a keyword in your URL use {keyword} syntax. You can add text before or after the keyword if the keyword is not empty with syntax {prepend:keyword:append}. For example {-hey:meta_title} will add "-hey-my-title" in the URL if the meta title is set. Friendly URL and rewriting Apache option must be activated on your web server to use this functionality.

Route to products	{category:/}{id}-{rewrite}{-:ean13}.html
	Keywords: id*, rewrite, ean13, category, categories, reference, meta_keywords, meta_title, manufacturer, supplier, price, tags
Route to category	{id}-{rewrite}
	Keywords: id*, rewrite, meta_keywords, meta_title
Route to category with attribute selected_filter for the module block layered	{id}-{rewrite}{/:selected_filters}
	Keywords: id*, selected_filters*, rewrite, meta_keywords, meta_title
Route to supplier	{id}__{rewrite}
	Keywords: id*, rewrite, meta_keywords, meta_title
Route to manufacturer	{id}_{rewrite}
	Keywords: id*, rewrite, meta_keywords, meta_title
Route to CMS page	content/{id}-{rewrite}
	Keywords: id*, rewrite, meta_keywords, meta_title
Route to CMS category	content/category/{id}-{rewrite}
	Keywords: id*, rewrite, meta_keywords, meta_title
Route to modules	module/{module}{/:controller}
	Keywords: module*, controller*

Once you have updated your fields, do not forget to save your changes, then on the "Save" button in the "Set up URLs" section in order to regenerate your .htaccess file, which is necessary for your friendly URLs.

Robots file generation

A robots.txt file enables you to block specific automated bots and web spiders which crawl the Web in order to find more web pages to add to their company's servers. Some bots you want to have full access to your website, such as Google's or Yahoo!'s, and some others you would rather not, such as spam bots, content thiefs, e-mail collectors, etc. Note that the worst of bots do not respect this file's directives, as it is purely advisory.

PrestaShop's robots.txt generation tool simply creates a file with exclusion directives for files and directories that are not meant to be public, and should not be indexed. These directives apply to all bots, good or bad: the generated file uses the "User-agent: *" string.

Clicking on the "Generate robots.txt" button replaces any existing robots.txt file with a new one. Therefore, if you want to add your own rules, do it after PrestaShop has generated its version of the file.

CMS - Managing Static Content

PrestaShop enables you create content pages as easily as you would create product pages, using its CMS tool. The pages will appear to customers in the "Information" block on your homepage and in the site menu. You can add CMS pages in the top menu using the "Top horizontal menu" module (which you can configure from the "Modules" page).

The "CMS" page presents you all the content pages that were previously created on your shop, for the currently selected category (by default, the home page is the only category).

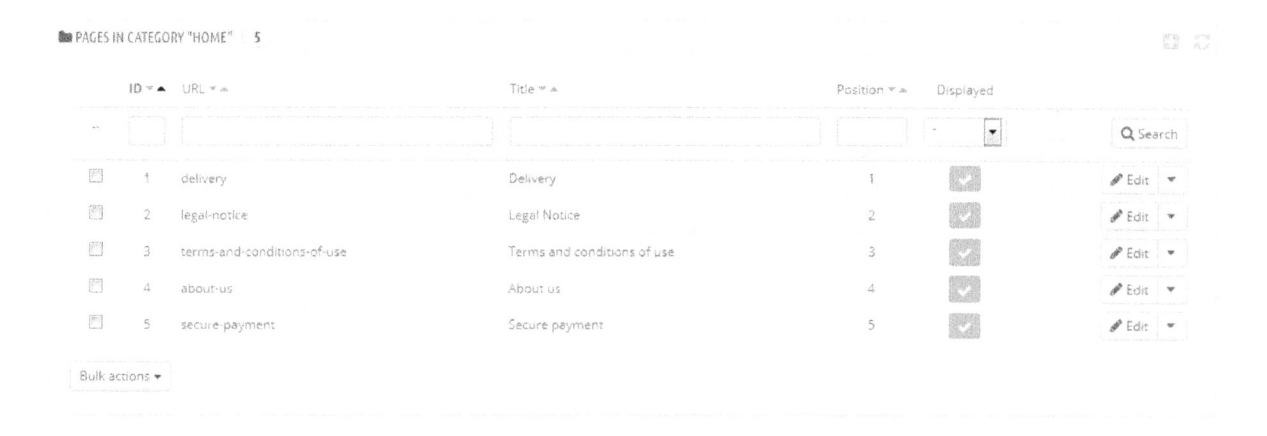

ID	URL	Title	Position	Displayed	
1	delivery	Delivery	1	✓	Edit
2	legal-notice	Legal Notice	2	✓	Edit
3	terms-and-conditions-of-use	Terms and conditions of use	3	✓	Edit
4	about-us	About us	4	✓	Edit
5	secure-payment	Secure payment	5	✓	Edit

Do not forget to create one version of each page for each of your supported languages! As usual, click on the language selector for each field in order to change language.

Creating a New CMS Category

Click the "Add new" button to create a CMS category – actually, a sub-category of the root category, "Home". You can create as many categories as needed.

CMS CATEGORY

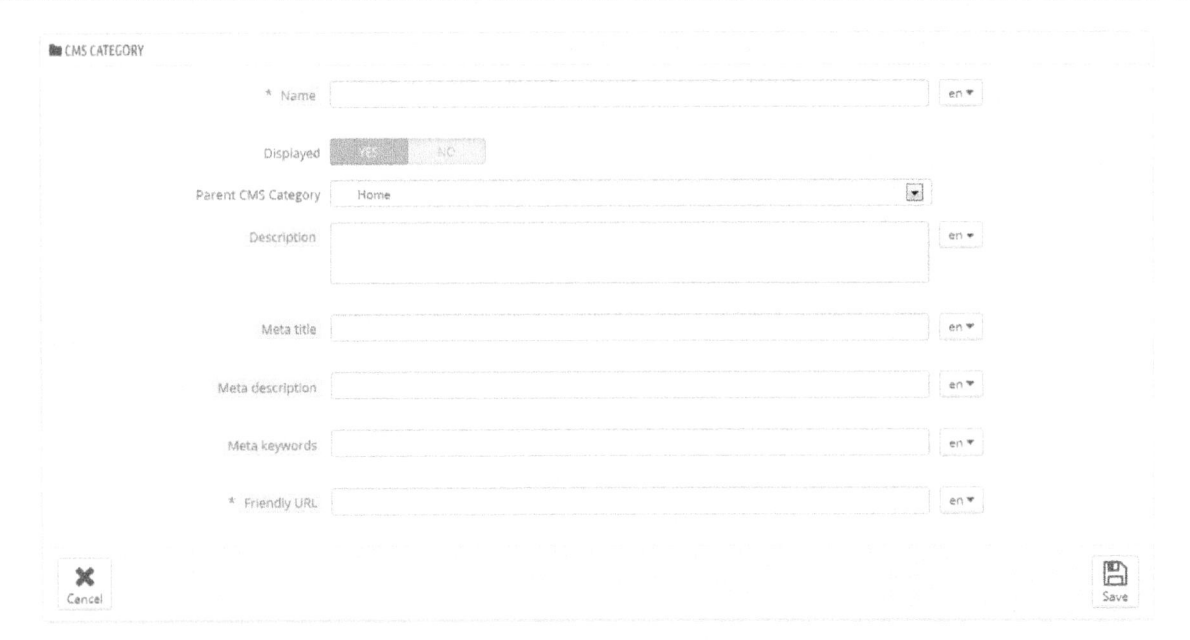

The form is quite basic:

- **Name**. Make sure to use a short and straightforward word.
- **Displayed**. Whether the category and its pages are available to the public, or hidden.
- **Parent CMS category**. The category under which this category is placed. By default, "Home". You can have an unlimited number of levels of sub-categories.
- **Description**. Do fill this field in all languages, as some theme can display that information to customers.
- **Meta title**. The name of the category, as displayed in the browser.
- **Meta description**. Used to describe the content of this category for search engines.
- **Meta keywords**. Used by search engines to understand what type of information the category is composed of.
- **Friendly URL**. Makes it easier for search engines to index your content, and for visitors to understand what they will find in the category. This field is automatically filled as you enter the category name, but you can still edit it manually.

When you save the category, PrestaShop takes you back to the tables, this time using the newly created category as its base. Therefore, you will not see any

sub-category or sub-pages in here unless you create some.
In order to go back to the root category, click on "Home" in the "Current category" section at the top. You can then edit each pages from the root category and move them into your newly created category if you feel like it.

> In order to create sub-categories, simply change the "Parent CMS Category" option from "Home" to the wanted parent category for the category you are creating.

Creating a New CMS Page

Click the "Add New" button to reach the content creation form:

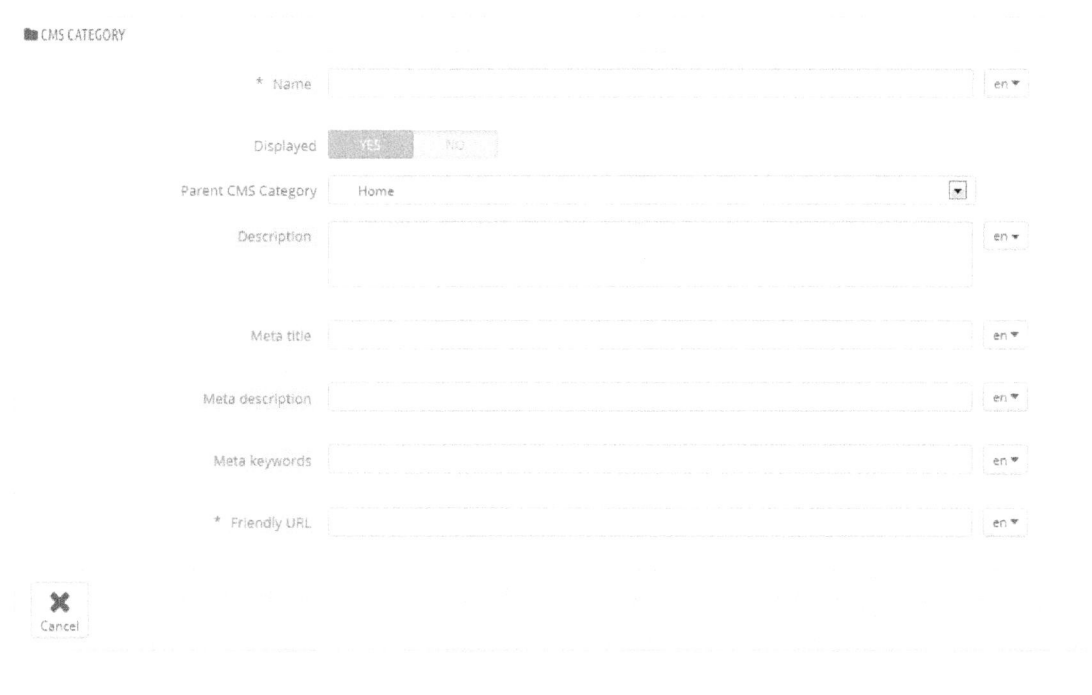

- **CMS Category**. The default category is the home-page of your shop. If you want to have this page in another category, you must first have created.
- **Meta title**. The name of the page, as displayed in the browser.
- **Meta description**. Used to describe the content of this page for search engines.
- **Meta Keywords**. Used by search engines to understand what types of information the page is composed of.

- **Friendly URL**. Makes it easier for search engines to index your content, and for visitors to understand what they will find in the category. This field is automatically filled as you enter the category name, but you can still edit it manually.
- **Page content**. This is the main content of your page. In this WYSIWYG editor, you can put as much text as necessary, even images or videos using the "Insert Image" or "Insert Embedded Media".
- **Indexation by search engine**. Indicates whether search engines should register this page or not.
- **Displayed**. You can choose to have you page public only once you are done proofreading it, and keep it as a draft for the moment. A draft is invisible to the public.

Once all the fields are filled out, click on "Save." If activated, you can then view the result directly on your online shop.

Images Preferences

The "Images" preference page enables you to configure the various image sizes that your customers will see on your shop.

> When you upload an image on PrestaShop, PrestaShop automatically generates various sizes of this image, including thumbnails and a mobile version (depending on what this image will apply to). Therefore, you only have to upload one "master" version of your image, big enough to be resized into all the images sizes.
>
> If you want to make sure your image is correctly resized, you should upload an image that fits the size ratio of the various image sizes. If your uploaded image does not have the same width-to-height ratio than the settings in place, you are taking the risk to see whitespace on the resized image.

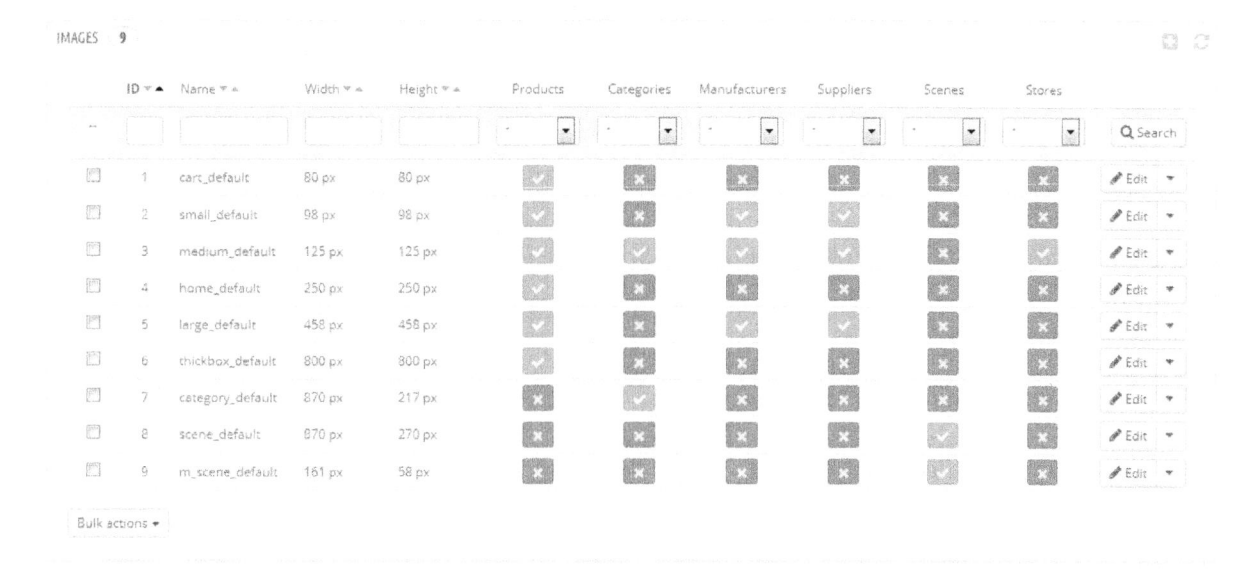

	ID	Name	Width	Height	Products	Categories	Manufacturers	Suppliers	Scenes	Stores	
	1	cart_default	80 px	80 px	✓	✗	✗	✗	✗	✗	Edit
	2	small_default	98 px	98 px	✓	✗	✓	✓	✗	✗	Edit
	3	medium_default	125 px	125 px	✓	✓	✓	✓	✗	✓	Edit
	4	home_default	250 px	250 px	✓	✗	✗	✗	✗	✗	Edit
	5	large_default	458 px	458 px	✓	✗	✓	✓	✗	✗	Edit
	6	thickbox_default	800 px	800 px	✓	✗	✗	✗	✗	✗	Edit
	7	category_default	870 px	217 px	✗	✓	✗	✗	✗	✗	Edit
	8	scene_default	870 px	270 px	✗	✗	✗	✗	✓	✗	Edit
	9	m_scene_default	161 px	58 px	✗	✗	✗	✗	✓	✗	Edit

You can enable image size for specific types of content, directly in the image sizes list.

> In the "Products" page under the "Preferences" menu, you can choose to have a zoom appear when the cursor hovers over a product's image.

Add a New Images Size

You can easily add a new image size, and even set to which type of content it applies.

Click the "Add new" button, then:

1. Type the size's name, width and height.
2. Choose to which type of content it applies.
3. Validate.

Images preferences

- **Image quality**. You have the choice between two of the major file formats: JPEG and PNG. Both are well established among browsers. JPEG has a good compression ratio, but can result in visible artifacts. PNG's compression algorithm is not as good as JPEG's, but there are comparatively fewer visible artifacts; nonetheless, older browsers might not recognize this format.
  Choosing between one and the other is often a matter of taste. That being said, JPEG remains the recommended choice. If you would rather prevent information loss because of a format change, choose the second option, "Use PNG only if the base image is in PNG format".

PNG format is not compatible with the "Watermark" module.

- **JPEG quality**. Do not choose anything below 80 or at worst 75, for fear of visible compression artifacts.

- **PNG quality**. Do not choose anything over 6 or at worst 7, for fear of visible compression artifacts.
- **Image generated by**. This feature allows you to position the product image in its pre-established space:
    - Choose "height" in order to fill the frame height (the width is then recalculated to maintain the same height/width ratio as in the file of origin).
    - Choose "width" so that the image fills the width of the frame (the height is then recalculated to maintain the same proportion).
    - Choose "auto" so that the width and height are calculated to maximize the space it can occupy in the frame.
- **Maximum size of product pictures**. Your customers can upload pictures for customized products. By default, PrestaShop sets this value to the PHP maximum setting – this can mean several megabytes: for instance, 8,388,608 bytes means 8 Mb. You can expand this value if necessary, but make sure that your PHP installation is able to take file uploads of this size.
- **Product picture width**. By default, customers can upload image with a maximum width of 64 pixels.
- **Product picture height**. By default, customers can upload image with a maximum height of 64 pixels.

Regenerate Images

You may be dissatisfied with your shop's current thumbnails size. This section makes it possible for you to regenerate them all – or only those for a specific type of content:

1. Change the image size settings in the table at the top of the "Images" preference page.
2. Select which content's images should be regenerated.
3. Indicate whether the previous thumbnails should be kept or not.
4. Click "Regenerate thumbnails".

> Manually-uploaded thumbnails will be erased and replaced by automatically-generated thumbnails.

Store Contacts Preferences

PrestaShop provides a complete physical store locating tool for your customers, with detailed contact information.

Customers can reach the Store Locator page from the front-office.

Obviously, this feature is only useful if you do have physical stores, where customers can come buy products.

> You cannot disable this feature, but you can make it inaccessible to customers:
>
> - Delete all the stores listed in the "Store Contacts" administration page. The Stores block will not appear anymore on the front-page.
> - Go the "Modules" page from the "Modules" menu. Find the "Store Locator" module and disable it.
> - Disable the link in the footer: in the "Stores Contacts" administration page, choose "No" for the "Display in the footer" option.
>
> If you do have stores in your database but you do not want the Stores block to be displayed in the front-page, either temporarily or permanently:
>
> 1. Go to the "Positions" page in the "Modules" menu.
> 2. Find the "Right column blocks" section, and delete the "Store locator block" from the list, either by click its trashcan icon, or by checking its checkbox and clicking on the "Unhook the selection" button at the top of the page.
> 3. Reload the front-page: the Store Locator block should not be here anymore. If it is still here, it might be because of the cache: go to the

> "Performance" page of the "Advanced parameters" menu, disable the cache and force the theme compilation temporarily. Once all this is done, reload the front-page.
>
> You can put the block back in the right column from the "Positions" page:
>
> 1. Click on the "Transplant a module" button at the top right of the page.
> 2. Choose the "Store locator block" module in the list.
> 3. Choose the "displayRightColumn (Right column blocks)" hook.
> 4. Save the page. Reload the front-page: the Stores block should be back in the right column.

Store list

You can choose how these stores are displayed in the front-office. The customer can access them through the "Our stores" link (depending on the theme)

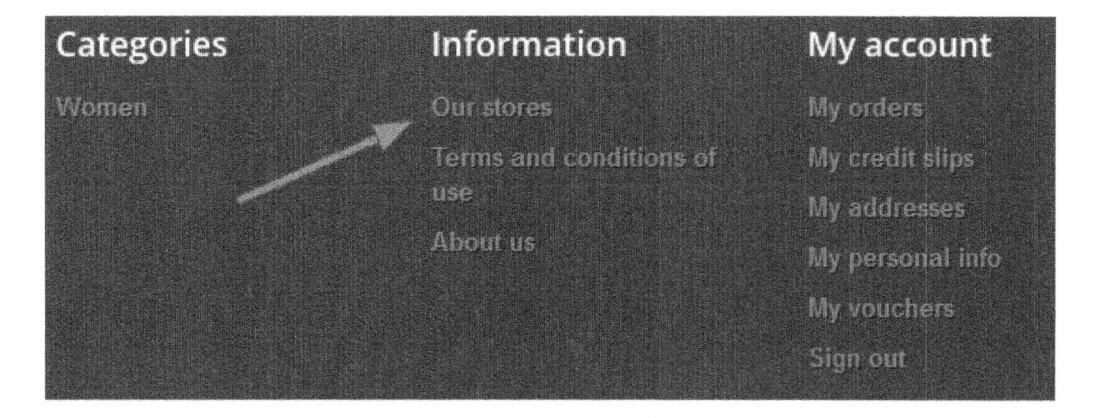

Categories	Information	My account
Women	Our stores	My orders
	Terms and conditions of use	My credit slips
		My addresses
	About us	My personal info
		My vouchers
		Sign out

All your stores are listed in a handy list, giving every store's information as well as an indicator telling whether the store is currently active or not – you might for instance want to gather the information for a new store in advance, in order to have its page ready for the launch.

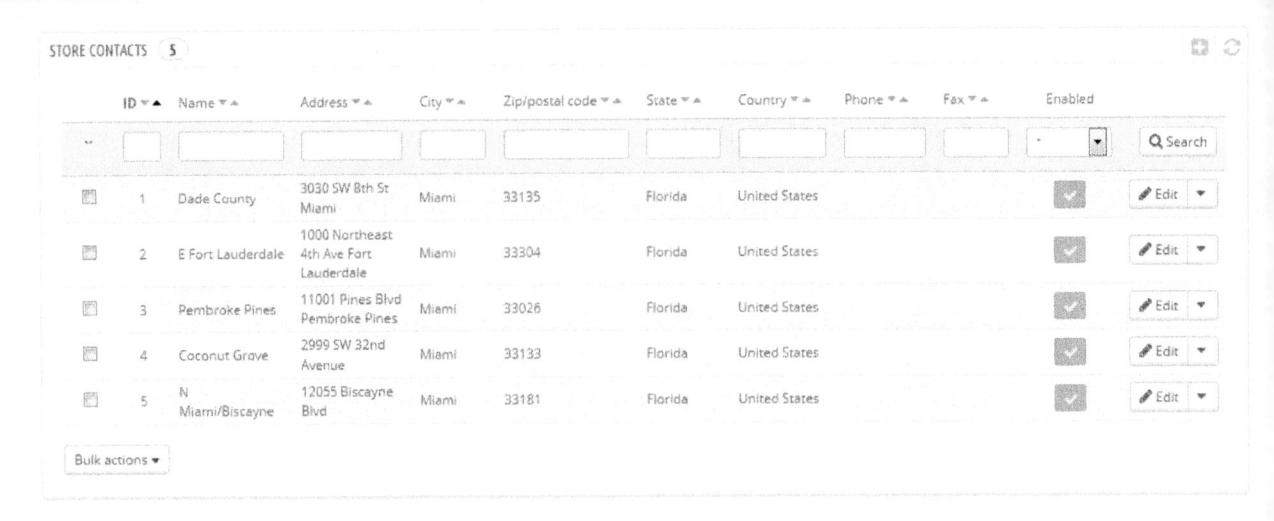

	ID	Name	Address	City	Zip/postal code	State	Country	Phone	Fax	Enabled	
	1	Dade County	3030 SW 8th St Miami	Miami	33135	Florida	United States			✓	Edit
	2	E Fort Lauderdale	1000 Northeast 4th Ave Fort Lauderdale	Miami	33304	Florida	United States			✓	Edit
	3	Pembroke Pines	11001 Pines Blvd Pembroke Pines	Miami	33026	Florida	United States			✓	Edit
	4	Coconut Grove	2999 SW 32nd Avenue	Miami	33133	Florida	United States			✓	Edit
	5	N Miami/Biscayne	12055 Biscayne Blvd	Miami	33181	Florida	United States			✓	Edit

Adding a new physical store

As usual, click "Add New" to reach the store creation form.

STORES

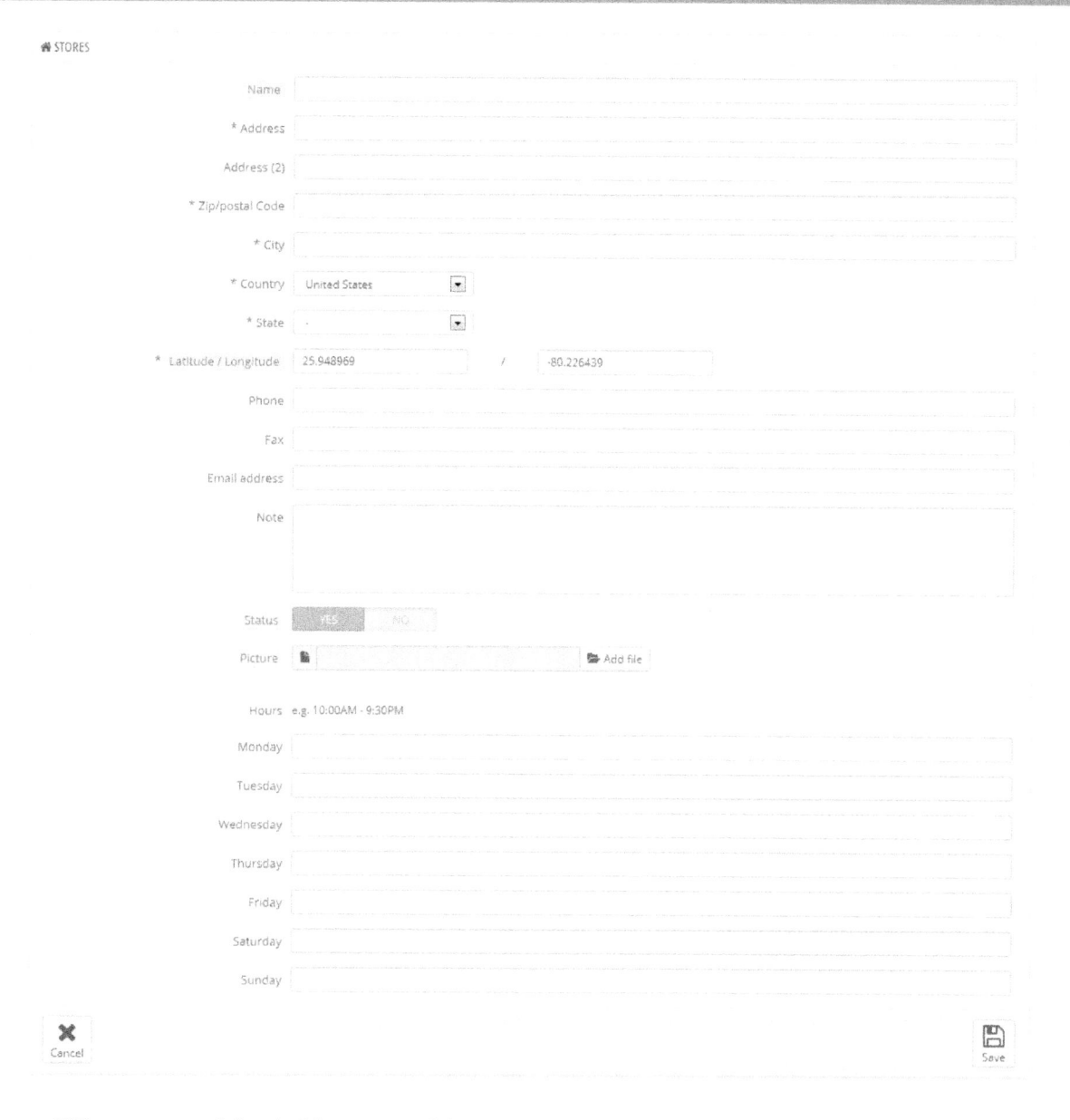

Name	
* Address	
Address (2)	
* Zip/postal Code	
* City	
* Country	United States
* State	-
* Latitude / Longitude	25.948969 / -80.226439
Phone	
Fax	
Email address	
Note	
Status	YES NO
Picture	Add file
Hours	e.g. 10:00AM - 9:30PM
Monday	
Tuesday	
Wednesday	
Thursday	
Friday	
Saturday	
Sunday	

Cancel   Save

Fill as many of the fields as possible, as they will be displayed to your customers within the map.

OUR STORE(S)!

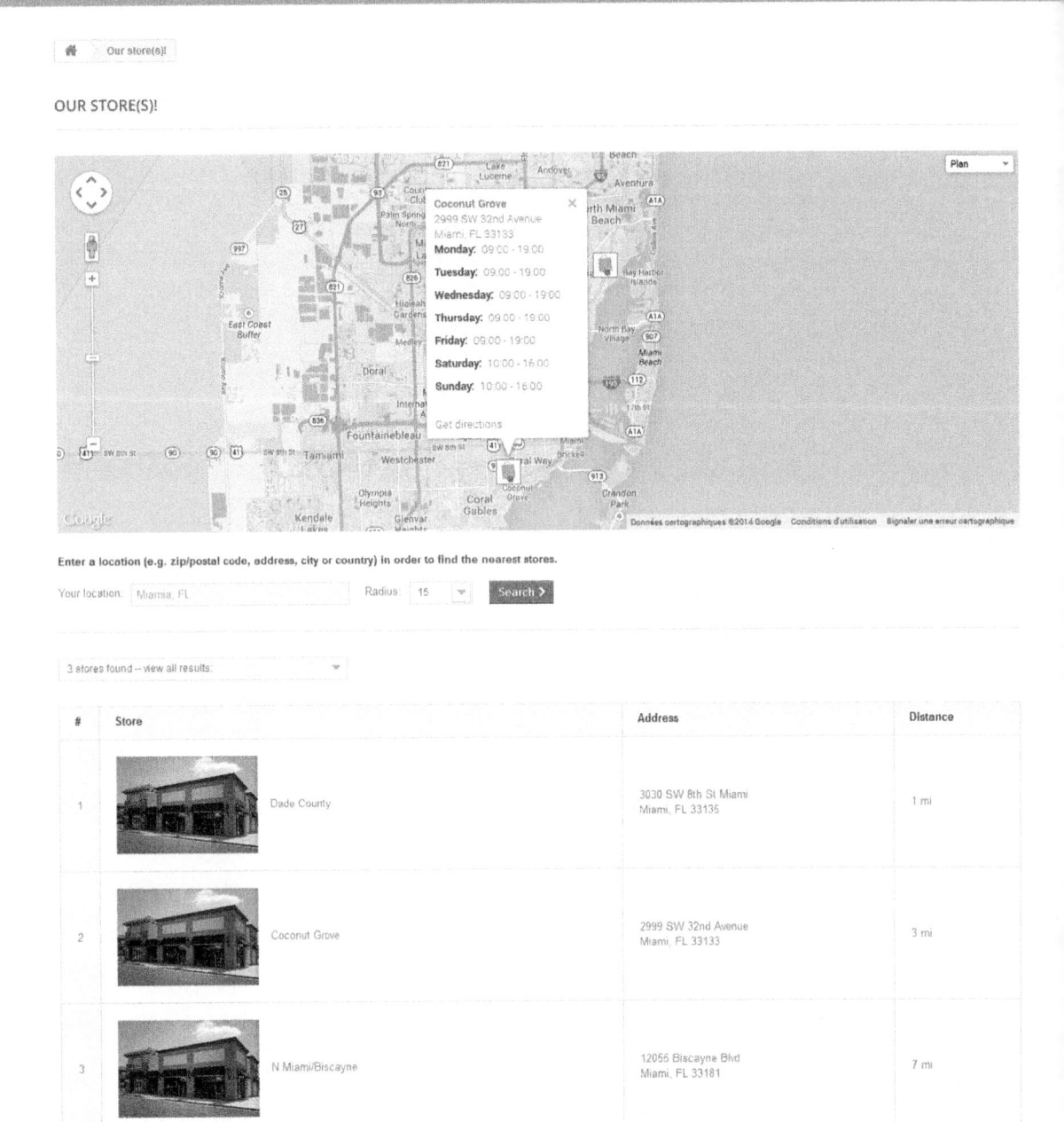

One very important field is the "Latitude/Longitude" one, as this is what PrestaShop uses to indicate the location of your store. You can use Steve Morse's online tool to get the lat/long coordinates of a given address: http://stevemorse.org/jcal/latlon.php.

Make sure to add a picture of the store front, as this is how your customers will be able to find it once in the street.

Finally, the business hours are an essential part of any physical store, and you should be as precise as possible about them.

Parameters

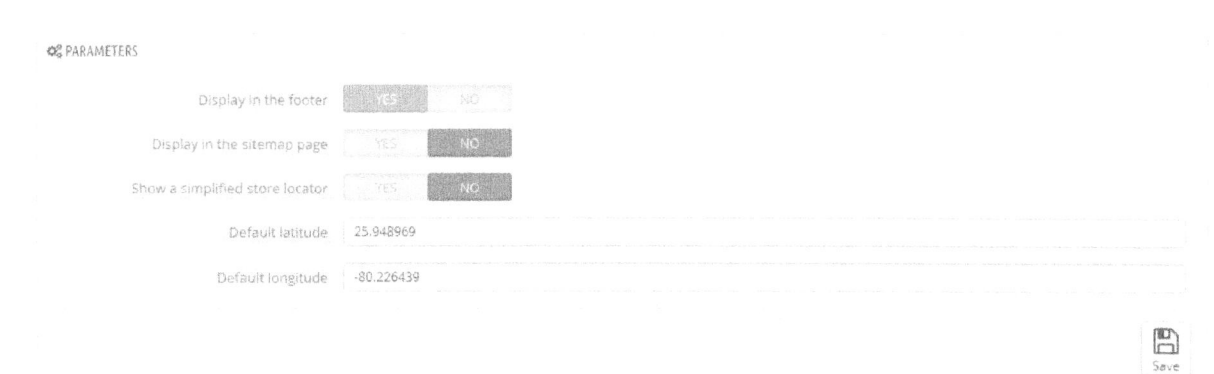

Display in the footer	YES / NO
Display in the sitemap page	YES / NO
Show a simplified store locator	YES / NO
Default latitude	25.948969
Default longitude	-80.226439

- **Display in the footer**. By default, PrestaShop displays a link to the store locator, titled "Our stores", in your shop's footer. In the default theme, it appears in the "Information" block, below the special product listing pages (best sellers, new products, specials, etc.). You can choose not to have that link appear here.
- **Display in the sitemap page**. You can choose to add the "Our stores" link in your shop's sitemap page, which lists all the pages on your site (not to be confused with your Google Sitemap file, which is for SEO purpose).
- **Show a simplified store locator**. The store locator presents itself as an interactive map with a search field. You can choose to make that interface much simpler by only displaying a list of stores.
- **Default Latitude** and **Default longitude**. The default starting position of your map. Very useful when you have many stores and you would rather primarily point customers to a specific area.

Contact details

This section enables you to give the main details of your company, rather than those of a specific shop. You should fill all the fields with information on your headquarters, as this is certainly the address customers will use to contact you, or even visit you.

These fields should be carefully filled:

- **Shop name**. The name of your store. Keep it short, as it will be used in all your correspondence and page titles.
- **Shop email**. The official contact address for your business. Use the general contact e-mail address that the customers should see when they receive an e-mail from your shop.
- **Registration**. Indicate your company's legal registration numbers, which depends on your country's legal system (Duns number in the USA, SIRET number in France, CNPJ number in Brazil, etc.). This shows that you are a fully registered business, thus giving a more reassuring opinion of your shop to your potential customers.
- **Shop address line 1 / Address line 2 / Postal code/Zip code / City / State / Country**. Use the official contact address of your business. The "State" option only appears when the selected country has states set in your database (through the "States" page in the "Localization" menu)
- **Phone**. The official contact phone number for your business. If you'd rather customers not call you, do not put anything in there.
- **Fax**. The official contact fax number for your business.

> Do not use a colon (":") in your store's name, as it might prevent some features from working (for instance, e-mail sending might fail).
>
> You can replace the colon with a dash if you need to have two sections in the title. For instance, use "MyStore – The best place for items to buy" instead of "MyStore: The best place for items to buy".

Search Preferences

The "Search" page enables you to configure your shop's search features.

Aliases list

When customers make a request using your shop's internal search engine, they may make mistakes in spelling. If PrestaShop does not display the right results, the "alias" feature can address them. You will be able to take words containing spelling errors, and point them to the real products sought by customers.

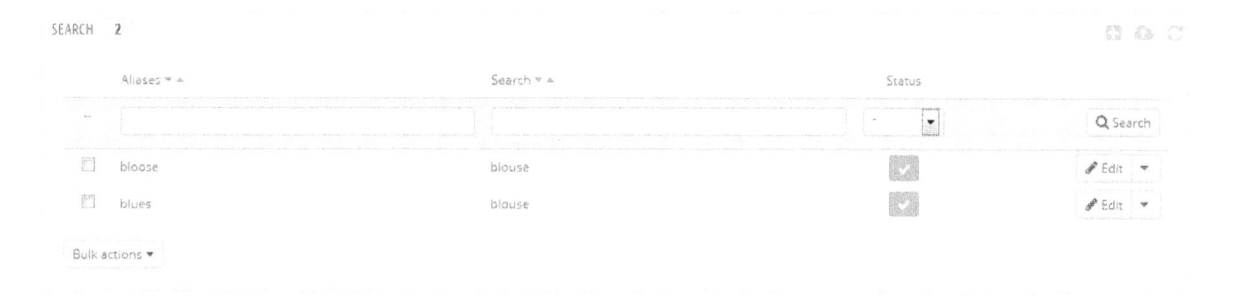

Aliases	Search	Status	
bloose	blouse	✓	Edit
blues	blouse	✓	Edit

To create a new useful alias, you should first find the spelling errors most often typed by your users:

1. Go to the "Shop search" tab of the "Stats" page, under the "Stats" menu. You can see the words typed by your customers as well as the most frequent errors.
2. Take the most frequent ones, and add them to your list of aliases, in order to point user to the correct products.
3. Click the "Add new" button on the "Search" preference page.

The creation form is very straight forward: indicate the typo you want corrected, and the correct word it should lead to.

Q ALIASES

* Alias
* Result

For instance, let's say your visitors frequently type "player" as "palyer" and "plaier". You can create an alias for each of these typos, which will match the word "Player". Your aliases can be used as soon as they are saved.

We also invite you to consult the sections of this guide on product and category meta tags, to better understand how to display products based on words typed by your customers. See the "Adding Products and Product Categories" and "A Look inside the Catalog" chapters.

Indexation

This section provides information on the number of products that can be searched through your shop's search function, and compares it to the number of products present in the database. If the values do not match, you must select the "Add missing products to the index" option. Only the new products will be indexed.

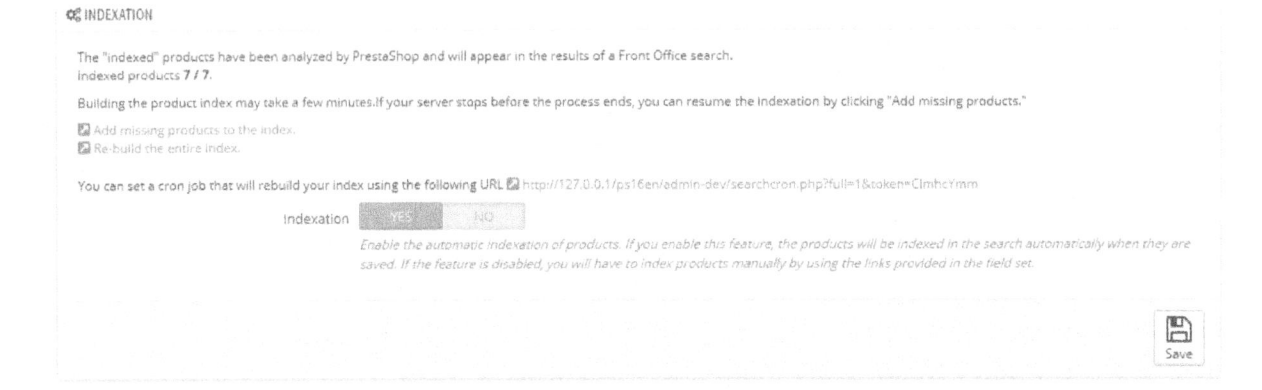

INDEXATION

The "indexed" products have been analyzed by PrestaShop and will appear in the results of a Front Office search.
Indexed products 7 / 7.

Building the product index may take a few minutes. If your server stops before the process ends, you can resume the indexation by clicking "Add missing products."

- Add missing products to the index.
- Re-build the entire index.

You can set a cron job that will rebuild your index using the following URL http://127.0.0.1/ps16en/admin-dev/searchcron.php?full=1&token=ClmhcYmm

Indexation   YES   NO

Enable the automatic indexation of products. If you enable this feature, the products will be indexed in the search automatically when they are saved. If the feature is disabled, you will have to index products manually by using the links provided in the field set.

Save

If you have made several changes to already indexed products, you might prefer to choose to re-build the whole index. The "Re-build entire index" process takes more time, but it is more thorough.

PrestaShop also gives you the URL to let you create a cron task for regular re-building of the index. If you do not know about cron and crontab, ask your web host about it.

Finally, the "Indexation" option enables you to have a product be indexed as soon as it is created/modified, thus rending the above links and cron link useless.

Search options

This section enables you to configure the behavior of your shop's search function:

- **Ajax search**. Enabling it displays a list of 10 results from the moment your customers type a few letters into the search bar, right under the search bar.
- **Instant search**. Enabling it displays a list of results from the moment your customers type a few letters into the search bar, directly within your shop's main content area. This setting is disabled by default, because visitors are not always used to have their whole content changed just be entering a few letters in the shop's search bar. Therefore, use with caution.
- **Minimum word length**. You can choose the minimum size at which a word may be registered in the search index and found by your customers. This feature allows you to eliminate short words in the search, such as prepositions or articles (the, and, of, etc.).
- **Blacklisted words**. You can choose the terms that must not be found by your visitors. Enter them directly into the field, separated by "|".

Weight

PrestaShop enables you to prioritize certain data when a search is performed on your shop.

WEIGHT

The "weight" represents its importance and relevance for the ranking of the products when completing a new search.
A word with a weight of eight will have four times more value than a word with a weight of two.

We advise you to set a greater weight for words which appear in the name or reference of a product. This will allow the search results to be as precise and relevant as possible.

Setting a weight to 0 will exclude that field from search index. Re-build of the entire index is required when changing to or from 0

Product name weight	6
Reference weight	10
Short description weight	1
Description weight	1
Category weight	3
Manufacturer weight	3
Tags weight	4
Attributes weight	2
Features weight	2

Save

As indicated in the section, the search "weight" of a product represents its importance and relevance for the ranking of the products when customers try a new search. An item with a weight of 8 will have 4 times more value than an item with a weight of 2.

For instance, by default "Product Name Weight" is at 6, "Tags weight" is at 4, and both "Short description weight" and "Description weight" are at 1. This means a product with "ipod" in its name will appear higher in the search results than another product which has "ipod" only in its tags. Meanwhile, a product which only has "ipod" in any of its description will have the lowest rank in the search results.

You have many factors that you can assign a weight to: short description, category, tags, attributes, etc. You will find that the display order of results can be reversed because you changed the weight of the various fields. Fine-tuning these settings will be more visible on a large catalog with many references.

Once your changes are saved, they take effect immediately.

Maintenance Settings

This very simple preference page will be invaluable when you want to make changes to your shop without your customers noticing. For instance, when you are adding several new products at once, or when you want to change the theme and make several tests before making it available to the world.

This page only has two options:

- **Enable Shop**. You can use this option to disable your shop temporarily, for instance when you need to perform maintenance on your shop.

> The webservice will still be active, so your data will still be available to those with a key. If you want to also disable the webservice, go to the "Webservice" preference page, in the "Advanced parameters" menu.

- **Maintenance IP**. The maintenance IP allows people to access the shop even if it is disabled. This means that you can prevent everyone on the Internet from accessing your shop, but still allow access to the computers used by your team-members and yourself. To discover the IP address of a machine, go to http://www.whatismyip.com/ from that machine. Click "Add my IP" if you only want to add the IP of your current computer. If you want to add more IP addresses, separate them with commas ",".

Geolocation Preferences

Geolocation is "the identification of the real-world geographic location of an object, such as a radar, a mobile phone or an Internet-connected computer" (read more on http://en.wikipedia.org/wiki/Geolocation). In our case, geolocation is used to discover the location of a visitor, using his or her computer's IP and other tools. One of the uses of geolocation is to block visitors from certain cities/countries.

As indicated the first time you open the "Geolocation" page, in order to use geolocation, you need download a special file first:
http://geolite.maxmind.com/download/geoip/database/GeoLiteCity.dat.gz. This file is the GeoLite City database from MaxMind, an accurate database of cities and locations. Download it by clicking on the link, and then decompress it into the /tools/geoip/ directory of your PrestaShop installation.

Once the file is in place, enable the "Geolocation by IP address" option, and you are set.

Options

You can choose which countries can access your shop (by default, all of them), and set PrestaShop's behaviors for restricted and unrestricted countries (or "other" countries). You choose between these three options:

- Visitors cannot see your catalog.
- Visitors can see your catalog but cannot make an order. In effect, you shop is in "Catalog mode".
- All features are available (only for unrestricted countries).

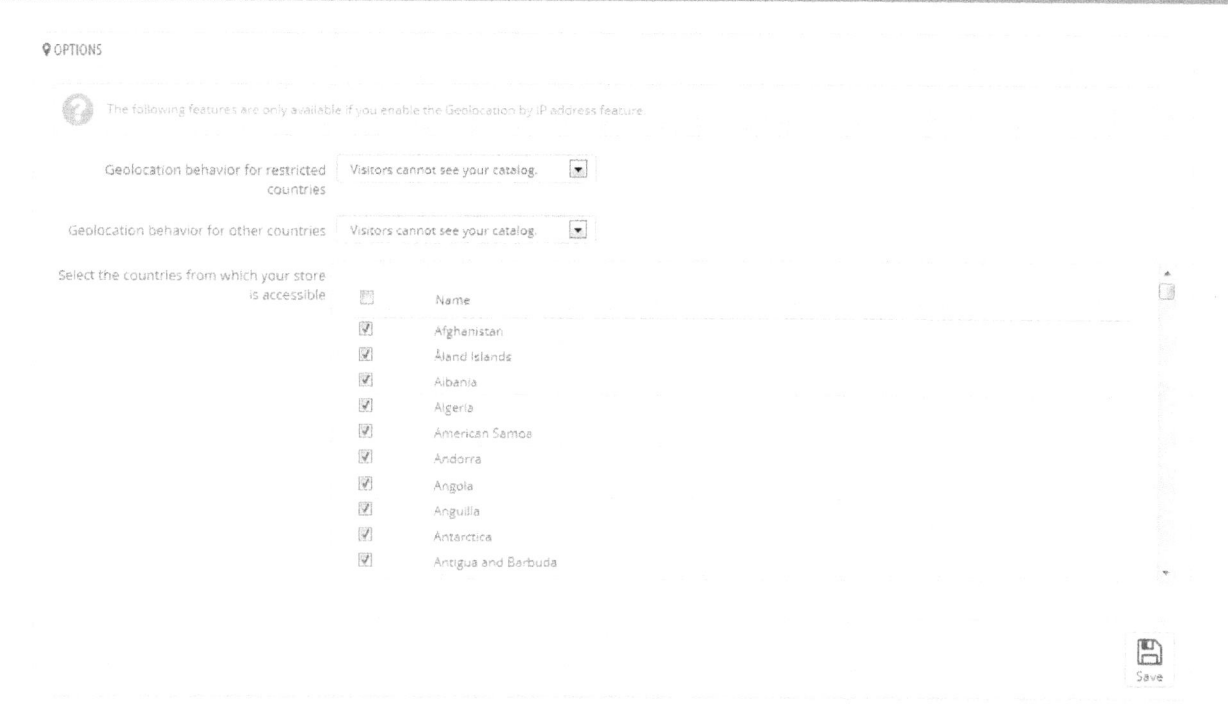

You can select or deselect all countries at once by checking the box at the top of the list. When selecting countries that can access your online shop, make sure to not block any country by mistake, as you would lose all potential sales to its inhabitants!

Whitelist of IP address

This section enables you to accept specific IPs address despite a blockade. It can be useful in case of spammers, bots or attacks. It is already filled with a list of known good IPs. Add as many as needed, one per line, and click "Save".

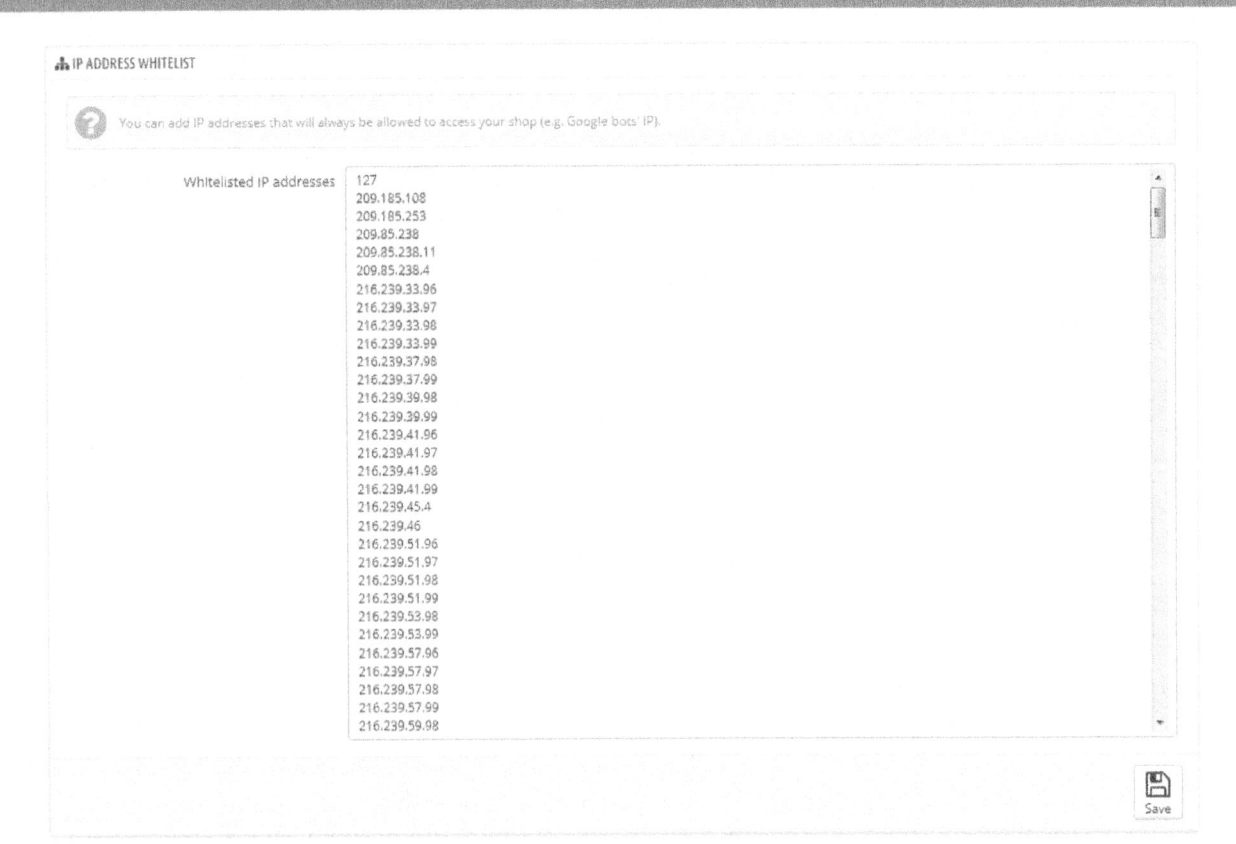

IP ADDRESS WHITELIST

You can add IP addresses that will always be allowed to access your shop (e.g. Google bots' IP).

Whitelisted IP addresses:
```
127
209.185.108
209.185.253
209.85.238
209.85.238.11
209.85.238.4
216.239.33.96
216.239.33.97
216.239.33.98
216.239.33.99
216.239.37.98
216.239.37.99
216.239.39.98
216.239.39.99
216.239.41.96
216.239.41.97
216.239.41.98
216.239.41.99
216.239.45.4
216.239.46
216.239.51.96
216.239.51.97
216.239.51.98
216.239.51.99
216.239.53.98
216.239.53.99
216.239.57.96
216.239.57.97
216.239.57.98
216.239.57.99
216.239.59.98
```

Save

Understanding the Advanced Parameters

Configuration Information

This page serves as a handy reminder of your PrestaShop configuration: version, server info, PHP version, a MySQL version. All these prove really useful when you need to report an issue to the PrestaShop developers, or simply your webmaster or web host.

CONFIGURATION INFORMATION

This information must be provided when you report an issue on our bug tracker or forum.

SERVER INFORMATION

Server information: Windows NT build 7601 (Windows 7 Business Edition Service Pack 1) AMD64
Server software version: Apache/2.4.4 (Win64) OpenSSL/1.0.1d PHP/5.4.12
PHP version: 5.4.12
Memory limit: 128M
Max execution time: 30

DATABASE INFORMATION

MySQL version: 5.6.12-log
MySQL engine: InnoDB
Tables prefix: ps_

STORE INFORMATION

PrestaShop version: 1.6.0.5
Shop URL: http://127.0.0.1/ps16en/
Current theme in use: default-bootstrap

MAIL CONFIGURATION

Mail method: You are using the PHP mail function.

YOUR INFORMATION

Your web browser: Mozilla/5.0 (Windows NT 6.1; WOW64; rv:28.0) Gecko/20100101 Firefox/28.0

CHECK YOUR CONFIGURATION

Required parameters: OK
Optional parameters: OK

There is one last section, titled "List of changed files". Right after you have first installed PrestaShop, the only thing that this section displays is "No change has been detected in your files".

But after you've installed some modules and a couple of themes, made advanced changes to some override classes or deleted files altogether, this list will show the difference between your current installation of PrestaShop and what it used to look like in its pristine state. This helps you see what changes have been made to your installation... and therefore what to take into account if you want to update your store manually, or if you are moving files to a new server.

> Even with a fresh installation, this section might indicate ".gitattributes", ".gitignore", "CONTRIBUTING.md", "CONTRIBUTORS.md" or "README.md" as missing files. These are Git-specific files, and PrestaShop does not use them, so you should not worry about them.

Performance parameters

This page combines many tools and tips that might help you improve your shop's performance server-wise – not sales-wise, although a server that performs well is able to serve more customers, and therefore make more sales.

Smarty

Smarty is the name of the template language used by PrestaShop's themes. You can learn more about it at http://www.smarty.net/.

There are two options:

- **Template cache**. For better front-end performance, PrestaShop caches your HTML pages.
    - **Never recompile template files**. Only enable this if you are making edits theme, and need to see your changes every time you reload your page.
    - **Compile templates if the files have been updated**. PrestaShop is able to see when a theme file has changed, but this might not always work as expected.
    - **Force compilation**. The normal behavior: HTML pages are compiled and cached, even if the theme has changed.
- **Cache**. This option makes it possible for you to disable all file caches, and not just the one pertaining to template files. Only disable this if you debugging a theme or a module for PrestaShop. Otherwise, you should leave it enabled.
  The "Clear Smarty cache" makes it possible to delete the cache in a single click instead of having to go delete files on your FTP server.

Debug mode

New in 1.6.

When in debug mode, you can choose to lessen the impact of certain features on PrestaShop, in order to best pinpoint where an error comes from:

- **Disable non PrestaShop modules**. PrestaShop's own module are heavily tested and should present no issue whatsoever. If you enable this setting, you will be able to tell if the problem comes from PrestaShop's own code (core or module), or from a third-party module.
- **Disable all overrides**. Many features in PrestaShop can be overridden. If you enable this settings, all overriding code will be disabled, and you will be able to tell if the problem comes from PrestaShop's own code, or from a third-party override.

Optional features

Some PrestaShop features can be disabled if you do not use them, as they can slow down your shop.

> If your catalog currently has products which make use of these features, then you will not be able to disable them. You will have to delete some data before you can turn them off.

You can disable the following features:

- **Combinations**. Product combinations enable you to have a whole product line out of a single product: varying size, colors, capacity, etc.
- **Features**. Product features enable you to indicate the product's specific information: weight, material, country of origin, etc.
- **Customer groups**. Customer groups enable you to group customers in order to give them certain privileges and restrictions: discount, module restrictions, etc.

Combine, Compress and Cache (CCC)

CCC is a set of tools aimed at minimizing server load and theme loading time.

It does what it says: it combines textual files of the same type into one bigger files, which makes for fewer files to download; it then compresses the file using the common Zip algorithm, which makes for faster downloads; finally, it caches the compressed file, so that the server does not have to do this process every time a page is loaded, which relieves the burden on the server's processor.

> Your theme must completely compatible with at least PrestaShop 1.4, otherwise CCC will not work as expected. This is why most options are disabled by default.

- **Smart cache for CSS**. CSS files are text-based, and can be safely combined and compressed.
- **Smart cache for JavaScript**. JavaScript files are also text-based, but their combination can sometimes prove problematic. Make sure to test everything before leaving that setting enabled.

- **Minify HTML**. The HTML code generated by Smarty can be minified, meaning that PrestaShop will remove all whitespace in order to save a few bytes. This is mostly safe.
- **Compress inline JavaScript in HTML**. Some themes have JavaScript code directly within. You can either leave it alone, or have them compressed. Again with JavaScript compression, make sure to test everything before leaving that setting enabled.
- **Apache optimization**. This setting will change your web server's configuration file in order to make it more efficient for CCC.

Media servers

This section enables you to redirect part of your traffic (image and video files, for instance) to other servers under your control, through other domains or sub-domains – most often, the files are hosted on a CDN (Content Delivery Network). By default, PrestaShop supports up to 3 media servers.

Putting your store's domain name in those fields is not the proper way to get fantastic performance. That being said, it is easy to set up a media server, and the benefits are real and almost immediate. Here is how:

1. Open an account at a new host, preferably one who is specialist of distributed content. The most popular are Akamai (http://www.akamai.com/), Amazon (with its AWS services, among which is CloudFront: http://aws.amazon.com/) or CloudFlare (http://www.cloudflare.com/). You should also ask your own host, maybe it has a CDN service you can subscribe to.
2. Copy your media files to that host's server. This means that the CDN server must contain an exact copy of the following folders from you

store's main server: /img, /themes and /modules.
Reminder: you must make it so that these folders are always synchronized: even if you add new products or change your theme, the CDN server must contain the latest version of all these files.
3. Once the CDN server is in place, add the web address (as given by your CDN host) in the first field, "Media server #1". If that host allows for more web addresses, add them.

In case you would rather that your files are still visually downloaded from your domain name rather that from an unknown domain name, follow this process:

1. Create a subdomain for your store's domain name, for instance http://cdn1.example.com (the way to do that depend on your host, ask him about it).
2. Put a .htaccess file at the root of the subdomain. That file should contain a single line:

   Redirect Permanent / http://cdn-adress.com

   Replace the http://cdn-adress.com with the one from your CDN server. This way, you are creating an automatic redirection from your subdomain to your CDN server.

3. Once the subdomain is in place, add it in the first field, "Media server #1". If that host allows for more web addresses, create as many subdomains to your store's main domain name.

Ciphering

Ciphering means encrypting data so as to render it unreadable to unwanted eyes. Your costumers' account details, as well as your own, are protected by cyphering.

CIPHERING

Algorithm   ● Use Rijndael with mcrypt lib. (you must install the Mcrypt extension.)
            ○ Use the custom BlowFish class.

Save

Here you can choose the algorithm you prefer:

- **Use Rijndael with mcrypt lib**. Default choice. Fast and secure, but requires you to have the Mcrypt extension installed with PHP.
- **Keep the custom BlowFish class**. Better security, but performance takes a toll, as it takes more time to validate the authentication, for each page load. Your customers might appreciate the added security, but might not like the time spent waiting for the page to load – although the time difference is really unnoticeable to most.

Therefore, choose wisely. If you change this configuration, all cookies will be reset.

Caching

Your server's cache stores static versions of your dynamic web page, in order to serve these to your customers and thus reduce server load and compiling time.

> Most of the time, you should first check with your web host about this setting, as it requires special settings on the server.

This section enables you to choose to enable caching, and then choose the caching method:

- **File system**. The static files are simply stored as any other file, on your server. This displays a field set to "1" by default. This is the file-system directory depth. Only change this value when you know what you are doing.
- **Memcached**. A distributed caching system. Very effective, above all with multiple servers, but you need to make sure that your servers/hosts support it – most probably, if your PHP configuration features the

Memcached PECL extension, you are good to go (you can download it here: http://pecl.php.net/package/memcache). You can add Memcached servers by clicking on the "Add server" link.
- **APC**. Alternative PHP Cache is free, open and robust, but only works with one server – which is the usual case when you start your online business. Again, check for the availability of the APC PECL extension on your server: http://pecl.php.net/package/APC.
- **Xcache**. Xcache is a new cache system, which is specific to the Lighttpd server – hence, it will not work with the popular Apache server. Read more about it at http://xcache.lighttpd.net/.

E-Mail Parameters

Your shop sends many messages throughout all the steps of registration and placing an order. Here, you can configure how these messages will be sent.

E-mail

This is where you decide how your e-mails are sent and received.

The form has three sets of options:

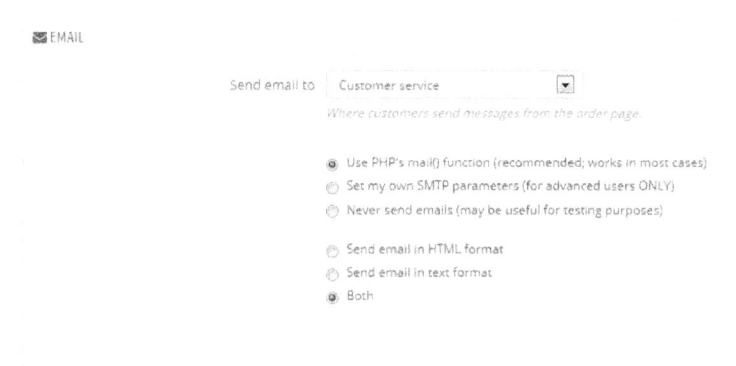

✉ EMAIL

Send email to   Customer service ▾
Where customers send messages from the order page.

◉ Use PHP's mail() function (recommended; works in most cases)
◯ Set my own SMTP parameters (for advanced users ONLY)
◯ Never send emails (may be useful for testing purposes)

◯ Send email in HTML format
◯ Send email in text format
◉ Both

💾 Save

- **Send e-mail to**. This is a front-end setting. At the end of the checkout process, a client can leave a message to you staff. You can choose to whom this message will be sent by selecting from the drop-down list.
- E-mail parameters: how e-mails are technically sent. Choose among the three. See below for more information.

- **E-mail format**: how e-mail are visually sent. Choose among the three. See below for more information.

Technical configuration

Configure PrestaShop to send emails to your customers. We strongly advise you that you consult your web host to determine which settings to use for this feature. The options are:

- **Never send e-mails**. Keep this setting for testing purpose. Once your shop is public, you should never use this setting.
- **Use the PHP mail() function**. This option is recommended by default. In the event that this does not work, then use the SMPT option below.
- **Set my own SMTP parameters**. In this case, a new section appears, with more fields. The information for these fields should be provided by your web host: mail domain name, SMTP server, SMTP user, etc. Make sure to transcribe exactly what your web host provides you with.

The SMTP configuration information can be provided to you either by:

- Your system administrator,
- Your host,
- Your ISP,
- Your e-mail provider.

Your web host can tell you whether or not your username is mandatory, as well as the password information, and the encryption to use.

For example, in the case of Gmail (the e-mail service offered by Google), you might have to enter information such as the following one:

- SMTP server: smtp.gmail.com
- User: my.user.name@gmail.com (example)
- Password: RT22UE87 (example)
- Encryption: SSL
- Port: 465

Visual configuration

There are two formats available for e-mails: HTML is great to look at, but might not work everywhere; text is dull to look at, but work everywhere.

You can choose to use only one of the two, or both. Both is the recommended way.

Test your email configuration

Once you have configured your e-mails using one of the two available methods, enter your own e-mail address in this section, then click the "Send an e-mail test" button.
Now check the inbox of the address provided to verify that you indeed have received the test e-mail, in the correct format. If you have not received it, update your configuration with the correct information.

Multistore Parameters

This page is only available when you enable the multistore feature.

Turning your single-shop PrestaShop installation into a multi-shop one is very simple:

1. Go to the "Preferences" menu and select the "General" page.
2. Find the "Enable multistore" option, select "Yes".
3. Save your changes.

The "Advanced Parameters" menu will now feature the "Multistore" page, which is presented in details in the "Managing multiple shops" chapter of this guide.

CSV Import Parameters

The CSV import page enables you to easily fill your product catalog when you have a very large amount of products, or to import data that you exported and converted from another e-commerce tool.

IMPORT

> You can read information on CSV import at http://doc.prestashop.com/display/PS16/CSV+Import+Parameters
> Read more about CSV format at http://en.wikipedia.org/wiki/Comma-separated_values

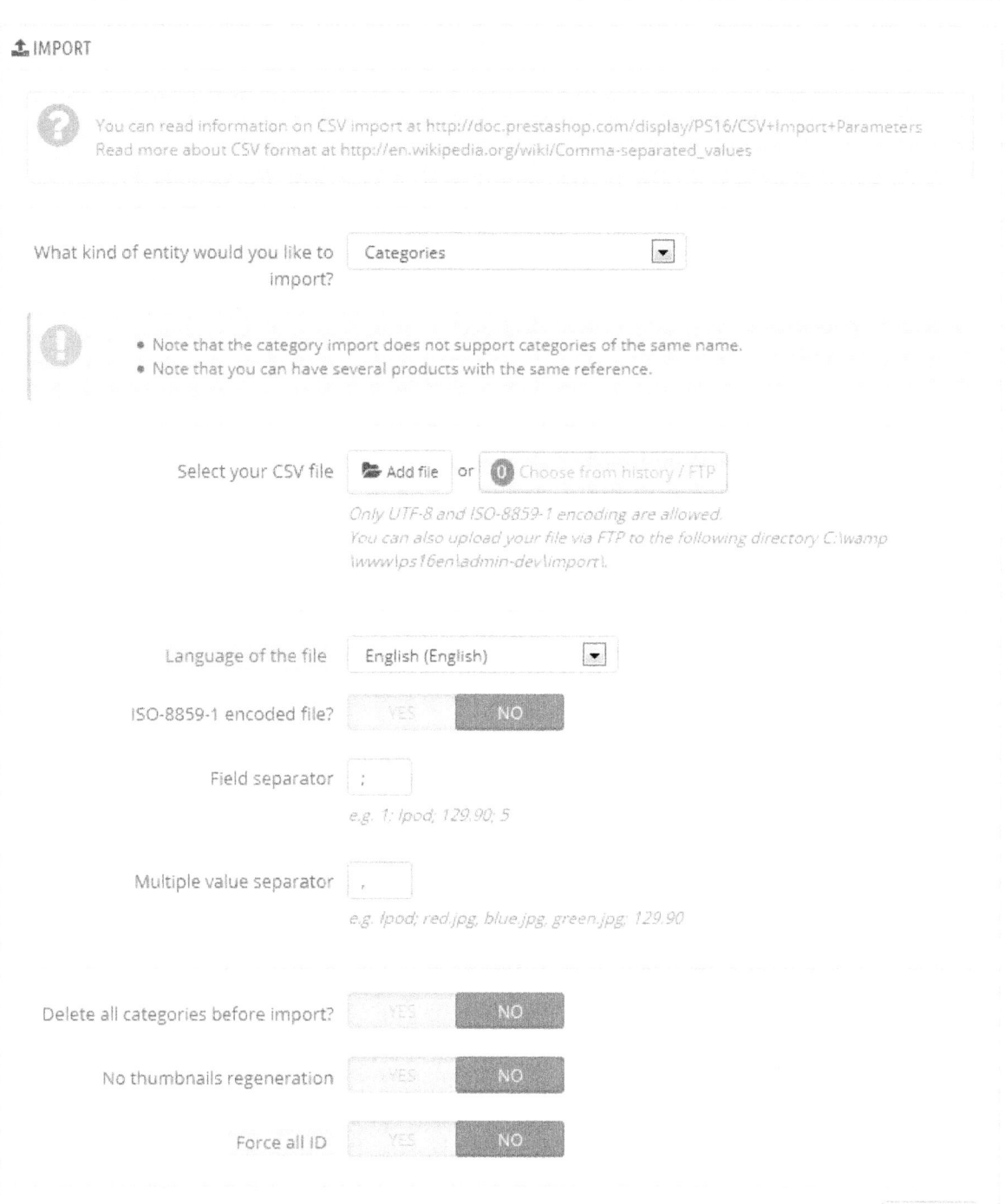

What kind of entity would you like to import? **Categories**

- Note that the category import does not support categories of the same name.
- Note that you can have several products with the same reference.

Select your CSV file: **Add file** or **Choose from history / FTP**

Only UTF-8 and ISO-8859-1 encoding are allowed.
You can also upload your file via FTP to the following directory C:\wamp\www\ps16en\admin-dev\import\.

Language of the file: **English (English)**

ISO-8859-1 encoded file? YES / **NO**

Field separator: `;`

e.g. 1; Ipod; 129.90; 5

Multiple value separator: `,`

e.g. Ipod; red.jpg, blue.jpg, green.jpg; 129.90

Delete all categories before import? YES / **NO**

No thumbnails regeneration YES / **NO**

Force all ID YES / **NO**

→ Next step

> CSV is an acronym of "Comma-separated values". It is a popular plain-text format when there is a need to import, export or simply store data in a non-proprietary format. Almost all data handling tool support CSV format, in various incarnations. You can read more about the CSV format on Wikipedia: http://en.wikipedia.org/wiki/Comma-separated_values.

The import process requires preparation, and starts with a form made of primary settings:

- **What kind of Entity would you like to import?**. Entities are the types of data that you can import. The "Available fields" on the right updates when you choose an entity, so that you know the kind of data that your CSV file should contain.
  PrestaShop enables you to import the following types of data:
    - Categories,
    - Products,
    - Combinations,
    - Customers,
    - Addresses,
    - Manufacturers,
    - Suppliers,
    - Alias,
    - Supply order (if Advanced Stock Management is enabled),
    - Supply order details (if Advanced Stock Management is enabled).
- **Select your CSV file**. You can import more than one file at a time, but make sure that they all contain the same type of data.

> You can download sample files for each type of data from the "Download sample CSV files" section on the right. This helps you compare these sample files with your own files, so that you can make sure that the files you are about to import are indeed ready to be imported to PrestaShop. These files are actually stored in the /docs/csv_import folder of your installation of PrestaShop.

- **Language of the file**. Data can only be imported for a single language at a time. If your data exists in more than one language, you should split it into as many files.
- **ISO-8859-1 encoded file?**. By default, the import files should use UTF-8 encoding. But if your files use ISO-8859-1 and you would rather not convert them, you can check this box.
- **Field separator**. Not all CSV file use commas to separate their values: some use tabulations, others semicolons, etc. You can indicate what your files use in this field.
- **Multiple value separator**. When an attribute can support more than one value, these values need to be separated with a specific separator. After reviewing your files, indicate your separator here.
- **Delete all ___ before import?**. This option will erase all previously existing entries of the type of data you are importing. Thus you will start with a clean slate.
- **Use product reference as key?**. Product import only. You can choose to have the product key be determined by PrestaShop, or instead use the product's reference as the ID. In this case, make sure the file does contain references for all your importer products.
- **No thumbnails regeneration**. Category and product import only. You can choose to have PrestaShop regenerate the thumbnails that are linked from your CSV file (in the "Image URL" or "Image URLs" fields).
- **Force all ID**. You can either keep the imported IDs, or let the importer auto-increment them.

When changing the Entity setting, the section on the right, titled "Available fields", changes to present the expected data fields. Although the importing tool helps you by taking care of matching your file's fields with PrestaShop's, you should strive to make your data more import-friendly by following the naming scheme and order of the presented fields. If not, the import will be more tedious, but not impossible.

Some fields have a little information popup available (represented by a "i" logo), which you can display by hovering the mouse cursor over it. They mostly pertain to PrestaShop's multistore or advanced stock management features. Make sure to read them all in order to better build/edit your data files.

AVAILABLE FIELDS

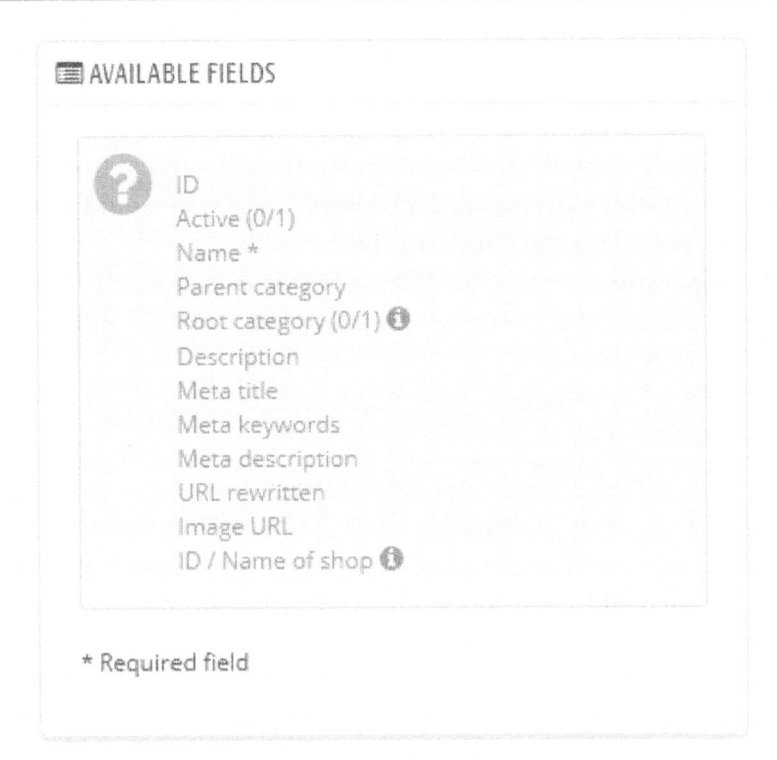

ID
Active (0/1)
Name *
Parent category
Root category (0/1)
Description
Meta title
Meta keywords
Meta description
URL rewritten
Image URL
ID / Name of shop

* Required field

Data format

Imported data file must be in text-file, using a CSV-based format and the accompanying .csv file extension. We recommend using a semicolon ";" as a field separator. If you textual data (product description and such) contains semicolons, you should either remove them, or choose another separator in the "Field separator" option.

You can create a CSV file using any text editor (we recommend Notepad++: http://notepad-plus-plus.org/), but we do advise you to use a spreadsheet program, then save your work in the CSV format. Using a spreadsheet program enables you to have an easier and more visual grasp of your data, in comparison to the plain text file. You can use the commercial Microsoft Excel (http://office.microsoft.com/en-us/excel/ or the free OpenOffice.org http://www.openoffice.org/ Calc.

Here is a sample import file, with a list of products:

"Enabled";"Name";"Categories";"Price";"Tax rule ID";"Buying price";"On sale";"Reference";"Weight";"Quantity";"Short desc.";"Long desc";"Images URL"

1;"Test";"1,2,3";130;1;75;0;"PROD-TEST";"0.500";10;"'Tis a short desc.";"This is a long description.";"http://www.myprestashop/images/product1.gif"

0;"Test 02";"1,5";110;1;65;0;"PROD-TEST2";"0.500";10;"'Tis also a short desc.";"This is a long description too.";"http://www.myprestashop/images/product2.gif"

1;"Test 03";"4,5";150;1;85;0;"PROD-TEST3";"0.500";10;"'Tis a short desc. again";"This is also a long description.";"http://www.myprestashop/images/product3.gif"

Note that this is only a regular sample files built for this demonstration; it is purposefully not optimized for PrestaShop importation. If you need a sample file you can learn from, use the ones you can download from the "Upload" button's form.

The first row should be a descriptive name for the data column (you will be able to skip it during the import process). There must be the same number of columns on each row.

You should remember that:

- The price column will use your store's default currency.
- Categories are to be specified using their existing IDs (so you should have imported them first), and separated with a comma (by default).
- The URL of the image must be an absolute link. In other words, it should be the link that may be used in a web browser in order to display the image. For instance: http://www.myprestashop/images/productXXX.gif.
- The file's character encoding should be UTF-8. If not, use ISO-8859-1 and check the "ISO-8859-1 encoded file?" option.
- Dates use the ISO 8601 format, without a time zone designator (the time zone is the one for your store): 2013-06-21 15:07:27.

Uploading the file

Once you have all your data in CSV format, you can upload them to your store's database using the form in this page.

You have two ways to register files to import:

- Using your browser: click the "Add file" button, find your file then validate. Do this as many times as necessary to list all your import files.
- Using your FTP client: upload the files in the /admin-dev/import folder of your PrestaShop installation. Reload the import page: the "Choose from history/FTP" button should now indicate a number. Click the button to display the list of available files (including the ones you previously uploaded using the browser), then click the "Use" button for the file you wish to import.

Once your files are all listed in the "Select your CSV file" section, you can proceed with the rest of the form:

1. **Select the type of data contained in your file**, using the drop-down list named "What kind of Entity would you like to import?". Once you have selected the type of data, the list of the available fields appears on the right, which helps you refine your CSV file – at least for the order of the columns, which will soon prove handy.
2. **Select the language of the imported content**. If the target language is not available, you must install it first, in the "Languages" page under the "Localization" menu.
3. **Select the file encoding**. Simply indicate if the file uses ISO-8859-1 or not. If not, then it is assumed the files use UTF-8.
4. **Select the field separators**. We suggest that you leave the default values ("field separator" with a semicolon ";", "multiple value separators" with a comma ","). But obviously, if your CSV file is built differently, you should change these values accordingly.
5. If you want to remove all the products in your catalog before importing, select the appropriate option.
6. Once all your choices have been made, click "Next step".

> All import files are uploaded directly in the admin folder's /import sub-folder. If the CSV File drop-down menu gets too crowded, you can delete old imports directly using your FTP client.

When clicking the "Next step" button, the page reloads with the data mapping tool. This interface helps you map you file's data columns with the ones required by PrestaShop.

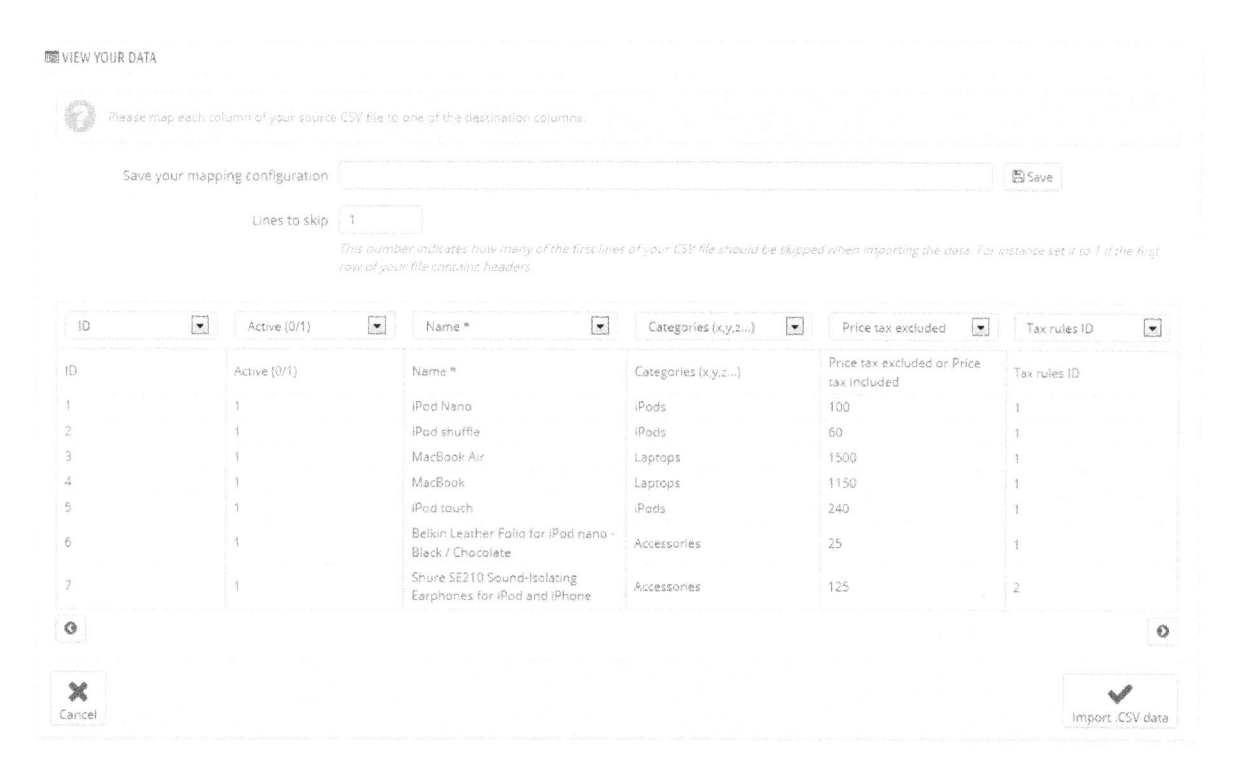

VIEW YOUR DATA

Please map each column of your source CSV file to one of the destination columns.

Save your mapping configuration [   ] 💾 Save

Lines to skip [1]
This number indicates how many of the first lines of your CSV file should be skipped when importing the data. For instance set it to 1 if the first row of your file contains headers.

ID	Active (0/1)	Name *	Categories (x,y,z...)	Price tax excluded	Tax rules ID
ID	Active (0/1)	Name *	Categories (x,y,z...)	Price tax excluded or Price tax included	Tax rules ID
1	1	iPod Nano	iPods	100	1
2	1	iPod shuffle	iPods	60	1
3	1	MacBook Air	Laptops	1500	1
4	1	MacBook	Laptops	1150	1
5	1	iPod touch	iPods	240	1
6	1	Belkin Leather Folio for iPod nano - Black / Chocolate	Accessories	25	1
7	1	Shure SE210 Sound-Isolating Earphones for iPod and iPhone	Accessories	125	2

✖ Cancel   ✔ Import .CSV data

Presented in this table are the rows from your CSV file, placed under arbitrary columns matched to PrestaShop's database needs. It is up to you to make sure that all the columns from your CSV file are matched with the correct column header, using each header's drop-down selector, so as to import your content correctly.

For instance, with our sample file:

- **First column**. We marked it as "Enabled", PrestaShop presents "ID" as a header. Click on the header's drop-down menu, and select "Active (0/1)".

- **Second column**. Marked "Name", header indicates "Active (0/1)". Let's change the header for "Name *".
- **Third column**. You get the idea...

The screen cannot contain more than 6 columns, so click the ">" and "<" buttons to see the other columns, and make sure to match them all correctly.

In our example, we used the first row as for column names. Since we do not want these imported, enter "1" in the "Lines to skip" text-field.

Once you are done matching your columns, click the "Import .CSV data" button (top right of the screen), and PrestaShop will start the importing process. When the process is done, you are sent to the main screen, which should either confirm that everything has indeed been imported, or give you a notice of all the encountered problems. In this second case, you should review your CVS file and make sure to correct everything.

Mapping configurations

The mapping process can be a tedious task if you cannot customize your CSV files columns order according to that used by the PrestaShop importer, and even more so if you have to do that repeatedly or frequently. That is why PrestaShop includes a small tool to save the current mapping order that you have set up using all the headers drop-down selectors.

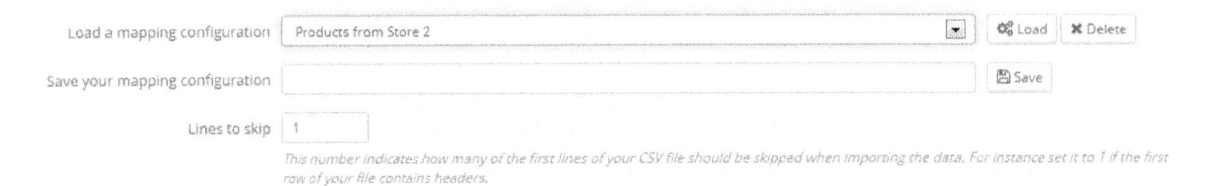

Load a mapping configuration	Products from Store 2	Load	Delete
Save your mapping configuration		Save	
Lines to skip	1		

This number indicates how many of the first lines of your CSV file should be skipped when importing the data. For instance set it to 1 if the first row of your file contains headers.

The tool is a simple field at the top of the matching tool. You can do the three basic actions (only one if there is no mapping configuration saved yet):

- **Saving**. Enter a descriptive name in the field, and click "Save". The interface updates to feature the saved configuration in its drop-down list.
- **Loading**. Select a mapping configuration in the drop-down list, and click "Load".

- **Deleting**. Select a mapping configuration in the drop-down list, and click "Delete".

DB Backup

A backup is the action of saving the content of your database into files that you store in a safe place. The point is that you can revert to them in case your database fails on you.

> You must perform regular backups of your shop, so that in case of a crash, you can reboot your shop quickly and in the best conditions. The database contains all the information in your shop, many of which are indispensable for PrestaShop to work correctly – and that's not talking about your products, categories and other data you added since the installation.
>
> The more often you perform backup, the safer you are. Once a week is a minimal frequency.

To create database backups of your shop, you have several solutions. You can use tools such as phpMyAdmin (reserved for advanced users), or use the one integrated into PrestaShop: the "DB backup" page.

The page starts with two big notices. You should read both completely in order to have a better idea of what the page does:

- The "Disclaimer" section gives you a series of reminders about backups, which you should read every time you make a backup. The section ends with the "I have read the disclaimer, please create a new backup" button, which you have to click in order to create a backup. Once created, the backup appears in a new "Download section" at the top of the page (click the button in order to download the backup file to your computer), and in the list below the notices.
- The "How to restore" section gives you tips on how to get your data back into PrestaShop in case of failure. You should commit this to memory, or at least save this information somewhere in case a database crash makes it impossible for you to access the PrestaShop administration – and thus the DB backup page – again.

The table below the notices lists all the backups that have already been made, indicating the date of creation, age, file name and size.
At the right of each row are the available actions:

- **View**. Enables you to download this backup.
- **Delete**. Enables you to delete this backup. Be careful, there is no turning back.

DB BACKUP				
Date	Age	File name	File size	
04/09/2014 11:46:30	< 1 Hour	1397058390-50ef8bb8.sql.gz	98.96 Kb	View

After each backup process, you should download the generated backup file by clicking on its "View" icon, or simply by using the link in the notification box at the top. Put your backup file in a safe place, for you might need it at any given time. Furthermore, you can find these backups directly on your server, in the /backup folder, under your custom-named /admin folder.

Your database is saved using the standard SQL format and its .sql file extension, and compressed using the BZip2 algorithm (simply put, a variant of the popular Zip format. Read more: http://en.wikipedia.org/wiki/Bzip2) and its .bz2 file extension. That gives a file archive with the .sql.bz2 file extension

Backup Options

At the bottom of the screen, two options are available:

- **Ignore statistics tables**. PrestaShop stores your site's statistics in a handful of database tables, and these can grow big quite quickly. While it can be sound to keep your stats in a safe place, they also make for huge files to download, while you are probably more interested in a backup of your products, categories, customers, orders, etc.
  By default, PrestaShop backups all tables, but if you are short on disk space on your web server, change this option to "Yes".
- **Drop existing tables during import**. When importing a backup file, the system can either overwrite the existing live tables with the content of the ones that were backed up, or delete all existing in order to replace

them with the content of the backup. The first case can result in doubles, which is why this option is enabled by default.

BACKUP OPTIONS

- Multistore: YES / **NO**
  Check / Uncheck all (If you are editing this page for several shops, some fields may be disabled. If you need to edit them, you will need to check the box for each field)

- Ignore statistics tables: YES / **NO**
  Drop existing tables during import.
  ps_connections, ps_connections_page, ps_connections_source, ps_guest, ps_statssearch

- Drop existing tables during import: YES / NO

Save

SQL Manager

The SQL manager is a complex feature, which should be reserved to technical people who know how to explore a database using the SQL language. In return for this complexity, it can be extremely powerful and prove immensely useful to those who master it.

ID	Name	Request	
2	Active French products	SELECT p.id_product, pl.name, pl.link_rewrite, pl.description FROM ps_product p LEFT JOIN ps_product_lang pl ON (p.id_product = pl.id_product) WHERE p.active = 1 AND pl.id_lang = 2	Export ▼

This tool enables you to perform SQL queries directly on the PrestaShop database, and save them for use at any later time. Indeed, PrestaShop presents its database data in many ways, but you might need something more, or more simply, something rawer than PrestaShop's clean interface. Using the SQL manager you can perform complex queries which build upon tables of data in the way YOU need them.

For instance, using this tool and your knowledge of SQL, you could create a reusable query giving you an updated list of the clients who are subscribed to your newsletter, or get a list of products in HTML or CSV format.

> For security reasons, some types of queries are not allowed: UPDATE, DELETE, CREATE TABLE, DROP, etc. In short, you can only read data (SELECT query).
>
> Also, secure keys or passwords are hidden (***********).

Creating a new query

As usual, the "Add New" button leads to the creation form. It has two main fields:

- **Name**. Make the name as long and descriptive as necessary.
- **Request**. The SQL query itself. You are free to perform JOINs or other intricate selections.

⚙ REQUEST

* Name	Active French products
* Request	SELECT p.id_product, pl.name, pl.link_rewrite, pl.description FROM ps_product p LEFT JOIN ps_product_lang pl ON (p.id_product = pl.id_product) WHERE p.active = 1 AND pl.id_lang = 2

✖ Cancel   💾 Save

Additionally, the "List of MySQL Tables" section helps you explore the database, and makes it easier for you to build your queries. It gives you a handy and clickable selector of all the currently available database tables. Select a table to make PrestaShop display its attributes and types, then click "Add attribute" to send its name into the "Request" field.

LIST OF MYSQL TABLES		LIST OF TABLES ATTRIBUTES		
		Attribute	Type	Action
ps_pagenotfound		id_product	int(10) unsigned	Add attribute
ps_paypal_usa_transaction		id_supplier	int(10) unsigned	Add attribute
ps_product		id_manufacturer	int(10) unsigned	Add attribute
ps_product_attachment		id_category_default	int(10) unsigned	Add attribute
ps_product_attribute		id_shop_default	int(10) unsigned	Add attribute
ps_product_attribute_combination		id_tax_rules_group	int(11) unsigned	Add attribute
ps_product_attribute_image		on_sale	tinyint(1) unsigned	Add attribute
ps_product_attribute_shop		online_only	tinyint(1) unsigned	Add attribute
ps_product_carrier		ean13	varchar(13)	Add attribute
ps_product_comment				
ps_product_comment_criterion				

○ Add table

Saving the form sends you back to the main page, with its list of queries.

Starting a query

Each saved query in the table has four icons to the right of its row:

- **Export**. Performs the query, and has it downloaded by you in CSV format.
- **View**. Performs the query, and has it displayed in an HTML table, right within the PrestaShop interface.
- **Edit**. You can edit a query as often as necessary, in order to refine it and get better results.
- **Delete**. Once a query is not used anymore (or simply because it does not work), you can delete it by clicking this button and confirming your choice.

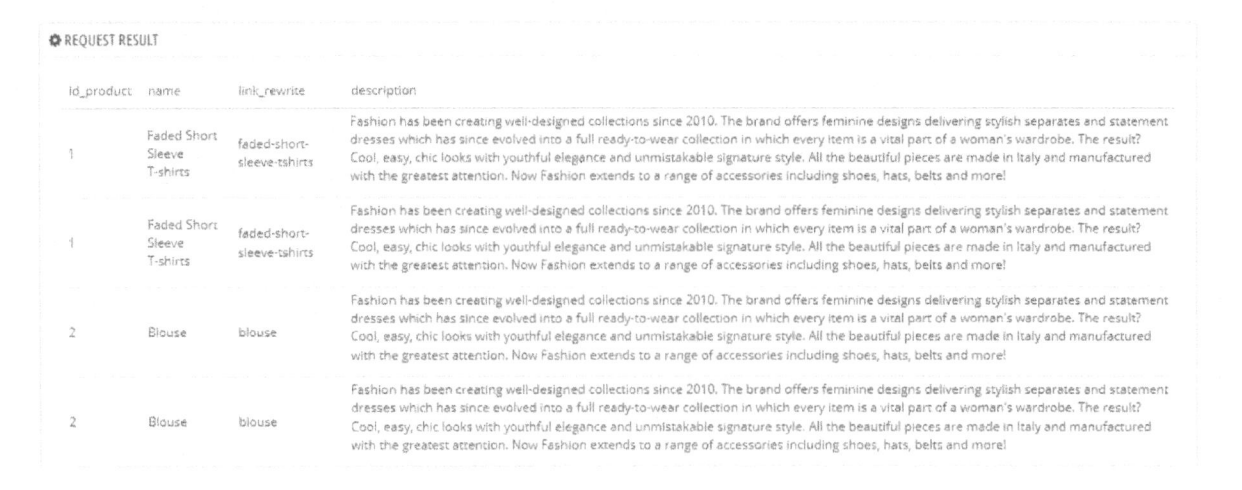

Settings

There is only one setting at this time:

- **Select your default file encoding**. You can configure the character encoding of the downloaded CSV file. The default, UTF-8, is recommended, but you can select ISO-8859-1 if need be.

Some sample queries

The possibilities are endless, but here are a few sample queries to help you build your own.

Listing all the e-mails address of all the customers

    SELECT email FROM ps_customer

Listing all the e-mails address of all the customers who are subscribed to your newsletter

    SELECT email

FROM ps_customer

WHERE newsletter = 1

Listing all the products which are active and have a description in French (id_lang = 4)

SELECT p.id_product, pl.name, pl.link_rewrite, pl.description

FROM ps_product p

LEFT JOIN ps_product_lang pl ON (p.id_product = pl.id_product)

WHERE p.active = 1

AND pl.id_lang = 4

Listing all the orders, with details about carrier, currency, payment, total and date

SELECT o.`id_order` AS `id`,

CONCAT(LEFT(c.`firstname`, 1), '. ', c.`lastname`) AS `Customer`,

ca.`name` AS `Carrier`,

cu.`name` AS `Currency`,

o.`payment`, CONCAT(o.`total_paid_real`, ' ', cu.`sign`) AS `Total`,

o.`date_add` AS `Date`

FROM `ps_orders` o

LEFT JOIN `ps_customer` c ON (o.`id_customer` = c.`id_customer`)

LEFT JOIN `ps_carrier` ca ON (o.id_carrier = ca.id_carrier)

LEFT JOIN `ps_currency` cu ON (o.`id_currency` = cu.`id_currency`)

Logs parameters

Errors happen. Most of the time, you are not aware of them because PrestaShop handles them silently. But you might want to know about them, in order to be able to correct the most regular ones, and insure a better stability for your shop.

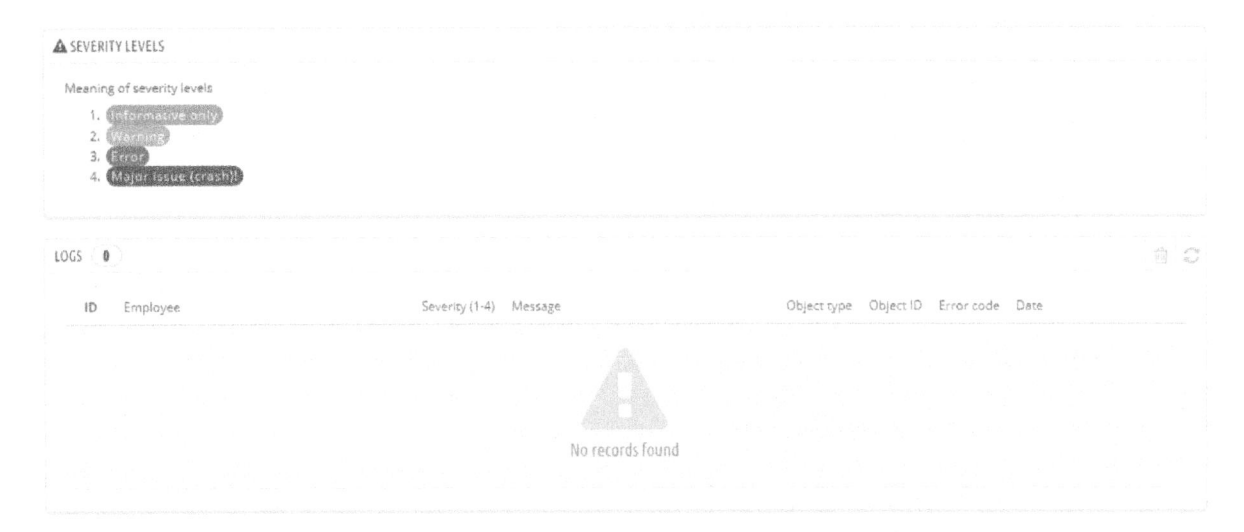

The "Logs" page is where you can have a look at the PHP errors which plague your shop. They are listed in the page's central table, and are presented in 4 levels:

- **1: Informative only**. Run-time notices. Indicate that the script encountered something that could indicate an error, but could also happen in the normal course of running a script.
- **2: Warning**. Run-time warnings (non-fatal errors). Execution of the script is not halted.
- **3: Error**.
- **4: Major issue (crash)!**. Fatal run-time errors. These indicate errors that cannot be recovered from, such as a memory allocation problem. The execution of the script is halted.

These explanations are the official ones from the PHP manual. Read more: http://www.php.net/manual/en/errorfunc.constants.php.

Logs be e-mail

The error levels also serve as values for the "Logs by e-mail" feature. PrestaShop adds one last value, 5, which indicates that the administrator does not want to receive any notification, either for minor or major errors.

LOGS BY EMAIL

Minimum severity level: 5

Save

The error logging tool enables you to receive an e-mail notification when an error occurs. Notifications are sent to the shop owner's e-mail address, and you can configure the degree of importance at which you should start receiving such e-mails:

- "1" if you want to know about everything, even the tiniest information.
- "3" if you only want to know about issues (errors and major issues).
- "4" if you only want to keep the major issues.
- "5" is the default, meaning that no notification is sent.

Webservice Parameters

In this page, you can enable your shop's webservice, so that third-party tools can access your data. This potentially makes it possible for interesting tools to help you or your customers make better use of your shop (such as mobile applications).

> A web service is a method of communication between two electronic devices over a network. It relies on a known set of methods, formats and access rights, so as be able to use the webservice's content on any other authorized tool, and build upon the original content. Read more about it on Wikipedia: http://en.wikipedia.org/wiki/Web_service.

The page starts by listing the currently existing webservice keys in a table, if there is any. A webservice key is a unique access that you grant to a developer, which can be used to tie a tool to your shop. Share them sparingly, as you might not always want everyone to access your data.

Key	Key description	Enabled	
WIXDR8H2LYTPSCEB9GNY24XEKF99FFHJ	Frank B's iPhone app.	✓	Edit

Not any app can access your shop through the PrestaShop webservice: you decide which can, and what they are allowed to do. Every app has a unique connection key, with specific access rights.

Adding a new key

The "Add new" button takes you to the webservice key creation form:

- **Key**. A unique key. You can either create your own, or choose to use a generated one, for instance by clicking the "Generate" button or by using any online key generator. Generated keys are most of the time safer, because they are harder to guess.
- **Key description**. A reminder of who that key is for, and what it gives access to.
- **Status**. You can disable a key anytime. This enables you to only temporarily grant access to your data from a certain key.
- **Permissions**. You do not have to share ALL your date with each key. You can choose among a wide array of permissions, either by section or by type of access. You might want some applications to only be able to view a handful of items, while some others (for instance, ones that you would use to manage the shop remotely) should be able to edit and delete just about everything. Choose wisely.

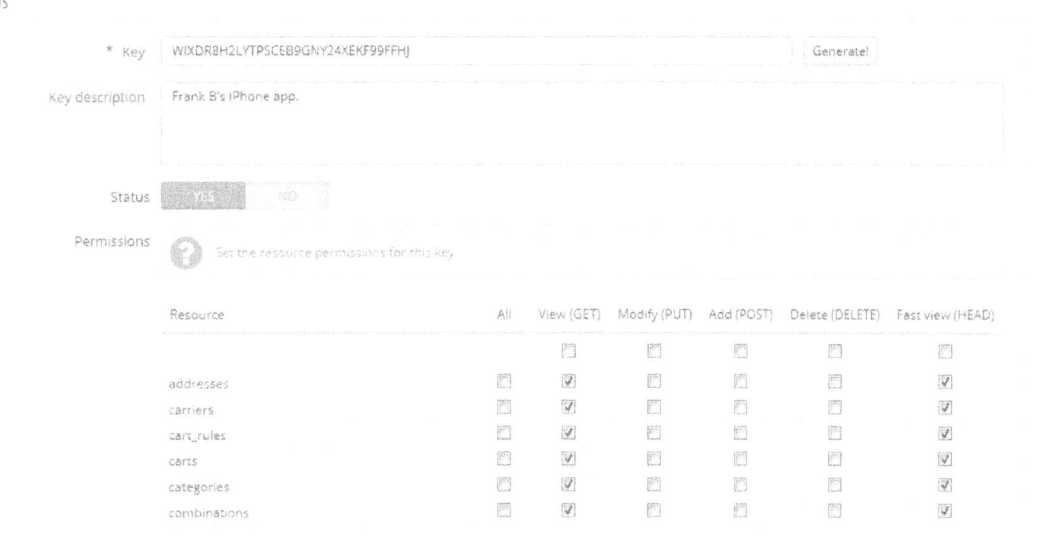

Configuration

> For security reasons, make sure your shop's server supports secure SSL connection!

The configuration is pretty easy:

- **Enable PrestaShop's webservice**. If you do not want anyone to access your shop through third-party tools and applications, just keep it disabled.
- **Enable CGI mode for PHP**. The CGI mode is a special setting for the Apache server, where you tell it to use PHP as a CGI script rather than an Apache module. While the CGI mode has a reputation of being more secure, it has been found to have a security flaw as recently as May 2012. Ask your web host for advices.

CONFIGURATION

Enable PrestaShop's webservice — YES / **NO**

Before activating the webservice, you must be sure to

1. Check that URL rewriting is available on this server.
2. Check that the five methods GET, POST, PUT, DELETE and HEAD are supported by this server.

Enable CGI mode for PHP — YES / **NO**

Before choosing "Yes", check that PHP is not configured as an Apache module on your server.

Developers can find our documentation on how to build a tool around PrestaShop's webservice at this address:
http://doc.prestashop.com/display/PS16/Using+the+PrestaShop+Web+Service

Administering the Back-Office

The "Administration" menu contains a special set of preference pages: rather than giving options that impact the customer or your front-end, they are all about the inner workings of your shop, and even your business itself. In effect, these pages enable you to set how the PrestaShop software will work for you, and how you and your team will be able to use it.

Administration Preferences

The "Preferences" administration page contains general options and settings on the way PrestaShop itself works. It has four sections.

General

This section is for the more general settings:

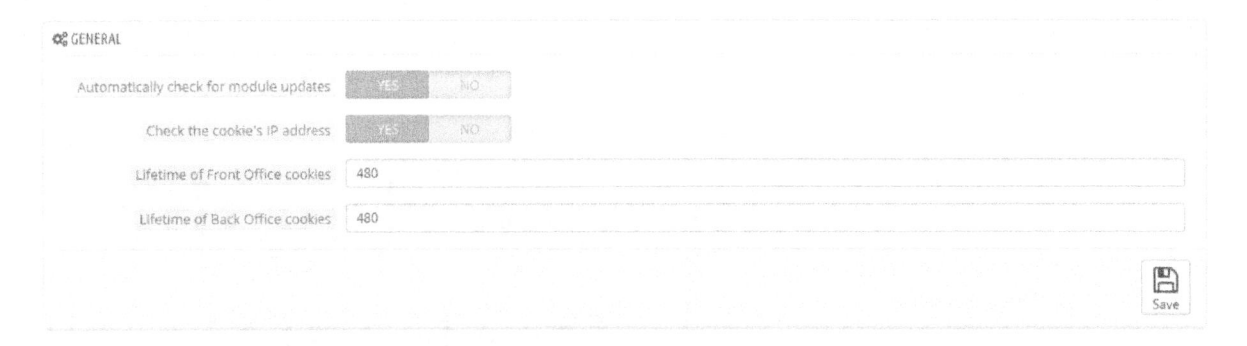

- **Automatically check for module updates.** You can ask PrestaShop to regularly check if there are new versions of your modules available from the Addons website. If so, the "Modules" page will display a "Update it!" button for installed modules, right next to their "Uninstall" button.
- **Check the IP address on the cookie.** This is an added security measure: you can tell PrestaShop to check that the user comes from the IP stored in his or her browser's cookie.
- **Lifetime of the Front Office cookie.** By default, the longevity of a PrestaShop cookie is 480 hours (20 days). You can reduce it if you feel your security needs it.
- **Lifetime of the Back Office cookie.** By default, the longevity of a PrestaShop cookie is 480 hours (20 days). You can reduce it if you feel your security needs it.

Upload quota

This page helps you define the authorized size of uploaded files from your own team – not from your customers.

There are three options, one being general and the two others being more specific:

- **Maximum size for attachment**. The default value is directly taken from your server's settings, but you can lower it if necessary.
- **Maximum size for a downloadable product**. If you sell virtual products (services, booking and downloadable products), this setting can limit the size of the files your team can upload – and thus the size of the final product. Plan in advance so that you never leave one of your team members blocked.
- **Maximum size for a product's image**. Likewise, you can limit the size of image that you or your team can upload to your shop. This can serve as a handy reminder that team-members should strive to reduce the size of image, as it is often not useful to upload anything more than 600x600 (which is roughly 200 kB when correctly compressed). See the "Images" preferences page for the image sizes your shop is set to use. This has the added benefit of saving on both server space and bandwidth usage, as well as processor power (since PrestaShop resizes uploaded image to give you thumbnails and more).

Help

To help you with your everyday usage of PrestaShop, the development team has added many tips & tricks within the interface.

You can have them displayed using one of these two options:

- **Back Office help boxes**. This will display yellow help boxes below some of the more obscure form fields.
- **Hide optimization tips**. This will display a box with configuration tips on the homepage of the PrestaShop back-office.

Notifications

Notifications are numbered bubbles that are displayed at the very top of any administration page when you have loaded it, right next to the shop's name. They display the number of new items since the last you clicked on them.

You can choose not to receive them for some content types:

- **Show notifications for new orders**. Clicking it display a larger bubble containing the name of the customers that registered since last time. From there on, you can either open any customer's single page, or open the "Customers" page to get the complete list.
- **Show notifications for new customers**. Clicking it display a larger bubble containing the numbers, amounts and customer names for the order that were last placed on your shop. From there on, you can either open any order's single page, or open the "Orders" page to get the complete list.
- **Show notifications for new messages**. Clicking it display a larger bubble containing the e-mail of the persons who last sent you a message using the contact form on your shop. From there on, you can either open any message, or open the "Customer Service" page to get the complete list.

Quick Access Configuration

PrestaShop has handy shortcuts to your most important pages, which can be accessed through the "Quick Access" menu, at the top right of every page of the PrestaShop back-office (right next to the username).

The "Quick Access" administration page enables you to create customized shortcuts, and make your navigation within the administration area even more relevant to you and your team.

```
QUICK ACCESS MENU
                    * Name  [                                              ] en ▼
                    * URL   [                                              ]
          Open in new window  YES  NO

  ✗                                                                    💾
Cancel                                                                Save
```

The page displays all the shortcuts that have already been created. By default, they are:

- **New category**. This special link takes you directly to the category creation form.
- **New product**. This special link takes you directly to the product creation page.
- **New voucher**. This special link takes you directly to the voucher/cart rule creation page.

Pages that open in a new tab/window will have a green "Enabled" in the "New window" column.

You can create as many shortcuts as needed – just do not overdo it, obviously, since this would render the "Quick access" menu slower to read.

Adding a new link

Let's create a shortcut the order creation page, from which you can create a new order, and even add new customers and their addresses on the fly.

As usual, clicking the "Add New" button takes you to the creation form:

- **Name**. Give the shortcut a unique name. Make it short and descriptive.
- **URL**. Indicate the page's address. Here is how you can use even pages with complex links as quick links:
    1. While keeping the link creation page open, go to the "Orders" page under the "Orders" menu in a new browser tab.
    2. Copy its web address from the browser's address bar. For instance, http://www.myprestashop.com/admin8945/index.php?controller=AdminOrders&token=f326b0419984706791c03f7e96599147.
    3. Remove the whole &token=xxx part and keep the specific bits (i.e., do not keep the domain and /admin8945 folder). In our case: index.php?controller=AdminOrders.
    4. Paste the result in the "URL" field of the creation form.
- **Open in new window**. Indicate whether you want to have this tab open in a new window or not. In general, link to the back-office should be kept within the same tab/window, and links leading outside of the back-office (front-office, other site altogether) should open in a new window/tab.

Note that you can create links to other websites, for instance your PayPal account or your webmail. Simply paste the complete URL in the "URL" field, including the http:// prefix.

Employees Accounts Configuration

The "Employees" administration page lists all the user accounts that have access to your shop's back-office. By default you will find the account that was created during the store's installation, which is automatically set as SuperAdmin. The SuperAdmin has access to all of PrestaShop's features without restriction.

EMPLOYEES	1					
ID	Last Name	First Name	Email address	Profile	Can log in	
1	Borderie	Xavier	xavier.borderie@prestashop.com	SuperAdmin	✓	Edit

You should make sure to create a new employee account for every actual employee that has anything to do you with your online business. This means that you should never have a general use account that everyone can use, because you need to keep track of who did what on your shop. Indeed, employees can edit orders, accept payments and refund customers, and you need to know who did what. Having a personal administration account for each employee is a good way for you to ensure that your team manages your shop responsibly.

Adding a new employee

The "Add New" button takes you to the employee creation form.

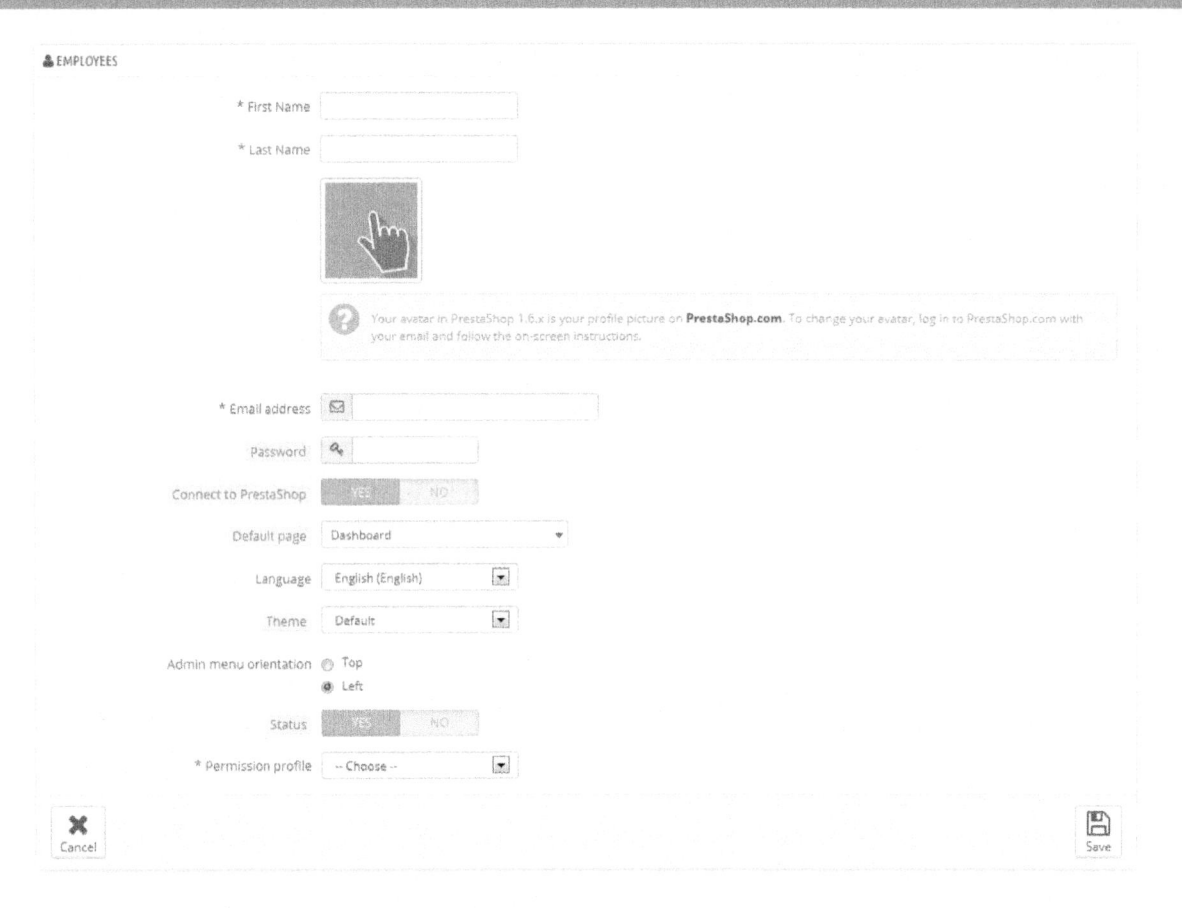

It has a dozen settings:

- **First name** and **Last name**. The name does not appear to customers, but is very helpful when you need to know who did what on your shop.
- **Password**. Try your best to not make it obvious. You do not want an employee's account to be used by unknown people.
- **Connect to PrestaShop**. You can tie your installation of PrestaShop to the central PrestaShop.com server in order to receive tips and tricks from the PrestaShop team.
- **E-mail address**. If allowed to, the employee will receive customer's e-mails and PrestaShop's notifications on this address. It is also used as the account's login identifier.
- **Default page**. You can decide which page the user sees right after logging in. This could be the Stats page for SuperAdmins, or the Orders page for salespersons.

- **Language**. The default language, since your business might be done in English, but your logisticians might be from another country. Make sure to add the necessary languages, using the "Languages" page under the "Localization" menu.
- **Theme**. The back-office of PrestaShop can use a different theme than the default one. You can choose which one to use here.
- **Admin menu orientation**. Each employee can set his own way of displaying the menu: at the top of the screen, or on the left.
- **Status**. You can temporarily and definitively disable an account. This enables you to create temporary accounts, for instance when you need help during the holidays or the shopping season.
- **Permission profile**. It is very important that you assign a correct profile to each employee account. A profile is tied to a set of permissions and access rights, and you should get to know the existing ones, listed in the "Profiles" page under the "Administration" menu (see below for more information). The profile determines which part of your shop's back-office the employee has access to; for instance, when the employee logs in, only the pages/menus that have been configured as accessible to his or her profile will be displayed. This is a very important setting.

The profile avatar (the image that represents you in the back-office) is tied to the user's account on the PrestaShop forum,. Therefore, if you want to customize this image, you must first create an account on the forum:

Employees options

The section at the bottom of the "Employees" page, right below the employees list, has two options available:

- **Password regeneration**. Enables you to set the frequency at which an employee can change his or her password.
- **Memorize the language used in Admin panel forms**. If "Yes", enables employees to save their own default form language.

Employee Profiles

PrestaShop enables you to assign specific duties and rights to each employee who helps you manage the online shop. For example, the administrator will have access to the entire store, without restriction, while an employee can only have access to the catalog or orders.

By default, PrestaShop has 4 profiles ready to use:

- **SuperAdmin**. The highest rank. It has all the rights and can access everything on the PrestaShop installation.
- **Logistician**. Those in charge of packing and sending orders. Can only access the orders, shipping and stock management pages, and part of the catalog and customer pages.
- **Translator**. Those who are tasked in translating your shop's textual content. Can access products and categories, CMS content and the "Translations" page.
- **Salesman**. Your salespersons, if any. In addition to the translator's access rights, can also access the customer pages, the modules and webservice, and some stats.

You can see the details of the access rights by reviewing each profile in the "Permissions" page (see below).

> The SuperAdmin profile cannot be deleted, only renamed.
>
> There should be at least one employee with a SuperAdmin profile.

Adding a new profile

You can add as many profiles as needed.

Adding a new profile is pretty straightforward: simply click the "Add new" button, enter a unique name for the new profile, and save.

The more complex part comes when setting the new profiles access rights. This is done in the "Permissions" page.

Profile permissions

Permissions are the central part of PrestaShop's profiles. They enable you to see very precisely what an employee account can and cannot do on your shop.

The "Permissions" administration page is built using tabs:

- On the left of the screen, as many tabs as there are available profiles.
- On the remaining right of the screen, PrestaShop display the clicked profile's permissions. This tab contains two tables side by side.

When you click any profile (except SuperAdmin), the two tables appear to give you access to their criteria:

- On the left, menu-related permissions: you can decide what the profile can do with menus. In effect, you could prevent a profile from editing the content of a page, or even hide the menu entirely.
- On the right, module-related permissions: while you might allow some profiles to see the available modules, you might prefer that only the most trustworthy employees should be able to configure some key modules.

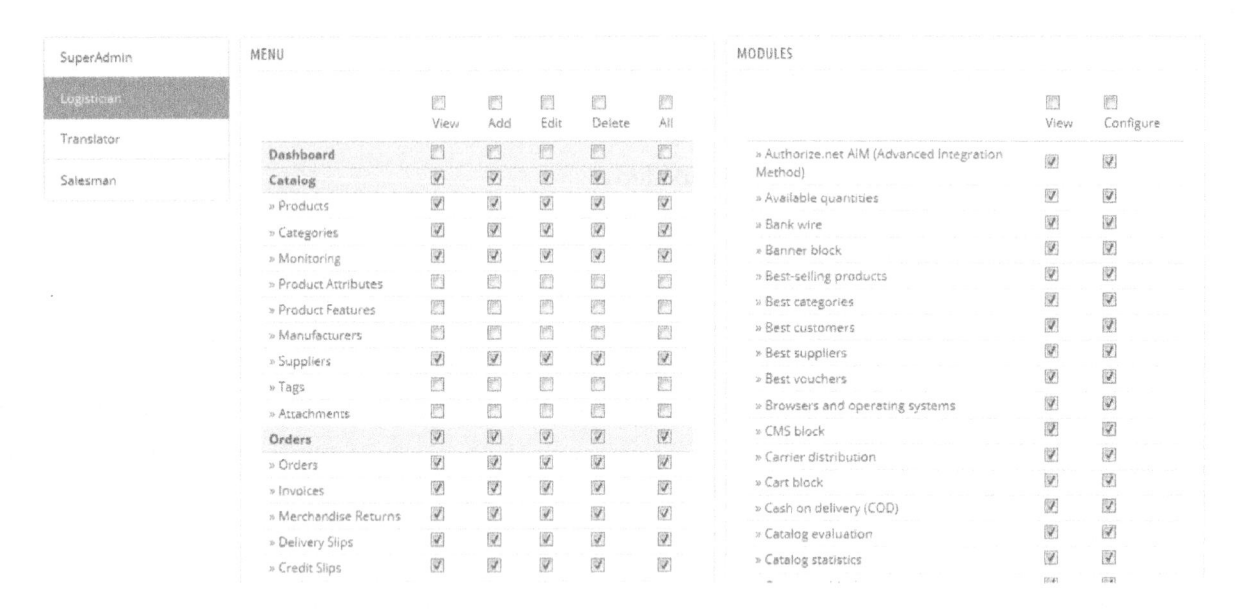

For each of the menu criteria, you have 5 options:

- **View**. Employee can view information.
- **Add**. Employee can add new information.
- **Edit**. Employee can change information.
- **Delete**. Employee can delete information.
- **All**. Enable all the above options for the current row.

Meanwhile, the module criteria have only 2 options:

- **View**. Employee can view the module's configuration.
- **Configure**. Employee can configure the module.

> The SuperAdmin permissions cannot be changed: the profile simply has all the rights for every criterion.

Setting permissions for a new profile

For this example we will create a new profile, "Order Preparer". First create the profile in the "Profiles" page, by filling the "Name" field. As soon as it is saved, it appears in the list of profiles.

Then you need to assign permissions to this new profile. Go to the "Permissions" page, and click on the tab for the new profile: the list of criteria appears. By default, a new profile has access to none of the back-office pages, and can only view the impact of some modules on the back-office (for the pages he or she has permissions to view).

You have two ways to fill the criteria, depending on the limits or freedom you want the profile to have:

- Click the permission checkboxes one by one until it has enough access rights to get the job done.
- Have all the checkboxes checked, then remove permissions one by one until it has only the ones necessary.

You have two ways to have checkboxes checked in batches:

- Per column: at the top of each column, a checkbox makes it possible to have all of the column's checkboxes checked at once. Unchecking it unchecks all the currently checked boxes.
- Per row: if you click on the "All" checkbox for a given row, all the checkboxes this row will be checked. Unchecking it unchecks all the currently checked boxes.

You can then uncheck selected rows rather than spending time checking each needed rows one by one.

To avoid mistakes during the configuration of your permissions, PrestaShop automatically saves your settings every time you make a change. This means you do not have to click any "Save" button. Once you have assigned the profile its rights, you can return to the "Employees" administration page and start assigning that new profile to the employees who need it.

Administration Menus Configuration

PrestaShop's back-office menu organization is not set in stone: while the default arrangement is built in order to have the most useful pages readily available, you might have a different opinion, and may want to change the organization, in part or in full.

This administration page enables you to move, edit, disable and even create pages.

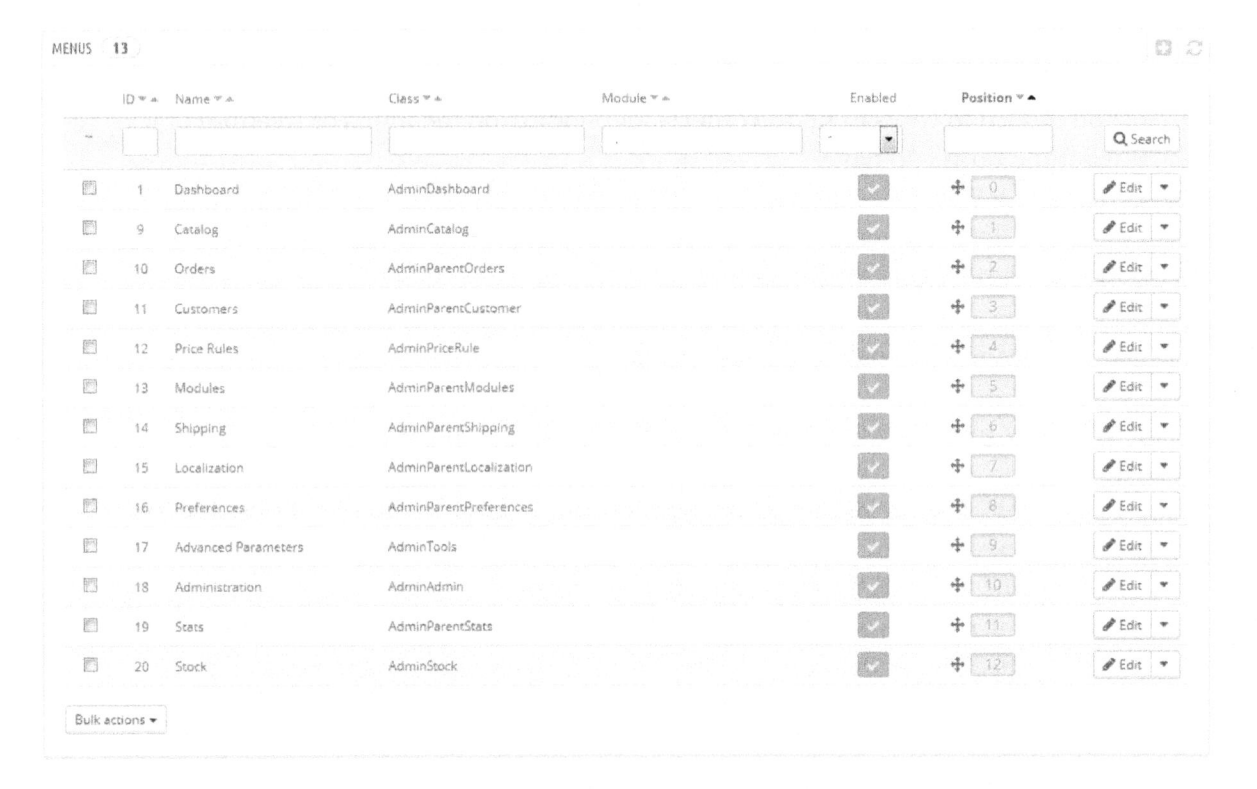

Moving menus

Menus can be moved directly from the list. You can either click on the arrows in the "Position" column, or drag the row itself and drop it in the position you want it to have. As soon as you drop the row, PrestaShop saves the location automatically. You can drag the row when the mouse cursor is over the "Position" column.

You can disable a menu simply by clicking on the green "Yes" in the "Enabled" column. Note that this will disable the menu for all back-office users. If you want to hide a menu from a specific set of users, edit their profile's permissions, in the "Permissions" administration page.

Moving pages

To access a menu's pages, click the "Details" action in the action menu. A new list appears with the pages in that menu, with the same columns.

Pages can be moved within a menu directly from the list. You can either click on the arrows in the "Position" column, or drag the row itself and drop it in the position you want it to have. As soon as you drop the row, PrestaShop saves the location automatically. You can drag the row when the mouse cursor is over the "Position" column.

You can also move a page to a different menu altogether. This cannot be done directly from the list; you must open the page's editing form, where you will find the "Parent" option. Change that option to another menu name, save your changes, and when returning to the "Menus" page, the page will have moved menu.

You can disable a page simply by clicking on the green "Yes" in the "Enabled" column. Note that this will disable the page for all back-office users. If you want to hide a page from a specific set of users, edit their profile's permissions, in the "Permissions" administration page.

Creating a new page or menu

Click on the "Add New" button to reach the page creation form.

This form has a handful option, some of which might prove complicated:

- **Name**. Give it a unique name, because it will serve as an internal identifier.
- **Class**. In short, a PrestaShop back-office page is based on specific internal PHP files, which are called "admin controllers", and are most often stored in the /controllers/admin folder of your PrestaShop installation. When creating a new page, you must know which controller to target, and most importantly the name of its class – which is the name of its PHP file.
  For instance, if you want to create a page displaying PrestaShop's backup administration page, you must first find its controller name (in this case, AdminBackupController), and copy it in the "Class" field.
- **Module**. In some cases, the administration controller for which you want to create a page comes from a module. In that case, you must also indicate the identifier for the module (in most cases, its folder name) and copy it in the "Module" field, in lowercase. This way, PrestaShop will know that it should not look for the controller in the /controllers/admin folder, but rather in the /modules/NAME-OF-THE-MODULE/ folder.
- **Status**. You can disable a page at any time, but do note that it affects all the back-office users.
- **Parent**. You can choose any menu, but for consistency's sake, make sure to pick one to which the page you are creating is relevant.

If you want to create a new menu page, choose "Home" as the parent.

Merchant Expertise

This page is generated by the module of the same name. It was specifically designed to help PrestaShop users keep track of their progress as e-merchants, see how much they've grown and progressed over the days, months and years. It is installed by default.

This module adds system of badges and points, broken down into three levels, all of which are integral to success in the e-commerce world:

- **Features**. Your use of key e-commerce features such as Site Performance, Catalog Size, Employees and SEO.
- **Achievements**. Your completion of specific key e-commerce goals such as number of Customers, Orders and Revenue.
- **International**. Tracks your presence in key International Markets such as the Americas, Oceania, Asia, Europe, Africa and Maghreb.

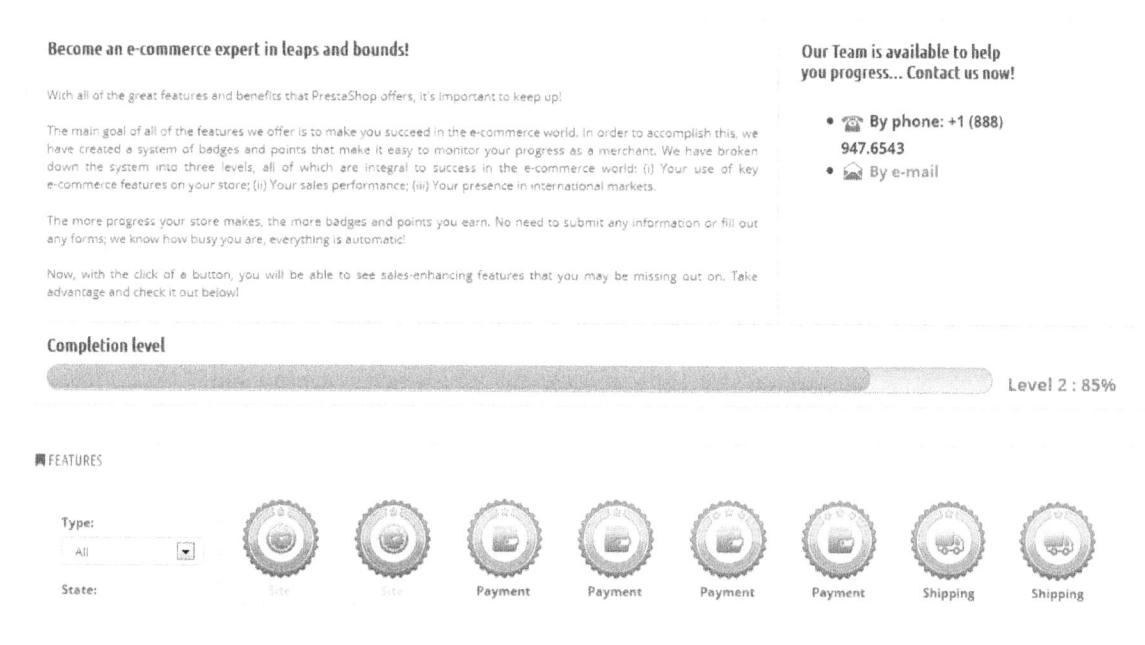

The more progress your store makes, the more badges and points you earn. There is no need to submit any information or fill out any forms. We know how busy you are; everything is done automatically. Use this tool to drive your business, view your progress and reflect on your great achievements.

Understanding Statistics

One of the greatest aspects of PrestaShop is its unrivaled power in digging up information on customer behavior. Let's see how this is done.

Contrary to the popular saying, statistics are not akin to "lies and damned lies". The numbers PrestaShop provides you with are rock-solid information which you can count on to improve your shop, change the way products are presented or adapt their prices, remove products that do not sell or simply push forward those that do. All this and more can be deduced from the data that PrestaShop automatically gathers for you, and which is presented in a dozen of entries, with graphics and data tables helping you making decisions.
The point to all this is to help you make a solid decision when you need to target your audience.

In addition to this, PrestaShop has a built-in referrer management system, which makes it possible for you to easily create affiliate campaigns.

Statistics

This section presents in details the usefulness of the various available statistics. By clicking on each of the categories at your disposal in the sidebar of the "Stats" page, the main page reloads with the most current numbers.

For some of the stats, a complete explanation is given, helping you understand the data given to you so that you can use the information to improve your shop and its conversion rate.

> Statistical data is gathered starting on the day you have installed PrestaShop. If you would prefer this data to be gathered starting with the opening day of you shop (and therefore, delete all your test data), you can use the "Auto-clean period" at least 24 hours before the definitive launch. See below.

Main interface

By default, the page displays the Stats Dashboard, an overview of the main numbers gathered by PrestaShop stat system since you launched your online shop.

| Day | Month | Year | Day-1 | Month-1 | Year-1 | | From | 2014-03-0 | To | 2014-04-01 | 🖫 Save |

📊 STATS DASHBOARD

All amounts listed do not include tax.

Display: Per day

	Visits	Registrations	orders	Items	% Registrations	% Orders	Sales
2014-04-01	2	1	0	0	50 %	0 %	$0.00

	Visits	Registrations	orders	Items	% Registrations	% Orders	Sales
Total	2	1	0	0	--	--	$0.00
Average	2	1	0	0	50 %	0 %	$0.00
Forecast	2	1	0	0	--	--	$0.00

▼ Conversion

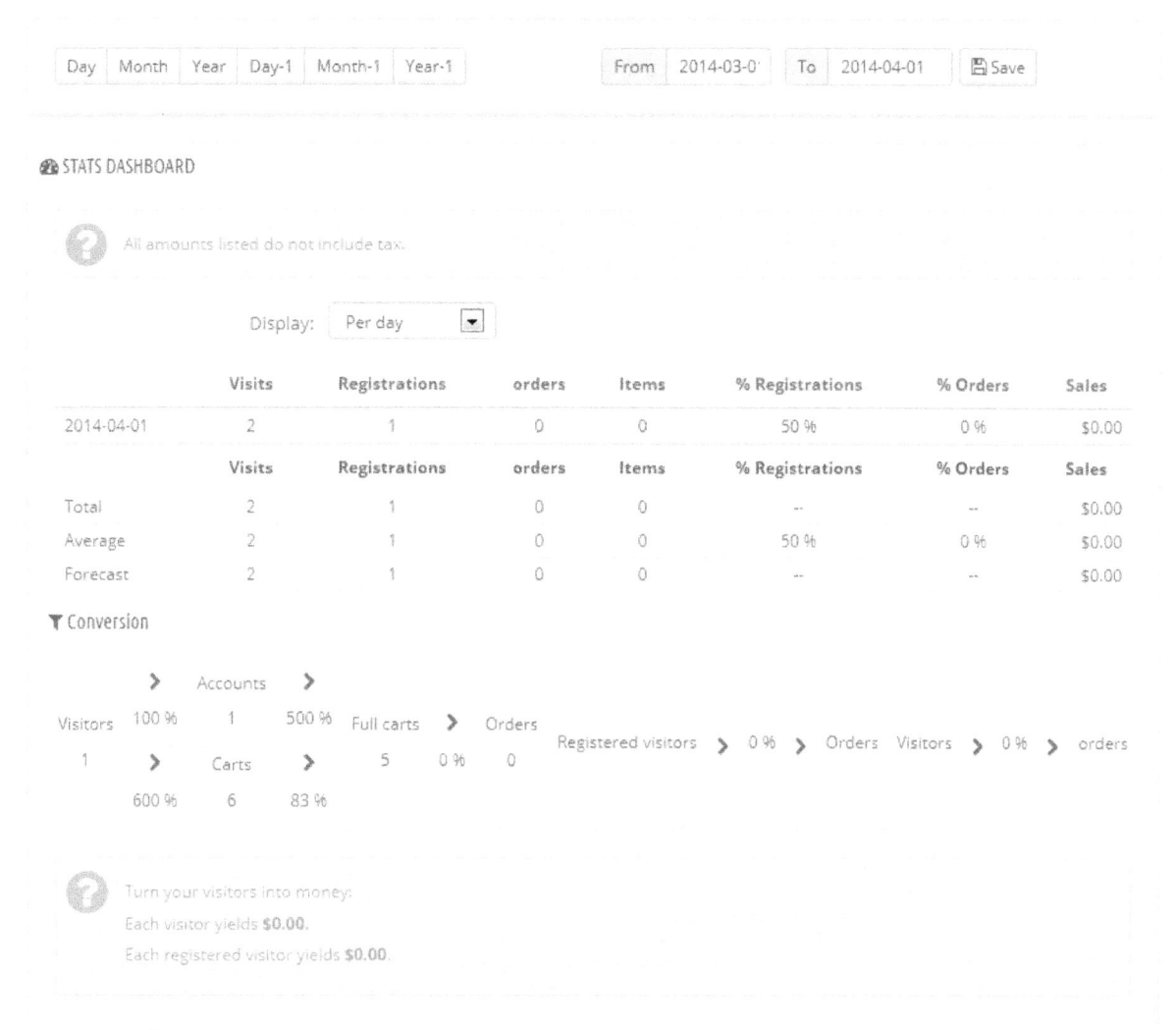

Visitors 1 > 100 % > 600 % Accounts 1 > Carts 6 > 500 % > 83 % Full carts 5 > 0 % Orders 0 > Registered visitors > 0 % > Orders Visitors > 0 % > orders

Turn your visitors into money:
Each visitor yields $0.00.
Each registered visitor yields $0.00.

▣ Payment distribution

At the top of the page is a single bar which helps you choose the period of time for the currently displayed statistics. Three sets of options are available:

- Current day, month or year.
- Previous day, month or year.
- Precise date selection.

The dashboard contains 8 sections:

- The main statistics. This truly is the heart of your statistics. Within a single table, PrestaShop gives an overview of the most important

numbers that were gathered for the selected period of time: visitors, new registrations, new orders, number of items bought for all orders combined, percentage of registration per visitors, percentage of orders per visitors, amount of used coupons, amount of all sales combined.
You can change the granularity using the drop-down selector, at the top right of the section. The available period sizes are: daily, weekly, monthly, and yearly.
The three lines at the bottom of the table are not affected by the selected period: total, average and forecast numbers enable you get a better estimate of where your shop is headed to.

- **Conversion**. This section gives you an idea of how much a visitor or a registered customer are worth on your shop, based the number of orders they place, basically. It is a nice indicator of how your shop is doing.
- **Payment distribution**. This section presents which payment methods are most often chosen by your paying customers. Based on these figures, you may wish to adapt your shop or your business in order to better cater for the most popular methods, or to push forward a specific method that you would prefer that your customers choose.
Using the "Zone" drop-down selector at top right of the section, you can limit the numbers to a specific geographical zone, and thus see which method works best or worst depending on the region.
- **Category distribution**. This section gives category-specific information. For each category, it presents you with useful numbers: products, sales, percentage of global for the whole shop, percentage of sales for the whole shop, average product price. If you notice that a category is way more successful than others, you might want to push your promotion efforts on it. On the other hand, you could try bolstering the numbers of disappointing category by releasing vouchers or other doing other promotional actions...
Using the "Zone" drop-down selector at top right of the section, you can limit the numbers to a specific geographical zone, and thus see which category is most successful depending on the region.
- **Language distribution**. You customers can choose their preferred language when registering, and you can see the language distribution with this section. Make sure to have all your products correctly translated for at least the two most popular languages.

- **Zone distribution**. You can filter other section by zones, and this section directly gives you a per-zone run down of your number of registered customers and placed sales (and their respective percentages).
- **Currency distribution**. If you accept more than one currency, this section helps you see which one is the most used by your paying customers.
  Using the "Zone" drop-down selector at top right of the section, you can limit the numbers to a specific geographical zone, and thus see which currency is most successful depending on the region.
- **Attribute distribution**. This is more of an internal statistic, enabling you to see which attribute and attribute group is the most used within your products.

Navigating the statistics

Most of the statistical data can be downloaded as CSV files, by clicking on the "CSV Export" button.

- **Available quantities**. This section gives you an overview of the value of your current stock.
- **Best categories**. This section presents your shop's performance by category. You can find out how many products in each category have been sold, the revenue generated, and the number of pages viewed. Make sure to regularly check the consistency of your results between different categories in order to adjust your shop's cohesiveness.
- **Best customers**. This section lists the best customers in your shop. It displays their e-mail address, as well as the number of time they have visited the website, and how much they have spent so far. Keep an eye on this page in order to keep track of, and take care of, your best customers. By clicking on the buttons at the top of the columns, you can choose how you would like to sort this data.
- **Best suppliers**. This section gives statistics on your suppliers by providing the quantities sold and the revenue generated.
- **Best vouchers**. This section displays the most popular coupons, vouchers, cart rules and catalog price rules that you created and distributed, whether personally or through a promotional campaign. The table also displays the turnover, and the number of coupons used.

Available quantities
Best categories
Best customers
Best suppliers
Best vouchers
Best-selling products
Browsers and operating systems
Carrier distribution
Catalog evaluation
Catalog statistics
Customer accounts
Newsletter
Pages not found
Product details
Registered customer information
Sales and orders
Search engine keywords
Shop search
Stats Dashboard
Visitors online
Visitors origin
Visits and Visitors

- **Best-selling products**. This section displays your best performing products. You can view the turnover achieved, the average daily sales, number of page views, and the quantity left in your current stock. With this table, you can identify your core products and decide whether to perform actions such as increasing or decreasing your prices or giving discounts on a specific product.
- **Browsers and operating systems**. This section informs you of the web browsers that visitors and customers use to browse your shop. You should verify that your shop is perfectly compatible with these browsers, or at least the three most popular ones. It also tells you if visitors are browsing your shop from their mobile devices (such as a smartphone). If this number is significant, you should think of having a mobile version of your shop.

Finally, you can see what operating systems your visitors are using. Make sure that your shop is fully compatible with all of your visitors' platforms.

- **Carrier distribution**. This page indicates which carriers are used most by your visitors. You can filter all results by order status. If you learn that a carrier is not often used, despite being fast and efficient, it might be appropriate to display it more prominently during checkout, to increase customer satisfaction.
- **Catalog evaluation**. This section gives an overview of your catalog's performance. You can find out if each product is active, or if its description is correctly entered in all of your shop's active languages. You can also see if all your products have enough images their sales

performance, and current stock status. The overall score for each product is displayed using a colored icon. You can define your criteria by filling in the table at the top of the page, then saving your settings.

- **Catalog statistics**. This section contains practical information on the products sold in your online shop, and your catalog as a whole. The figures can be filtered by category using the drop-down selector at the top right of the section. You can act on your catalog's performance by considering the following indicators:
    - **Products available**. The amount of available products in this category (by default, all categories).
    - **Average price (base price)**. Average product price in the selected category.
    - **Product pages viewed**. Number of pages that were visited by your potential customers. Compare this data between different categories to see which has the most product views, or on the contrary which ones do not attract many customers. Use this information to make some improvements in your catalog.
    - **Products bought.** The amount of products purchased in each category.
    - **Average number of page visits**. The global number of visits for the products in the selected category.
    - **Average number of purchases**. The global return for the product sales in the selected category.
    - **Images available**. Indicates how many images are tied to the selected category's products. A quick way to know if some products lack images is when there are fewer images as there are products.
    - **Average number of images**. Number of images divided by the number of products in the selected category.
    - **Products never viewed**. Some of your products might never have been viewed by visitors. Check their pages to try and understand why.
    - **Products never purchased**. Some of your products have never been bought by customers. This is a serious issue, and you should take time to understand why.
    - **Conversion rate**. Indicates the relationship between the number of visitors and the number of purchases. It is important that this value be as high as possible.

- o A table at the bottom of the page tells you what products in this category have never been purchased. You may want to consider changing their price or writing a more attractive description.
- **Customer accounts**. This page displays a graph with the number of customer accounts created in your online shop. With this information, you can measure the impact of your marketing campaigns. You can see the number of visitors who subscribed but actually never purchased anything, as well as the number of customers who created an account and bought an item immediately after registering.
- **Newsletter**. This page displays newsletter subscription statistics. You can use this database to keep customers informed. The newsletters usually help increase traffic to your shop. If you want to improve subscription, consider adding coupons/voucher/cart rules codes to each newsletter. You can see all of your subscribers' addresses via the "Newsletter" module, in the "Modules" page.
- **Pages not found**. This page tells you which pages of your catalog people have attempted to access but could not find (resulting in what is called "HTTP 404" errors). This is useful for finding potential technical problems that may hinder your sales.
- **Product details**. This page shows you all the products in your shop by the reference number, name, and available stock. You can sort your results by selecting from the drop-down menu above the product category you want to view. Click on a product to access its statistics. You can then view a chart with two sets of data: sales made and number of visits to the product page. The conversion rate of the product will also be displayed.
- **Registered Customer Information**. This section is divided into 5 charts.
  - o **Gender Distribution**. You can see how your customers are distributed among the various social titles that you have set – by default, Mr., Ms. and Miss, but there can be many others, such as Dr. or Sr. Therefore, you cannot trust this graph to show you the gender distribution... unless you have reduced your social titles to just two gendered ones.
  - o **Age Ranges**. You can learn about the distribution of your customers according to their age. If you see that the age range of your customers is not what you imagined it would be, think about adjusting your marketing approach.

- o **Country Distribution**. You can quickly consult in which countries your customers are living. This can help you focus marketing efforts on a single country.
- o **Currency Distribution**. You can see what currencies are used to shop for items in your shop, and in what proportions.
- o **Language Distribution**. You can see in what languages your shop is consulted most often, and thus decide whether or not you should improve your shop's translations in a given language.
- **Sales and orders**. Those two graphs present the evolution of your shop's sales and orders. They can be filtered by country, using the drop-down menu at the top right.
    - o The first graph indicates the total number of valid orders, as well as the total number of products ordered. With this graph, you can analyze which periods gave you the biggest return in terms of quantity of orders.
    - o The second graph helps you visualize your sales graphically. It can analyze the periods of time when you had the greatest sales. This enables you, for instance, to have a better idea of when to start your marketing campaigns.
- **Search engine keywords**. This page tells you what keywords typed into a search engine brought visitors to your online shop. This enables you to know which terms make your shop easily identifiable. Conversely you can see which keywords are absent from this list, and are thus not effective.
- **Shop search**. This section presents two indicators.
    - o The first one is a chart which shows the distribution of keywords typed into your shop's search bar. This allows you to see which products your visitors are most looking for – and therefore, the one you should have plenty of stock of.
    - o The second is a table summarizing your visitors' searches. You can see which keywords are being used, how often they were typed, and how many results were available. It is important that all of your customers' requests get a result. To improve your shop, be sure to add the products that meet the customers' demands (searches) or add additional tags to your products that are easily identifiable.

- **Stats Dashboard**. This is the stats homepage itself. It presents a bird's eye view of you shop's stats. Clicking this last option simply takes you back to the global stats dashboard.
- **Visitors online**. This section indicates the number of visitors currently on your shop. You can see their names and the pages that they are currently looking at. The data is updated live, as visitors browse your shop.
- **Visitors origin**. This page uses a graph to give you the top ten sites and search engines that have sent visitors to you. Usually, search engines play a very important role. If you create a marketing campaign by publishing articles on other sites, you can see what impact it had on your shop. Below the graph are the names of the sites that brought you your audience, with the number of visitors from each on the right hand column.
- **Visits and Visitors**. This page gives you statistics on visitors to your shop and the number of times they visit. The larger the number, the more popular your shop is. The graph helps you understand the behavior of your visitors. Basically you will see how many visits your shop gets, and you can compare it to the number of visitors (PrestaShop can recognize when the same person visits your shop multiple times, hence why the number of visits will be much higher than the number of visitors). The greater the difference between the two numbers, the more you are succeeding in creating a faithful base of core customers.

Search Engines

A lot of you visitors will come from search engines. In order to know what they were looking for, and how you can improve your shop for their search queries, you need to know their queries.

This page presents a table of all the search engines that your installation of PrestaShop supports – meaning that PrestaShop is able to recognize it, and to extract the query that the visitor from that a given search engine used to find your shop.

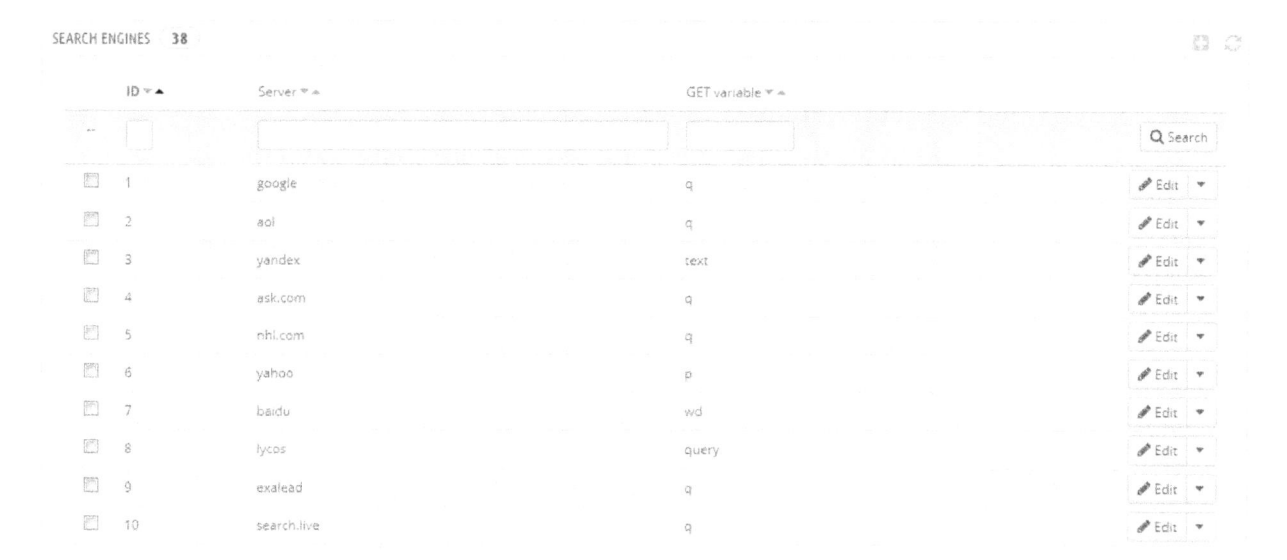

	ID	Server	GET variable	
	1	google	q	Edit
	2	aol	q	Edit
	3	yandex	text	Edit
	4	ask.com	q	Edit
	5	nhl.com	q	Edit
	6	yahoo	p	Edit
	7	baidu	wd	Edit
	8	lycos	query	Edit
	9	exalead	q	Edit
	10	search.live	q	Edit

While Google has the biggest share of search engines users, there are many other search engines that people could use to find your website. Therefore, you have to be able to retrieve their search requests too. When an unknown search engine is starting to bring regular visitors, it is high time that you add it to your database – otherwise, those visitors would be marked in your statistics as coming from "Other search engines", which is not helpful at all.

Adding a Search Engine

It is very simple to add a new search engine to your list.

Let's say you want to add DuckDuckGo, a search engine that emphasizes its respect for data privacy:

1. Get the full referrer URL for the search. For instance, http://duckduckgo.com/?q=kids+shoes

2. Take the domain name, which is specific to that search engine, and put it in the "Server" field. In our case, "duckduckgo".
3. Find the query variable:
    1. Find the query string. It should be a set of letters, followed by an "=" sign, followed by the query itself, closed by a "&" or the end of the string. In our case, it is "q=kids+shoes".
    2. The query variable is the set of letters before the "=" sign. In our case: "q". Put that in the "$_GET variable" field.
4. Click the "Save" button, and from now on, PrestaShop will be able to recognize visitors from DuckDuckGo.

Referrers

A referrer means a website that brings you at least one visitor. This website features a link to your shop, and thus it helps you build an audience and eventually make more sales.

ID	Name	Visitors	Visits	Pages	Reg.	Ord.	Sales	Avg. cart	Reg. rate	Order rate	Click	Base	Percent	
1	Frank's website	0	0	0	0	0	0.00	0.00	--	--	0.00	0.00	0.00000000	View

Some referrers are more important to you than others: you might have partners that have links to your shop on their own website, and both you and your partners would certainly want to know how many visitors those links brought you. You could even pay your partners to display a link to your shop, depending on how much you value your traffic.

This, in effect, is called affiliation, and the "Referrers" page helps you build a complete affiliate program, to which even your partner can connect to see the number of visits and sales their links have generated. Registered affiliates generate traffic to your shop, you want to reward them for those visitors, and the affiliate program is how both of you can access the figures the reward is based on.

PrestaShop's referrer tool can be likened to that of a statistical dashboard open to others than only your staff members. When you create an affiliate campaign for a site, you can grant that site access to all of the activity it will have made for

your site, through a password-protected URL:
http://example.com/modules/trackingfront/stats.php.

> In the list of referrers, the Click, Base and Percent values are calculated depending on the actual clicks, sales and percent of sales from the referrer site.

Adding a new referrer

The affiliate space enables you to create privileged access for your partners. They will have access to all statistics on the flow of visitors from their site to your online shop. To create their privileged space, you need to create their account in your affiliation program, then define how you will pay based on traffic and sales generated.

To create a new affiliate partner, click on the "Add new" button, which will take you to the affiliate creation form.

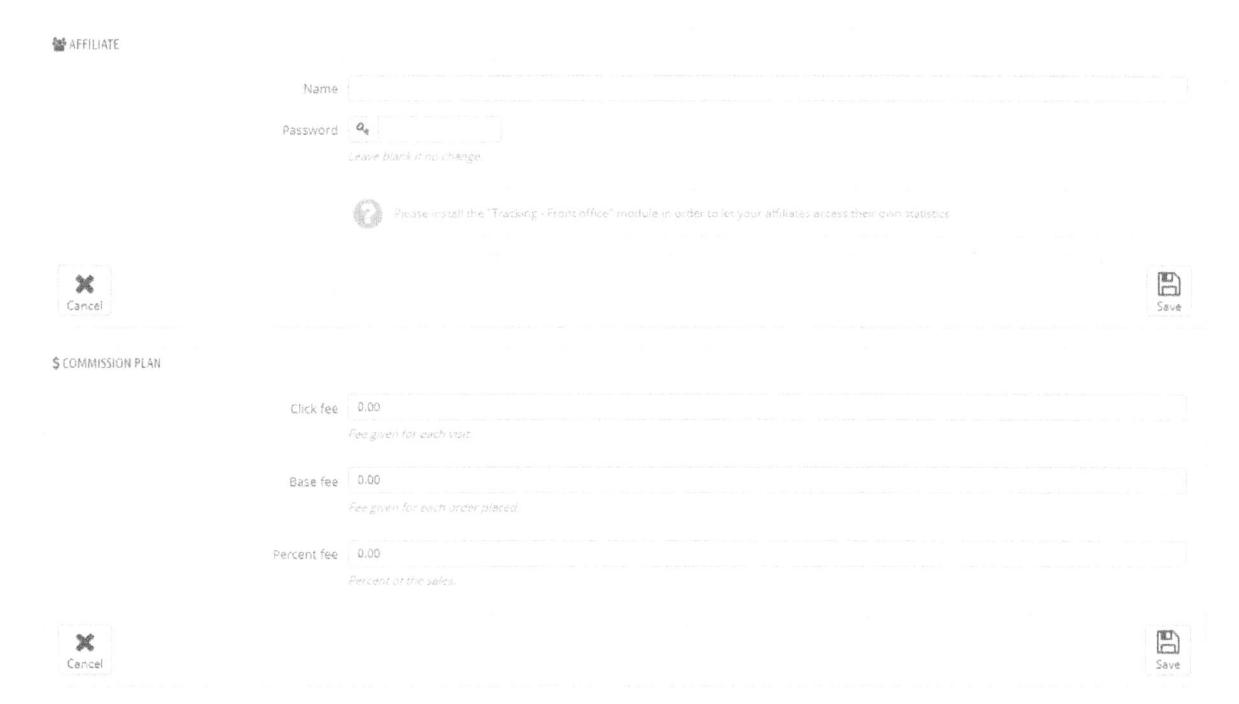

Each section is important:

- **Affiliate**. The account of the partner in your affiliation program.

- **Name**. To connect to your affiliation back-office, your partner needs a login name; you can use a simple name or an e-mail, but make sure to use something both you and your partner can remember easily.
- **Password**. The first time you create the account, PrestaShop saves the password along the login name. When you need to edit the account (for instance, when needing to change the commission), the password will be blank. This does not mean there is no password; if you fill the blank field when editing the account, it will change the password.
- **Commission plan**. This is where you indicate the fees of your affiliate – meaning the money you will owe your partner for actions of visitors from their site.
    - **Click fee**. This defines how much you estimate a visitor from this partner's site is worth. Every time a visitor from your partner's site comes to your shop by clicking on their link, the partner earns the marked amount.
    - **Base fee**. You can also reward your partners if visitors from their sites do buy one of your products. Note that this is only valid if the purchase is made during the browsing session that follows the click on the partner's link.
    - **Percent fee**. In addition to the base fee, or as a replacement, you can reward partners with a percentage of the sales made during the browsing session of visitors from their sites.
- **Technical information - Simple mode**. This is very important, as this is what will make the system differentiate this partner from other referrer links. Once configured, you should make a couple of test in order to make sure that you are indeed tracking the affiliate correctly.
    - **HTTP referrer**. In the "Include" field, set the partner's domain name that you want to track as your affiliate domain.
    - **Request URI**. In the "Include" field, set the last part of the query string. The system will track referrers that use a special query string. For instance, you can track referrers that use the ?prestaff= argument in their URL. This can help you further differentiate referrers.
- **Technical information - Expert mode**. While the simple mode matches words using MySQL's "LIKE" function, the expert mode enable you to use MySQL regular expressions. This can prove very powerful but also

very hard to maintain. Be sure to master the subject of regular expressions before putting anything in these fields.

The "Help" section gives you some precious indications on how to best configure your affiliate. Read it through.

Settings

The referrer settings are mostly tools to help you make the best of your affiliate program.

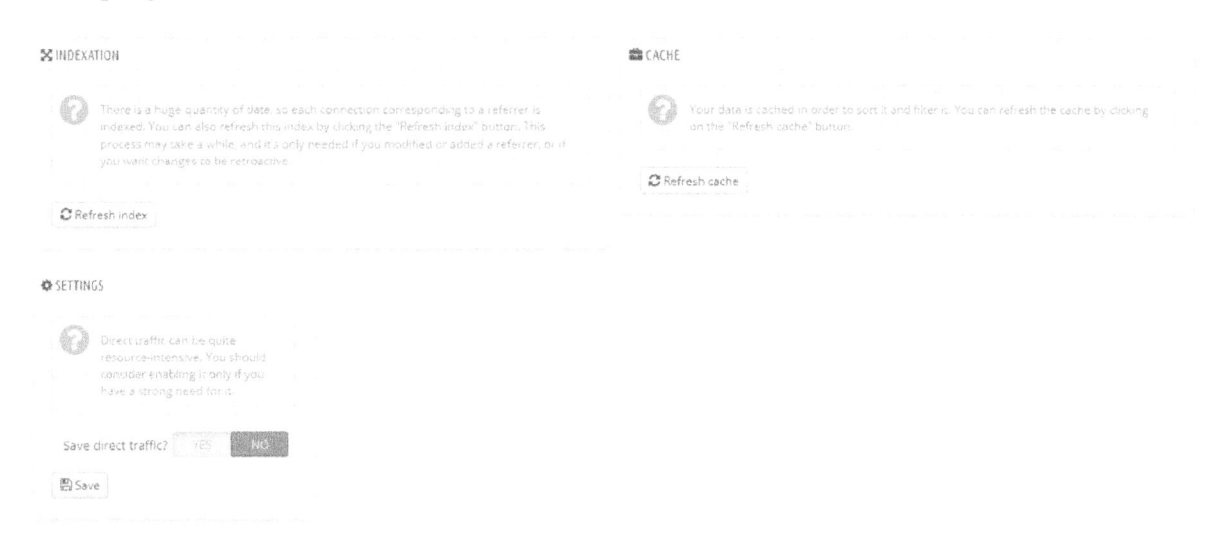

There are three possibilities:

- **Save direct traffic?**. Direct traffic represents visitors who arrive on your shop directly, by typing your URL in their browser. While these are important because they are visitor who really know about your shop and are interested in your products (contrary to visitors with referrer, who might have simply stumble upon your shop by chance), saving this traffic can put a huge toll on your database. This is why this traffic is not saved nor analyzed by default. Only enable this option if you know what you are doing.
- **Indexation**. You must click once on the "Refresh index" button when you add a new referrer and you want to analyze your past traffic for this new referrer.
- **Cache**. PrestaShop caches the data it gathers. You can use the "Refresh cache" button to regularly refresh your data cache.

Advanced Stock Management

PrestaShop features a complete stock management feature: more than just merely listing how much of a specific product you have currently available, this menu enables you to list warehouses and get a proper view of your stock, its movement, your coverage, your stock orders, etc.

Not all merchants will have a need for this feature. It is therefore optional, and the classic "available quantity management" tool is still available.

You can enable the advanced management menu by going to the "Products" preferences page, at the bottom of which is the "Products stock" section. Select "Yes" for the "Enable advanced stock management" option.

General Concepts

In order to avoid confusion with the classic stock management feature from version 1.4 of PrestaShop and see the possibilities offered by the advanced management feature introduced with version 1.5, you should picture two distinct concepts: product quantity available for sale, and physical products.

Product quantity available for sale

This is the same as the stock management feature from PrestaShop 1.4.x. It is the product quantity that is displayed in the shop for each product and product combination. This is the quantity that defines whether the product can be ordered or not (unless the "Allow ordering of out-of-stock products" option is enabled). That quantity can be manually changed for each product and product combination.

Since PrestaShop 1.5.x, that quantity can be automatically set according to the physical stock of the affected product. In a multistore scenario, the quantity is to be defined for each shop.

Consequently, what used to be called "stock" in PrestaShop 1.4.x is called "quantity of product available for sale" since PrestaShop 1.5.x.

Product stocks (physically stored)

This is the physical management of the stored products from a warehouse (or more). This is the new concept introduced as "stock" in PrestaShop 1.5.x.

This new stock management feature includes stock movement, stock valuation, stock transfer between warehouses, integration in the multistore feature and supply order management.

It also makes it possible to take into account the notion of actual stock. At a given time, a product can be available as a physical stock, but not available for sale because some client orders are still waiting for shipping. That same product can also have a supply order in progress, and thus not yet accounted for in the physical stock.

Real stock is therefore made of stock that is physically available in a warehouse, to which we add the quantity presently ordered from suppliers, and from which we subtract the quantity presently ordered by clients and which have not yet been shipped.

Using the new stock management feature

Do I have to use the new stock management feature?

There is no obligation to use the new stock management feature, just as there is no obligation to use the "quantity available for sale" management feature.

To activate both the "quantity available for sale" management feature and the stock management feature, go to the "Products" preference page, scroll down to the "Products stock" section, and choose "Yes" for the two stock management options. You have to first enable basic stock management in order to enable advanced stock management.

> The advanced stock management feature, or even the standard stock management feature and your warehouses, is independent from the multistore feature. Consequently, no matter which shop you are administrating in the PrestaShop back-office, when you use the "Stock" menu, you are always managing the stock in a global way.

I do not want to change anything to my settings in PrestaShop 1.4.x/15.x. What should I do?

If you would rather not use the new advanced stock management feature from PrestaShop 1.5, and simply are satisfied with the "classic" way that PrestaShop handles product quantity management, you just have to enable the old-style stock management manager, and not the advanced stock management feature: go to the "Products" preference page, scroll down to the "Products stock" section, and choose "Yes" for the "Enable stock management" option, leaving the "Enable advanced stock management" option set to "No".

The "available for sale quantity" management feature is now centralized in the "Quantities" tab from the product sheet: create a new product or edit an existing one, and the "Quantities" tab is available on the left, among the other tabs.

Does the new stock management feature apply to my needs?

The new stock management feature enables you to manage a stock of products. This feature applies to your business if:

- You manage a stock of products which you sell on your shop(s).
- You use at least one storage place (warehouse) which you manage yourself.
- You order most or all of your products to one or more suppliers.
- You need statistics about the state of your stock and of your warehouse(s).

This feature does not apply to your business if:

- You do not manage your stock of products yourself.
- You already use a stock management system/tool/program that you are satisfied with, and you wish to keep using it without changing anything.

Presenting the Stock Management Interface

Stock management is essential from the moment you start selling products whose quantity is depleting at each sale.

If you wish to use the advanced stock management, you must:

- Associate your products with warehouses.
- Associate your warehouses with carriers.
- Associate your warehouses with the appropriate shops.

Stock management within PrestaShop runs through several screens, and can use one of two levels.

These levels are:

- No stock management: there is no product quantity, PrestaShop assumes that a product's stock is infinite. Use this if you only sell virtual products (files, services, etc.).
- Simple stock management: for every product you sell, you can indicate the currently available quantity (including product combinations). Use this if you have few products or a simple storing location.
- Advanced stock management: for every product you sell (and its combinations), you can indicate where the available quantity is located in an unlimited number of warehouses (with varying carriers and valuation methods). You can also see your stock movements, the current status of your stock, you stock coverage, and you can place an order to your product suppliers.

These screens are:

- Preferences > Products > "
- Catalog > Products > product's page: one to two tabs are added to the creation/edition page of a product :
    - Quantities:
        - In Simple mode: you can manually indicate the quantity of each product.
        - In Advanced mode: quantities are handled from PrestaShop's "Stock" menu.
    - Warehouses: in Advanced mode, you can indicate the location of a product or is combinations within a warehouse.
- Stock: in Advanced mode, you can make use of all the stock management pages (warehouse creation, stock movement, stock status, stock coverage, supplier order).

The following section describe these pages one by one.

Stock management from the product sheet

Quantities management

In PrestaShop 1.4, you could manually set the quantity of product available for sale.

> In PrestaShop 1.5 and 1.6, you can still set the quantity manually for each product. But once advanced stock management is also enabled, you can also automatically set the quantity depending on the current quantity status of the physical product. Note that it is possible to enable advanced stock management globally, yet only use it for one product or just a few.

When the "Enable stock management" option is enabled (in the "Preferences > Products" page), all the products get a new tab in their administration page, called "Quantities". This clear and simple interface enables you to manage the available quantities for sale on your shop(s) for a given product, and any potential combination.

With only this option enabled, you can manage the product quantities for individual products, one by one.

If you prefer to have all your product quantities managed directly from PrestaShop's advanced stock management feature rather than on a product basis, you have to enable another option from the "Preferences > Products" page: "Enable advanced stock management".

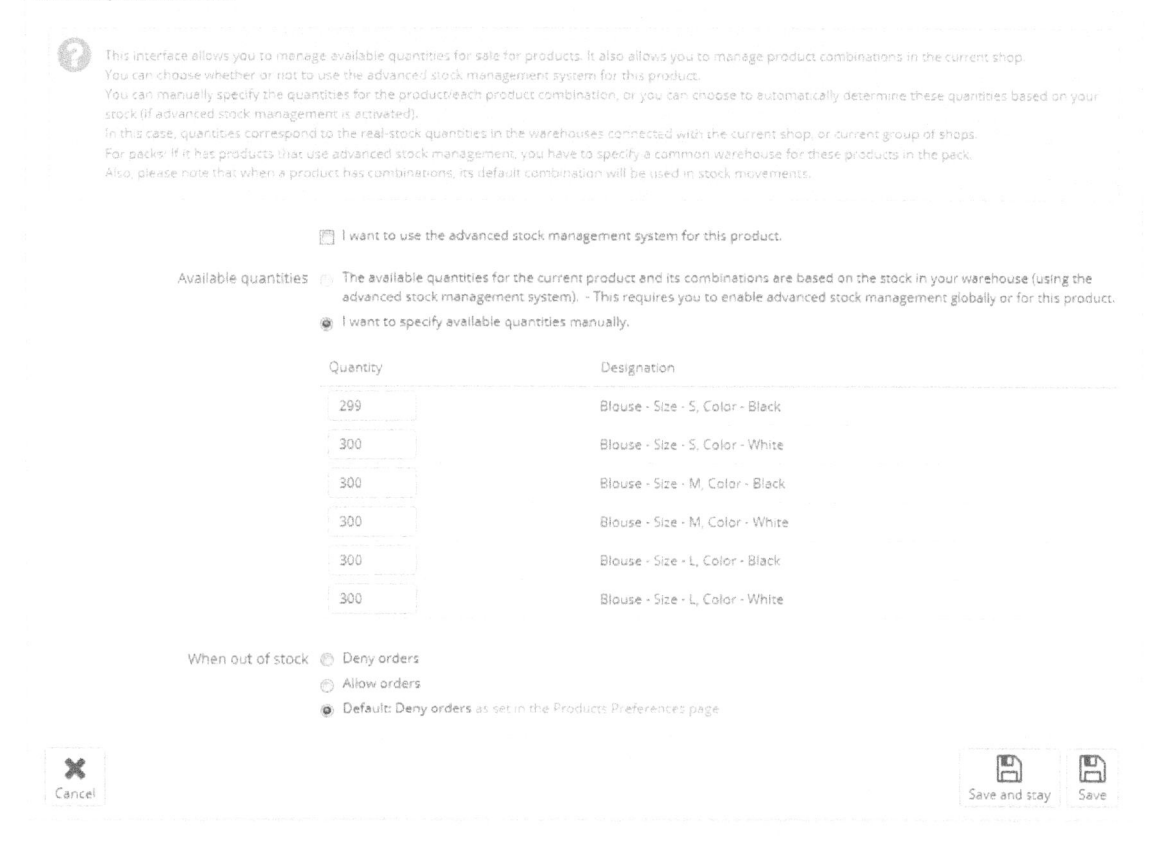

AVAILABLE QUANTITIES FOR SALE

[Screenshot of the Available Quantities for Sale interface showing options for advanced stock management, a table of quantities (299, 300, 300, 300, 300, 300) for Blouse combinations (Size S/M/L, Color Black/White), and "When out of stock" options: Deny orders, Allow orders, Default: Deny orders.]

The "Quantity" tab opens with an explanatory section, which we urge you to fully read. That section is followed by the quantities management interface itself, which opens with three options:

- **I want to use the advanced stock management system for this product.**
- **The available quantities for current product and its combinations are based on stock in your warehouses.**
- **I want to specify available quantities manually**.

By default, the third option is ("I want to specify available quantities manually") is enabled. As long as you haven't check the first option ("I want to use the advanced stock management system for this product"), quantities are managed the same way they were in version 1.4 of PrestaShop, which means that you have add the quantities manually, and PrestaShop will remove quantities for each sale.

If you'd rather synchronize the available quantities with your warehouse stock (or that of several warehouses), you have to change the quantities management method:

1. Check the "I want to use the advanced stock management system for this product" box in order the change method.
2. This makes the second option, "Available quantities for current product and its combinations are based on stock in the warehouses", finally available. Select it in order to synchronize the available quantity for this product with your warehouse stock.

As soon as you have selected the second option, the table's "Quantity" column cannot be edited anymore: quantities are now directly handled from the advanced stock management feature rather than from each product's "Quantities" tab.

> Product packs are a special case. Since it is not yet possible to add product combinations to a pack, the PrestaShop developers have decided that when necessary, PrestaShop would use the default combination when decrementing the physical stock.
>
> Also, a notice indicates the recommended maximal number of packs.

The rest of the tab explained in the "Managing the Catalog" chapter of this guide.

Supplier management

You can now set more than one supplier for a given product. For each supplier associated to a product, you can set the supplier's reference number and a default purchase price for that product as well as its combination. This information is used when making an order to the supplier.

SUPPLIERS OF THE CURRENT PRODUCT

This interface allows you to specify the suppliers of the current product and eventually its combinations.
It is also possible to specify supplier references according to previously associated suppliers.

When using the advanced stock management tool (see Preferences/Products), the values you define (prices, references) will be used in supply orders.

Please choose the suppliers associated with this product. Please select a default supplier, as well.

Selected	Supplier Name	Default
☑	Fashion Supplier	○

+ Create a new supplier

PRODUCT REFERENCE(S)

You can specify product reference(s) for each associated supplier. Click "Save and Stay" after changing selected suppliers to display the associated product references.

FASHION SUPPLIER

Product name	Supplier reference	Unit price tax excluded	Unit price currency
Blouse - Size - S, Color - Black		0	Dollar
Blouse - Size - S, Color - White		0	Dollar
Blouse - Size - M, Color - Black		0	Dollar
Blouse - Size - M, Color - White		0	Dollar
Blouse - Size - L, Color - Black		0	Dollar
Blouse - Size - L, Color - White		0	Dollar

Warehouses management

If advanced stock management is enabled, a "Warehouses" tab appears in the product sheet, where you can indicate which warehouse(s) the product and each of its combinations can be stored in. You can even indicate the location for the product and its combinations.

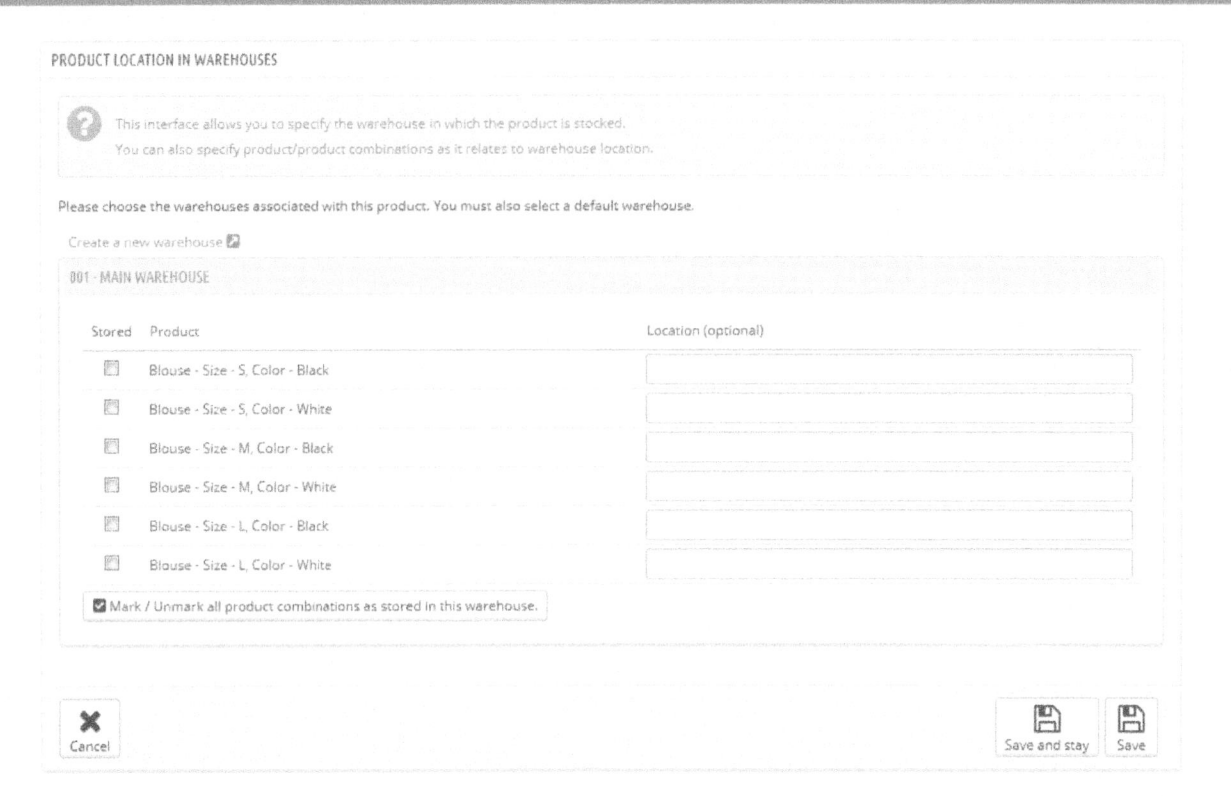

You must first create at least one warehouse (see below) before associating a product to it and setting the product location in it. This step is essential: it is important to at least set one warehouse in which a product can be stored. This will have considerable impact on the order preparation in the multi-shipping context.

Warehouses management

The advanced stock management feature makes it possible to create one or more warehouses. In order to create one, go to the "Warehouse" page under the "Stock" menu.

Once you start creating a new warehouse, you must fill in the following fields:

- **Reference** and **Name**. The warehouse's unique reference identifier and name. Make sure to use something recognizable: you must be able to easily differentiate to warehouses from a drop-down list.
- **Address**, **Postcode/Zip Code**, **City** and **Country**. The warehouse's physical address. This information will be used on the purchase order to suppliers.
- **Manager**. A person in charge of the warehouse, chosen among your shop's registered employees. If the employee's account is not yet created, you must create it first.
- **Carriers**. The carriers who you authorize for orders shipping from this warehouse. Maintain the "Shift" key pressed while clicking to select more than one carrier.
- **Management type**. A method of accounting valuation, based on your country's regulations. See the "Stock management rules" part of this chapter for more information.
- **Stock valuation currency**. A valuation currency for this warehouse's stock (among the registered currencies).

It is not possible to change a warehouse's valuation method and currency once it has been set. If you need to change that information, you will have to recreate the warehouse, and delete the wrong one. You can only delete a warehouse if it does not contain any product anymore.

Be careful of the carriers you choose to authorize, as this will a huge impact on the order preparation in the multishipping scenario.

WAREHOUSE INFORMATION

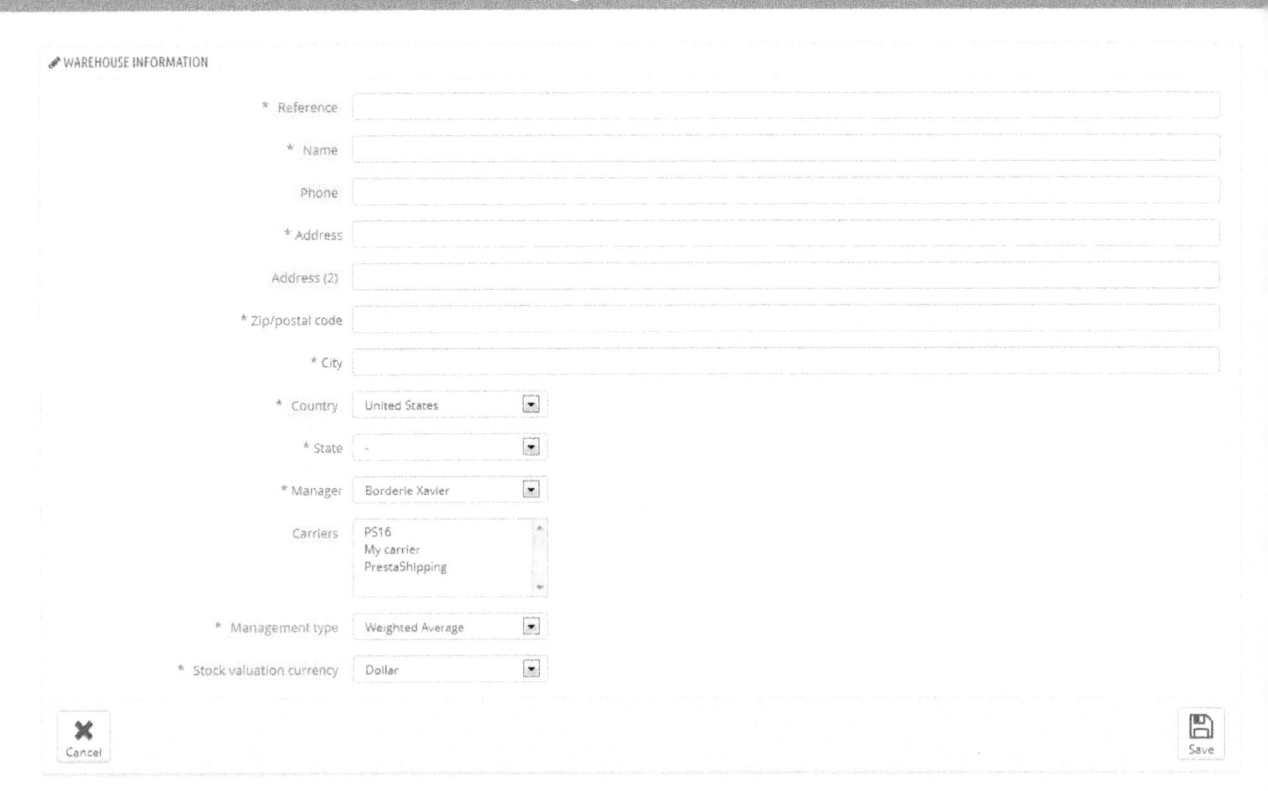

* Reference	
* Name	
Phone	
* Address	
Address (2)	
* Zip/postal code	
* City	
* Country	United States
* State	-
* Manager	Borderie Xavier
Carriers	PS16 My carrier PrestaShipping
* Management type	Weighted Average
* Stock valuation currency	Dollar

[Cancel] [Save]

In the situation where you manage more than one shop, you will also have to associate each shop to one or more warehouses. This enables you to set from which warehouse the client orders for a given shop can be sent.

Once the warehouse has been created, you are taken back to the list of warehouses. Click the "View" icon on the right of its row to access a bird's eye view of its information, including the references of all the products stored in it, the sum of all the available quantities, a global accounting valuation, details of the stored products, and the history of the stock movements for that warehouse.

INFORMATIONS GÉNÉRALES

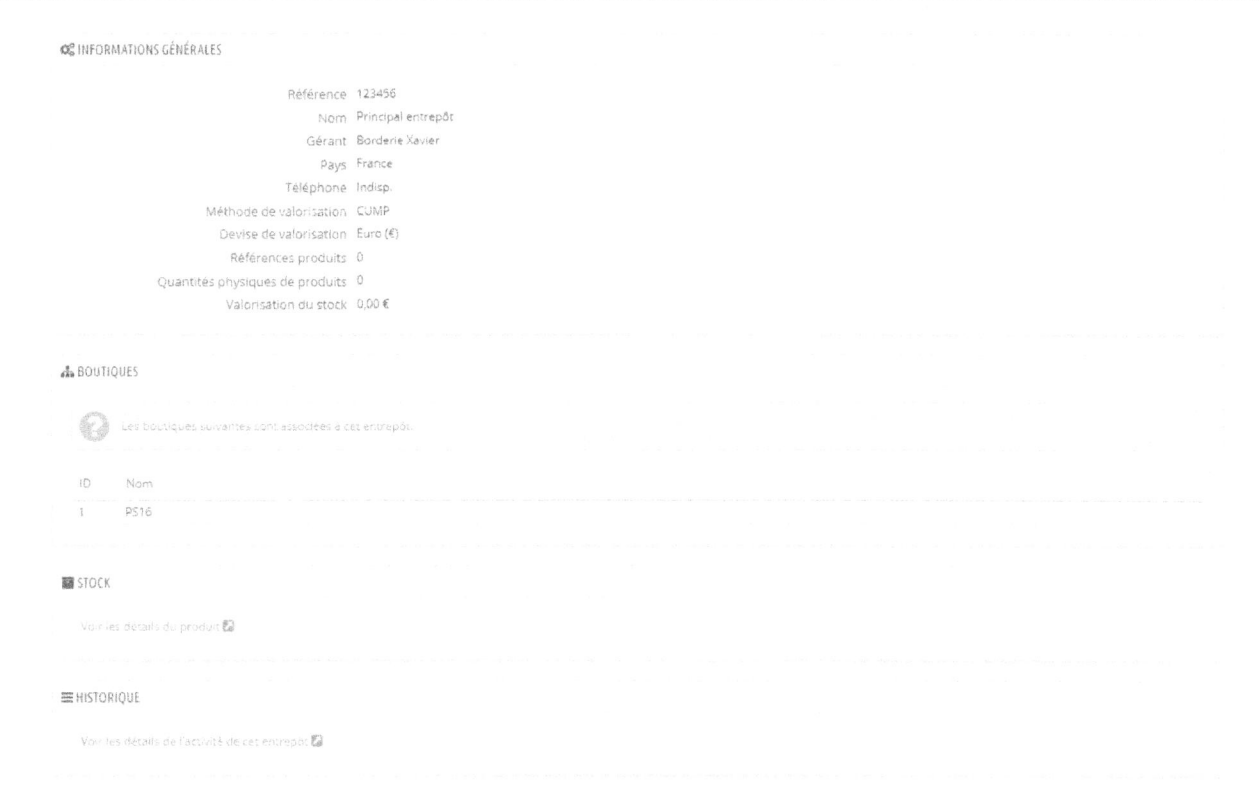

Référence	123456
Nom	Principal entrepôt
Gérant	Borderie Xavier
Pays	France
Téléphone	Indisp.
Méthode de valorisation	CUMP
Devise de valorisation	Euro (€)
Références produits	0
Quantités physiques de produits	0
Valorisation du stock	0,00 €

BOUTIQUES

Les boutiques suivantes sont associées à cet entrepôt.

ID	Nom
1	PS16

STOCK

Voir les détails du produit

HISTORIQUE

Voir les détails de l'activité de cet entrepôt

Each warehouse page also contains two links at the bottom:

- **See product details**. Takes you to the warehouse's "Instant Stock Status" page.
- **See warehouse's activity details**. Takes you to the warehouse's "Stock Movement" page.

Stock management

Now that you have created one or more warehouses, you have to set stock for each of them. To that end, go to the "Stock Management" page under the "Stock" menu.

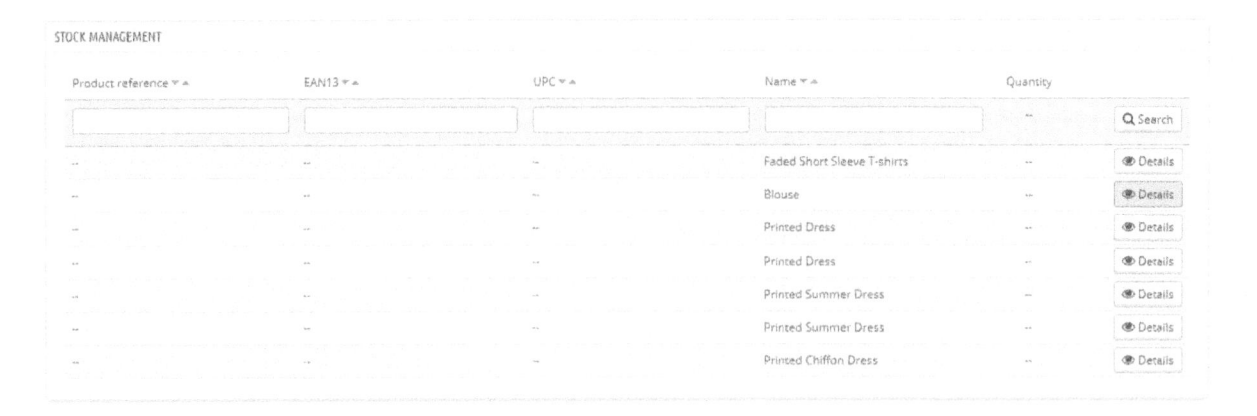

All available products from your catalog are listed in this interface. If you have any combination of product, you can manage them from the "Details" action.

In your daily activities, you can use this interface in order to manually:

- **Add stock**. This button adds stock for a specific product in a given warehouse.
- **Remove stock**. This button removes stock for a specific product in a given warehouse.
- **Transfer stock**. This button transfers stock from one warehouse to another.

The last two actions only appear if there already is some stock of the chosen product in any warehouse.
The "Transfer stock" only appears if you have at least two registered warehouses.

Adding stock to a warehouse

To add more stock to a product, use the "Add stock" action (up arrow) for said product or product combination. A new page opens, containing a form where the most important information is displayed in order to help you identify a product with certainty (reference, EAN13 and UPC code, and name). This information cannot be changed from this form, therefore it is grayed out.

You must then set:

- **Quantity to add**. This must be a positive number. You cannot remove stock by using a negative number.
- **Usable for sale?**. Whether that quantity of stock is usable for sale, or simply stored until you make a decision about it. In the second case, it is considered "reserved".
- **Warehouse**. The warehouse where the stock is to be added. The form lets you add product stock to only one warehouse at a time. If you need to add stock for this product in more than one warehouse, you must make the entire adding process again for each warehouse.
- **Unit price (tax excl.)**. The unit price for the product at the time of the addition. This is for valuation purpose.
- **Currency**. The currency of the unit price. If the currency is not available, you can create one from the "Currencies" page, under the "Localization" menu, or import from the "Localization" page under the "Localization"

menu, by importing the localization pack of the country whose currency you want to use.
- **Label**. A label for the stock movement that you are generating, for future reference. This is purely informational.

> When hovering the "Quantity to add" and "Unit price (tax excl.)" fields with the mouse cursor, the interface will display a reminder of their values the last time you added some stock.

Removing stock from a warehouse

When you want to remove a certain quantity of product stock, you must use the "Remove stock" action (down arrow, available only when there already are products in stock). A new page opens, containing a form where the most important information is displayed in order to help you identify a product with certainty (reference, EAN13 and UPC code, and name). This information cannot be changed from this form, therefore it is grayed out.

You must then set:

- **Quantity to remove**. This must be a positive number. You cannot add stock by using a negative number.
- **Usable for sale**. Whether this quantity should be removed from the usable quantity or from the whole physical quantity (including the reserved one).
- **Warehouse**. From which warehouse that quantity should be removed. The form lets you remove product stock from only one warehouse at a time. If you need to remove stock for this product in more than one warehouse, you must make the entire removing process again for each warehouse.
- **Label**. A label for the stock movement that you are generating, for future reference. This is purely informational.

Transferring stock from one warehouse to another

The stock transfer enables you to transfer stock from one warehouse to another, or from one status to another (usable in store / reserved) within a single warehouse. Click on the "Transfer stock" action (sideways arrows, available only when there already are products in stock). A new page opens, containing a form where the most important information is displayed in order to help you identify a product with certainty (reference, EAN13 and UPC code, and name). This information cannot be changed from this form, therefore it is grayed out.

You must then set:

- **Quantity to transfer**. This must be a positive number.
- **Source warehouse**. The warehouse from which you want to transfer some products, or where you want to change the status of some of the stock.
- **Is this product for sale in your source warehouse?**. Whether the quantity to remove from the "source" warehouse should be from the "usable for sale" stock or the "reserved" stock.
- **Destination warehouse**. The warehouse to which you want to transfer some products. If you simply want to change the status of some of the stock from your source warehouse, make sure to select the same warehouse in this form.
- **Is this product usable for sale in your destination warehouse?**. Whether the quantity to add to the "destination" warehouse is usable for sale or reserved. This is also the option to use when you simply want to change the status of some of the stock in the source warehouse:
    - If you do not want to change status while moving warehouses: make sure both "Use for sale?" option are set alike.
    - If you do want to change status, whether within the same warehouse or while moving warehouses: make sure both "Use for sale?" option are set differently.

For these operations, all that is related to valuations is run automatically according to the management method chosen for each warehouse. Currency conversions work the same.

Stock Movement

This interface enables you to view the stock movement history. You can display all of the stock movements, or only those tied to one warehouse. Filters can be applied to refine your search.

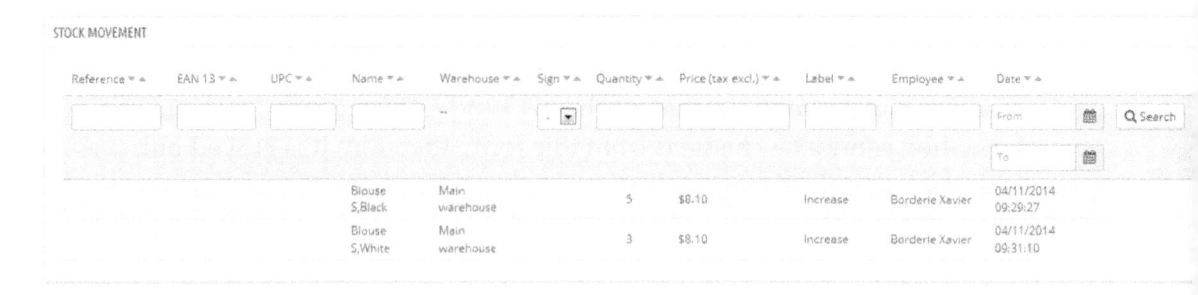

When the "Filter movements by warehouse" drop-down list is set to a warehouse, you can make a CSV export of the obtained list.

Instant Stock Status

This interface enables you to have an instant overview of your stock, either globally or per warehouse. The numbers are current.

For each product or product combination in stock, the following indicators are available:

- Unit price (tax excluded).
- Product valuation depending on the physical quantity of stock. The sum (for all prices) is not available for all warehouses, please filter by warehouse.
- Physically available stock.
- Stock that is usable for sale.
- Real quantity (physical usable quantity - client orders + supply Orders).

As appropriate, and depending on the chosen valuation method, the breakdown of the unit prices and of the associated valuations is available by clicking on the "Details" action.

Moreover, for a given warehouse, you have two ways to export the current list in CSV format:

- Export the indicators tied to the quantities.
- Export the indicators tied to the valuation (prices).

Stock Coverage

This interface enables you to overview the coverage of your stock. The coverage indicates how many days your current stock can last. This information is very useful, as it helps you predict the necessary restocking. Coverage is calculated according to previously registered stock movements.

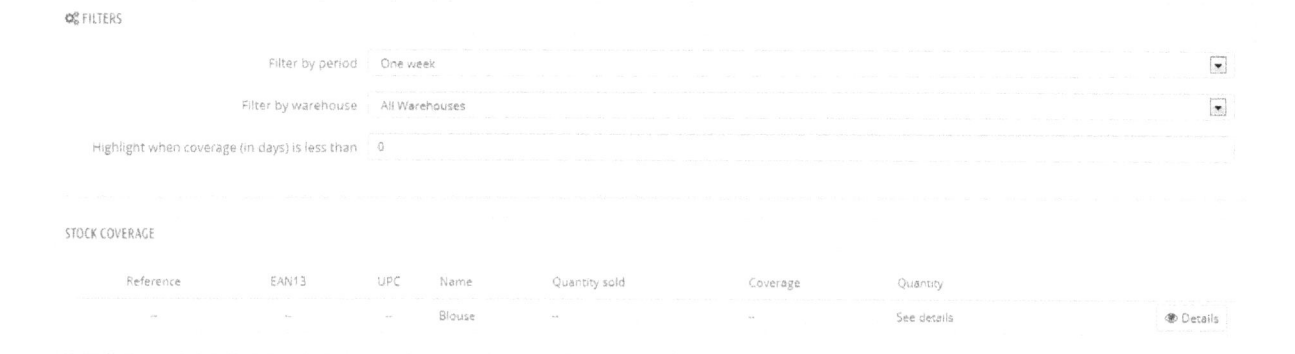

You can get the stock coverage for all the warehouses, or for a single warehouse. You can also set the time period (one week, two weeks, three weeks, one month, six months, a year) of registered stock movement which is to be taken into account when calculating the coverage.

Finally, you can highlight the stock coverage which is below a given number of days. This will highlight the relevant products, helping you identify them quicker.

In order to view the stock coverage of product combinations, you have to click the "Details" action of the product.

> It is possible to receive notifications of the stock coverage for a product. The e-mail notification module (mail alerts) can take product stock coverage into account. It is thus possible to set a number of coverage days below which you will receive a notification. See the configuration for this module.

Supply orders

One of the major features of the stock manager is the ability to place orders to suppliers so as to better manage your restocking.
This interface enables you to manage all your supplier orders, as well as reusable order templates.

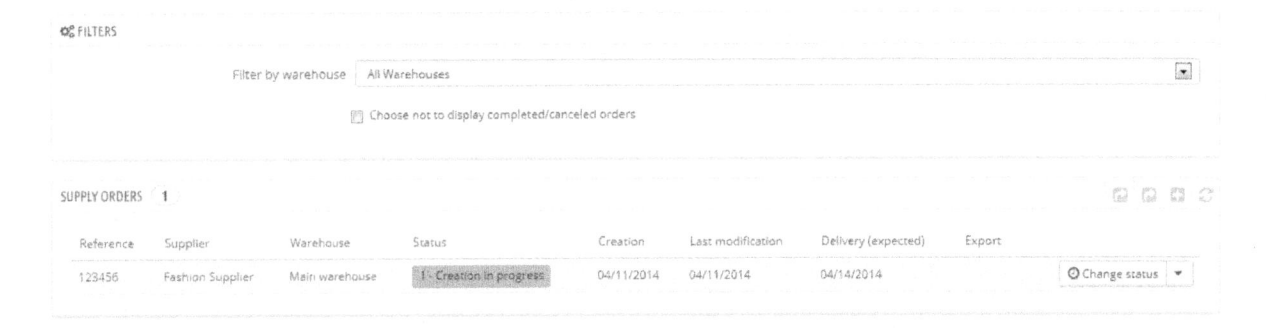

Reference	Supplier	Warehouse	Status	Creation	Last modification	Delivery (expected)	Export	
123456	Fashion Supplier	Main warehouse	1 - Creation in progress	04/11/2014	04/11/2014	04/14/2014		Change status

The order template creation process is the same as the order creation process (except for the "Expected delivery date" field). We will therefore only explain the order creation process.

Creating a new order

The creation of an order for a supplier can be broken down in two steps: creating the order, then adding products to it.

ORDER INFORMATION

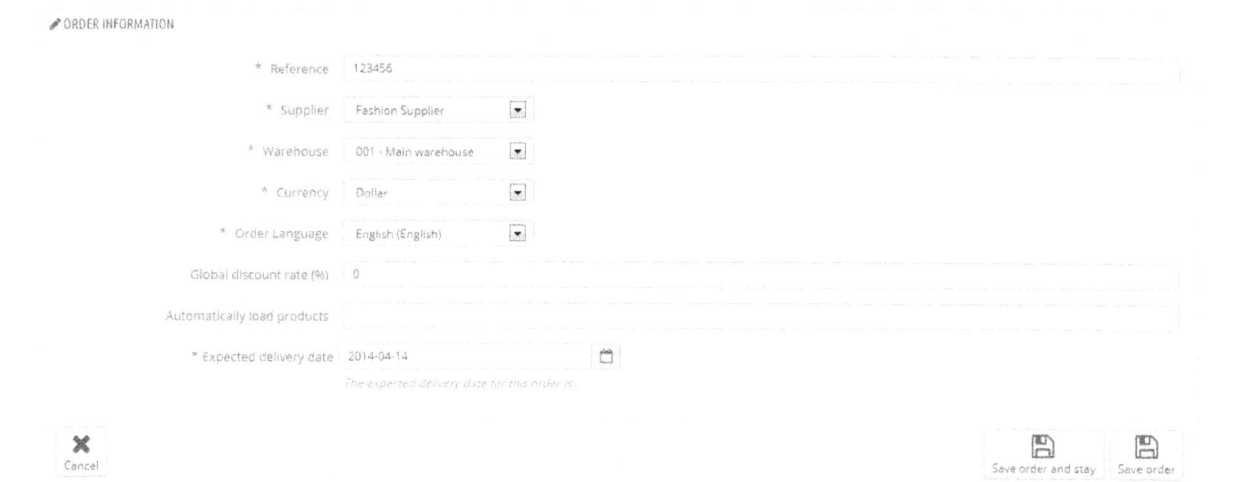

* Reference	123456
* Supplier	Fashion Supplier
* Warehouse	001 - Main warehouse
* Currency	Dollar
* Order Language	English (English)
Global discount rate (%)	0
Automatically load products	
* Expected delivery date	2014-04-14

The expected delivery date for this order is...

[Cancel]   [Save order and stay]   [Save order]

So, the first step is to define the order's headers:

- Set the unique reference number. This is an administrative number; do not put any seemingly unique number.
- Select the supplier. If the supplier you want is not in the drop-down list, you must create it in the "Suppliers" page, under the "Catalog" menu.
- Select the warehouse which will take delivery of the order. You must have created at least one warehouse.
- Select the currency in which the order will be formalized. If needed, you can create or import a currency using, respectively, the "Currencies" or "Localization" page under the "Localization" menu.
- Select the language in which the order will be formalized. If needed, you can create or import a language using, respectively, the "Languages" or "Localization" page under the "Localization" menu.
- If needed, set the global discount on the order (in percentage). You can just leave it at "0" if you do not have a discount on this order.
- If needed, set the physical quantity of a product below which all the products have to be restocked, and are therefore to be added to the order automatically. Each pre-added product will be ordered with a quantity equal to the entered quantity, minus the already available quantity.
- Set the expected delivery date.

The second step consists of adding actual products to the order. To make that second step, you can either:

- Click on the "Save order and stay" button.
- Click on the "Save order" button. You are taken back to the list of supply orders: click on the "Edit" action for the order you just created.

The interface of the order creation form has been updated with a second form below the previously-filled fields. You must use that second form to add products to your order, using the integrated search engine. The products that you add appear in a new list.

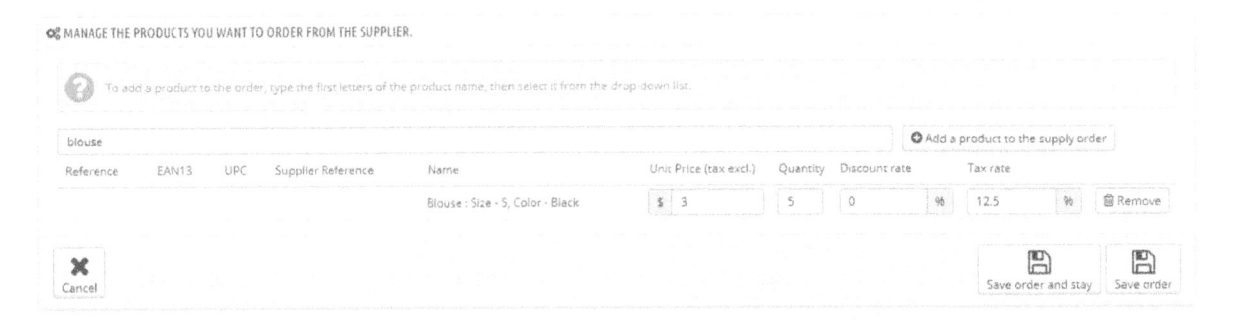

For each product, you must set or update the unit purchase price (tax excluded), the quantity to order, any applicable tax rate, and any product-specific discount.

Once the order is created, it appears in the list with the "Creation in progress" status. This status enables you to view and edit the information that were previously entered as well as add products to the order. You will not be able to change the order once you change its status to "Order validated".

> You can never delete a supply order: you can only cancel it.

You need to follow through for the whole order process, always indicating its status change in PrestaShop's interface. This is what the first action button of the list ("Change state") is for: click on it to reach the status changing form. See the "Changing the status of a supplier order" section below for more information on the available statuses, and see the "Registering the reception of products" to understand how to follow through on a supply order.

The "+" icon in the supply order list displays the order's history, which enables you to see who did what and when.

Order template creation

The whole point of creating a template is to serve as a basis for new orders.

Reference	Supplier	Warehouse	Creation	
123	Fashion Supplier	Main warehouse	04/11/2014	View

STOCK: SUPPLY ORDER TEMPLATES 1

The supply order template creation process is the same as the one for a real order, except that:

- You do not have to set a planned delivery date.
- The "Automatically load products" value will be the quantity to order for the loaded products, not the stock/typed value difference.

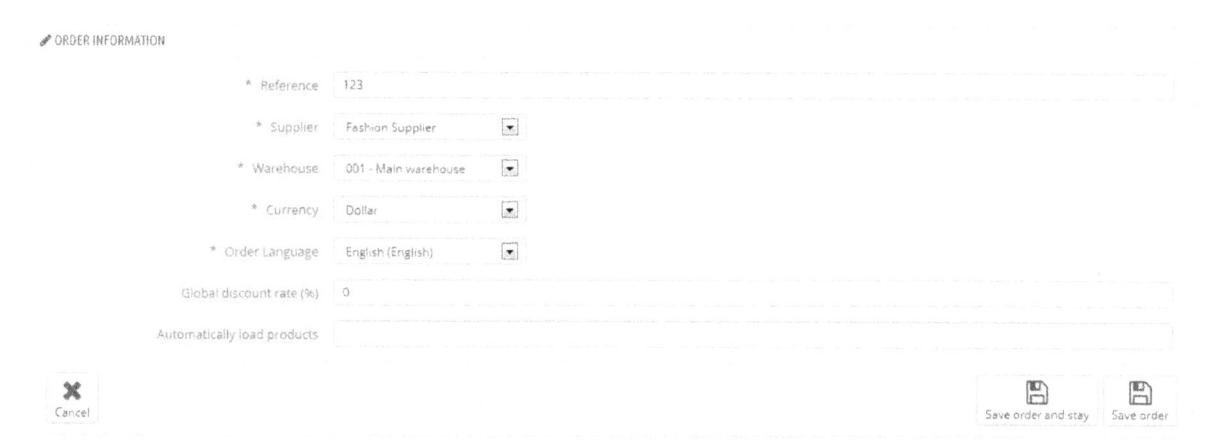

ORDER INFORMATION

* Reference	123
* Supplier	Fashion Supplier
* Warehouse	001 - Main warehouse
* Currency	Dollar
* Order Language	English (English)
Global discount rate (%)	0
Automatically load products	

Cancel / Save order and stay / Save order

Moreover, contrary to an ordinary supply order:

- A template does not have a status.
- A template can be deleted.
- A template has no edit history.

Once you have created your template, you only need to use the "Use this template to create a supply order" action from the template list (the "two windows" icon) to start creating an order.

Changing the status of a supply order

Each order has many available actions (in the "Actions" column of the order list). One of them enables you to edit the status: the "Change state" one. There are six possible default statuses, but you can add your own (see the "Configuration" section of this chapter).

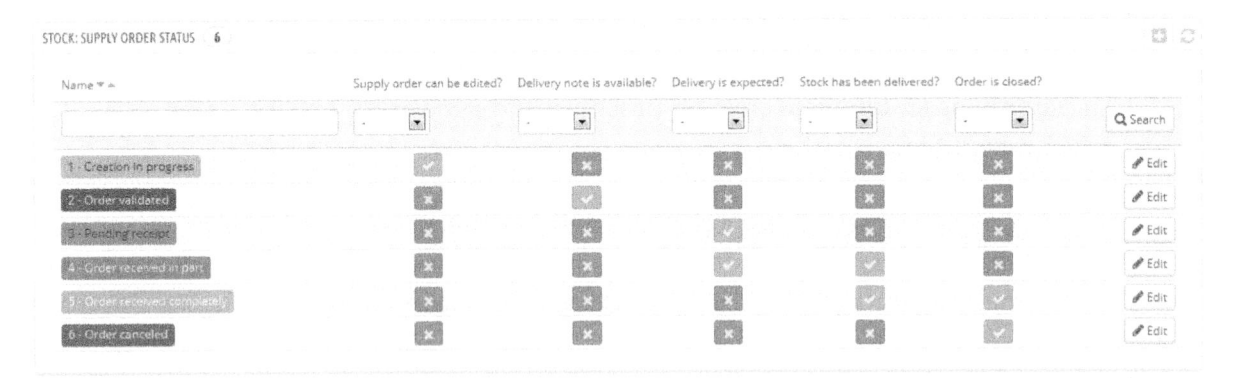

An order's status helps you understand your stock movements at a glance thanks to their color code. Here is the significance of the six default statuses:

1. **Creation in progress**. This is when you are in the first step of the creation step, where you can edit everything.
2. **Order validated**. This status validates the order and freezes the information it contains (purchase prices, quantities, etc.). At this step, a new action appears in the "Actions" column, which enables you to edit the invoice that is sent to the supplier in PDF format.
3. **Pending receipt**. As soon as the supplier has received and validated your invoice, you have to change the supply order's status to "Pending receipt".
4. **Order received in part**. As soon as a delivery is made, you must switch the order to this status. There can be multiple deliveries, and a delivery history is logged for each product. The restocking is made with each delivery.
5. **Order received completely**. Once an order is completely delivered, or partially because of a partial cancellation, it should be switched to this status. Stocks are unaffected in this case, and it is possible to perform actions on the order.

6. **Order canceled**. This status is to be given to canceled orders, whatever the reason. Stocks are unaffected in this case, and it is not possible to perform actions on the order.

With each status change, the status drop-down selector evolves in order to present only the possible status changes, in regard to the current status. The unavailable statuses are grayed out.

Details of a supplier order

Clicking the "View" icon from the list of supply orders enables you to get a synthetic view of your order.
You can also download the invoice generated as a PDF file (provided the order is validated by you) from the list of orders or from the status change page.

The "Details" action enables you to display the status change history for the current order.

Registering the reception of products

You must change the status of your supply order within PrestaShop as soon as actions are taken in the real world. This is done using the "Change state" action in the "Actions" column from the list of orders. The form in this page always preselects the next logical status, but you are free to choose any of the other statuses available.

While you are preparing the supply order, keep its status to "Creation in progress". Once you are done preparing the order, switch it to "Order validated", then print the invoice PDF and send it to your supplier. As soon as your supplier confirms the reception of the invoice, change the status to "Pending receipt".

During the "Pending receipt" and "Order received in part" statuses, a new action is available in the "Actions" column. Using the "truck" icon, the "Update ongoing receipt of products" action enables you to register the reception of products for a given order during the current day.
The form that opens after clicking that "truck" action enables you to see how many items were expected, and to indicate the quantity of product delivered for each product that day. Click the "Update selected" button to mark the selected

products as received with the number of items you indicated in the "Quantity received today?" field. The checkbox on the left of each row must be checked for PrestaShop to take that line into account.

> This step can be done as many times as necessary, and it is possible to receive and incorporate more stock than planned.
>
> If you receive less stock than expected, PrestaShop automatically changes the order's status to "Order received in part".

For each product, a reception history is available ("+" action), as well as an indication of the received quantity, the expected quantity, and the remaining quantity. If the "received quantity" is equal to the "expected quantity", the corresponding row is highlighted in green. If you received more than expected, it is in red.

When all the products from the order have been received, you must manually change the supply order's status to "Order received completely". This ends the supply order process, and a new "Export" action appears, which you can use to download a CSV file of all the information pertaining to that order.

CSV export

Using the supply orders interface, you can filter the list of orders or the details of these orders so that you may export it, according to the current filters (reference, supplier, etc.).
Moreover, you can choose not to display the orders that are completed or canceled, using the appropriate checkbox.

Configuration

The configuration page enables you to customize the way certain parts of the advanced stock manager work:

- The available statuses for a supply order.
- The labels for the stock movements.
- The default statuses for some stock movements which are used throughout the solution.

Adding a new default order status

You can add custom statuses corresponding to your business line. You cannot delete a default status.

The list on the main page enables you to get a better perspective of the available statuses, and how they can impact an order.

Click the "Add new" button to reach the creation form.

A status has a label, a color, and enables you to define whether:

- The order can be edited. As long as the order is editable, it cannot be sent to the supplier.
- The order delivery note can be generated.
- Product reception is ongoing, meaning that you have not yet received all the ordered products.
- Product delivery is still pending, meaning that you are still waiting for any product to arrive.

Adding a stock movement label

It is possible to add more labels to stock movements. Click the "Add new" button from the "Stock movement labels" section to access the creation form.

You simply have to set a name for the label, and indicate whether it pertains to stock increase or decrease. Those labels can be used when adding/removing/transferring stock manually (as explained earlier).

Changing default supply order labels

It is possible to choose the default stock movement labels in the following standard cases:

- Increasing stock (manually).
- Decreasing stock (manually).
- Decreasing stock following the shipment of a client order.
- Increasing stock following the delivery of products from a supplier's order.

Stock Management Rules

In this section, we will explain the management rules that are automatically applied to stock management.

Each stock entry and exit must be valued. That is why each unit product stock must be associated with a tax-excluded unit price (either purchase price or production cost), whether through supplier order, or manual entry. Each product exit must also be valued.

There are three main valuation methods that you can choose, depending on your business activity or on the tax laws of each warehouse's country or origin:

- FIFO (first in, first out).
- LIFO (last in, first out).
- AVCO (Average Cost, or Weighted Average Cost per Unit).

With the FIFO and LIFO methods, each unit product from the stock has a purchase price that has been fixed when it entered the stock. This way, for a given reference available in 100 units, 40 units can have a purchase price of X, and 60 can have a purchase price of Y. When an order is made, and depending on the chosen method, you know which product to use and with which purchase price, which enables you to precisely manage a potential order return and put the products back into stock with their original purchase price.

The table below gives you an example of the FIFO method of stock valuation. In this example, you have a two-input table (price and quantity per type of stock movement). You add more columns as we receive new products with new prices.

Price	4	6	7
Initial stock	1000		
Entry		500	
Exit	(700)		
Exit	(300)	(400)	
Entry			900
Instant state	0	100	900

The stock value during the instant state in this case is 6,900.

The table below illustrates how the FIFO method can be used to value stock. We use the same entry and exit values as in the previous example. The principle remains the same as in the FIFO example, except that during exits, we primarily use the units that were the last to be entered in the stock.

Price	4	6	7
Initial stock	1000		
Entry		500	
Exit	(200)	(500)	
Exit	(700)		
Entry			900
Instant state	100	0	900

The stock value during the instant state in this case is of 6,700.

The third most frequently used method for stock valuation is Weighted Average Cost (AVCO). The AVCO calculation is done after each new entry in the stock.

For a given product, the AVCO calculation is done using this formula:

AVCO = (QS * previous AVCO + QA * UP) / (QS + QA)
Unless QS is negative or null, in which case AVCO = UP.

With:

- QS = Quantity of products currently in stock, or initial stock.
- QA = Quantity of products to be added to stock.
- UP = Unit Price (tax-excluded purchase price, or production cost).

The table below illustrates the evolution of the AVCO with the example of a product initially with 20 units in stock, and purchased at a price of 2. The new entry/exit will be valued as follows:

	Entry	Entry UP	Exit	Exit UP	AVCO	Stock valuation
Initial stock	20	2			2	40
X Date			12	2	2	16
Y Date	20	3.4			3*	84
Z Date			10	3	3	54

*: Calculation details: ((8 remaining product in stock * 2) + (20 products to add * 3.4)) / 28 total products = 3.

At the Y date, we calculated the AVCO according to the number of products added in the stock their unit prices. Therefore, all products in stock now have a reassigned unit value, which depends on the new AVCO.

Managing Multiple Shops

One of the great features of PrestaShop is called "multistore", meaning the ability to manage multiple shops from the same back-office.

Thanks to this feature, you can manage many customized shops, which share many common elements. For more efficiency, you can even create groups of shops.

How to decide if you need the multistore feature

You may find yourself wanting to use the multistore feature, when in fact it is not necessary. For instance, if you want a multilingual shop, or if you need to use more than one currency, or if you would like to have a different graphic template for each category.

Here are two questions that you should ask yourself before deciding to enable the multistore feature:

- Do you want your shops to have a different price for the same product (besides special discounts for a client or group of clients).
  If the answer is 'yes', then you need to use the multistore feature.

- When a client buys from one shop, would you want him or her to not have access that shop's order history and invoices from the other shop (even if the client have the same login credentials on both shops). **If the answer is 'yes', then you need to use the multistore feature**: the shops will not share their carts and orders, and customers putting items in their cart for shop 1 will not see these items in their cart for shop 2.

If the answer is 'no' to both questions, then the multistore feature is not for you.

Enabling the multistore feature

Turning your single-shop PrestaShop installation into a multi-shop one is very simple:

1. Log-in to your shop's administration.
2. Go to the "Preferences" menu and select the "General" page.
3. Find the "Enable multistore" option, select "Yes".
4. **Save your changes**.

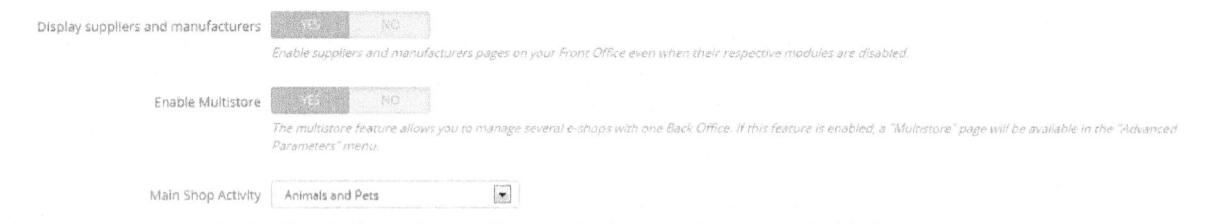

There you go: the multistore feature is now in place, starting with the addition of the "Multistore" page under the "Advanced parameters" menu. This is the page were you will manage the various shops created with this PrestaShop installation.

The multistore interface

Managing your stores

The "Multistore" page comprises three mains sections:

- **Multistore tree**. Gives you a bird's eye view of your shop groups, their shops, and even the various URLs tied to a single shop.
  By default, there is only one shop, in the default group: the main shop.
- **Shop groups** table. Lists the available shop groups. You can edit them by click on the 'edit' icon on the right.
- **Multistore options**. Lists the available options for the existing shops.
- **Default shop**. The default shop is the one which will serve a central hub for all the other ones, shares its details with other shops (products, carriers, etc.), and is the one that appears when you log in the administration.

One back-office to rule them all

When the multistore feature is enabled for your PrestaShop installation, many aspects of PrestaShop become customizable on a per-shop or per-shop-group basis.

To help you understand which shop your changes are applied to, PrestaShop adds a dropdown selector at the top of each screen, where you can choose the scope of application of your changes:

- Apply to all of your shops on this installation of PrestaShop.
- Apply to only the shops of the selected shop group.
- Apply to only the selected shop.

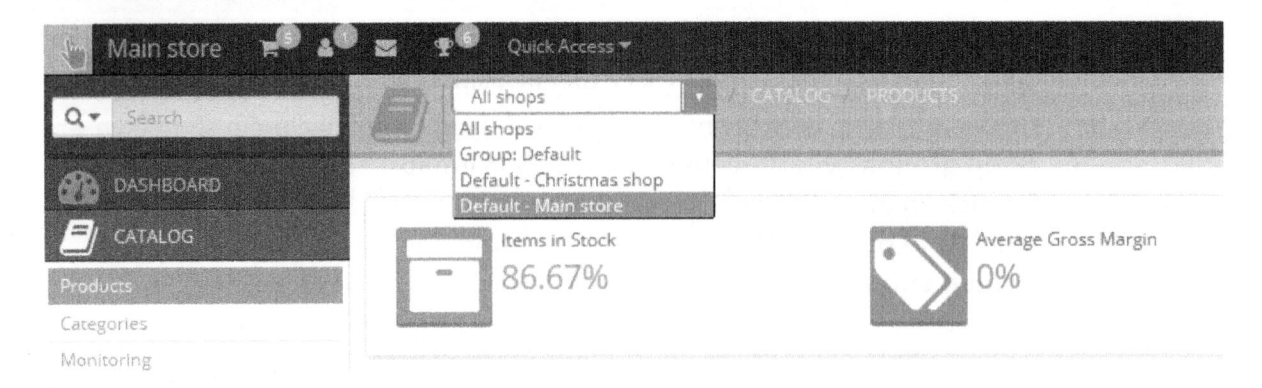

This shop selector helps you know on which shop(s) you are currently working.

That being said, once the multistore mode is in place, many of the regular settings can only be changed on a global (all shops) scale (most notably the settings pages: localization, preferences, advanced preferences, administration) and will therefore present the options as disabled in any other selection. Still, you can choose to edit those settings on a more local (per group shop or even per shop) scale if it is needed.

Indeed, settings pages will look regular when the shop selector is on "All shops", while in any other selection (shop group or single shop) they get additional options:

- A "Yes/No" option at the top of each section of the settings page.
- A check box next to each option.

They both serve the same purpose: letting you enable the options that would otherwise be disabled in the current shop context. You can pick the options that you want to enable, or you can enable all the options of the section by switching the Yes/No option. Once enabled, it is up to you to change the value of each

PrestaShop 1.6 User Guide

options: clicking the checkbox or switching the Yes/No option does not change any settings, it just allows you to change it in that context.

> Nevertheless, some options cannot be edited on a local context: they will display "You can't change the value of this configuration field in the context of this shop."

The following table indicates whether the item can also be customized for a single shop, for a group of shops, or for all shops at once.

Item	Per shop	Per shop group	All shops
Employees	X	X	X
Customer groups	X	X	X
Products	X	X	X
— Prices	X	X	X
— Combinations and prices	X	X	X
— Languages	X	X	X
— Multiple images (**except for the main image**)	X	X	X
— Available quantity for sale, provided that: • The "Share quantity available for sale" option is checked for the group, • The group does not share its quantity available for sale outside of the group.	X	X	
— All other information (description, tags, friendly URL, etc.)	X	X	X
Catalog values and attributes	X	X	X
Discounts: cart rules	X		
Discounts: catalog price rules	X		
Taxes: tax rules	X	X	X
Categories (**except for the main image**)	X	X	X
Carriers	X	X	X

PrestaShop 1.6 User Guide

Warehouses	X	X	X
Advanced stock management	X		
Suppliers	X	X	X
Manufacturers	X	X	X
CMS pages	X	X	X
Contacts	X	X	X
Countries A country's status (enabled or disabled) is common to all shop it is associated to.	X	X	X
Currencies	X	X	X
Languages	X	X	X
Modules	X	X	X
— Hooks and exceptions	X	X	X
— Enabling/disabling	X	X	X
— Configuration (for instance, PayPal login credentials)	X		
Payment modules	X	X	X
— Per-country restrictions	X		
— Per-currency restrictions	X		
— Per-customer group restriction	X		
Friendly URLs	X		
Scenes	X	X	X
Web service account	X	X	X
Homepage image slider	X		

Notes

Categories: A product can only appear in a given category of a shop if it has been associated to this category in that shop's context. In other words: if shop A and shop B have the C category in common, we can associate the P product to

> the C category for the A shop's context, and P will not appear in category C on shop B.
>
> **Carriers**: You can manage the carriers association on a per-shop basis, a per-shop-group basis or for all shops; but you cannot customize a carrier on a per-shop basis. You must duplicate the carrier if you want to use the same carrier with different price ranges on two shops.
>
> **Warehouses**: While advanced stock management can only be used for a single shop at a time, warehouses can be used with shop groups, and you can simply manage the warehouses in order to have advanced stock management.

For each shop, you can set specific price for every products, share part of the catalog or the whole of it, change product images, etc.

You can choose to share the customer accounts between your shops, enabling your customers to use the credentials between all shops, and even be transparently signed-in to each.

With advanced stock management, you can do a fine-grained management of the associations between yours shops and your warehouses.

Creating a new shop group

Having shop groups enables you to share certain characteristics between the shops in that group: catalog, employees, carriers, modules, etc. It allows you to manage a set of shops as easily as you would a single shop, while still being able to fine-tune the details of each shop manually.
Applying new parameters to all the shops in a group only requires a single action. When in multistore mode, a drop-down menu is available on most of the administration pages, and enables you to filter your changes by shop or shop group.

> Technically speaking, when selecting a shop group in the multistore drop-down menu, the displayed entities reflect the **union** of the entities pertaining to the shops in that group.

> Generally speaking, parameters are applied to all the entities belonging to the selected entity in the multistore drop-down menu. This is explained in details later in this chapter.

Clicking the "Add new shop group" button brings a form with few options but a lot of text: you should make sure to read each description from beginning to end, as they help you make a decision about these options. Since some are non-reversible (you cannot disable them once they are enabled), it is important to know exactly what you enable.

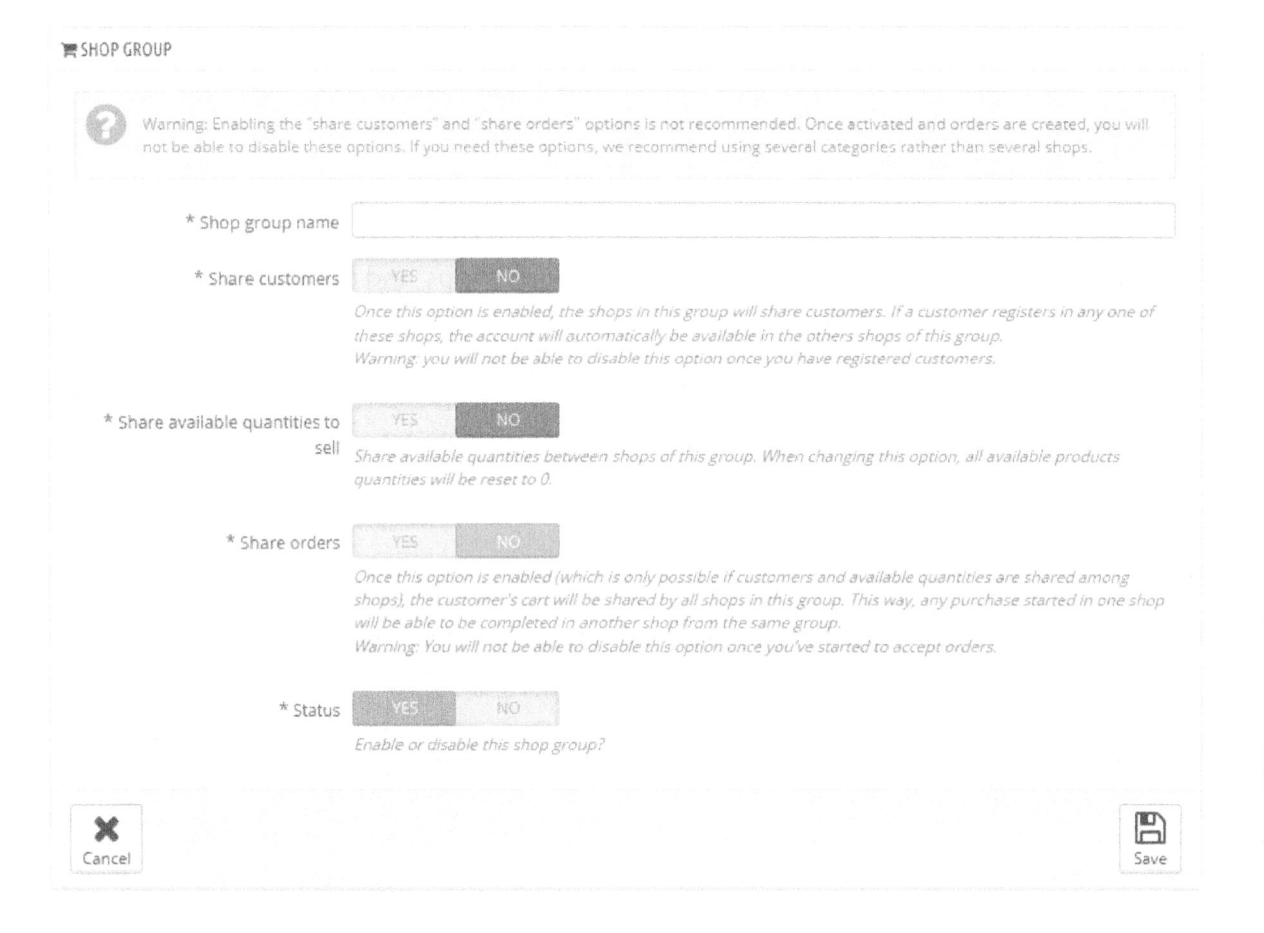

SHOP GROUP

Warning: Enabling the "share customers" and "share orders" options is not recommended. Once activated and orders are created, you will not be able to disable these options. If you need these options, we recommend using several categories rather than several shops.

* Shop group name

* Share customers — YES / **NO**
Once this option is enabled, the shops in this group will share customers. If a customer registers in any one of these shops, the account will automatically be available in the others shops of this group.
Warning: you will not be able to disable this option once you have registered customers.

* Share available quantities to sell — YES / **NO**
Share available quantities between shops of this group. When changing this option, all available products quantities will be reset to 0.

* Share orders — YES / **NO**
Once this option is enabled (which is only possible if customers and available quantities are shared among shops), the customer's cart will be shared by all shops in this group. This way, any purchase started in one shop will be able to be completed in another shop from the same group.
Warning: You will not be able to disable this option once you've started to accept orders.

* Status — **YES** / NO
Enable or disable this shop group?

[Cancel] [Save]

The available settings are:

- **Shop group name.** The name is private, customers will not see it. Still, make sure to use a telling name: the more shop groups you will have,

the more you will need to be able to find a given group quickly. You can edit the name at any time.
- **Share customers**. Once enabled, you cannot disable this option. This is great when you want to allow your customers to use the same login credentials on all shops of this shop group.
- **Share available quantities to sell**. You can have different quantities of the same product for sale on your shops. With this option, all the shops from this group will share the same available quantity of products. This can make it easier to manage said quantities.
- **Share orders**. Once enabled, you cannot disable this option. This option can only be enabled if both "Share customers" and "Share available quantities to sell" options are enabled. With this option, customers who are logged on any shop from this group will be able to see their order history for all the shops in the group.
- **Status**. Choose to enable this group right away, or later. You can enable/disable a shop group at any time.

Two shop groups cannot share customers, carts or orders.

Existing shop groups can be edited from the shop groups list on the "Multistore" front page: simply click on the 'edit' icon on the right of the shop's row to open the form. As expected, you cannot edit the "Share customers" and "Share orders" options.

Creating a new shop

The shop creation tool, located in the "Multistore" page, enables you to simply and precisely define both the front-office appearance of your shop (namely, its theme) and the elements you wish to import from your main shop into this new one.

SHOP

* Shop name

This field does not refer to the shop name visible in the front office.
Follow this link to edit the shop name used on the Front Office.

Shop group | Default

Warning: You won't be able to change the group of this shop if this shop belongs to a group with one of these options activated: Share Customers, Share Quantities or Share Orders.

Category root | Home

This is the root category of the store that you've created. To define a new root category for your store, Please click here.

Associated categories

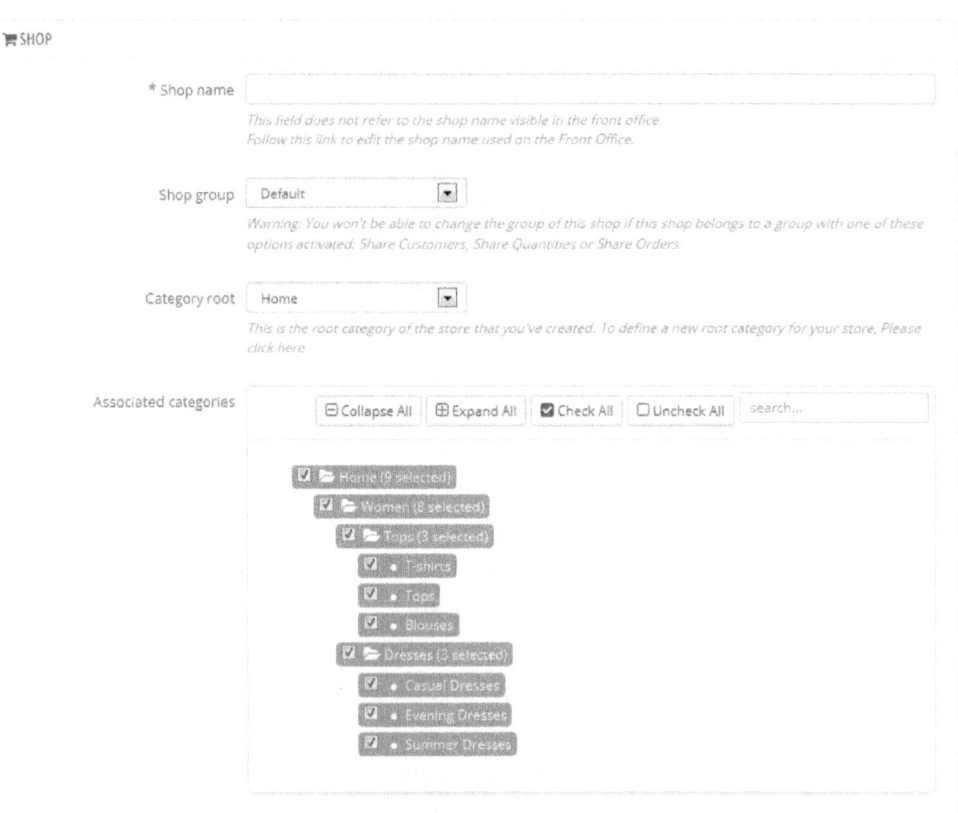

[Collapse All] [Expand All] [✓ Check All] [Uncheck All] [search...]

- ✓ 📂 Home (9 selected)
  - ✓ 📂 Women (8 selected)
    - ✓ 📂 Tops (3 selected)
      - ✓ • T-shirts
      - ✓ • Tops
      - ✓ • Blouses
    - ✓ 📂 Dresses (3 selected)
      - ✓ • Casual Dresses
      - ✓ • Evening Dresses
      - ✓ • Summer Dresses

By selecting associated categories, you are choosing to share the categories between shops. Once associated between shops, any alteration of this category will impact every shop.

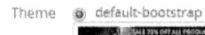

Theme ● default-bootstrap

[Cancel]   [Save]

Clicking the "Add new shop" button opens brings a form with two sections. The first one has 5 options:

- **Shop name**. The name is public: customers will see it in many places, such as the site title or the e-mail references. Make sure to make it clear that it describes this specific shop.
- **Shop Group**. A shop can only belong to one shop group. Also, it must belong to a group: it cannot exist outside of a shop group – even if it's the only shop in that group.
  Note: you will not be able to move the shop to any other group if you create it within a shop group which has any of its three options enabled ("Share customers", "Share available quantities to sell" or "Share orders").
- **Category root**. While your main shop has the catalog root as its category root, any other shop can either use the same root, or use any category of the catalog as its root – in effect using a sub-set of the main catalog as its own catalog.
- **Associated categories**. In addition to being able to limit a shop's catalog to a sub-set of the main catalog (see the "Category root" option above), you can choose to only make some sub-categories of the main category available in this new shop.
- **Theme**. You can use any of the available themes as the theme for this shop. In effect, this makes it possible for you to have the very same catalog available in two completely different shops, with a different theme, URL or even prices.

The second section, "Import data from another shop", is where you define which data of the main shop you want to use as the data of this new shop.

IMPORT DATA FROM ANOTHER SHOP

Import data: YES / NO

Choose the shop (source): Main store

Choose data to import:
- ☑ Attribute groups
- ☑ Available quantities for sale
- ☑ CMS block
- ☑ CMS pages
- ☑ Carriers
- ☑ Cart rules
- ☑ Combinations
- ☑ Contact information
- ☑ Countries
- ☑ Currencies
- ☑ Customer groups
- ☑ Discount prices
- ☑ Employees
- ☑ Features
- ☑ Image slider for your homepage
- ☑ Images
- ☑ Languages
- ☑ Manufacturers
- ☑ Meta
- ☑ Module hooks
- ☑ Modules
- ☑ Products
- ☑ Referrers/affiliates
- ☑ Scenes
- ☑ Stores
- ☑ Suppliers
- ☑ Tax rules groups
- ☑ Top horizontal menu
- ☑ Warehouses
- ☑ Webservice accounts
- ☑ Zones

[Cancel] [Save]

It has two options:

- **Import data**. If disabled, your shop will not share any data with any other shop, and the section will close itself. While this is helpful when you want to manage two entirely different shops with a single installation of PrestaShop, this also means you will have to configure both shops from A to Z, whereas sharing data means you would not have to recreate carriers, currencies or modules, for instance. Make sure to think your choice through, as you will not be able to revert back.

- **Choose the shop (source)**. If you do wish to import data, you must indicate from which of the existing shops you want to import that data. If you already have defined a sub-shop of the main shop, this can help you make a "copy" of that sub-shop, instead of having to set the various import options again.
- **Choose data to import**. This is where you decide what kind of data you want to import from the source shop. At the very least, you should import all the modules, even if it means disabling some, as the whole front-office is displayed through modules and some major parts of the back-office also rely on modules.

When you create a product in a new shop and that product already exists in another shop, PrestaShop will try its best to suggest the existing product, so that you will not have to recreate everything.

When saving the shop, PrestaShop warns you that it does not yet have a URL. Click on the red warning to add one (see below).

Setting a shop's URL

Each shop can have its own web address (URL) – or even several addresses – entirely independent from the main shop (the first shop that you have installed). You must define at least one web address for each shop.

Two shops cannot share the same address. If you try to give a new shop an address that is already in use by another shop, PrestaShop will display an error. On the other hand, you can have as many shops on one domain name as you want:

- Using subfolders: http://www.example.com/men/, http://www.example.com/women/, http://www.example.com/kids/, http://www.example.com/pets/, etc.

> In the case of subfolder stores, make sure to create two URLs for each store: one with the "www.", one without it!
>
> For instance: http://www.example.com/men/ and http://example.com/men/
>
> Otherwise, customers trying to access your secondary store without the "www." in the URL will be redirected to your main store.

- Using subdomains: http://men.example.com/, http://women.example.com/, http://kids.example.com/, http://pets.example.com/, etc.

> Do not create any subdomain or subfolder yourself, either on your server or your computer: PrestaShop takes care of creating the path for you on your server. When the customer requests this path, PrestaShop will recognize the shop and serve the files and data for the correct store automatically.

Of course, a shop can also have its own domain name.

> **Using a domain name**
>
> In case you want to use a different domain name for your supplemental shop rather than a subdomain/subfolder, you must configure your domain to point to the folder where PrestaShop is located. The URL rewriting is then done by PrestaShop itself.
>
> Alternatively, you can create an alias for your domain name that redirects to absolute URL where your installation of PrestaShop is located. The way to achieve this depends on the control panel and options that your hosting company provides you with: "Alias" for Plesk, "Forward" for CPanel, "Aliasdomain" for ISPConfig, etc.

To add a URL to shop, select the shop in the "Multistore tree" selector, and then click on the "Add new URL" button. PrestaShop will load a screen with two sections and eight options:

- **URL options**.

- **Shop**. A reminder of the shop to which you are adding a URL. You may also simply switch to another shop.
- **Main URL**. By enabling this, you indicate that you want all the other URLs for this shop to redirect to this main URL (this will switch any other Main URL to be a normal URL).
- **Status**. You can disable and enable a URL at any time.
- **Shop URL**.
- **Domain**. The shop's domain name itself. It does not have to be limited to the domain name: you can indicate a sub-domain if you need to. Just make sure to not add 'http://', or any '/'. Example: www.example.com or kids.example.com.
- **Domain SSL**. If your SSL domain is different from your main domain, be sure to indicate it in that field. Example: www.example.com or kids.example.com.
- **Physical URI**. Here you must set the physical path to your actual installation on your server. If the shop is at the root of the domain or subdomain, leave this field empty. Example: / or /kids/.
- **Virtual URI**. You can make the shop transparently available to customers using this option: through the power of URL rewriting, you can have your shop be displayed without the need to create a sub-folder. Of course, URL rewriting must be enabled in PrestaShop (meaning Friendly URLs, see the "SEO & URLs" page of the "Preferences" menu). Example: /shoes/. Note that this only works for subfolder shops, not subdomain shops.
- **Your final URL will be**. Gives you the impact that your URL settings above will have on the complete web address to your shop.

URL OPTIONS

Shop: Main store

Main URL: YES / **NO**

If you set this URL as the Main URL for the selected shop, all URLs set to this shop will be redirected to this URL (you can only have one Main URL per shop).

The selected shop already has a Main URL. Therefore, if you set this one as the Main URL, the older of the two will be set as the normal URL.

Enabled: **YES** / NO

[Cancel] [Save]

SHOP URL

Domain: 127.0.0.1

Domain SSL: 127.0.0.1

Physical URL: /ps16en/

This is the physical folder for your store on the server. Leave this field empty if your store is installed on the root path (e.g. if your store is available at www.my-prestashop.com/my-store/, you input my-store/ in this field).

Virtual URL:

You need to activate URL Rewriting if you want to add a virtual URL.

Your final URL will be: http://127.0.0.1/ps16en/

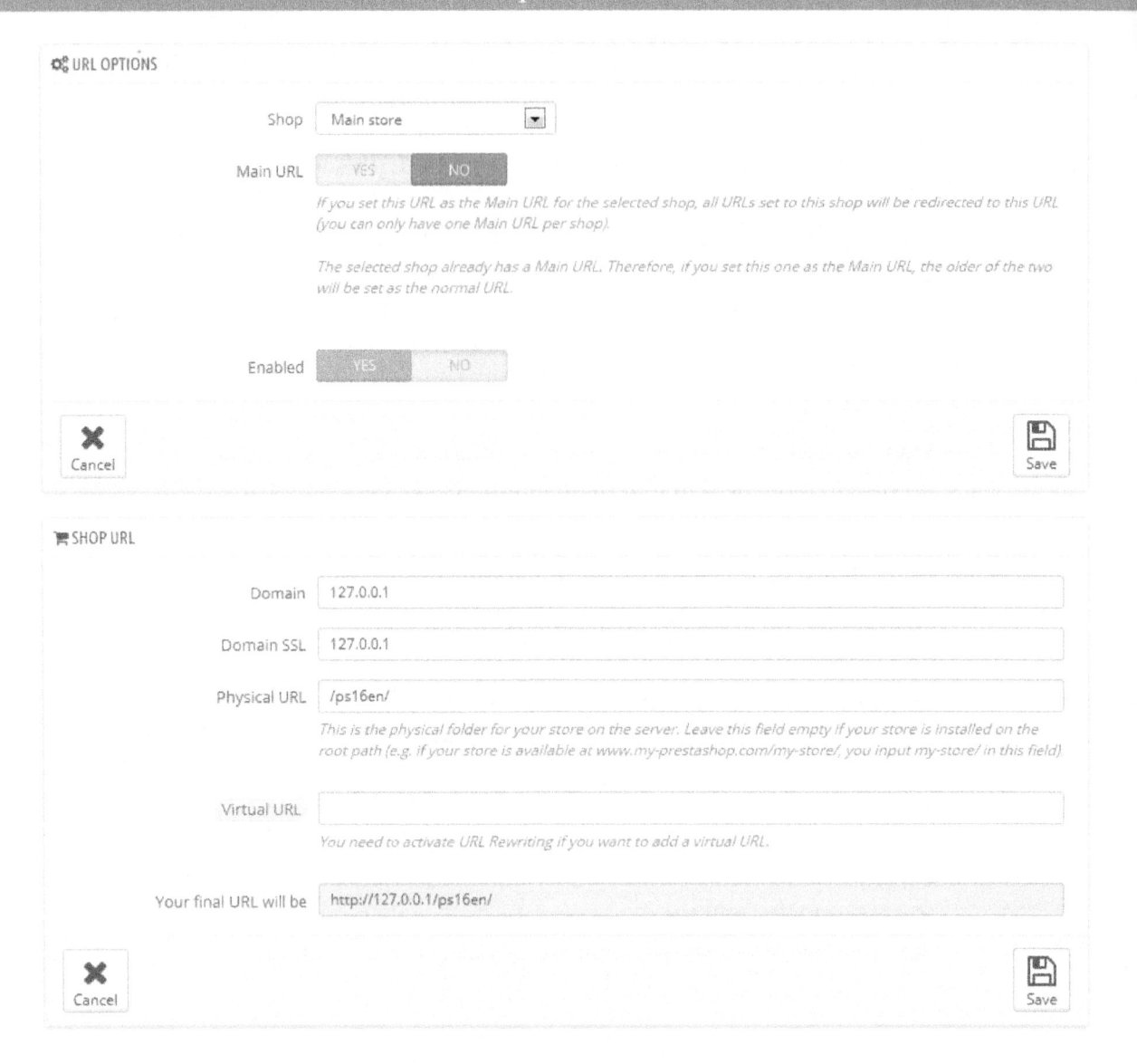

[Cancel] [Save]

Sample Usages and Specifics

Managing a catalog in multistore mode

In multistore mode, some of the PrestaShop administration pages feature a prominent drop-down menu, titled "Multistore configuration for". This menu gives you the context of what you are doing: it enables you to set the shop or shop group to which the changes you are making are to be applied.

For instance, when creating a new product, the selection in this menu will determine whether the product will be available for all shop, only one shop group, or a single shop.

When editing a product, PrestaShop displays notifications to help you understand the scope of your changes. For instance, when editing a product while in the "Shop A" context, the notification will say "Warning, if you change the value of fields with an orange bullet, the value will be changed for all other shops for this product", with said orange bullet appearing on all the implicated fields, such as "Type of product", "Reference", the package's size, etc.

Likewise, if you change a product while in the "All shops" context or in the context of a shop group, some fields will be disabled: since they have a global impact, you cannot edit them. If you really need to edit this content, each field has a box that you can check to edit that field in all the shops under this context.

> If you edit a disabled field, the product is created in all the shops of the context which do not already have it in their own catalog. Make sure to double check your context.

Data exchange between stores

Duplicating data between stores

Duplicated data in PrestaShop are set during the setup of any individual shop, by importing all or some of the content from an existing shop into the new one. The content that can be imported is varied: products, categories, employees, modules, cart rules, suppliers, etc. Data importation is done once and for all: once a store has been created, you cannot easily import data again from another store.

Sharing data between stores and store groups

Stores can share data. Shared data are fundamentally handled at the store group level: one of the important things to understand when dealing with PrestaShop's multistore mode is that all the stores within a store group can share the same details share data – or more precisely, three types of content: customers, available quantities, and orders. Once the store group is set, the sharing of data between its stores is mostly finished: while you can change the setting for the available product quantities, you cannot change the customers and orders settings anymore as soon as any store within the group as at least one customer or one order.

Sharing products and categories

When you create a new store within a group, you can choose to have all or some of the categories in the new store be exact duplicates of the categories in any other store on your installation of PrestaShop.

When creating a category, either for a specific store or for all the stores in the PrestaShop installation, PrestaShop registers the category for all the stores – it is simply hidden from any store where it has not been set.

By associating the new stores with a given category, any change in this category will impact all the stores which are associated with it, even if the stores are from different store groups. You can therefore change the category's content once and for all from one place, including its products.

Sharing customers and customer groups

As indicated above, stores within the same store group can share clients: all you have to do it set the proper option when creating the store group.

Groups are less detailed: if you change one of the default customer group in one store, the change is applied to all the other stores, regardless of the store group.

If you want to have different customer group for each store, you must create a new group and use the "Multistore configuration for" selector to associate the group with the current store or store group.

Using a different theme for each shop/shop group

To install a theme on PrestaShop, you must use the "Theme Import/Export" module to import the theme's zip file. Once that file is uploaded, the module will ask you some module-specific questions. When in multistore mode, it will also ask you whether you want to enable this theme with all stores in your PrestaShop installation, only some store groups, or only some specific stores –

with the current stores being already selected. The theme will still be available for the non-selected stores, but will be disabled.

This setting can be changed: once a theme is installed on your PrestaShop, you can use the "Themes" page in the "Preference" menu to change the theme of the current store, or of the current store group, depending on how the "Multistore configuration for" selector is set.

Using specific settings for each shop/shop group

"Multistore configuration for" selector is the go-to option when you want your changes to have an impact on a given store or set of stores. It should even be the first option to look at when an administration screen opens up, as PrestaShop will change the available options depending on the context you are in: store, store group or all stores.

This makes it possible for you to:

- Using different image formats for each shop/shop group
- Activating/configuring a module on a per-shop basis
- Positioning/displaying front-office blocks on a per-shop basis
- ...and so much more!

Managing CMS pages in multistore mode

When viewing the list of CMS pages in the "All shops" context, all the CMS pages from all shops are displayed. Likewise, when in a shop group context, the pages for all the shops in that group are displayed.

When creating a page in a shop group context, all the shops in this group will display this page, yet the page will be unique: editing it in one shop will apply the changes in all the shops from this group.
On the creation page, a section appears with a list, indicating which ones will be impacted.

Managing discounts in multistore mode

When creating cart rules or catalog price rules in a multistore context, an additional condition is available, with which you can choose the shops on which the rule should be available.

Web-service and multistore

Access to the web-service is also highly configurable, both at the shop level and at the shop group level. When creating a web-service key, you can choose to associate it to all shop, some shop groups, or select shops.

Lightning Source UK Ltd.
Milton Keynes UK
UKOW05f0952250116

267053UK00011B/473/P